A Manual for Writers of Research Papers, Theses, and Dissertations

9th Edition

A Manual for Writers of Research Papers, Theses, and Dissertations

Chicago Style for Students and Researchers

Kate L. Turabian | *9th Edition*

Revised by | Wayne C. Booth, Gregory G. Colomb, Joseph M. Williams, Joseph Bizup, William T. FitzGerald, and the University of Chicago Press Editorial Staff

The University of Chicago Press | Chicago and London

Portions of this book have been adapted from *The Craft of Research*, 4th edition, by Wayne C. Booth, Gregory G. Colomb, Joseph M. Williams, Joseph Bizup, and William T. FitzGerald, © 1995, 2003, 2008, 2016 by The University of Chicago; and *The Chicago Manual of Style*, 17th edition, © 2017 by The University of Chicago.

The University of Chicago Press, Chicago 60637
The University of Chicago Press, Ltd., London
© 2007, 2013, 2018 by The University of Chicago

Published 2018
Printed in the United States of America

27 26 25 24 23 22 21 20 19 18   1 2 3 4 5

ISBN-13: 978-0-226-49442-5 (cloth)
ISBN-13: 978-0-226-43057-7 (paper)
ISBN-13: 978-0-226-43060-7 (e-book)
DOI: https://doi.org/10.7208/chicago/9780226430607.001.0001
Library of Congress Cataloging-in-Publication Data

Names: Turabian, Kate L., author. | Booth, Wayne C., editor. | Colomb, Gregory G., editor. | Williams, Joseph M., editor. | Bizup, Joseph, 1966– editor. | FitzGerald, William T., editor.
Title: A manual for writers of research papers, theses, and dissertations : Chicago Style for students and researchers / Kate L. Turabian ; revised by Wayne C. Booth, Gregory G. Colomb, Joseph M. Williams, Joseph Bizup, William T. FitzGerald, and the University of Chicago Press editorial staff.
Other titles: Chicago guides to writing, editing, and publishing.
Description: Ninth edition. | Chicago ; London : The University of Chicago Press, 2018. | Series: Chicago guides to writing, editing, and publishing | Includes bibliographical references and index.
Identifiers: LCCN 2017047620 | ISBN 9780226494425 (cloth : alk. paper) | ISBN 9780226430577 (pbk. : alk. paper) | ISBN 9780226430607 (e-book)
Subjects: LCSH: Dissertations, Academic—Handbooks, manuals, etc. | Academic writing—Handbooks, manuals, etc.
Classification: LCC LB2369 .T8 2018 | DDC 808.06/6378—dc23
LC record available at https://lccn.loc.gov/2017047620

♾ This paper meets the requirements of ANSI/NISO Z39.48-1992 (Permanence of Paper).

Contents

Part I

Research and Writing

Wayne C. Booth, Gregory G. Colomb, Joseph M. Williams,
Joseph Bizup, and William T. FitzGerald

Part II

Source Citation

Part III
Style

A Note to Students

Known by many as simply "Turabian" in honor of its original author, *A Manual for Writers of Research Papers, Theses, and Dissertations* is the authoritative student resource on "Chicago style." This book has helped generations of students successfully research, write, and submit papers in virtually all academic disciplines. Its guidelines for source citations and style have been condensed and adapted for student writers from another, more comprehensive reference work, *The Chicago Manual of Style*.

Part 1 covers every step of the research and writing process. It provides practical advice to help you formulate the right questions, read critically, and build arguments. It also shows you how to draft and revise your papers to strengthen both your arguments and your writing.

Part 2 offers a comprehensive guide to the two methods of Chicago-style source citation, beginning with helpful information on general citation practices in chapter 15. In the humanities and most social sciences, you will likely use the notes-bibliography style detailed in chapters 16 and 17; in the natural and physical sciences and some social sciences, you will more likely use the author-date style described in chapters 18 and 19.

Part 3 covers Chicago's recommended editorial style, which will help you bring consistency to your writing in matters such as punctuation, capitalization, and abbreviations; this section also includes guidance on incorporating quotations into your writing and on properly presenting tables and figures.

The appendix presents formatting and submission requirements for theses and dissertations that many academic institutions use as a model, but be sure to follow any local guidelines provided by your institution.

Preface

Students writing research papers, theses, and dissertations in today's colleges and universities inhabit a world filled with digital technologies that were unimagined in 1937—the year dissertation secretary Kate L. Turabian first assembled a booklet of guidelines for student writers at the University of Chicago. The availability of word-processing software and new digital sources has changed the way students conduct research and write up the results. But these technologies have not altered the basic task of the student writer: doing well-designed research and presenting it clearly and accurately while following accepted academic standards for citation, style, and format.

Turabian's 1937 booklet reflected guidelines found in an already classic resource for writers and editors published by the University of Chicago Press that would ultimately be known as *The Chicago Manual of Style* (CMOS). The Press began distributing Turabian's booklet in 1947 and first published the work in book form in 1955, under the title *A Manual for Writers of Term Papers, Theses, and Dissertations*. Over time, Turabian's book has become a standard reference for students of all levels at universities and colleges across the country. Turabian died in 1987 at age ninety-four, a few months after publication of the book's fifth edition.

Beginning with that edition, members of the Press editorial staff have carried out the revisions to the chapters on source citation, style, and paper format. For the seventh edition (2007), Wayne C. Booth, Gregory G. Colomb, and Joseph M. Williams expanded the focus of the book by adding extensive new material adapted from their book *The Craft of Research*, also published by the University of Chicago Press and now in its fourth edition (2016). Among the new topics covered in their chapters were the nature of research, finding and engaging sources, taking notes, developing an argument, drafting and revising, and presenting evidence in tables and figures. Following the deaths of this remarkable trio of authors, whose collective voice will always animate this work, Joseph Bizup and William T. FitzGerald have with this edition assumed the mantle of revising their chapters for a new generation of students, as they had previously for *The Craft of Research*.

Part 1, now aligned with the most recent edition of that book, incorporates updated advice for writers and responds to recent developments in information literacy, including the use of digital materials. Part 2 offers a comprehensive guide to the two Chicago styles of source citation—the notes-bibliography format used widely in the humanities and most social sciences and the author-date format favored in many of the sciences and some social sciences. Thoroughly updated guidance related to online citation practices has been supplemented throughout by new examples featuring the types of sources students are most likely to consult. Part 3 addresses matters of spelling, punctuation, abbreviation, and treatment of numbers, names, special terms, and titles of works. The final two chapters in this section treat the mechanics of using quotations and graphics (tables and figures), topics that are discussed from a rhetorical perspective in part 1. Both parts 2 and 3 have been updated for this edition in accordance with the seventeenth edition (2017) of *The Chicago Manual of Style*. The recommendations in this manual in some instances diverge from CMOS in small ways, to better suit the requirements of academic papers as opposed to published works.

The appendix presents guidelines for paper format and submission that have become the primary authority for dissertation offices throughout the United States. These guidelines have been updated to reflect the nearly universal electronic submission of papers and to feature new examples from recently published dissertations. This appendix is intended primarily for students writing PhD dissertations and master's and undergraduate theses, but the sections on format requirements and electronic file preparation will also aid those writing class papers. An extensive bibliography, organized by subject area and fully updated, lists sources for research and style issues specific to various disciplines.

The guidelines in this manual offer practical solutions to a wide range of issues encountered by student writers, but they may be supplemented—or even overruled—by the conventions of specific disciplines or the preferences of particular institutions, departments, or instructors. All of the chapters on style and format remind students to review the requirements of their university, department, or instructor, which take precedence over the guidelines presented in this book.

Updating a book that has been used by millions of students over eighty years is no small task, and many people participated in preparing this ninth edition. The Press staff welcomed Bizup and FitzGerald to their new role in revising part 1. Russell David Harper, the principal reviser of the sixteenth and seventeenth editions of CMOS, revised parts 2 and 3 and the appendix. Several recent PhD recipients from the University of Chicago allowed the use of excerpts from their dissertations in the appendix, where they are credited individually.

Within the Press, the project was developed under the guidance of editors Mary E. Laur and David Morrow, editorial director Christie Henry, and editorial associates Rachel Kelly and Susan Zakin. Lucy Johnson and Kristin Zodrow offered additional research support. Ruth Goring edited the manuscript, June Sawyers proofread the pages, and James Curtis prepared the index. Michael Brehm provided the design, while Joseph Claude supervised the production. Carol Kasper, Jennifer Ringblom, Lauren Salas, and Carol Fisher Saller brought the final product to market.

The University of Chicago Press Editorial Staff

Part I | Research and Writing

Wayne C. Booth,
Gregory G. Colomb,
Joseph M. Williams,
Joseph Bizup, and
William T. FitzGerald

Overview of Part I

We know how daunting it can feel to start a substantial research project, whether it's a doctoral dissertation, a master's or senior thesis, or just a long class paper. But you can handle any project if you break it into its parts, then work on them one step at a time. Part I of this book shows you how.

We first discuss the aims of research and what readers will expect of any research paper (a term we use broadly to refer to all varieties of research-based writing). We then focus on how to find a research question and problem whose answer is worth your time and your readers' attention; how to find and use information from sources to back up your answer; and then how to plan, draft, and revise your paper so your readers will see that your answer is based on sound reasoning and reliable evidence.

Several themes run through this part.

- You can't plunge into a project blindly; you must plan it, then keep the whole process in mind as you take each step. So think big, but break the process down into small goals that you can meet one at a time.
- Your best research will begin with a question that *you* want to answer. But you must then imagine readers asking questions of their own: *So what if you don't answer it? Why should I care?*
- From the outset, you should try to write every day, not just to record the content of your sources but to clarify what you think of them. You should also write down your own developing ideas to get them out of the cozy warmth of your head and into the cold light of day, where you can see if they still make sense. You probably won't use much of this writing in your final draft, but it is essential preparation for it.
- No matter how carefully you do your research, readers will judge it by how well you present it, so you must know what they will look for in a clearly written paper that earns their respect.

If you're an advanced researcher, skim chapters 1–4. You will see there much that's familiar; but if you're also teaching, it may help you explain what you know to your students more effectively. Many experienced researchers tell us that chapters 5–12 have helped them not only to explain to others how to conduct and report research, but also to draft and revise their own writing more quickly and effectively.

If you're just starting your career in research, you'll find every chapter of part 1 useful. Skim it all for an overview of the process; then as you work through your project, reread chapters relevant to your immediate task.

You may feel that the steps described here are too many to remember, but you can manage them if you take them one at a time, and as you do more research they'll become habits of mind. Don't think, however, that you must follow these steps in exactly the order we present them. Researchers regularly think ahead to future steps as they work through earlier ones and revisit earlier steps as they deal with a later one. (That explains why we so often refer you ahead to anticipate a later stage in the process and back to revisit an earlier one.) And even the most systematic researcher has unexpected insights that send her off in a new direction. Work from a plan, but be ready to depart from it, even to discard it for a new one.

If you're a very new researcher, you may also think that some matters we discuss are beyond your immediate needs. We know that a ten-page class paper differs from a dissertation. But both require a kind of thinking that even the newest researcher can start practicing. You begin your journey toward full competence when you not only know what lies ahead but also can start practicing the skills that experienced researchers began to learn when they were where you are now.

No book can prepare you for every aspect of every research project. And this one won't help you with the specific methodologies in fields such as psychology, economics, and philosophy, much less physics, chemistry, and biology. Nor does it tell you how to adapt what you learn about academic research to business or professional settings.

But it does provide an overview of the processes and habits of mind that underlie all research, wherever it's done, and of the plans you must make to assemble a paper, draft it, and revise it. With that knowledge and with help from your teachers, you'll come to feel in control of your projects, not intimidated by them, and eventually you'll learn to manage even the most complex projects on your own, in both the academic and the professional worlds.

The first step in learning the skills of sound research is to understand how experienced researchers think about its aims.

1

What Research Is and How Researchers Think about It

Whenever we read about a scientific breakthrough or a crisis in world affairs, we benefit from the research of others, who likewise benefited from the research of countless others before them. When we walk into a library, we are surrounded by more than twenty-five centuries of research. When we go on the internet, we can read the work of millions of researchers who have posed questions beyond number, gathered untold amounts of information from the research of others to answer them, and then shared their answers with the rest of us. We can carry on their work by asking and, we hope, answering new questions in turn. Governments spend billions on research, businesses even more. Research goes on in laboratories and libraries, in jungles and ocean depths, in caves and in outer space, in offices and, in the information age, even in our own homes. Research is in fact the world's biggest industry.

So what, exactly, is it?

1.1 What Research Is

You already have a basic understanding of research: answering a question by obtaining information. In this sense, research can be as simple as choosing a new phone or as complex as discovering the origin of life. In this book we use *research* in a specific way to mean a process of systematic inquiry to answer a question that not only the researcher but also others want to solve. Research thus includes the steps involved in presenting or reporting it. To be a true researcher, as we are using the term, you must share your findings and conclusions with others.

If you are new to research, you may think that your paper will add little to the world's knowledge. But done well, it will add a lot to *your* knowledge and to your ability to communicate that knowledge. As you learn to do your own research, you also learn to use and judge that of others. In every profession, researchers must read and evaluate the work of others before they make a decision. This is a job you will do better after you have learned how others judge yours.

This book focuses on research in the academic world, but every day we read or hear about research that affects our lives. Often we get news of research secondhand, and it can be difficult to know what reasoning and evidence support a claim. But research doesn't ask for our blind trust or that we accept something on the basis of authority. It invites readers to think critically about evidence and reasoning.

That is how *research-based writing* differs from other kinds of persuasive writing: it must rest on shared facts that readers accept as truths independent of your feelings and beliefs. Your readers must be able to follow your reasoning from evidence they accept to the claim you draw from it. Your success as a researcher thus depends not just on how well you gather and analyze data but also on how clearly you report your reasoning so that your readers can test and judge it before making your claims part of their knowledge and understanding.

1.2   How Researchers Think about Their Aims

All researchers collect information, what we're calling *data*. But researchers do not merely gather facts on a topic—*stories about the Battle of the Alamo*, for example. They look for specific data to test and support an answer to a question that their topic inspired them to ask, such as *Why has the Alamo story become a national legend?* In doing so, they also imagine a community of readers who they believe will share their interest and help them test and support an answer to that question.

Experienced researchers, however, know that they must do more than convince us that their answer is sound. They must also show us why their question was worth asking, how its answer helps us understand some bigger issue in a new way. *If we can figure out why the Alamo story has become a national legend, we might then answer a larger question: how have regional myths shaped the American character?*

You can judge how closely your thinking tracks that of an experienced researcher by describing your project in a sentence like this:

1. Topic: I am working on X (*stories about the Battle of the Alamo*)
    2. Question: because I want to find out Y (*why its story became a national legend*)
        3. Significance: so that I can help others understand Z (*how such regional myths have shaped the American character*).

That sentence is worth a close look, because it describes not just the progress of your research but your personal growth as a researcher.

1. Topic: "I am working on X . . .": Those new to research often begin with a simple topic like *the Battle of the Alamo*. But too often they stop there, with nothing but a broad topic to guide their work. Beginning this way, they may pile up dozens or hundreds of notes but then can't decide what data to keep or discard. When it comes time to write, their papers become "data dumps" that leave readers wondering what all those data add up to.

2. Question: ". . . because I want to find out Y . . .": More experienced researchers begin not just with a topic but with a *research question*, such as *Why has the story of the Alamo become a national legend?* They know that readers will think their data add up to something only when they serve as evidence to support an answer. Indeed, only with a question can a researcher know what information to look for and, once obtained, what to keep—and not just data that support a particular answer but also data that test or discredit it. With sufficient evidence to support an answer, a researcher can respond to data that seem to contradict it. In writing a paper, the researcher tests that answer and invites others to test it too.

3. Significance: ". . . so that I can help others understand Z": The best researchers understand that readers want to know not only that an answer is sound but also why the question is worth asking: *So what? Why should I care why the Alamo story has become a national legend?* Think of it this way: what will be lost if you *don't* answer your question? Your answer might be *Nothing. I just want to know.* Good enough to start but not to finish, because eventually your readers will want an answer beyond *Just curious.*

Answering *So what?* is tough for all researchers, beginning and experienced alike, because when you only have a question stemming from a topic of personal interest, it's hard to predict whether others will find its answer significant. Some researchers therefore work backwards: they begin not by following their own curiosity but by crafting questions with implications for bigger ones that others in their field already care about. But many researchers, including us, find that they cannot address that third step until they finish a first draft. So it's fine to *begin* your research without being able to answer *So what?*, and if you are a student, your teacher may even let you skip that last step. But if you are doing advanced research, you *must* take it, because your answer to *So what?* is what makes your research matter to others.

In short, not all questions are equally good. We might ask how many cats slept in the Alamo the night before the battle, but so what if we find out? It is hard to see how an answer would help us think about any larger issue worth understanding, so it's a question that's probably not worth asking (though as we'll see, we could be wrong about that).

How good a question is depends on its significance to some community of readers. Exactly what community depends on your field but also on how you frame your research. You can try to expand your potential readership by connecting Z to even broader questions: *And if we can understand what has shaped the American character, we might understand better who Americans think they are. And when we know that, we might better understand why others in the world judge them as they do.* Now perhaps political scientists will be as interested in this research as historians. On the other hand, if you try to widen your audience too much, you risk losing it altogether. Sometimes it's better to address a smaller community of specialists.

We can't tell you the right choice, but we can tell you two wrong ones: trying to interest everyone (some people just won't care no matter how you frame your research) or not trying to interest anyone at all.

1.3   Conversing with Your Readers

When you can explain the *significance* of your research, you enter into a kind of conversation with your research community. Some people, when they think of research, imagine a lone scholar or scientist in a hushed library or lab. But no places are more crowded with the presence of others than these. When you read a book or an article or a report, you silently converse with its authors—and through them with everyone else they have read. In fact, every time you go to a written source for information, you join a conversation between writers and readers that began millennia ago. And when you report your own research, you add your voice and hope that other voices will respond to you, so that you can in turn respond to them. And so it goes.

Experienced researchers understand that they are participating in such conversations and that genuine research must matter not only to the researcher but also to others. That is why our formula—*I am working on X to find out Y so that others can better understand Z*—is so powerful: because it makes informing others the end of research.

But these silent conversations differ from the face-to-face conversations we have every day. We can judge how well everyday conversations are going as we have them, and we can adjust our statements and behavior to repair mistakes and misunderstandings as they occur. But in writing we don't have that opportunity: readers have to *imagine* writers in conversation with one another, as well as with themselves, and writers have to imagine their readers and their relationship to them. In other words, writers have to offer readers a social contract: *I'll play my part if you play yours.*

Doing this is one of the toughest tasks for beginning researchers: get that relationship wrong and your readers will think you are naive or, worse, won't read your work at all. Too many beginning researchers offer their readers a relationship that caricatures a bad classroom: *Teacher, I know less than you. So my role is to show you how many facts I can dig up. Yours is to say whether I've found enough to give me a good grade.* Do that and you turn your project into a pointless drill, casting yourself in a role exactly opposite to that of a true researcher. In true research, you must switch the roles of student and teacher. You must imagine a relationship that goes beyond *Here are some facts I've dug up about fourteenth-century Tibetan weaving. Are they enough of the right ones?*

There are three better reasons to share what you've found. You could say to your reader, *Here is some information that you may find interesting.* This offer assumes, of course, that your reader wants to know. You could also say not just *Here is something that should interest you* but *Here is something that will help you remedy a situation that troubles you.* People do this kind of research every day in business, government, and the professions when they try to figure out how to address problems ranging from insomnia to falling profits to climate change. In chapter 2 we call such situations and their consequences *practical problems.* When academic researchers address such practical problems, we say they are doing *applied* research. Most commonly, though, academic researchers do *pure* research that addresses what we call *conceptual problems*—that is, not troubling situations in the world but the limitations of our understanding of it (again see chapter 2). In this case, you say to your readers, *Here is something that will help you better understand something you care about.* When you make this last sort of appeal, you imagine your readers as a community of receptive but also skeptical colleagues who are open to learning from you and even changing their minds—if you can make the case.

We now understand the goal of research, at least in its pure form: it is not to have the last word but to keep the conversation going. The best questions are those whose answers raise several more. When that happens, everyone in the research community benefits.

2 Defining a Project: *Topic, Question, Problem, Working Hypothesis*

A research project begins well before you search the internet or head for the library and continues long after you have collected all the data you think you need. Every project involves countless specific tasks, so it is easy to get overwhelmed. But in all research projects, you have just five general aims:

- Ask a question worth answering.
- Find an answer that you can support with good reasons.
- Find good data that you can use as reliable evidence to support your reasons.
- Draft an argument that makes a good case for your answer.
- Revise that draft until readers will think you met the first four goals.

You might even post those five goals in your workspace.

Research projects would be much easier if we could march straight through these steps. But you will discover (if you have not already) that the research process is not so straightforward. Each task overlaps with others, and frequently you must go back to an earlier one. The truth is, research is messy and unpredictable. But that's also what makes it exciting and ultimately rewarding.

2.1   Find a Question in Your Topic

Researchers begin projects in different ways. Many experienced researchers begin with a question that others in their field want to answer: *What caused the extinction of most large North American mammals?* Others begin with just basic curiosity, a vague intellectual itch that they have to scratch. They might not know what puzzles them about a topic, but they're willing to spend time to find out whether that topic can yield a question worth answering.

They realize, moreover, that the best research question is not one whose answer they want to know just for its own sake; it is one that helps them and others understand some larger issue. For example, if we knew why North American sloths disappeared, we might be able to answer a larger question that puzzles many historical anthropologists: *Did early Native Americans live in harmony with nature, as some believe, or did they hunt its largest creatures to extinction? And if we knew that, then we might also understand . . .* (So what? again. See 1.2.)

Then there are those questions that just pop into a researcher's mind with no hint of where they'll lead, sometimes about matters so seemingly trivial that only the researcher thinks they're worth answering: *Why does a coffee spill dry up in the form of a ring?* Such a question might lead nowhere, but you can't know that until you see its answer. In fact, the scientist puzzled by coffee rings made discoveries about the behavior of fluids that others in his field thought important—and that paint manufacturers found valuable. If you cultivate the ability to see what's odd in the commonplace, you'll never lack for research projects as either a student or a professional.

If you already have a focused topic, you might skip to 2.1.3 and begin asking questions about it. If you already have some questions, skip to 2.1.4 to test them using the criteria listed there. Otherwise, here's a plan to help you search for a topic.

2.1.1 Search Your Interests

Beginning researchers often find it hard to pick a topic or believe they lack the expertise to research a topic they have. But a research topic is an interest stated specifically enough for you to imagine *becoming* a local expert on it. That doesn't mean you *already* know a lot about it or that you'll know more about it than others, including a teacher or advisor. You just want to know more about it than you do now.

If you can work on any topic, we offer only a cliché: start with what interests you. Ask these questions:

- What special interests do you have—chess, old comic books, scouting? The less common, the better. Choose one and investigate something about it that you don't know.
- Where would you like to travel? Find out all you can about your destination. What particular aspect surprises you or makes you want to learn more?
- Can you find an online discussion list or social media page focused on issues that interest you?
- Visit a museum or a "virtual museum" on the internet with exhibitions that appeal to you. What catches your interest that you would like to know more about?
- Have you taken positions on issues in your field or in debates with others but found that you couldn't back up your views with good reasons and evidence?
- What issues in your field do people outside your field misunderstand?
- What topic is your instructor or advisor working on? Would she like you to explore a part of it? Don't be too shy to ask.
- Does your library have rich resources in some field? Ask your instructor or a librarian.
- What intrigues you in your reading? What connections do you see among different things you are reading?
- What other courses will you take in your field or out of it? Find a textbook and skim it for study questions.
- If you have a job in mind, what kind of writing might help you get it? Employers often ask for samples of an applicant's work.

Once you have a list of possible topics, choose one or two that interest you most and explore their research potential. Sometimes beginning researchers choose a topic because they already know what they want to say about it, even before they've done any research. That's a mistake: the best topics provoke good questions; the worst come with ready-made answers. To gauge a topic's potential, do these things:

■ In the library, look up your topic in a general guide such as *CQ Researcher* and skim the subheadings. In an online database such as Academic Search Premier, you can explore your topic through subject terms. If you have a narrower focus, you can do the same with specialized guides such as *Women's Studies International*. At most libraries today, such guides are found online.

■ On the internet, google your topic, but don't surf indiscriminately. Look first for websites that are roughly like the sources you would find in a library, such as online encyclopedias. Read the entries on your general topic, and then copy their lists of references for a closer look. Few experienced researchers trust Wikipedia as a reliable source to cite as evidence, but most would use the site to find ideas and more specific sources.

■ Finally, think ahead: you may be in for a long relationship with your topic, so be sure it interests you enough to get you through the inevitable rocky stretches.

2.1.2 Make Your Topic Manageable

If you pick a topic that sounds like an encyclopedia entry—*bridges, birds, masks*—you'll find so many sources that you could spend a lifetime reading them. You must carve out of your topic a manageable piece. Before you start searching, limit your topic to reflect a special interest in it: What is it about, say, masks that made you choose them? What particular aspect of them interests or puzzles you? Think about your topic in a context that you know something about, and then add words and phrases to reflect that knowledge:

masks in religious ceremonies
masks as symbols in Hopi religious ceremonies
mudhead masks as symbols of sky spirits in Hopi fertility ceremonies

You might not be able to focus your topic until after you start reading about it. That takes time, so start early (you can do much of this preliminary work online):

■ Begin with an overview of your topic in a general encyclopedia (in the bibliography, see items in category 2 in the general sources); then read about it in a specialized one (see items in category 2 in your field).

■ Skim a survey of your topic (encyclopedia entries usually cite a few).

■ Skim subheads under your topic in an annual bibliography in your field (in the bibliography, see items in category 4 in your field). That will also give you a start on a reading list.

■ Search the internet for the topic (but evaluate the reliability of what you find; see 3.3.2).

Especially useful are topics that spark debate: *Fisher claims that Halloween masks reveal children's archetypal fears, but do they?* Even if you can't resolve the debate, you can learn how such debates are conducted (for more on this, see 3.1.2).

2.1.3 Question Your Topic

Once they have a focused topic, many new researchers start plowing through all the sources they can find, taking notes on everything they read. They then dump it all into a report with little sense of purpose or direction. Experienced researchers, however, document information not for its own sake but to support an answer to a question they (and they hope their readers) think worth asking. So the best way to begin working on a focused topic is to pose questions that direct you to just the information you need to answer them.

Do this not just once, early on, but throughout your project. Ask questions as you read, especially *how* and *why* (see also 4.1.1–4.1.2). Try the following kinds of questions (the categories are loose and overlap, so don't worry about keeping them distinct).

1. Ask how the topic fits into a larger context (historical, social, cultural, geographic, functional, economic, and so on):
   - How does your topic fit into a larger story? *What came before masks? How did masks come into being? Why? What changes have they caused in other parts of their social or geographic setting? How and why did that happen? Why have masks become a part of Halloween? How and why have masks helped make Halloween the biggest American holiday after Christmas?*
   - How is your topic a functioning part of a larger system? *How do masks reflect the values of specific societies and cultures? What roles do masks play in Hopi dances? In scary movies? In masquerade parties? For what purposes are masks used other than disguise? How has the booming market for kachina masks influenced traditional designs?*
   - How does your topic compare to and contrast with other topics like it? *How do masks in Native American ceremonies differ from those in Africa? What do Halloween masks have to do with Mardi Gras masks? How are masks and cosmetic surgery alike?*

2. Ask questions about the nature of the thing itself, as an independent entity:
   - How has your topic changed through time? Why? What is its future? *How have Halloween masks changed? Why? How have Native American masks changed? Why?*

- How do the parts of your topic fit together as a system? *What parts of a mask are most significant in Hopi ceremonies? Why? Why do some masks cover only the eyes? Why do so few masks cover just the bottom half of the face?*
- How many different categories of your topic are there? *What are the different kinds of Halloween masks? What are the different qualities of masks? What are the different functions of Halloween masks?*

3. Turn positive questions into a negative ones: *Why have masks not become a part of Christmas? How do Native American masks not differ from those in Africa? What parts of masks are typically not significant in religious ceremonies?*

4. Ask speculative questions: *Why are masks common in African religions but not in Western ones? Why are children more comfortable wearing Halloween masks than are most adults? Why don't hunters in camouflage wear masks?*

5. Ask *What if?* questions: how would things be different if your topic never existed, disappeared, or were put into a new context? *What if no one ever wore masks except for safety reasons? What if everyone wore masks in public? What if movies and TV were like Greek plays and all the actors wore masks? What if it were customary to wear masks on blind dates? In marriage ceremonies? At funerals?*

6. Ask questions that reflect disagreements with a source: if a source makes a claim you think is only weakly supported or even wrong, make that disagreement a question (see also 4.1.2). *Martinez claims that carnival masks uniquely allow wearers to escape social norms. But I think religious masks also allow wearers to escape from the material realm to the spiritual. Is there a larger pattern of all masks creating a sense of alternative forms of social or spiritual life?*

7. Ask questions that build on agreement: if a source offers a claim you think is persuasive, ask questions that extend its reach (see also 4.1.1). *Elias shows that masked balls became popular in eighteenth-century London in response to anxiety about social mobility. Is the same anxiety responsible for similar developments in other European capitals?* You can also ask a question that supports the same claim with additional evidence. *Elias supports his claim about masked balls entirely with published sources. Is it also supported by evidence from unpublished sources such as letters and diaries?*

8. Ask questions analogous to those that others have asked about similar topics. *Smith analyzed the Battle of Gettysburg from an economic point of view. What would an economic analysis of the Battle of the Alamo turn up?*

9. Look for questions that other researchers pose but don't answer. Many journal articles end with a paragraph or two about open questions, ideas for more research, and so on. You might not be able to do all the research they suggest, but you might carve out a piece of it.

10. Find a professional discussion forum on your topic, then "lurk," just reading the exchanges to understand the kinds of questions being asked. If you can't find one using a search engine, ask a teacher or visit websites of professional organizations in your field. Look for questions that spark your interest. If questions from students are welcomed, you can even post one yourself, so long as it is very specific and narrowly focused.

2.1.4   Evaluate Your Questions

After asking all the questions you can think of, evaluate them. Not all questions are equally good. Look for questions whose answers might make you (and your readers) think about your topic in a new way. Avoid questions like these:

■ Their answers are settled fact that you could just look up. *What was Audre Lorde's first published poem?* Questions that ask *how* and *why* call for interpretations, not just the discovery of facts. That's why they invite deeper thinking than questions beginning *who, what, when,* or *where,* and deeper thinking leads to more interesting answers.

■ Their answers can't be plausibly disproved. *How important are masks in Inuit culture?* The answer is obvious: *Very.* If you can't imagine disproving a claim, then proving it is pointless. (On the other hand, world-class reputations have been won by those who questioned a claim that seemed self-evidently true—for instance, that the sun circled the earth—and dared to disprove it.)

■ Their answers would be merely speculative. *Would church services be as well attended if the congregation all wore masks?* If you can't imagine finding data that would settle the question, it's not a question you can answer.

■ Their answers are dead ends. *How many black cats slept in the Alamo the night before the battle?* It's hard to see how an answer would help us think about any larger issue worth understanding better, so the question is probably not worth asking.

■ Their answers require different capacities from the ones you have. *How do Japanese translations of* The Great Gatsby *treat early twentieth-century America?* If you can't read Japanese, this question is not for you to answer.

■ Their answers require more or different resources—materials, technology, money, especially time—than you have. *How is childhood repre-*

sented in the Victorian novel? Can you read enough of them in the time you have to arrive at a reasonable answer?

Don't reject a question because you think someone must already have asked it. Until you know, pursue its answer as if you asked first. Even if someone has answered it, you might come up with a better answer or at least one with a new slant. In fact, in the humanities and social sciences the best questions usually have more than one good answer. You can also organize your project around comparing and contrasting competing answers and supporting the best one (see 6.2.5).

The point is to find a question that *you* want to answer. Too many students, both graduate and undergraduate, think that the aim of education is to learn settled answers to someone else's questions. It's not. It is to find your own answers to your own questions. To do that, you must learn to wonder about things, to let them puzzle you—particularly things that seem commonplace.

2.2 Understanding Research Problems

In chapter 1 we gave you a formula that expresses how experienced researchers think about their work:

1. Topic: I am working on X (*stories about the Battle of the Alamo*)
   2. Question: because I want to find out Y (*why its story became a national legend*)
      3. Significance: so that I can help others understand Z (*how such regional myths have shaped the American character*).

When you can state that significance from the point of view of your readers, you have more than a question: you have posed a *research problem* that they recognize needs a solution.

Among researchers, the term *problem* has a special meaning that sometimes confuses beginners. In our everyday world, a problem is something we try to avoid. But in academic research, a problem is something we seek out, even invent. Indeed, without a problem to work on, a researcher is out of work.

Experienced researchers often talk about their problems in shorthand. When asked what they are working on, they often answer with what sounds like a general topic: *adult measles, mating calls of Wyoming elk.* As a result, beginners may think that having a topic to read about is the same thing as having a problem to solve. But without a specific question to answer and a reason to find that answer significant, researchers have no way of knowing when they have enough. So they can be tempted to throw in everything just to be safe.

To avoid the judgment that your paper is just a *data dump*, you need a problem, one that focuses on finding just those data that will help you solve it. To find one, you need to know how problems work.

2.2.1 Understanding Practical and Conceptual Problems

There are two kinds of research problems: *practical* and *conceptual*. Each of them has a two-part structure:

- a situation or *condition*, and
- undesirable *costs* or *consequences* caused by that condition.

Your research question is about your problem's condition; its significance follows from your problem's cost or consequence.

What differentiates practical and conceptual problems is the nature of those conditions and costs/consequences. The condition of a practical problem can be any state of affairs in the world that troubles you or, better, your readers: a traffic jam, foreign competition, a disease we can't effectively treat. The cost of a practical problem is always some tangible effect we don't like: inconvenience, expense, pain, even death. Practical problems are often a matter of perspective: if my company's products are outselling yours, that's a problem for you but not for me.

The condition of a conceptual problem is always some version of not knowing or understanding something. A conceptual problem does not have a tangible cost but a consequence. This consequence is a particular kind of ignorance: a lack of understanding that keeps us from understanding something else that is even more significant. Put another way, because we haven't answered one question, we can't answer another that is more important.

In short, practical problems concern what we should *do*; conceptual problems concern what we should *think*. Practical problems are most common in the professional world; conceptual problems are most common in academe.

2.2.2 Distinguishing Pure and Applied Research

We call research *pure* when it addresses a conceptual problem that does not have any direct practical consequences, when it only improves the understanding of a community of researchers. We call research *applied* when it addresses a conceptual problem that does have practical consequences. You can tell whether research is pure or applied by considering the significance of your project: is it about understanding or doing?

1. *Topic:* I am studying how readings from the Hubble telescope differ from readings for the same stars measured by earthbound telescopes

2. *Question*: because I want to find out how much the atmosphere distorts measurements of electromagnetic radiation
   3. *Practical Significance*: so that astronomers can use data from earthbound telescopes to *measure* more accurately the density of electromagnetic radiation.

Applied research is common in academic fields such as business, engineering, and medicine and in companies and government agencies that do research to understand what must be known before they can solve a problem.

Some new researchers may be uneasy with pure research because the consequence of a conceptual problem—not knowing something—seems so abstract. Since they are not yet part of a community that cares deeply about understanding its part of the world, they feel that their findings aren't good for much. So they try to show the importance of their conceptual answer by cobbling onto it an implausible practical use:

1. *Topic*: I am studying differences among nineteenth-century versions of the Alamo story
   2. *Question*: because I want to find out how politicians used stories of such events to shape public opinion
      3. *Potential Practical Significance*: in order to protect ourselves from unscrupulous politicians.

Most readers will find the link between this research question and its asserted significance a stretch. But for researchers in American history, the question does not need to have practical significance. As the term *pure* suggests, many researchers value the pursuit of knowledge "for its own sake" as a reflection of humanity's highest calling to know more.

So if you are doing academic research, resist the urge to turn a conceptual problem into a practical one—unless you've specifically been asked to do so. You are unlikely to solve any genuine practical problem in a course project. And in any case, most academic researchers see their mission not as fixing the problems of the world but as understanding them better (which may or may not lead to fixing them).

2.3   Propose a Working Hypothesis

Before you get deep into your project, try one more step. It is one that some beginners resist but that experienced researchers usually attempt. Once you have a question, imagine some plausible answers, no matter how sketchy or speculative. At this stage, don't worry whether they're right. That comes later.

For example, suppose you ask, *Why do some religions use masks in cer-emonies while others don't?* You might speculate:

Maybe cultures with many spirits need masks to distinguish them.
Maybe masks are common in cultures that mix religion and medicine.
Maybe religions originating in the Middle East were influenced by the Jewish prohibi-tion against idolatry.

Even a general answer can suggest something worth studying:

Maybe it has to do with the role of masks in nonreligious areas of a culture.

Try to imagine at least one plausible answer, no matter how tenta-tive or speculative. If one answer seems promising, call it your *working hypothesis* and use it to guide your research. You can, of course, start gath-ering data with no more than a question to guide you, but even a tenta-tive working hypothesis will help you think about the kind of data you'll need as evidence to support it: numbers? quotations? observations? im-ages? historical facts? In fact, until you have a hypothesis, you can't know whether any data you collect are relevant to your project.

If you can't imagine any working hypotheses, reconsider your ques-tion. You may even decide to start over with a new topic. That costs time in the short run, but it may save you from a failed project. Under no circumstances should you put off thinking about a hypothesis until you begin drafting your paper or, worse, until you've almost finished it. You might not settle on the *best* answer to your question until you're well into writing your paper, for writing is an act of discovery. But you can't wait until that last draft to start thinking about *some* answer.

2.3.1   Beware the Risks in a Working Hypothesis

Don't settle on a final answer too soon: working hypotheses are meant to change. But many new researchers and some experienced ones are afraid to consider *any* working hypothesis early in their project, even one they hold lightly, because they fear it might bias their thinking. There is some risk of that, but a working hypothesis need not close your mind to a bet-ter one. Even the most objective scientist devises an experiment to test for just a few predicted outcomes, often just one. A working hypothesis is a risk only if it blinds you to a better one or if you can't give it up when the evidence says you should. So as in all relationships, don't fall too hard for your first hypothesis: the more you like it, the less easily you'll see its flaws. Despite that risk, it's better to start with a flawed hypothesis than with none at all.

2.3.2 If You Can't Find an Answer, Argue for Your Question

We have focused so much on questions that you might think your project fails if you can't answer yours. Not so. Much important research explains why a question no one has yet asked should be asked: *Do turtles dream? Why is yawning contagious?* Papers addressing such questions don't argue for answers; they explain why the question is important and what a good answer might look like.

Or perhaps you find that someone has answered your question, but incompletely or even—if you're lucky—incorrectly. If you can't find the right answer, you still help your research community by showing that a widely accepted one is wrong. You can even organize your paper around a working hypothesis you abandon. If after lots of research, you can't confirm it, you can explain why that answer seemed reasonable at the time but turned out to be wrong and so isn't worth the time of other researchers. That in itself can be a valuable contribution to the conversation on your topic. (See 10.1.1–10.1.2 for how to use an apparently good idea that turns out to be wrong.)

Only by asking question after question will you develop the critical imagination you need to excel at research. Experienced researchers know there are few, if any, final answers, because there are no final questions. They know that it's as important to ask a new question as it is to answer an old one, and that one day their new question will become old and yield to a newer researcher's still newer one. That's how the conversations of research communities progress.

2.4 Build a Storyboard to Plan and Guide Your Work

For a short paper, you might not need a detailed plan—a sketch of an outline might do. But for a long project, you'll usually need more, especially for one as long as a thesis or dissertation. The first plan that comes to mind is usually an outline, with its Is and IIs and As and Bs and so on (see 23.4.2.2). If you prefer an outline, use one, especially if your project is relatively short. The problem is that an outline can force you to specify too much too soon and so lock up a final form before you've done your best thinking.

To avoid that risk, many researchers, including those outside the academic world, use a *storyboard* to plan and guide their work. A storyboard is like an outline spread over several pages, with lots of space for adding data and ideas as you go. But it is more flexible than an outline because storyboard pages can be moved around, allowing you to try out new ways of organizing your ideas. You can spread its pages across a wall, group related pages, and put minor sections below major ones to create a "picture" of your project that shows you at a glance the design of the whole and your progress through it. For this reason, a storyboard is useful at every stage of your project. It can help you plan your research, develop your argument, organize your paper, write a first draft, and test a final one.

Someday you may have the time to amble through sources, reading just what interests you. Such random browsing has opened up many important lines of research. But if your paper is due in a month or so, or even sooner, you need a plan. A storyboard is a simple and reliable device to help you create one.

2.4.1 State Your Question and Working Hypotheses

To start a storyboard, state at the top of its first page your question and working hypothesis as precisely as you can. Then add plausible alternatives and new hypotheses as you think of them, and cross off those you prove wrong. But save them, because you might be able to use one of them in your introduction (see 10.1.1).

2.4.2 State Your Reasons

We say more about the structure of arguments in chapter 5. For now, the commonsense understanding of an argument as a claim supported by reasons and evidence is enough. Put at the top of separate pages each reason that might support your best hypothesis, even if you have only one or two. Imagine explaining your project to a friend. You say, *I want to show that Alamo stories helped develop a unique Texan identity*, and your friend asks, *Why do you think so?* Your reasons are the general statements that you offer to support your answer: *Well, first, the stories distorted facts to emphasize what became central to Texan identity; second, the stories were first used to show that Texas (and the Wild West) was a new kind of frontier; third, . . .* and so on.

If you can't think of more than one or two reasons, put placeholders at the tops of pages: *Reason 3: Something about Alamo stories making Texans feel special.* If you know only *how* you want a reason to support your answer, state that: *Reason 4: Something to show that Alamo stories were more than just myth.* Each reason, of course, needs support, so for each reason, ask, *Why do I think that? What evidence will I need to prove it?* That will help you focus your search for evidence (see 2.4.3 and 5.4.2).

If you're new to your topic or early in your project, your reasons may be only educated guesses that you'll later change. But a list of reasons, no matter how speculative, can not only guide your research but also focus your thinking and help you anticipate the argument you will eventually make.

2.4.3 **Sketch the Kind of Evidence You Should Look For**

Every field prefers its own kinds of evidence—numbers, quotations, observations, historical facts, images, and so on. So for each reason, sketch the kind of evidence that you think you'll need to support it. Even imagine what the most convincing evidence would look like. If you can't imagine the kind of evidence you'll need, leave that part of the page blank, then read secondary sources to find out the kind of evidence researchers in your field typically use (see 3.1.2).

2.4.4 **Look at the Whole**

Lay the pages on a table or tape them on a wall. Then step back and look at their order. When you plan a first draft, you must put its parts in some order, so you might as well think about one now. Can you see a logic in your storyboard? Cause and effect? Narrative time? Relative importance? Complexity? Length? (See 6.2.5 for more principles of order.) Try out different orders. This storyboard isn't your final plan; it's only a tool to guide your thinking and organize what you find. When you fill a page, try drafting that section, because writing out your ideas can improve your thinking at every stage of your project.

2.5 Join or Organize a Writing Group

One of the best ways to stay on track with your project is to join or organize a writing group. In many fields, especially in the humanities and social sciences, scholars read, think, and write mostly alone. But it doesn't have to be that way, at least not entirely. Find someone other than your instructor or advisor to talk with about your progress, to review your drafts, even to pester you about how much you have written. That person might be a generous friend or, better, another writer with whom you can trade feedback on ideas and drafts.

Better yet is a writing group: four or five people working on their own projects who meet regularly to discuss each other's work. Early on, start each meeting with a summary of each person's project in that three-part sentence: *I'm working on the topic X, because I want to find out Y, so that I (and you) can better understand Z.* As your projects develop, start with an "elevator story," a short summary of your research that you might give someone in the elevator on the way to the meeting. It should include that three-part sentence, a working hypothesis, and the major reasons supporting it (see 13.4). In later stages, share outlines and drafts so that the members of the group can serve as surrogate readers. If your group has a problem with your draft, so will your final readers. Your group can even help you brainstorm when you bog down. All of this support is valuable.

But for many writers, a writing group is valuable simply for the discipline it imposes. It is easier to meet a schedule when you know you must report your progress to others.

Writing groups are standard practice for those preparing theses or dissertations. But the rules may differ for class papers. Some teachers worry that writing groups or writing partners might provide more help than they should. So if you join a group, be clear with your teacher about what it will do. If you don't, she may decide the assistance you have received is inappropriate (see 7.10).

3 Finding Useful Sources

Once you have a research question and perhaps a working hypothesis, you can start looking for the data you'll need to test your hypothesis and develop your argument. In this chapter we explain how to find those data in sources and in the next how to work with them. But don't think of finding sources and reading them as separate steps. Once you have a promising source, read it to find other sources. And as you fill your storyboard with notes, you'll discover gaps and new questions that only more sources can fill. So while we discuss finding and using sources as distinct steps, you'll more often do them repeatedly and simultaneously.

3.1   Three Kinds of Sources and Their Uses

Sources are conventionally categorized into three kinds: *primary*, *secondary*, and *tertiary* (think first-, second-, and thirdhand). Their boundaries are fuzzy, but knowing these categories can help you conduct your research.

3.1.1   Consult Primary Sources for Evidence

Primary sources are "original" materials that provide you with the "raw" data or evidence you will use to develop, test, and ultimately justify your hypothesis or claim. In history, primary sources are artifacts or documents that come directly from the period you are studying: letters, diaries, objects, maps, even clothing. In literature or philosophy, your main primary sources are usually the texts you are analyzing, and your data are the words on the page. In the arts, your primary source would be the works of art you are interpreting. In social sciences, such as sociology or political science, census or survey data would also count as primary sources, as would data obtained through observation or experiment in many fields. The primary sources for those collected data are reports of original research in scholarly journals or government and commercial databases.

3.1.2   Read Secondary Sources to Learn from Other Researchers

Secondary sources are books, articles, papers, or reports that are based on primary sources and intended for scholarly or professional audiences. An article in a scholarly journal analyzing Alamo stories would be a secondary source for researchers working on those stories. The body of secondary sources in a field is sometimes called that field's *literature*. The best secondary sources are books from reputable university presses and articles or reports that have been *peer reviewed*, meaning that they were vetted by experts in the field before they were published (see 3.3.2). Secondary sources also include specialized encyclopedias and dictionaries that offer essays written by scholars in a field.

You use secondary sources for three purposes:

1. *To keep up with current research.* Researchers read secondary sources to keep up with the work of other researchers, to inform and refine their thinking, and to motivate their own work by adding to a published line of research.

2. *To find other points of view.* A research paper is not complete until the researcher acknowledges and responds to the views of others and to his readers' predictable questions and disagreements. You can find most of those other points of view in secondary sources. What alternatives to your ideas do they offer? What evidence do they cite that you must acknowledge? Some new researchers think they weaken their case if they mention any view opposing their own. The opposite is the truth. When you acknowledge competing views, you show readers that you not only know those views but can confidently respond to them. (For more on this, see 5.4.3.)

3. *To find models for your own research and analysis.* You can use secondary sources to find out not just *what* others have written about your topic but *how* they have written about it, as models for the form and style of your own paper. Imagine a secondary source as a colleague talking to you about your topic. As you respond, you'd want to sound like someone who knows the field, and so you'd try to learn how she reasons, the language she uses, the kinds of evidence she offers, and the kinds she rarely or never uses. The "conversation" would be in writing, so you'd even imitate stylistic details such as whether she writes in long paragraphs or breaks up her pages with subheads and bullet points (common in the social sciences, less common in the humanities).

You can also use a secondary source as a model for your conceptual analysis. If, for example, you were analyzing Alamo stories, you might study how a source treats Custer's Last Stand. Is its approach psychological, social, historical, political? Its particular reasons or evidence will probably be irrelevant to your project, but you might support your answer with the same kinds of data and reasoning, perhaps even following the same organization.

So if you come across a source that's not exactly on your topic but treats one like it, skim it to see how that researcher thinks about his material and presents it. (You don't have to cite that source if you use only its general logic, but you may cite it to give your own approach more authority.)

You can even borrow evidence from secondary sources to use in your own arguments, but you should do so only if you do not have access to the primary sources from which that evidence was originally taken. If you're doing advanced work, check the accuracy of important quotations, facts, or numbers you draw from secondary sources.

Of course, if you were studying how the Alamo story has been analyzed, then secondary sources offering those analyses would be your primary sources.

If you're new to a field, you may find secondary sources hard to read: they assume a lot of background knowledge, and many aren't clearly written (see 11.2). If you're working on a topic new to you, you might begin with an overview in a specialized encyclopedia or reliable tertiary source.

3.1.3   Read Tertiary Sources for Introductory Overviews

Tertiary sources are books and articles that synthesize secondary sources for general readers. They include textbooks, encyclopedias (including Wikipedia), and dictionaries, as well as articles in publications for broad audiences, like *Time* and the *Atlantic*. In the early stages of research, you can use tertiary sources to get a broad overview of your topic. But if you are making a scholarly argument, you should rely on secondary sources because these make up the conversation in which you are seeking to participate. If you cite tertiary sources in a scholarly argument, you will mark yourself as a novice or outsider, and many readers won't take you—or your argument—seriously.

3.2   Search for Sources Systematically

Knowing where to begin your search for sources can be overwhelming at first. It is tempting to simply enter terms into a familiar search engine (e.g., Google) and see what comes up. We do this too, but we also know that there are more systematic and productive ways for discovering useful, credible sources. Make the library the focus of your search strategies even as you draw on the expertise of others inside or outside the academic community and use the resources of the internet.

3.2.1   Ask a Librarian

The best advice we can offer is to draw on the research expertise of librarians. Both general reference librarians and (in larger libraries) subject area specialists can help you refine your search parameters and direct you to the right tools for your specific research question. They can help you use the catalog to locate materials held by your library or by other libraries (and obtainable through interlibrary loan). These same librarians typically design research guides that identify reference works and online databases for specific fields. If you're a new researcher, seize every opportunity to learn online search techniques in your field.

And don't be shy. Librarians love to assist researchers of all levels and at all stages of the research process. They can help you formulate your research question and plan, develop search terms, and inventory your results to ensure you haven't overlooked something of value. The only embarrassing question is the one you failed to ask. If you already have a research question, share it: *I'm looking for data on X because I want to find out* . . . If you have a working hypothesis and reasons, share them too: *I'm looking for data to show Y [your reason] because I want to claim Z [your hypothesis].* Rehearse your questions to avoid wasting your time and theirs.

3.2.2 Consult Reference Works

Researchers in all fields share common values and habits of thought, but every field has its own ways of doing things. To learn about the ways of your field, browse the shelves in your library's reference room that hold guides to your field's particular research methods, databases, and special resources (in the bibliography, see items in category 3 in your field). At least familiarize yourself with the following resources (in the bibliography, see category 4 for lists of sources in your field; many are also online):

- a bibliography of works published each year in your field, such as *Philosopher's Index* or *Education Index*
- summary bibliographies of works on a specific topic collected over several years (*Bibliographic Index* is a bibliography of bibliographies)
- annual literature reviews; look for a title in your field beginning with *Reviews in* . . .
- specialized reference works such as the *Encyclopedia of Philosophy* or the *Concise Oxford Dictionary of Literary Terms*, where you may find an overview of your topic and often a list of standard primary and secondary sources (in the bibliography, see items in categories 1 and 2 in your field).

3.2.3 Explore Online Databases

What sets libraries apart from the internet are subscriptions to indexes and databases. After books, these are arguably a library's most valuable assets, since they give researchers access to materials they could not obtain otherwise. Each library's subscriptions will differ, with major research libraries offering the most comprehensive access to specialized indexes and databases. However, academic libraries and many public libraries offer powerful online tools that greatly extend their actual collections. You will certainly want to make use of these general and specialized resources in your research. At least become familiar with the major databases to which your library subscribes, such as Academic Search Premier, MLA International Bibliography, or PubMed. Many academic databases either provide abstracts or direct you to articles that include abstracts. Looking at these can help you decide if an article itself is worth reading carefully. Some databases allow you to access full-text articles or books. But beware: if your library does not subscribe to a particular journal included in a database, you might be asked to pay a fee to access a full-text article. Before doing so, *always* speak with a librarian about other means of access.

3.2.4   Search Your Library Catalog

In your research, you will likely use your library's catalog in two ways: keyword searching and browsing. When you have examined some sources to identify a list of *keywords* related to your topic, you are ready to use these terms to search the catalog. In most libraries you must choose the category (books, articles, journals, etc.) you wish to use for your search.

If your sources include books, you can use the Library of Congress subject headings, found either on the back of their title page or on their "details" page in the online catalog, to search for related materials. For example, the online entry for this book includes these two topics:

1. Dissertations, Academic. 2. Academic writing.

If you search an online catalog, you will find all the books on that subject in that library. A book may be cross-listed under multiple subject headings. In that case, look at titles listed under those headings as well. You can also *browse* the catalog for books with similar *call numbers*.

Also search your online catalog using keywords from your question or working hypothesis—*Alamo, Texas independence, James Bowie*. If you find too many titles, start with those published in the last ten or fifteen years by well-known university presses. For a wider selection, search WorldCat if your library subscribes. Otherwise, search the Library of Congress catalog at https://www.loc.gov. It has links to large university catalogs. Start early if you expect to get books on interlibrary loan.

If most sources on your topic are articles, locate a recent one in your library's online databases. Its database entry will include a list of keywords. Search for them to find more articles on your topic. In most cases you can just click on them. Use the keywords to search the library catalog as well. Some databases also provide abstracts of journal articles that you can skim for search terms.

3.2.5   Search Guides to Periodical Literature

If you've done research before, you're probably familiar with annual guides such as *Readers' Guide to Periodical Literature*, which cites sources such as magazines and newspapers. Most specialized fields also have yearly guides to secondary sources, such as *Art Abstracts, Historical Abstracts,* and *Abstracts in Anthropology* (in the bibliography, see items in category 4 in your field). Most are available online or in other digital forms.

All those resources will direct you to more sources, but none of them can substitute for the kind of in-library search that turns up an unexpectedly useful source.

3.2.6 Prowl the Stacks

Doing research online is faster than on foot, but if you never go into the stacks of your library (assuming you have access), you may miss crucial sources that you'd find only there. More important, you'll miss the benefits of serendipity—a chance encounter with a source that you find only in person. If you can get to the stacks, find the shelf with books on your topic, then scan the titles on that shelf and the ones above, below, and on either side, especially for books with new bindings published by university presses. Then turn around and skim titles behind you; you never know. When you spot a promising title, skim its table of contents, then its index for keywords related to your question or its answer. Then skim its bibliography for titles that look relevant to your project. You can do all that faster with books on a shelf than you can online.

If the book looks promising, skim its preface or introduction. If it still looks promising, set it aside for a closer look. Even if it doesn't seem relevant, record its Library of Congress call number and bibliographic data (author, title, publisher, date of publication and so on; see part 2 of this manual for the details), and in a few words summarize what the book seems to be about. A month later, you might realize that it's more useful than you thought.

You can check tables of contents for many journals online, but browsing in the journals area of a library can be more productive. Find the journals that have promising articles. Skim tables of contents for the prior ten years. Most volumes include a yearly summary table of contents. Then take a quick look at the journals shelved nearby. Skim their most recent tables of contents. You will be surprised at how often you find a relevant article that you would have missed had you done your work entirely online.

If you are new to a field, you can get a rough impression of the academic quality of a journal by its look. If it's on glossy paper with lots of illustrations, even advertisements, it might be more journalistic than scholarly. Those are not infallible signs of unreliable scholarship, but they are worth considering.

3.2.7 Follow Bibliographic Trails

Most sources will give you trailheads for bibliographic searches. When you find a book or article that seems useful, skim its bibliography or works cited. Its index will list the authors cited most often. Journal articles usually begin with a review of previous research, all cited. Finally, look for recent PhD dissertations even marginally related to your topic. Almost every dissertation reviews research in its first of second chapter. By following these bibliographic trails, you can navigate the most difficult research territory, because one source leads to another, and another . . .

3.2.8 Search the Internet

Your practical experience using the internet for everyday research might lead you to believe that it is comprehensive and reliable, but that would be a mistake. Your library's catalog and databases provide access to information that you cannot get through a search engine. When doing research online, maintain a healthy skepticism: most of what we retrieve using Google or some other search engine is perfectly reliable, but not everything is. In contrast to your library's catalog and databases, the internet is essentially unmonitored. There is no one to vouch for the credibility of materials posted to countless websites. And finally, keep in mind that companies offering free search engines make their money by acquiring data about you through online behavior and by selling advertising, and that webmasters routinely modify their sites to make them appear higher in search results.

But if you keep these limitations in mind, the internet can be an enormously valuable resource. In particular, you can do useful preliminary work with a scholarly search engine such as Google Scholar or with a tertiary source such as Wikipedia (which you should never cite as a reference). Of course, the internet can also be a primary source if you are researching the internet itself, including social media.

3.2.9 Look for Someone Who Knows Something about Your Topic

You might also ask around or search online to find someone who knows something about your topic and standard reference works on it: advanced students, faculty, even people outside the academic community. You won't always find someone, but you might get lucky.

3.3 Evaluate Sources for Relevance and Reliability

You will probably find more sources than you can use, so you must evaluate their usefulness by skimming quickly for two criteria: relevance and reliability.

3.3.1 Evaluate Sources for Relevance

Once you decide a book might be relevant, do this:

- Skim its index for your keywords, then skim the pages on which those words occur.

- Skim the first and last paragraphs in chapters that use a lot of your keywords.
- Skim the book's introduction, especially its last page, where authors and editors often outline their text.
- Skim its last chapter or conclusion, especially the first and last several pages.
- Skim prologues, summary chapters, and so on.
- Check the bibliography for titles relevant to your topic.

Be sure that you're looking at a book's most recent edition. Researchers change their views over time, refining them, even rejecting earlier ones. If your source is an e-book, still follow these steps, but you can also search the whole text for your keywords. If you are an advanced researcher, read book reviews of promising sources (see section 4 of the bibliography of resources in your field).

If your source is a journal article, do this:

- Read the abstract, if it has one.
- Skim the introduction and conclusion; if they are not marked off by headings, skim the first six or seven paragraphs and the last four or five.
- Skim for section headings, and read the first and last paragraphs of those sections.
- Check the bibliography for titles relevant to your topic.

If your source is online, do this:

- If it looks like a printed article, follow the steps for journal article, and also search for your keywords.
- Skim sections labeled "Introduction," "Overview," "Summary," or the like. If there are none, look for a link labeled "About the Site" or something similar.
- If the site has a link labeled "Site Map" or "Index," check it for your keywords and skim the referenced pages.
- If the site has a search function, type in your keywords.

3.3.2   Evaluate Sources for Reliability

You can't judge a source until you read it, but there are signs of its reliability:

1. **Is the source published by a reputable press?** Most books and journals published by university presses, whether in print or in electronic editions, are reliable, especially if you recognize the name of the university. You can also trust some commercial presses in some fields, such as Norton in literature, Ablex in sciences, or West in the law. Be

skeptical of a commercial book that makes sensational claims, even if its author has a PhD after his name. Be especially careful on contested social issues such as gun control or climate change. Many books and articles are published by individuals or organizations driven more by ideology than by evidence.

2. **Is the book or article peer reviewed?** Most reputable presses and jour-nals ask experts to review a book or article before it is published; this is called *peer review.* Essay collections published by university presses are often but not always peer reviewed; sometimes they are reviewed only by the named editor or editors. Few commercial magazines use peer review, and fewer still check an author's facts. If a book or article hasn't been peer reviewed, use it cautiously.

3. **Is the author a reputable scholar?** This is a hard question to answer if you are new to a field. Most established scholars are reliable, but use good judgment: even reputable scholars can have axes to grind, especially if their research is supported by a special interest group.

4. **If the source is available only online, is it sponsored by a reputable organization?** A website is only as reputable as its sponsor. You can usually trust one that is sponsored and maintained by a reputable organization. Some sites run by individuals are reliable; most are not. Do a web search for the name of the sponsor.

5. **Is the source current?** You must use up-to-date sources, but what counts as current depends on the field. In computer science, a journal can be out of date in months; in the social sciences, ten years pushes the limit. Publications have a longer shelf life in the humanities: liter-ary or art criticism, for example, can remain relevant for decades, even centuries.

6. **If the source is a book, does it have notes and a bibliography?** If not, be suspicious, because you have no way to follow up on anything that the source claims.

7. **If the source is a website, does it include bibliographic data?** You can-not judge the reliability of a site that does not indicate who sponsors and maintains it, who wrote what's posted there, and when it was posted and last updated.

8. **If the source is a website, does it approach its topic judiciously?** Your readers are unlikely to trust a site that engages in heated advocacy, attacks other researchers, makes wild claims, uses abusive language, or makes errors of spelling, punctuation, and grammar.

The following criteria are especially important for advanced re-searchers.

9. **If the source is a book, has it been well reviewed?** Many fields have indexes to published reviews that tell you how others evaluate a source.
10. **Has the source been frequently cited by others?** You can roughly estimate how influential a source is by how often others cite it. To determine that, consult a citation index (in the bibliography, see section 4 in your field). If you find that a source has been cited repeatedly by other scholars, you can infer that experts in the field regard it as reliable and significant. Such sources are said to have an "high impact factor."

Those signs don't guarantee that a source is reliable, but they should give you reasonable confidence in it. If you can't find reliable sources, acknowledge the limits of the ones you have. Of course, you may find an exciting research problem when you discover that a source thought to be reliable is not.

3.4 Look beyond the Usual Kinds of References

For a class paper, you'll probably use sources typical in your field. But if you are doing an advanced project such as an MA thesis or PhD dissertation, search beyond them. If, for example, you were doing a project on the economic effects of agricultural changes in late sixteenth-century England, you might read some Elizabethan plays, look at woodcuts of agricultural life, find commentary by religious figures on rural social behavior. Conversely, if you were working on visual representations of daily life in London, you might work up the economic history of the period and place. When you look beyond the standard kinds of references relevant to your question, you enrich not only your analysis but also your range of intellectual reference and your ability to synthesize diverse kinds of data, a crucial competence of an inquiring mind. Don't ignore a work on your topic that is not mentioned in the bibliographies of your most relevant sources—you'll get credit for originality if you turn up good sources others have ignored.

3.5 Record Your Sources Fully, Accurately, and Appropriately

Once you decide a source is worth reading, record all of its bibliographic information. Your first obligation as a researcher is to cite your sources accurately and fully so that your readers can find them.

3.5.1 Determine Your Citation Style

Most fields require a specific citation style. The two most common ones are described in detail in part 2:

- *notes-bibliography style* (or simply *notes style*), used widely in the humanities and in some social sciences (see chapters 16 and 17)
- *author-date style*, used in most social sciences and in the natural sciences (see chapters 18 and 19)

If you are uncertain which style to use, consult your instructor or advisor. Before you start compiling your list of sources, read the general introduction to citations in chapter 15 and then, depending on the citation style you are required to use, read the introduction to notes style (chapter 16) or author-date style (chapter 18).

3.5.2   Record Complete Bibliographical Information

To save time and avoid errors, record all the citation information you will need when you first find a source. Most of this information appears on the title page of a book or at the head of a journal article. The specific information you need depends on the type of source, but for each source, answer the following:

- Who wrote or assembled the source?
  - author(s)
  - editor(s) (if any)
  - translator(s) (if any)
- What data identify the source?
  - title (including subtitle)
  - page numbers (if the source appears in a larger work)
  - volume number
  - issue number
  - edition number
- Who published the source and in what context?
  - publisher's name
  - place of publication
  - name of the journal, collection, or other work in which the source appears
- When was the source published?
  - year of publication
  - season, month, or specific day (and, in some cases, time)
  - for online sources, the date you accessed the material (whether or not you include this date in your citation)
- Where can the source be found?
  - for online sources, a URL or the name of the database
  - for physical items in a one-of-a-kind collection, the place that houses the collection

For your own use, you might record Library of Congress call numbers. You won't include them in bibliographic citations, but you may find them helpful if you must consult the source again.

If you access a printed text online, record the URL and any other data for the online version in addition to the full bibliographic data for the original source.

If you scan or photocopy a passage from a book, also scan or photocopy its title page and the bibliographic information on the reverse side. Then add the library call number if you know it.

At some point, you'll need to format this bibliographic information into your required citation style, so you should record your sources in that style now. (You can find templates and examples for notes style in figure 16.1 and chapter 17; for author-date style, refer to figure 18.1 and chapter 19.)

For many types of sources, you can copy and paste citation data online if you know where to look. And there are a number of programs that will help you collect and organize your citations and automatically insert them in your paper in the proper format. These are useful aids, but they are not perfect, so plan on double-checking your citations not only as you acquire them but also later, after they've been inserted in your paper.

4 Engaging Your Sources

Once you have a research problem, use it to guide your search for evidence, models, and arguments to respond to. But if you don't yet have one firmly in hand, you won't know which data, models, or arguments will prove relevant. So read sources not randomly but deliberately to find a problem. Look for claims that seem puzzling, inaccurate, or simplistic—anything you can disagree with. You're more likely to find a research problem when you disagree with a source, but you can also find one in sources you agree with.

Experienced researchers don't read passively; they engage their sources actively, entering into conversation with them. Once you find a source worth a close look, don't read it mechanically, just mining it for data to record. Note-taking is not clerical work. When you take notes on a source thoughtfully, you engage not just its words and ideas but also its implications, consequences, shortcomings, and new possibilities.

4.1 Read Generously to Understand, Then Critically to Engage

If you can, read promising sources twice. First, read generously. Pay attention to what sparks your interest. Reread passages that puzzle or confuse you. Don't look for disagreements right away, but read in ways that help the source make sense. Disagree too soon and you will misunderstand your source or exaggerate a weakness if it presents an argument that challenges yours.

Then, if a source seems important or challenges your own position, read it a second time slowly and more critically. When you read a passage, think not only about what it says but about how you would respond. Record those responses in your notes or—if you own the source or a copy of it—in the margins of the source. Test your understanding by summarizing; if you can't sum up a passage in your mind, you don't understand it well enough to disagree.

You probably won't be able to engage your sources fully until you've done a bit of reading and have developed your own ideas further. But from the outset, be on alert for ways to engage your sources, actively and creatively. At some point, the earlier the better, you must look for ways to go *beyond* your sources, too, even when you agree with them.

4.1.1 Look for Creative Agreement

It's a happy moment when a source confirms our views. But if we just passively agree, we don't develop our own ideas. So if you believe what a source claims, try to extend that claim: What new cases might it cover? What new insights can it provide? Is there confirming evidence the source hasn't considered? Here are some ways to find a problem through creative agreement.

1. **Offer additional support.** You can offer new evidence to support a source's claim.

   Smith uses anecdotal evidence to show that the Alamo story had mythic status beyond Texas, but editorials in big-city newspapers offer better evidence.

   ■ Source supports _____ with old evidence, but maybe you can offer new evidence.
   ■ Source supports _____ with weak evidence, but maybe you can offer stronger evidence.

2. **Confirm unsupported claims.** You can prove something that a source has only assumed or speculated.

   Smith recommends visualization to improve sports performance, but a study of the mental activities of athletes shows why that is good advice.

   - Source speculates _____ might be true, but you can offer evidence to show that it is.
   - Source assumes _____ is true, but maybe you can prove it.

3. **Apply a claim more widely.** You can extend a position to new areas.

   Smith argues that medical students learn physiological processes better when they are explained with many metaphors rather than with just one. The same appears to be true for engineers learning physical processes.

   - Source correctly applies _____ to one situation, but maybe it can apply to new ones.
   - Source claims that _____ is true in a specific situation, but maybe it's true in general.

4.1.2   Look for Creative Disagreement

If you read actively, you'll inevitably find yourself disagreeing with your sources. Don't brush those disagreements aside, because they often point to new research problems. So instead of just noting that you disagree with another writer's views, use that disagreement to encourage your own productive thinking. Look for these types (the list is not exhaustive, and some overlap).

1. **Contradictions of kind.** A source says something is one kind of thing, but maybe it's another kind.

   Smith says that certain religious groups are considered "cults" because of their strange beliefs, but those beliefs are no different in kind from standard religions.

   - Source claims that _____ is a kind of _____, but it's not.
   - Source claims that _____ always has _____ as one of its features or qualities, but it doesn't.
   - Source claims that _____ is normal/good/significant/useful/moral/interesting, but it's not.

   You can reverse those claims and the ones that follow to state the opposite:

   - Though a source says _____ is *not* a kind of _____, you can show that it is.

2. **Part-whole contradictions.** You can show that a source mistakes how the parts of something are related.

Smith has argued that coding is irrelevant to a liberal education, but in fact, it is essential.

   - Source claims that ___ is a part of ___, but it's not.
   - Source claims that one part of ___ relates to another in a certain way, but it doesn't.
   - Source claims that every ___ has ___ as one of its parts, but it doesn't.

3. **Developmental or historical contradictions.** You can show that a source mistakes the origin and development of a topic.

Smith argues that the world population will rise, but it won't.

   - Source claims that ___ is changing, but it's not.
   - Source claims that ___ originated in ___, but it didn't.
   - Source claims that ___ develops in a certain way, but it doesn't.

4. **External cause-effect relations.** You can show that a source mistakes a causal relationship.

Smith claims that legalizing marijuana will increase its use among teenagers, but evidence shows that it doesn't.

   - Source claims that ___ causes ___, but it doesn't.
   - Source claims that ___ causes ___, but it doesn't; they are both caused by ___.
   - Source claims that ___ is sufficient to cause ___, but it's not.
   - Source claims that ___ causes only ___, but it also causes ___.

5. **Contradictions of perspective.** Most contradictions don't change a conceptual framework, but when you can contradict a "standard" view of things, you urge others to think in a new way.

Smith assumes that advertising has only an economic function, but it also serves as a laboratory for new art forms.

   - Source discusses ___ from the point of view of ___, but a new context or point of view reveals a new truth. (The new or old context can be social, political, philosophical, historical, economic, ethical, gender specific, etc.)
   - Source analyzes ___ using theory / value system ___, but you can analyze it from a new point of view and see it in a new way.

As we said, you probably won't be able to engage sources in these ways until after you've read enough to form some views of your own. But if you keep these ways of thinking in mind as you begin to read, you'll engage your sources sooner and more productively.

Of course, once you discover that you can productively agree or disagree with a source, you should ask *So what?* So what if you can show that while Smith claims that easterners did not embrace the story of the Alamo enthusiastically, in fact many did?

4.2   Take Notes Systematically

Once you find and record a source you think you can use, you must read it purposefully and carefully. Then take notes in a way that will help you not only to remember and use what you have read but also to further your own thinking. Like the other steps in a research project, note-taking goes better with a plan.

4.2.1   Taking Notes on Paper

Years ago, the standard way to take notes on sources was to create a file of index cards (see figure 4.1). At the top left is the author, short title, and page number. At the top right are keywords that let the researcher sort and re-sort notes into different categories and orders. The body of the card summarizes the source, records a direct quotation, and includes a comment or thought about further research that is clearly distinguished from the quotation. At the bottom left is the call number for the source.

A card like this seems old-fashioned, but it provides a template for efficient note-taking:

Sharman, <u>Swearing</u>, p. 133   HISTORY/ECONOMICS (GENDER?)

Says swearing became economic issue in 18th c. Cites <u>Gentleman's Magazine</u>, July 1751 (no page reference): woman sentenced to ten days' hard labor because couldn't pay one-shilling fine for profanity.

"... one rigid economist practically entertained the notion of adding to the national resources by preaching a crusade against the opulent class of swearers."

[*Way to think about swearing today as econmic issue? Comedians more popular if they use bad language? Movies more realistic? A gender issue here? Were 18th-c. men fined as often as women?*]

GT3080/S6

Figure 4.1. Example of a note card

- Record complete bibliographic information for each source so that you can cite it properly and find it again easily.
- Separate notes on different topics, even if they come from the same source.
- Make sure your notes are accurate, because you need to be able to rely on them later. (If you want to quote more than a few lines, copy or save the passage or the whole document.)
- Clearly distinguish (1) what you quote from a source, (2) what you paraphrase or summarize from a source, and (3) your own thoughts. If you are writing on paper, use headings or brackets or distinct colors to differentiate these three different kinds of notes. You might also create a section specifically dedicated to *your own* responses, agreements, disagreements, speculations, and so on (see the italicized section in figure 4.1). That will encourage you to do more than simply record the content of what you read.

4.2.2 Taking Notes Electronically

When you take notes electronically, you have some options:

- You can use a word processor. Create a separate file (or at least a separate page) for each source, and be sure to unambiguously distinguish your words from those of your source. Though word processors are easy to use, they also limit your ability to index, organize, sort, and search your notes. For long or complex projects, you might consider other options.
- You can use a dedicated note-taking application to create and organize your notes. Such applications can help you to index, sort, and access your notes. But since they sometimes use proprietary formats, they can make it difficult to share your notes or use them with other programs.
- You can use a full-featured citation management program. In addition to allowing you to make your own notes, these programs can often pull information directly from online library catalogs and databases, and they can format and update your bibliographies as you write. Some will even store full electronic copies of your sources, creating a personal library for your project. But like note-taking applications, these programs sometimes use proprietary formats.

In electronic notes, as in notes on paper, you must clearly distinguish your own words and ideas from those of your source.

- Record quotations from your source in a distinctive color or font so that you can recognize them at a glance, and enclose them in large quotation marks in case the file loses its formatting.

■ Record paraphrases from your source in a second color or font so that you can't possibly mistake them for your own ideas, and enclose them in curly brackets in case the file loses its formatting.

■ Record your own thoughts in a third color or font, and enclose them in square brackets. Put longer responses in a separate section so there is no chance you will mistake your own ideas for your source's, or vice versa.

4.2.3   Decide Whether to Summarize, Paraphrase, or Quote

If you can photocopy, scan, or otherwise reproduce your source, or you know you can access it online when you write, you can focus less on preserving its exact words than on your engagement with it. Summarize the source, which will help you understand it, and note passages you might want to quote or paraphrase when you write. Note also your response to the source. Where did you find yourself agreeing or disagreeing with it?

If you can't preserve your source and you don't know whether you will be able to access it later, you have a tougher choice. It takes too long to transcribe the exact words of every passage you might want to use, so when taking notes, you must choose as you go whether to quote, paraphrase, or summarize. Every choice depends on how you plan to use your source:

■ Summarize when you need only the point of a passage, section, or even whole article or book. Summary is useful for context and for data or claims that are related—but not directly relevant—to your project. A summary of a source can never serve as good evidence (see 5.4.2).

■ Paraphrase when the specific words of a passage are less important than its meaning. Paraphrase doesn't mean changing just a word or two. You must replace most of the words and phrasing of the original with your own (see 7.9.2). As evidence, a paraphrase is never as good as a direct quotation.

■ Record exact quotations for these purposes:

   ■ The quoted words are evidence that backs up your reasons. If, for example, you claimed that different regions responded to the Battle of the Alamo differently, you would quote exact words from different newspapers. You would paraphrase them if you needed only their general sentiments.

   ■ The words are from an authority you plan to rely on or challenge.

   ■ The words are strikingly original or so compelling that the quotation can frame the rest of your discussion.

   ■ The words express a claim that you disagree with, and to be fair you want to state it exactly.

If you don't record important words now, you can't quote them later. So copy or photocopy more passages than you think you'll need (for more on photocopying, see 4.3.1).

Never abbreviate a quotation thinking you can accurately reconstruct it later. You can't. And if you misquote, you'll damage your credibility.

4.2.4 Guard against Inadvertent Plagiarism

For students and professionals alike, sloppy note-taking has caused grief ranging from ridicule for trivial errors to professional exile for inadvertent plagiarism. To avoid that risk, commit to heart these two iron rules for recording information in notes:

- *Always* unambiguously identify words and ideas from a source so that weeks or months later you cannot possibly mistake them for your own. As recommended above, record quotations and paraphrases with quotation marks, as well as in a font or color that unambiguously distinguishes them from your own ideas.
- *Never* paraphrase a source so closely that a reader can match the phrasing and sense of your words with those in your source (see 7.9.2).

In fact, rather than retyping quotations of more than a few lines, download or photocopy them. Add to the top of the downloaded or photocopied pages the name of the source and keywords for sorting.

This is important: *never* assume that you can use what you find online without citing its source, even if it's free and publicly available. You must acknowledge your use of *anything* you did not create yourself. (For more on plagiarism, see 7.9.)

4.3 Take Useful Notes

Readers will judge your work not just by the quality of your sources and how accurately you report them but also by how deeply you engage them. To do that, you must take notes in a way that not only reflects but encourages a growing understanding of your project.

4.3.1 Use Note-Taking to Advance Your Thinking

Many inexperienced researchers think that note-taking is a matter of merely recording data. Recording or photocopying can help you quote or paraphrase accurately, but if you don't *engage* your sources, you simply accumulate inert data. To advance your thinking, on any pages you've copied, annotate key sentences and passages by highlighting or labeling them in the margin. Mark ideas or data that you expect to use in your paper. Summarize what you have highlighted, or sketch a response to it, or add notes in the margin that help you interpret your highlighting. The more you write about a source now, the better you will understand it later.

4.3.2   **Take Notes Relevant to Your Question and Working Hypothesis**
For sources you think especially useful, record not just facts that you think you can use as evidence but also other information that helps you explain those facts and their relationship to your claim. You can create a template to help with this (see 4.2.1).

The first three items directly support or challenge your working hypothesis:

- reasons that support your hypothesis or suggest a new one
- evidence that supports your reasons
- views that undermine or even contradict your hypothesis (see 5.4.3)

These next items might not support or challenge your hypothesis, but they may help you explain its context or simply make your paper more readable:

- historical background of your question and what authorities have said about it, particularly earlier research (see 6.2.2 and 10.1.1)
- historical or contemporary context that explains the importance of your question
- important definitions and principles of analysis
- analogies, comparisons, and anecdotes that might not directly support your hypothesis but do explain or illustrate complicated issues or simply make your analysis more interesting
- strikingly original language relevant to your topic

4.3.3   **Get the Context Right**
You can't record everything, but you have to record enough to ensure that you accurately capture the source's meaning. As you use material from sources, record not just what they say but how they use the information. Here are some ways to guard against misleading your reader.

1. **When you quote, paraphrase, or summarize, be sure to capture the context.** When you note an important conclusion, record the author's line of reasoning:

     Not   Bartolli (p. 123): The war was caused by Z.

     But   Bartolli: The war was caused by X, Y, and Z (p. 123). But the most important cause was Z (p. 123), for two reasons: reason 1 (pp. 124-26); reason 2 (p. 126).

Sometimes you care only about a conclusion, but readers usually want to see how a conclusion emerges from the argument supporting it. So when you take notes, record not only conclusions but also the arguments that support them.

2. **When you record a claim, note its role in the original.** Is it a main point? A minor point? A qualification or concession? By noting these distinctions, you avoid this kind of mistake:

Original by Jones: "Researchers recognize that lung cancer has a number of causes, including genetic predisposition and exposure to environmental factors such as asbestos, radon, and fine particulates. But no one who has studied the data doubts that lung cancer's leading cause is smoking."

Misleading report about Jones: Smoking is just one cause of lung cancer among many. Jones, for example, claims that "lung cancer has a number of causes, including genetic predisposition and exposure to environmental factors such as asbestos, radon, and fine particulates."

Jones did not make that point at all. He *conceded* a point to set up a point he wanted to make. Anyone who deliberately misrepresents an author in this way violates basic standards of truth. But you can make such a mistake inadvertently if you note only a source's words and not their role in an argument.

3. **Record the scope and confidence of a claim.** These are not the same:

Chemicals in french fries cause cancer.

Chemicals in french fries may be a factor in causing cancer.

Some chemicals in french fries correlate with a higher incidence of cancer.

4. **Don't mistake a summary of another writer's views for those of an author summarizing them.** Some writers do not clearly indicate when they summarize another's argument, so it's easy to quote them as saying what they set out to disprove rather than what they in fact believe.

5. **Note *why* sources agree and disagree.** Two social scientists might claim that a social problem is caused by personal factors, not by environmental forces, but one might cite evidence from genetic inheritance while the other points to religious beliefs. How and why sources agree is as important as the fact that they do. In the same way, sources might disagree because they interpret the same evidence differently or take different approaches to the problem.

It is risky to attach yourself to what any one researcher says about an issue. It is not "research" when you uncritically summarize another's work. If you rely on at least two sources, you'll usually find that they do not agree entirely, and that's where your own research can begin.

4.4   Review Your Progress

Regularly review your notes and storyboard to see where you are and where you have to go. In a storyboard, full pages indicate reasons with support; empty pages indicate work to do. Consider whether your working hypothesis is still plausible. Do you have good reasons supporting it? Good evidence to support those reasons? Can you add new reasons or evidence?

4.4.1   Search Your Notes for an Answer

We have urged you to find a working hypothesis or at least a question to guide your research. But some writers start with a question so vague that it evaporates as they pursue it. If that happens to you, search your notes for a generalization that might be a candidate for a working hypothesis, then work backward to find the question it answers.

Look first for questions, disagreements, or puzzles in your sources and in your reaction to them (see 2.1.3 and 4.1). What surprises you might surprise others. Try to state that surprise:

I expected the first mythic stories of the Alamo to originate in Texas, but they didn't. They originated in . . .

That working hypothesis suggests that the Alamo myth began as a national, not a regional, phenomenon—a modest but promising start.

If you can't find a working hypothesis in your notes, look for a pattern of ideas that might lead you to one. If you gathered data with a vague question, you probably sorted them under predictable keywords. For masks, the categories might be their origins (*African, Indian, Japanese, . . .*), uses (*drama, religion, carnival, . . .*), materials (*gold, feather, wood, . . .*), and so on. For example:

Egyptians—mummy masks of gold for nobility, wood for others

Aztecs—masks from gold and jade buried only in the graves of the nobility

New Guinea tribes—masks for the dead from feathers from rare birds

Those facts could support a general statement such as *Mask-making cultures use the most valuable materials available to create religious masks, especially for the dead.*

Once you can generate two or three such statements, try to formulate a still larger generalization that might include them all:

Many cultures invest great material and human resources in creating masks that represent their deepest values._{generalization} Egyptians, Aztecs, and Oceanic cultures all created religious masks out of the rarest and most valuable materials.

If you think that some readers might plausibly disagree with that generalization, you might be able to offer it as a claim that corrects their misunderstanding.

4.4.2 Invent Your Question

Now comes a tricky part. It's like reverse engineering: you've found the answer to a question that you haven't yet asked, so you have to reason backward to invent the question that your new generalization answers. In this case, it might be *What signs indicate the significance of masks in the societies of those who make and use them?* As paradoxical as it may seem, experienced researchers often discover their question *after* they answer it, the problem they should have posed after they solve it.

4.4.3 Re-sort Your Notes

If none of that helps, try re-sorting your notes. When you first selected keywords for your notes, you identified general concepts that could organize not just your evidence but your thinking. If you chose keywords representing those concepts carefully, you can re-sort your notes in different ways to get a new slant on your material. If your keywords no longer seem relevant, review your notes to create new ones and reshuffle again.

4.5 Manage Moments of Normal Anxiety

As you get deeper into your project, you may experience moments when everything seems to run together into a hopeless muddle. That usually happens when you accumulate notes faster than you can sort them. Such moments can be stressful, but they can also be a sign that you are on the verge of a new insight or discovery.

You can minimize the anxiety by taking every opportunity to organize and summarize what you have gathered by *writing as you go* and by returning to the central questions: *What question am I asking? What problem am I posing?* Keep rehearsing that formula: *I am working on X to learn more about Y, so that my readers can better understand Z.* Writing regularly about these questions does more than help you stay focused; it also helps you think.

You can turn to friends, classmates, teachers—anyone who will serve as a sympathetic but critical audience. Explain how what you have learned bears on your question and helps you resolve your problem. Ask them, *Does this make sense? Am I missing something important? What else would you like to know?* You will profit from their reactions and even more from the mere act of explaining your ideas to nonspecialists.

5 Constructing Your Argument

Most of us would rather read than write. There is always another article to read, one more source to track down, just a bit more data to gather. But well before you've done all the research you'd like to do, there comes a point when you must start thinking about the first draft of your paper. You might be ready when your storyboard starts to fill up and you're satisfied with how it looks. You will know you're ready when you think you can sketch a reasonable case to support your working hypothesis (see 2.3). If your storyboard is full and you still can't pull together a case strong enough to plan a draft, you may have to rethink your hypothesis, perhaps even your question. But you can't be certain where you stand in that process until you at least try to plan that first draft.

In this chapter we explain how to build your argument; in the next, how to organize it. As you gain experience, you'll learn to combine those two steps into one.

5.1   **What a Research Argument Is and Is Not**

The word *argument* has negative associations these days because it evokes images of people shouting at one another. In that kind of argument the goal is to win, to bludgeon or intimidate one's opponent into assent or silence. But a research argument isn't like that. As we suggested in chapter 1, it is more like a conversation with a community of receptive but skeptical colleagues. Such readers won't necessarily oppose your claims (although they might), but they also won't accept them until they see good reasons based on reliable evidence and until you respond to their questions and reservations.

When you make (not *have*) an argument in a face-to-face conversation, you cooperate with your listeners. You state your reasons and evidence not as a lecturer would to a silent audience but as you would engage friends sitting around a table: you offer a claim and reasons to believe it; they probe for details, raise objections, or offer their points of view; you respond, perhaps with questions of your own; they ask more questions. At its best, it's an amiable but thoughtful back-and-forth that develops and tests the best case that you and they can make *together*.

In writing, even when done collaboratively, that kind of cooperation is harder. You must not only answer your imagined readers' questions but also *ask them on their behalf*—as often and as sharply as real readers will. Your aim isn't to think up clever rhetorical strategies that will persuade readers to accept your claim regardless of how good it is. It is to test your claim and especially its support, so that you offer your readers the best case you can make. In a good research paper, readers hear traces of that imagined conversation.

As we've said, reasoning based on evidence isn't the only way to reach a sound conclusion, sometimes not even the best way. We often make good decisions by relying on intuition, feeling, even spiritual inspiration. But when we try to *explain* why we believe our claims are sound and why others should too, we have no way to *demonstrate* how we reached them, because we can't offer intuitions, feelings, or inspirations as evidence for readers to evaluate. We can only say we had them and ask readers to take our claim on faith, a request that readers of research papers rarely grant.

When you make a research argument, therefore, you must lay out your reasons and evidence so that your readers can consider them; then you must imagine both their questions and your answers. Doing all this is hard, but remembering how arguments work in everyday conversations will help you.

5.2 **Build Your Argument around Answers to Readers' Questions**

Consider the kind of conversation you have every day:

Abby: I hear you had a hard time last semester. How do you think this one will go? [Abby *poses a problem in the form of a question.*]

Brett: Better, I hope. [Brett *answers the question.*]

Abby: Why so? [Abby *asks for a reason to believe* Brett's *answer.*]

Brett: I'm taking courses in my major. [Brett *offers a reason.*]

Abby: Like what? [Abby *asks for evidence to back up* Brett's *reason.*]

Brett: History of Art, Intro to Design. [Brett *offers evidence to back up his reason.*]

Abby: Why will taking courses in your major make a difference? [Abby *doesn't see the relevance of* Brett's *reason to his claim that he will do better.*]

Brett: When I take courses I'm interested in, I work harder. [Brett *offers a general principle that relates his reason to his claim that he will do better.*]

Abby: What about that math course you have to take? [Abby *objects to* Brett's *reason.*]

Brett: I know I had to drop it last time I took it, but I found a good tutor. [Brett *acknowledges* Abby's *objection and responds to it.*]

If you can imagine yourself in that conversation, you'll find nothing strange about assembling a research argument. That's because the five elements of any argument are just answers to the kinds of questions Abby asks Brett—and that you must ask yourself on your reader's behalf.

- Claim: What do you want me to believe? What is your point?
- Reason: Why do you say that? Why should I agree?
- Evidence: How do you know? Can you back it up?
- Acknowledgment and response: But what about . . . ?
- Warrant: How does that follow? Can you explain your reasoning?

Think of your research as the process of figuring out answers to those questions.

5.3 **Turn Your Working Hypothesis into a Claim**

We described the early stages of research as finding a question and imagining a tentative answer. We called that answer your *working hypothesis*. Now as we discuss building an argument to support that hypothesis, we change our terminology one last time. When you think you can back up your hypothesis with good reasons and evidence, you'll present that hypothesis as your argument's *claim*. A claim is an assertion (which could be one sentence or several) that demands support. Your *main claim* is the assertion supported by your whole research argument. Some call this assertion your *thesis*.

5.4 Assemble the Elements of Your Argument

At the core of your argument are three elements: your claim, your reasons for accepting it, and the evidence on which those reasons are based. To that core you'll add one and perhaps two more elements: one responds to questions, objections, and alternative points of view; the other answers those who do not understand how your reasons are *relevant* to your claim.

5.4.1 State and Evaluate Your Claim

Start a new first page of your storyboard (or outline). At the bottom, state your claim in a sentence or two. Be as specific as you can, because the words in this claim will help you plan and execute your draft. Avoid vague value words like *important, interesting,* and *significant*. Compare the two following claims:

Masks play a significant role in many religious ceremonies.

In cultures from pre-Columbian America to Africa and Asia, masks allow religious celebrants to bring deities to life so that worshipers experience them directly.

Now judge the *significance* of your claim (*So what?* again). A significant claim doesn't make a reader think *I know that,* but rather *Really? How interesting. What makes you think so?* (Review 2.1.4.) These next two claims are too trivial to justify reading, much less writing, an argument to back them up:

This paper discusses teaching popular legends such as the Battle of the Alamo to elementary school students. (*So what if it does?*)

Teaching United States history through popular legends such as the Battle of the Alamo is common in elementary education. (*So what if it is?*)

Of course, what your readers will count as interesting depends on what they know, and if you're early in your research career, that's something you can't predict. If you're writing one of your first papers, assume that your most important reader is you. It is enough if *you alone* think your answer is significant, if it makes you think, *Well, I didn't know that when I started.* As you become more experienced and come to understand your particular research community better, you'll learn to frame your arguments in terms of your readers' interests (see chapter 1). If, however, you think your own claim is vague or trivial, you're not ready to assemble an argument because you have no reason to make one.

5.4.2   Support Your Claim with Reasons and Evidence

At the core of every research argument is the answer to your research question, the solution to your problem—your main claim. You have to back up that claim with two kinds of support: reasons and evidence.

A reason is a statement that leads readers to accept a claim. We often join a reason to a claim with *because*:

Elementary schools should make teaching foreign languages a priority~claim~ because we acquire languages best and most easily when we are young.~reason~

You often need more than one reason to support a claim, and in a complex argument, your reasons will be claims themselves, requiring support with additional reasons in turn.

Evidence is the data on which you base your reasons. It may seem obvious that you must back up a claim with reasons and evidence, but it's easy to confuse those two words because we often use them as if they mean the same thing:

You have to base your claim on good reasons.

You have to base your claim on good evidence.

Reasons and evidence are not the same thing, and distinguishing them is crucial in making sound arguments. Compare these two sentences:

On what evidence do you base your reasons?

On what reasons do you base your evidence?

That second sentence is odd: we don't base evidence on reasons; we base reasons on evidence. We use our minds to *think up* reasons. We have to *search* for evidence "out there" in the world and then make it available for everyone to see. Reasons need the support of evidence; evidence should need no support beyond careful demonstration or a reference to a reliable source.

When assembling your evidence, be aware that what you think is a true fact and therefore hard evidence, your readers might not. For example, suppose a researcher offers this claim and reason:

Early Alamo stories reflected values already in the American character.~claim~ The story almost instantly became a legend of American heroic sacrifice.~reason~

To support that reason, she offers this "hard" evidence:

Soon after the battle, many newspapers used the story to celebrate our heroic national character._{evidence}

The researcher treats this statement as fact. But skeptical readers, the kind you should expect (even hope for), might ask *How soon is "soon"? How many is "many"? Which papers? In news stories or editorials? What exactly did they say? How many papers didn't mention it?* Such readers will accept that statement as evidence only when they're satisfied their questions about it have been answered.

To be sure, readers may accept a claim based only on a reason, without any evidence at all, if that reason comes from a trusted authority or seems clearly—or *self-evidently*—true:

We are all created equal,_{reason} so no one has a natural right to govern us._{claim}

In research papers written for introductory courses, it is often sufficient to support reasons only by what authoritative sources say: *Wilson says* X, *Yang says* Y, *Schmidt says* Z. But in advanced work, readers expect more: they want evidence drawn not just from secondary sources but from primary sources or your own observations, demonstrations, or experiments.

Review your storyboard: Can you support each reason with what your readers will think is evidence of the right kind, quantity, and quality? Might your readers challenge what you offer as evidence? If so, how? Do you need to offer a better demonstration or a better source? If so, you must produce more or better data or acknowledge the limits of what you have.

Your claim, reasons, and evidence make up the core of your argument, but it needs at least one more element, maybe two.

5.4.3 Acknowledge and Respond to Anticipated Questions and Objections

Careful readers will be fair, but they will also question every part of your argument. So you must anticipate as many of their questions as you can and then acknowledge and respond to the most important ones. Doing this may be hard because you know your own argument too well and may believe in it too much to seriously challenge it. Still, you must *imagine* your readers' questions and take their views into account. That's how you establish a cooperative relationship with your readers.

Readers can challenge both the *intrinsic* and *extrinsic* soundness of your argument: they might point to problems *inside* your argument, usually with its evidence, or they might raise questions from *outside* your argument by noting alternatives or exceptions. Try to imagine and respond to both sorts of challenges.

1. To address potential challenges to your argument's *intrinsic* sound-ness, imagine a reader making any of these criticisms, and then con-struct a subargument in response.

   Imagine a reader challenging the *nature* of your evidence:

   - "I want to see a different *sort* of evidence—hard numbers, not anec-dotes." Or ". . . stories about real people, not cold statistics."

   Imagine a reader questioning its *quality*:

   - "It isn't accurate. The numbers don't add up."
   - "It isn't precise enough. What do you mean by 'many'?"
   - "It isn't current. There's newer research than this."
   - "It isn't representative. You didn't get data on all the groups."
   - "It isn't authoritative. Smith is no expert on this matter."

   Now imagine a reader questioning its quantity (usually the stron-gest objection of all):

   - "You need more evidence. A single data point / quotation / number / anecdote is not sufficient."

   Most researchers have difficulty finding enough good evidence to make an airtight case, especially when working to a deadline. Research is always a compromise between being thorough and being timely. If you feel that your evidence is less than unassailable, you might want to admit its limitations candidly, before readers reject your argument because you overstated it.

   Next, imagine these kinds of reservations about your reasons and how you would answer them:

   - Your reasons are inconsistent or contradictory.
   - They are too weak or too few to support your claim.
   - They are irrelevant to your claim. (We discuss this matter in 5.4.4.)

2. To address potential challenges to your argument's *extrinsic* sound-ness, you have to step back and view your argument from other per-spectives. Doing this is difficult, but you must try. It's important to get into the habit of asking yourself, *What could cast doubt on my claim?*

   Those who see the world differently from you are likely to define terms differently, reason differently, even offer evidence that you find irrelevant. If you and your readers see the world differently, you must acknowledge and respond to these issues as well. Do not treat differ-ing points of view simply as objections. You will lose readers if you argue that your view is right and theirs is wrong. Instead, acknowledge the differences, then compare them so that readers can understand your argument on its own terms. They still might not agree, but you'll show them that you understand and respect their views; they are then more likely to try to understand and respect yours.

If you're a new researcher, you'll find these questions hard to imagine because you might not know how your readers' views differ from your own. Even so, try to think of plausible questions and objections. But if you're writing a thesis or dissertation, you are responsible not just for supporting your own claim but also for knowing the positions of others in your research community and the issues they are likely to raise. Whatever your level of experience, practice imagining and responding to objections and alternative arguments. By doing so, you'll cultivate a habit of mind that your readers will respect and that may keep you from jumping to questionable conclusions.

Add those acknowledgments and responses to your storyboard where you think readers will raise them.

5.4.4   Establish the Relevance of Your Reasons

The last element of an argument is called a *warrant*, and even experienced researchers find it hard to grasp. You add a warrant to your argument when you think a reader might reject your claim not because a reason supporting it is factually wrong or is based on insufficient evidence, but because it seems *irrelevant* and so doesn't count as a reason at all.

For example, imagine a researcher writes this claim.

The Alamo stories spread quickly$_{claim}$ because in 1836 the United States wasn't yet a confident player on the world stage.$_{reason}$

Imagine that she suspects that her readers will likely object, *It's true that the Alamo stories spread quickly and that in 1836 the United States wasn't yet a confident player on the world stage. But I don't see how not being confident is relevant to the story's spreading quickly.* The writer can't respond simply by offering more evidence that this country was not a confident player on the world stage or that the stories in fact spread quickly: her reader already accepts both as true. Instead, she has to explain the *relevance* of that reason—*why* its truth supports the truth of her claim. To do that, she needs a warrant.

5.4.4.1   HOW A WARRANT WORKS IN CASUAL CONVERSATION. Suppose you make this little argument to a new friend from a faraway land:

It's 5° below zero,$_{reason}$ so you should wear a hat.$_{claim}$

To most of us, the reason seems obviously to support the claim and so needs no explanation of its relevance. But suppose your friend asks this odd question:

So what if it is 5° below? Why does that mean I should wear a hat?

That question challenges not the *truth* of the reason (it is 5° below) but its *relevance* to the claim (you should wear a hat). You might think it odd that anyone would ask that question, but you could answer with a general principle:

Well, when it's cold, people should dress warmly.

That sentence is a warrant. It states a general principle based on our experience in the world: when a certain general condition exists (*it's cold*), we're justified in saying that a certain general consequence regularly follows (*people should dress warmly*). We think that the general warrant justifies our specific claim that our friend should wear a hat on the basis of our specific reason that it's 5° below, because we're reasoning according to this principle of logic: if a general condition and its consequence are true, then specific instances of it must also be true.

In more detail, it works like this (warning: what follows may sound like a lesson in Logic 101):

- In the warrant, the general condition is *it's cold*. It regularly leads us to draw a general consequence: *people should dress warmly*. We state that as a true and general principle: *When it's cold, people should dress warmly*.
- The specific reason, *it's 5° below*, is a valid instance of the general condition *it's cold*.
- The specific claim, *you should wear a hat*, is a valid instance of the general consequence, *people should dress warmly*.
- Since the general principle stated in the warrant is true and the reason and claim are valid instances of it, we're "warranted" to assert as true and valid the claim *wear a hat*.

But now suppose six months later you visit your friend and he says this:

It's above 80° tonight,_{reason} so wear a long-sleeved shirt._{claim}

That might baffle you: How could the reason (it's *above 80°*) be relevant to the claim (*wear a long-sleeved shirt*)? You might imagine this general principle as a warrant:

When it's a warm night, people should dress warmly.

But that isn't true. And if you think the warrant isn't true, you'll deny that the reason supports the claim, because it's irrelevant to it.

But suppose your friend adds this:

Around here, when it's a warm night, you should protect your arms from insect bites.

Now the argument would make sense, but only if you believe all this:

- The warrant is true (*when it's a warm night, you should protect your arms from insect bites*).
- The reason is true (*it's above 80° tonight*).
- The reason is a valid instance of the general condition (*80° is a valid instance of being warm*).
- The claim is a valid instance of the general consequence (*wearing a long-sleeved shirt is a valid instance of protecting your arms from insect bites*).
- No unstated limitations or exceptions apply (*a cold snap didn't kill all insects the night before, the person can't use insect repellent instead, and so on*).

If you believe all that, then you should accept the argument that when it's 80° at night, it's a good idea to wear a long-sleeved shirt, at least at that time and place.

We all know countless such principles, and we learn more every day. If we didn't, we couldn't make our way through our daily lives. In fact, we express our folk wisdom in the form of warrants, but we call them proverbs: *When the cat's away, the mice will play. Out of sight, out of mind. Cold hands, warm heart.*

5.4.4.2 **HOW A WARRANT WORKS IN AN ACADEMIC ARGUMENT.** Here is a more scholarly example, but it works in the same way:

Encyclopedias must not have been widely owned in early nineteenth-century America,_{claim} because wills rarely mentioned them._{reason}

Assume the reason is true: there is lots of evidence that encyclopedias were in fact rarely mentioned in early nineteenth-century wills. Even so, a reader might wonder why that statement is *relevant* to the claim: *You may be right that most such wills didn't mention encyclopedias, but so what? I don't see how that is relevant to your claim that few people owned one.* If a writer expects that question, she must anticipate it by offering a warrant, a general principle that shows how her reason is relevant to her claim.

That warrant might be stated like this:

When a valued object wasn't mentioned in early nineteenth-century wills, it usually wasn't part of the estate._{warrant} Wills at that time rarely mentioned encyclopedias,_{reason} so few people must have owned one._{claim}

We would accept the claim as sound *if and only if* we believe the following:

- The warrant is true.
- The reason is both true and a valid instance of the general condition of the warrant (encyclopedias were valued objects in the early nineteenth century).
- The claim is a valid instance of the general consequence of the warrant (not owning an encyclopedia is a valid instance of something valuable not being part of an estate).

And if the researcher feared that a reader might doubt any of those conditions, she would have to make an argument supporting it.

But that's not the end of the problem: is the warrant true *always and without exception*? Readers might wonder whether in some parts of the country wills mentioned only land and buildings, or whether few people made wills in the first place. If the writer thought that readers might wonder about such qualifications, she would have to make yet another argument showing that those exceptions don't apply.

Now you can see why we so rarely settle arguments about complex issues: even when we agree on the evidence, we can still disagree over how to reason about it.

5.4.4.3 **TESTING THE RELEVANCE OF A REASON TO A CLAIM.** To test the relevance of a reason to a claim, construct a warrant that bridges them. First, state the reason and claim, in that order. Here's the original reason and claim from the beginning of this section:

In 1836, this country wasn't a confident player on the world stage,reason so the Alamo stories spread quickly.claim

Now construct a general principle that includes that reason and claim. Warrants come in all sorts of forms, but the most convenient is the *When–then* pattern. This warrant "covers" the reason and claim.

When a country lacks confidence in its global stature, it quickly embraces stories of heroic military events.

We can formally represent those relationships as in figure 5.1.

To accept that claim, readers must accept the following:

- The warrant is true.
- The specific reason is true.
- The specific reason is a valid instance of the general condition side of the warrant.

When this **General Condition** exists,		this **General Consequence** follows._{warrant}
*When a country lacks confidence,*_{general condition}		*it quickly embraces stories of heroic military events.*_{general consequence}
*In 1836, this country wasn't a confident player on the world stage*_{specific reason}	so	*the story of the Alamo spread quickly.*_{specific claim}
This **Specific Condition** exists,_{reason}	so	this **Specific Consequence** follows._{claim}

Figure 5.1. Argument structure

- The specific claim is a valid instance of the general consequence side of the warrant.
- No limiting conditions keep the warrant from applying.

If the writer thought that readers might deny the truth of that warrant or reason, she would have to make an argument supporting it. If she thought they might think the reason or claim wasn't a valid instance of the warrant, she'd have to make yet another argument that it was.

As you gain experience, you'll learn to check arguments in your head, but until then you might try to sketch out warrants for your most debatable reasons. After you test a warrant, add it to your storyboard where you think readers will need it. If you need to support a warrant with an argument, outline it there.

5.4.4.4 WHY WARRANTS ARE ESPECIALLY DIFFICULT FOR RESEARCHERS NEW TO A FIELD. If you're new in a field, you may find warrants difficult for these reasons:

- Advanced researchers rarely spell out their principles of reasoning, because they know their colleagues take them for granted. New researchers must figure them out on their own. (It's like hearing someone say, "Wear a long-sleeved shirt because it's above 80° tonight.")

- Warrants typically have exceptions that experts also take for granted and therefore rarely state, forcing new researchers to figure them out as well.
- Experts also know when *not* to state an obvious warrant or its limitations, one more thing new researchers must learn on their own. For example, if an expert wrote *It's early June, so we can expect that we'll soon pay more for gasoline*, he wouldn't state the obvious warrant: *When summer approaches, gas prices rise.*

If you offer a well-known but rarely stated warrant, you'll seem condescending or naive. But if you fail to state one that readers need, you'll seem illogical. You just need to know when readers need one and when they don't. And that takes time and familiarity with the conventions of your field.

So don't be dismayed if warrants seem confusing; they're difficult even for experienced writers. But knowing about them should encourage you to ask this crucial question: in addition to the *truth* of your reasons and evidence, will your readers see their *relevance* to your claim? If they might not, you should consider making an argument to demonstrate it.

5.5 Prefer Arguments Based on Evidence to Arguments Based on Warrants

Finally, it's important to note that readers judge arguments based on warrants and arguments based on evidence differently.

- The first type of argument infers a claim from a reason and warrant. The claim in that kind of argument is believed to be *certainly* true.
- The second type supports a claim with reasons based on evidence. The claim in that kind of argument is considered to be *probably* true.

Contemporary readers generally trust the second kind more than the first. Compare these two examples:

We should do what we can to discourage teenagers from texting and driving.claim because that behavior increases the risk of having an accident.reason 1 Driving is difficult and texting a distraction,reason 2 supporting reason 1 and we know that when people are distracted while performing complex tasks, their performance suffers.warrant linking reason 2 and reason 1

We should do what we can to discourage teenagers from texting and driving.claim because distracted driving is a leading cause of teenage deaths.reason According to the CDC, motor vehicle accidents are responsible for over a third of all fatalities among people aged 12–19, and texting while driving exponentially increases the likelihood that any driver will be involved in one. Moreover, . . . evidence

If you are like most contemporary readers, you probably preferred the second of these arguments to the first. That's because its warrant is not controversial (and therefore goes without saying) and its claim is supported by a reason based on solid evidence. That first argument seems plausible because an uncontroversial (and therefore unstated) warrant connects reason 1 to the claim, and an explicit warrant connects reason 2 to reason 1 (reason 1 is the claim reason 2 supports). In other words, reason 1 and reason 2 are good instances of that warrant's general consequence and condition, respectively. Even so, as tight as that argument is, most readers still want some hard evidence.

In particular, you can rarely support a claim of fact with a warrant and reason alone. Generally, we can't just *reason* our way to the facts; we have to *discover* them through research. Except in a few fields—some branches of mathematics, philosophy, theology—the way to demonstrate a claim of fact is to show with evidence that what you are claiming is, *in fact*, the case.

All arguments rely on warrants, but readers of *research* arguments are likely to mistrust arguments from principle alone. So whenever you can, rely not on elaborate lines of reasoning based on warrants but on hard evidence.

5.6   Assemble an Argument

Here is a small argument that fits together all five parts:

Video games aimed at children can aid their intellectual development, but that contribution is largely offset by a factor that could damage their emotional development—too much violence.$_{\text{claim}}$ Example, parents and child psychologists agree, is a major influence on children's development. It seems plausible, then, that when children see images of degrading or disturbing behavior, they will be adversely affected by it.$_{\text{warrant}}$ In a single day, children see countless examples of violence.$_{\text{reason}}$ Every day the average child plays over three hours of video games and sees over twenty acts of violence (Duarte 2012).$_{\text{evidence}}$ Kim has shown that children don't confuse video-game violence with real life (2015),$_{\text{acknowledgment of alternative point of view}}$ but because of their interactivity, video-game violence may affect them nonetheless.$_{\text{response}}$ We cannot ignore the possibility that childhood exposure to violent video games encourages the development of violent adults.$_{\text{claim restated and amplified}}$

Most of those elements could be expanded to fill many paragraphs.

Arguments in different fields look different, but they all consist of answers to just these five questions:

- What are you claiming?
- What are your reasons?

- What evidence supports your reasons?
- But what about other points of view?
- What principle makes your reasons relevant to your claim?

Your storyboard should answer those questions many times. If it doesn't, your paper will seem incomplete and unconvincing.

6 Planning a First Draft

Once you have assembled your argument, you might be ready to draft it. But experienced writers know that the time they invest in planning a draft more than pays off when they write it. To draft effectively, you need more than just the elements of a sound argument; you need a plan to assemble those elements into a coherent draft. Some plans, however, are better than others.

6.1   Avoid Unhelpful Plans

When you are doing research, it is good to write early, but your early writing should not determine the plan for your final paper: the real purpose of that early writing is to help you *discover* your ideas, not to *communicate* them to your readers. If you find yourself adopting one of the following plans, pause. It means that you are not yet ready to draft your paper.

1. **Narrative of discovery.** If you find yourself telling the story of your project—*First I investigated . . . Then I compared . . .*—you are probably still

too close to the activity of research to put your readers' needs before your own. Most readers want to know your ideas, not necessarily the steps through which you arrived at them.

2. **Patchwork of sources.** If your draft is just a series of quotations, paraphrases, and summaries of sources, you are probably overwhelmed by your sources and have not yet developed a controlling claim of your own. Readers want to know that you've done your research thoroughly, but they also want to know what *you* think. Note: if you submit a paper that is stitched together from other sources, especially if you have cut-and-pasted from the web, you also risk being seen not just as an amateur but also as a plagiarist (see 7.9).

3. **Mirror of the assignment.** If you are writing for a course and your draft simply mirrors the organization of your assignment, you have to ask why. Are you just playing it safe or going through the motions? You owe it to yourself and your teacher to do more. Are you still developing your own ideas? Let the structure of your paper reflect them. Are you struggling to organize your paper another way? (See section 6.2.5 for some possibilities.)

6.2 Create a Plan That Meets Your Readers' Needs

Some fields stipulate the plan of a paper. In the experimental sciences, for example, readers expect papers to follow an organization like this:

Introduction—Methods and Materials—Results—Discussion—Conclusion

If your paper must follow a conventional plan, find a model in a secondary source or ask your mentor, teacher, or advisor for guidance. In most fields, however, you have to create a plan of your own, but that plan must make sense to your readers. To create one, start with your storyboard or outline.

6.2.1 Convert Your Storyboard into an Outline

If you prefer to work from an outline, you can turn your storyboard into one:

■ Start with a sentence numbered I that states your claim.
■ Add complete sentences under it numbered II, III, . . . , each of which states a reason supporting your claim.
■ Under each reason, use capital letters to list sentences summarizing your evidence; then list by numbers the evidence itself. For example (the data are invented for the illustration):

I.   Introduction: Educational benefits of writing on laptops are uncertain.
II.   Different uses have different effects.
    A. All uses increase number of words produced.
        1. Study II.A.1: 950 vs. 780
        2. Study II.A.2: 1,103 vs. 922
    B. Study II.B: Using laptops encourages writer's block.
III. Studies show limited benefit on revision.
    A. Study III.A: Writers using laptops are more wordy.
        1. Average of 2.3 more words per sentence
        2. Average of 20% more words per essay
    B. Study III.B: Writers need hard copy to revise effectively.
        1. 22% fewer typos when done on hard copy vs. computer screen
        2. 2.26% fewer spelling errors
IV. Conclusion: Disadvantages of laptops may outweigh advantages.

A sparer outline is just phrases, with no formal layers of I, A, 1, and so on.

Introduction: Benefits uncertain
Different uses / different effects
    More words
    Writer's block
Revision studies
    Study 1 longer sentences
    Study 2 longer essays
    Study 3 hardcopy better
Conclusion: Disadvantages outweigh advantages

When you start a project, a spare outline may be the best you can do, and for a short project it may be all you need, so long as you know the point of each item. But an outline of complete sentences is usually more useful. More useful yet is a storyboard, especially for a long project.

6.2.2   Sketch a Working Introduction

Writers are often advised to write their introduction last, but most of us need a working introduction to start us on the right track. Expect to write your introduction twice, first a sketch for yourself and later a final one for your readers. That final introduction will usually have four parts (see chapter 9), so you might as well sketch your working introduction to anticipate them.

1. At the top of the first page of your storyboard, sketch a *brief* summary of *only* the key points in *only* those sources most relevant to your argument. Include only the sources that you intend to challenge, modify,

or expand on. Then order those sources in a way that is useful to your readers: chronologically, by quality, significance, point of view, or the like. Don't just follow the order in which you happened to read them or record them in your notes.

2. Rephrase your research question as a statement about a flaw or gap that you see in your sources:

Why is the Alamo story so important in the United States' national mythology?

→ Few of these historians, however, have explained why the Alamo story has become so important in the United States' national mythology.

3. If you can, sketch an answer to *So what?* What larger issue will your readers not understand if you don't answer your question? You may be only guessing, but try to find *some* answer.

If we understood how such stories become national legends, we would better understand the United States' national values, perhaps even what makes the American character distinct.

If you can't think of any answer, skip it; we return to it in chapter 10.

4. State the answer to your question as your claim, or promise an answer in a launching point. You have two choices here:

   ▪ State your claim at the end of your introduction to frame what follows and again near the beginning of your conclusion.
   ▪ State it only in your conclusion, as a climax to your reasoning.

This is a crucial choice, because it creates your social contract with your readers (see 1.2). If you state your main claim toward the end of your introduction, you put your readers in charge: they know what's coming, and they can decide to read on—or not. On the other hand, if you wait until your conclusion to state your main claim, you create a more controlling relationship: you ask them to trust that they'll find your claim—when you eventually reveal it—worth the investment of their time. Most readers prefer to see your main claim at the end of your introduction, because that lets them read what follows faster, understand it better, and remember it longer. In your storyboard, put that claim at the bottom of your introduction page. Then restate it in different words at the top of your storyboard's conclusion page. If you can, make this concluding claim more specific than the one in the introduction.

Some new researchers fear that if they reveal their main point too early, readers will be "bored" and stop reading. Others worry about repeating themselves. Both fears are baseless. If you ask an interesting question, readers will want to see how well you can answer it, and knowing where your argument is going will help your readers follow it.

But if you do decide to announce your claim only in your conclusion, you still need a sentence at the end of your introduction that launches your reader into the body of your paper. That sentence should include the key terms that will run through your paper (see 6.2.3). You'll be better prepared to write that sentence after you draft your final introduction, so when planning, just put your main claim at the bottom of your storyboard's introduction page (you can move it later).

Finally, some writers add a "road map" at the end of their introduction:

In part 1, I discuss the issue of . . . Part 2 addresses . . . Part 3 examines . . .

Road maps are common in the social sciences, but many in the humanities find them clumsy. You can add a road map to your storyboard to guide your drafting, then cut it from your final draft. If you keep it, make it short.

6.2.3   Identify Key Concepts That Will Run through Your Paper

For your paper to seem coherent, readers must see a few key concepts running through all its parts. But readers won't recognize those repeated concepts if you refer to them in many different words. Readers need to see specific terms that repeatedly refer to those concepts, not every time you mention them but often enough that readers can't miss them. You might find them among the terms you used to categorize your notes, but they must include keywords from the sentences stating your problem and main point. On the introduction page, circle four or five words or phrases that express those concepts. Ignore words that name your general topic; focus on those relevant to your specific question:

gender, education level, major, choice of profession, wage gap

If you find few words or phrases that can serve as key terms, your topic and point might be too general (review 5.4.1).

You can also use this procedure to identify concepts that distinguish your sections from each other. Look at the reason you stated at the top of each reason page, and circle its important words. Some of those words should be related to the words circled in the introduction and conclusion, but others will be specific to that section. When you draft, you can use these lists of key terms to keep yourself on track and to recognize when you might be saying something new (see 7.3).

6.2.4 **Use Key Terms to Create Subheads That Uniquely Identify Each Section**

Even if papers in your field don't use subheads (see A.2.2.4 in the appendix), we recommend that you use them in your drafts. Create them out of your key terms. If you cannot find key terms that distinguish a section, consider its contribution to the whole: if little differentiates that section from others, readers may find it repetitive or irrelevant.

If your field avoids subheads, use them to keep yourself on track, and delete them from your last draft.

6.2.5 **Order Your Paper**

When you assembled your argument, you may not have put your reasons in any particular order (one benefit of a storyboard). But when you plan a draft, you must impose some order on them. That is not easy, especially when you're writing on a new topic in a new field.

The best order is the one that best meets your readers' needs. When you're not sure how to order your reasons, consider the following options.

You can organize your paper according to your subject matter:

- *Chronological.* This is the simplest: earlier-to-later or cause-to-effect.
- *Part by part.* If you can break your topic into its constituent parts, you can deal with each in turn, but you must still order those parts in some way that helps readers understand them: by their functional relationships, hierarchy, or the like.
- *Comparison and contrast.* Choose this form if you are comparing two or more entities, concepts, or objects. You have two options, and one is usually better than the other. If you were comparing Hopi masks to Inuit masks, you might decide to devote the first half of your paper to the former and the second half to the latter. But this kind of organization often results in a pair of disconnected summaries. Instead, try to treat the objects of comparison together, aligning parallel aspects as you go. In our example, you might write first about the masks' designs, then about the stages of their evolution, then about their use of symbolism, and so on.

You can also organize your paper to accommodate your readers' prior knowledge and to facilitate their efforts to grasp your argument:

- *Short to long, simple to complex.* Most readers prefer to deal with less complex issues before they work through more complex ones.
- *More familiar to less familiar.* Most readers prefer to read what they know about before they read what they don't.
- *Less contestable to more contestable.* Most readers move more easily from what they agree with to what they don't.

- *Less important to more important (or vice versa).* Readers prefer to read more important reasons first, but those reasons may have more impact when they come last.
- *Earlier understanding as a basis for later understanding.* Readers may have to understand some events, principles, definitions, and so on before they understand another thing.

Often these principles cooperate: what readers agree with and easily understand might also be short and familiar. But these principles may also conflict: readers might reject most quickly reasons that are most important. Whatever your order, it must reflect *your readers'* needs, not the order that the material seems to impose on itself (such as chronology), least of all the order in which those reasons occurred to you.

6.2.6   Make Your Order Clear with Transitional Words

Your readers must be able to recognize the order you choose. In your storyboard, start each page of reasons with words that make the *principle of* order clear: *First, Second, Later, Finally, More important, A more complex issue is . . . , As a result.* Don't worry if these words feel awkwardly obvious. At this point, they're more for your benefit than for your readers'. You can revise or even delete the clumsy ones from your final draft.

6.2.7   Sketch a Brief Introduction to Each Section and Subsection

Just as your whole paper needs an introduction that frames what follows, so does each of its sections. If a section is only a page or two, you need just a short paragraph; for a section several pages long, you might need to sketch in two or more paragraphs. This introduction should announce the key terms that are special to the section, ideally in a sentence at its end expressing the section's point, which might be a reason, a response to a different point of view, or a warrant you must explain.

6.2.8   For Each Section, Sketch Evidence, Acknowledgments, Warrants, and Summaries

In their relevant sections, sketch out the parts of your argument. Remember that many of those parts will themselves make points that must be supported by smaller subarguments.

6.2.8.1   EVIDENCE. Most sections consist primarily of evidence supporting reasons. Sketch the evidence after the reason it supports. If you have different kinds of evidence supporting the same reason, group and order them in a way that will make sense to your readers.

6.2.8.2 EXPLANATIONS OF EVIDENCE. You may have to explain your evidence—where it came from, why it's reliable, exactly how it supports a reason. Usually these explanations follow the evidence, but you can sketch them before if that seems more logical.

6.2.8.3 ACKNOWLEDGMENTS AND RESPONSES. Imagine what readers might object to in your argument and sketch responses. Responses are typically subarguments with at least a claim and reasons, often including evidence and even another response to an imagined objection to your response.

6.2.8.4 WARRANTS. If you think you need a warrant to justify the relevance of a reason, develop it before you state the reason. (If you're using a warrant only for emphasis, put it after the reason.) If you think readers will question the truth of the warrant, sketch a subargument to support it. If readers might think that your reason or claim isn't a valid instance of the warrant, sketch a subargument showing that it is.

6.2.8.5 SUMMARIES. If your paper is long and "fact heavy" with dates, names, events, or numbers, you might end each major section by briefly summarizing the progress of your argument. What have you established in that section? How does your argument shape up so far? If in your final draft those summaries seem clumsy, cut them.

Writers in different fields may arrange these elements in slightly different ways, but the elements themselves and their principles of organization are the same in every field and profession. What's crucial in every paper, regardless of field, is that you must order the parts of your argument not merely to reflect your own thinking but to help your readers understand it.

6.2.9 Sketch a Working Conclusion

You should have stated your concluding claim at the top of the conclusion page of your storyboard. If you can add to the significance of that claim (another answer to *So what?*), sketch it after the claim (see 10.2 for more on conclusions).

6.3 File Away Leftovers

Once you have a plan, you may discover that you have a lot of material left over that doesn't fit into it. Resist the impulse to shoehorn these leftovers into your paper just to show your work. In fact, if you don't have more leftovers than what you used, you may not have done enough research. Leftovers aren't waste: at a minimum, they helped you discover your ideas. You might decide that you need to use them after all. And they could even contain the seeds of another project.

7 Drafting Your Paper

Some writers think that once they have an outline or storyboard, they can draft by just grinding out sentences. If you've written a lot to explore your ideas, you may even think that you can plug that preliminary writing into a draft. Experienced writers know better. They know two things: exploratory writing is crucial but often not right for a draft, and thoughtful drafting can be an act of discovery that planning and storyboarding can prepare them for but never replace. In fact, most writers don't know what they *can* think until they see it appear in words before them. Indeed, you experience one of the most exciting moments in research when you discover yourself expressing ideas that you did not know you had until that moment.

So don't treat drafting as merely translating a storyboard or outline into words. If you draft with an open mind, you can discover lines of thought that you couldn't have imagined before you started. But like other steps in the process, even surprises work better with a plan.

7.1 Draft in the Way That Feels Most Comfortable

Writers draft in different ways. Some are slow and careful: they have to get every paragraph right before they start the next one. To do that, they need a meticulous plan. So if you draft slowly, plan carefully. Other writers let the words flow, skipping ahead when they get stuck, omitting quotations, statistics, and so on that they can plug in later. If they are stopped by a stylistic issue such as whether to represent numbers in words or numerals, they insert a "[?]" and keep on writing until they run out of gas, then go back and fix it. But quick drafters need lots of time to revise. So if you draft quickly, start early. Draft in whatever way works for you, but experienced writers usually draft quickly, then revise extensively.

7.2 Develop Effective Writing Habits

Most of us learn to write in the least efficient way—under pressure, rushing to meet a deadline, with a quick draft the night before and maybe a few minutes in the morning for proofreading. That rarely works for a short paper, almost never for a longer one. You need time and a plan that sets small, achievable goals but keeps your eye on the whole.

Most important, draft regularly and often, not in marathon sessions that dull your thinking and kill your interest. Set a small goal and a reasonable quota of words for each session, and stick to it. When you resume drafting, you need not start where you left off: review your storyboard to decide what you're ready to draft today. Review how it will fit into its section and the whole: *What reason does this section support? Where does it fit in the overall logic? Which key terms state the concepts that distinguish this section?* If you're blocked, skip to another section. Whatever you do, don't substitute more reading for writing. Chronic procrastinators are usually so intimidated by the size of their project that it paralyzes them, so they just keep putting off getting started. You can overcome that destructive habit by breaking your project into small, achievable goals (see 7.11).

7.3   Keep Yourself on Track through Headings and Key Terms

Here are two techniques you can use to keep yourself on track as you draft.

Use headings—ideally full sentences—to break your draft into manageable chunks and to show how your sections are related to one another. Even if papers in your field don't ordinarily use headings and subheadings, you can still use them as you draft and delete them later.

You can also use lists of key terms to keep yourself on track. As you draft, keep in front of you both the terms that should run through your whole paper and those specific to individual sections (see 6.2.3 and 6.2.4). From time to time, check how often you've used those words, both those that run through the whole paper and those that distinguish one section from another. If you find yourself writing something that lacks those terms, pause and reflect: are you just off track, or are you discovering something new? You need not stay yoked to your original plan: you are free to follow a new path to see where it leads, but do that as a choice—not just because you got lost along the way.

7.4   Quote, Paraphrase, and Summarize Appropriately

We covered this issue when we discussed note-taking (4.2.2). You should build most of your paper out of your own words that reflect your own thinking. But you'll support much of that thinking with the words of others, delivered in quotations, paraphrases, and summaries. As we've said, different fields use these techniques differently: researchers in the humanities quote more than do social and natural scientists, who typically paraphrase and summarize. But you must decide each case for itself, depending on how you use the information. Here again are some principles:

- Summarize when details are irrelevant or a source isn't important enough to warrant much space.
- Paraphrase when you can state what a source says more clearly or concisely or when your argument depends on the details in a source but not on its specific words.
- Quote for these purposes:
    - The words themselves are evidence that backs up your reasons.
    - The words are from an authority who backs up your claims.
    - The words are strikingly original or express your key concepts so compellingly that the quotation can frame an extended discussion.

▪ The words express a claim you disagree with, and to be fair you want to state it exactly.

Readers value research only to the degree that they trust its sources. So for every summary, paraphrase, or quotation you use, cite its bibliographic data in the appropriate style (see 15.5). Under no circumstances should you stitch together passages from the internet with a few sentences of your own. Teachers grind their teeth reading such papers, dismayed by their lack of original thinking. Readers of advanced projects reject such patchworks out of hand.

7.5   Integrate Quotations into Your Text

Signal direct quotations in one of two ways:

▪ For four or fewer quoted lines, run them into your text, surrounded by quotation marks.
▪ For five or more lines, set them off as an indented block.

You can insert run-in and block quotations in your text in three ways.

1. Drop in the quotation with a few identifying words (*Author says, According to Author, As Author puts it*, etc.).

   Diamond says, "The histories of the Fertile Crescent and China . . . hold a salutary lesson for the modern world: circumstances change, and past primacy is no guarantee of future primacy" (417).

2. Introduce the quotation with a sentence that interprets or characterizes it.

   Diamond suggests what we can learn from the past: "The histories of the Fertile Crescent and China . . . hold a salutary lesson for the modern world" (417).

3. Weave the grammar of the quotation into the grammar of your own sentence.

   Diamond suggests that the chief "lesson for the modern world" in the history of the Fertile Crescent and China is that "circumstances change, and past primacy is no guarantee of future primacy" (417).

You can modify a quotation, so long as you don't change its meaning and you signal deletions with three dots (called *ellipses*) and changes with square brackets. This sentence quotes the original intact:

As Hariman argues, "The realist style radically separates power and textuality, constructing the political realm as a state of nature and the political actor as someone either rationally calculating vectors of interest and power or foolishly believing in such verbal illusions as laws or ethical ideals" (4).

This version modifies the quotation to emphasize one part of it and to fit the grammar of the writer's sentence:

Hariman argues that "the realist style radically separates power and textuality, constructing . . . the political actor as someone either rationally calculating vectors of interest and power or foolishly believing in such verbal illusions as laws or ethical ideals" (4).

See chapter 25 for more on integrating quotations with your text.

When you refer to a source the first time, use the author's full name. Do not precede it with *Mr.*, *Mrs.*, *Ms.*, or *Professor* (see 24.2.2 for the use of *Dr.*, *Reverend*, *Senator*, and so on). When you mention a source thereafter, use just the author's last name:

According to Steven Pinker, "claims about a language instinct . . . have virtually nothing to do with possible genetic differences between people."[1] Pinker goes on to explain that . . .

Except when referring to royalty, never refer to an author only by his or her first name. You might write this:

In a recent speech, Prince Charles described his efforts to preserve the village pubs that are such a part of British culture.

But never this:

According to Steven Pinker, "claims about a language instinct . . ." Steven goes on to explain that . . .

7.6 Use Footnotes and Endnotes Judiciously

If you are using notes-style citations (see 3.5.1), you will have to decide as you draft how to use footnotes and endnotes (for their formal requirements, see chapter 16). You must cite every source in a note, of course, but you may also decide to use footnotes and endnotes for substantive material that you don't want to include in the body of your text but also don't want to omit. (You might also use such substantive notes in combination with parenthetical citations in author-date style; see 18.3.3.)

- If you cite sources in endnotes, put substantive material in footnotes. Otherwise you force readers to keep flipping to the back of your paper to check every endnote to see whether it is substantive or bibliographical.
- Use substantive footnotes sparingly. If you create too many, you risk damaging the flow of your writing with asides and digressions.

In any event, keep in mind that many readers ignore substantive footnotes on the principle that information not important enough for you to include in the main text is not important enough for them to read in a footnote.

7.7   Show How Complex or Detailed Evidence Is Relevant

By this point you may be so sure that your evidence supports your reasons that you'll think readers can't miss its relevance. But evidence never speaks for itself, especially not long quotations or complex sets of numbers. You must therefore speak for it: introduce it by stating what you want your readers to get out of it. For example, this passage bases a claim about Hamlet on the evidence of the following quotation:

When Hamlet comes upon his stepfather Claudius at prayer, he demonstrates cool rationality:claim

> Now might I do it [kill him] pat, now 'a is a-praying,
> And now I'll do't. And so 'a goes to heaven,
> And so am I reveng'd. . . . [Hamlet pauses to think]
> [But this] villain kills my father, and for that,
> I, his sole son, do this same villain send
> To heaven.
> Why, this is hire and salary, not revenge. (3.3)report of evidence

Since that quotation doesn't explicitly refer to Hamlet's rationality, readers might not see how it supports the claim. So show them what is means by introducing it with a reason:

When Hamlet comes upon his stepfather Claudius at prayer, he demonstrates cool rationality.claim He impulsively wants to kill Claudius but pauses to reflect: if he kills the praying Claudius, he will send his soul to heaven, but he wants Claudius damned to hell, so he coolly decides to kill him later:reason

> Now might I do it [kill him] pat, . . . report of evidence

Now we see the connection. This kind of explanatory introduction is even more important when you present data in a table or figure (see 8.3.1).

7.8   Be Open to Surprises

If you write as you go and plan your best case before you draft, you're unlikely to be utterly surprised by how your draft develops. Even so, be open to new directions from beginning to end:

- When your drafting starts to head off on a tangent, go with it for a bit to see whether you're onto something better than you planned.

- When reporting your evidence leads you to doubt a reason, don't ignore that feeling. Follow it up.
- When the order of your reasons starts to feel awkward, experiment with new ones, even if you thought you were almost done.
- Even when you reach your final conclusion, you may think of a way to restate your claim more clearly and pointedly.

If you get helpful new ideas early enough before your deadline, invest the time to make the changes. It is a small price to pay for a big improvement.

7.9   Guard against Inadvertent Plagiarism

It will be as you draft that you risk making one of the worst mistakes a researcher can make: leading readers to think that you're trying to pass off the work of another writer as your own. Do that and you risk being accused of plagiarism, a charge that, if sustained, could mean for a professional writer an irreparably damaged reputation, or for a student writer a failing grade or even expulsion.

Students know they cheat when, say, they submit as their own work papers bought online. Most also know they cheat when they pass off as their own long passages copied directly from their sources. For those cases, there's nothing to say beyond *Don't*.

But many inexperienced researchers fail to realize that they risk being charged with plagiarism even if they were not intentionally dishonest but only misinformed or careless. You run that risk when you do any of the following:

- You quote, paraphrase, or summarize a source but fail to cite it.
- You use ideas or methods from a source but fail to cite it.
- You use the exact words of a source and you do cite it, but you fail to put those words in quotation marks or in a block quotation.
- You paraphrase a source and cite it, but paraphrase too closely (see 7.9.2).

7.9.1   Signal Every Quotation, Even When You Cite Its Source

Even if you cite the source, readers must know exactly which words are yours and which you quote. If, however, you borrow only a few words, you enter a gray area. Read this:

Because technology begets more technology, the importance of an invention's diffusion potentially exceeds the importance of the original invention. Technology's history exemplifies what is termed an autocatalytic process: that is, one that speeds up at a rate that increases with time, because the process catalyzes itself (Diamond 1998, 301).

If you were writing about Jared Diamond's ideas, you would probably have to use some of his words, such as *the importance of an invention*. But you might not put that phrase in quotation marks, because it shows no originality of thought or expression.

Two of his phrases, however, are so striking that they do require quotation marks: *technology begets more technology* and *autocatalytic process*. For example:

The power of technology goes beyond individual inventions because "technology begets more technology." It is, as Diamond puts it, an "autocatalytic process" (301).

Once you cite those words, you can use them again without quotation marks or citation:

As one invention begets another one and that one still another, the process becomes a self-sustaining catalysis that spreads across national boundaries.

This is a gray area: words that seem striking to some are not to others. If you put quotation marks around too many ordinary phrases, readers might think you're naive, but if you fail to use them when readers think you should, they may suspect you of plagiarism. Since it's better to seem naive than dishonest, especially early in your career, use quotation marks freely. (You must, however, follow the standard practices of your field. Lawyers, for example, often use the exact language of a statute or judicial opinion with no quotation marks.)

7.9.2   Don't Paraphrase Too Closely

You paraphrase appropriately when you represent an idea in your own words more clearly or pointedly than the source does. But readers will think that you plagiarize if they can match your words and phrasing with those of your source.

For example, here is a passage from page 38 of Malcolm Gladwell's *Outliers: The Story of Success*:

Achievement is talent plus preparation. The problem with this view is that the closer psychologists look at the careers of the gifted, the smaller the role innate talent seems to play and the bigger the role preparation seems to play.

This too-close paraphrase is plagiarism:

Success seems to depend on a combination of talent and preparation. However, when psychologists closely examine the gifted and their careers, they discover that innate talent plays a much smaller role than preparation (Gladwell 2008, 38).

This paraphrase does not plagiarize:

As Gladwell (2008, 38) observes, summarizing studies on the highly successful, we tend to overestimate the role of talent and underestimate that of preparation.

This phrasing is not a close match to the original. And notice that we chose not to put *talent* or *preparation* in quotes. We decided that those words are common enough to use as our own.

To avoid seeming to plagiarize, read the passage, look away, think about it for a moment; *then, still looking away,* paraphrase it in your own words. Then check whether you can run your finger along your sentence and find synonyms for the same ideas in the same order in your source. If you can, try again.

7.9.3 Usually Cite a Source for Ideas Not Your Own

This rule is more complicated than it seems, because few ideas are entirely new. Readers don't expect you to cite a source for the idea that the earth is round. But they do expect you to cite a source for an idea when (1) it is associated with a specific person *and* (2) it is new enough *not* to be part of a field's common knowledge. For example, psychologists claim that we think and feel in different parts of our brains. No knowledgeable reader would expect you to cite a source for that idea, because it's so familiar that no one would think you are implying it is yours. On the other hand, some psychologists argue that emotions are crucial to rational decision-making. That idea is so new and tied to particular researchers that you'd have to cite them.

7.9.4 Don't Plead Ignorance, Misunderstanding, or Innocent Intentions

To be sure, what looks like plagiarism is often just honest ignorance of how to use and cite sources. Some students sincerely believe that they don't have to cite material downloaded from the Web because it's free and publicly available. They are wrong. Others defend themselves by claiming they didn't *intend* to mislead. The problem is that we read words, not minds. So think of plagiarism not as an *intended* act but as a *perceived* one. Here is the best way to think about this: If the author of the source you borrowed from were to read your paper, would she recognize any of it as hers, including paraphrases and summaries, or even general ideas or methods from her original work? If so, you must cite those borrowings.

7.10 Guard against Inappropriate Assistance

Experienced writers regularly show their drafts to others for criticism and suggestions, and you should too (see chapter 12). But check how much assistance is appropriate and how you should acknowledge the assistance you receive.

1. How much help is appropriate?

   ▪ For a class paper, most instructors encourage students to get general criticism and minor editing, but not detailed rewriting or substantive suggestions.

   ▪ For work submitted for publication, writers are free to get all the help they can from colleagues, reviewers, and others so long as these people don't become virtual ghostwriters.

   Theses and dissertations lie between these extremes. If you are in doubt, ask someone with authority—your teacher or your advisor—where the line is drawn. Then get all the help you can on the right side of it.

2. What help must you acknowledge?

   ▪ For a class paper, you usually aren't required to acknowledge general criticism, minor editing, or help from a school writing tutor, but you must acknowledge help that's special or extensive. Your instructor sets the rules, so ask.

   ▪ For a thesis, dissertation, or published work, you're not required to acknowledge routine help, though it's courteous and often politic to do so in a preface (see A.2.1.9 and A.2.1.10). But you must acknowledge special or extensive editing and cite in a note major ideas or phrases provided by others.

7.11 **Work Through Chronic Procrastination and Writer's Block**

If you can't seem to get started on a first draft or if you struggle to draft more than a few words, you may have writer's block. Writer's block is tremendously frustrating. Some cases of it arise from mental health issues related to school pressures, and for those you should consider seeking professional help. But most cases have causes you can address: you may be stuck because you have no goals or have goals that are too high; you may feel so intimidated by the size of the task that you don't know where to begin; you may feel that you have to make every sentence or paragraph perfect before you move on to the next one; you may just allow yourself to be easily distracted. Here are some good practices that can help with all of these causes:

▪ Create a routine and set small, achievable goals.
▪ Use devices to keep yourself moving, such as a progress chart or a timer for writing sessions.

- Write routinely as you research, not just after.
- Lower the bar by telling yourself that you're not writing a draft but only sketching out some ideas.
- Write without looking at the page or with your screen turned off.
- Disconnect your computer from your network, or turn off wifi.
- Find a writing partner or join a writing group.
- Visit your school's learning center or writing center, which will be staffed with consultants who can help.

And remember that if you take perfection as your goal, you will never finish or, worse, never start. We all have to compromise to get the job done.

On the other hand, sometimes writer's block is a sign that you need to let your ideas simmer in the back of your mind, where they might combine and recombine into something new and surprising. If you're stuck but have time (another reason to start early), do something else for a few hours: go on a run, read a book, take a nap. If you have even more time, put your draft aside for a day or two. Then return to the task to see if you can get back on track.

8 Presenting Evidence in Tables and Figures

If your data are in the form of numbers, most readers grasp them more easily if you present them graphically. But you face many choices of graphic forms, and some forms will suit your data and message better than others. In this chapter we show you how to choose the right graphic form and design it so that readers can see both what your data are and how they support your argument. (See pp. 426–28 in the bibliography for guides to creating and using graphics; see chapter 26 for details on formatting graphics.)[1]

8.1   Choose Verbal or Visual Representations of Your Data

Ordinarily, present quantitative data verbally when they include only a few numbers. (See chapter 23 for presenting numbers in text.) Present them graphically when most of your evidence is quantitative or you must communicate a large set of data. But when the data are few and simple, readers can grasp them as easily in a sentence as in a table like table 8.1.

---

1. A note on terminology: In this chapter we use the term *graphics* to refer to all visual representations of evidence. Another term sometimes used for such representations is *illustrations*. Traditionally, graphics are divided into *tables* and *figures*. A table is a grid with columns and rows that present data in numbers or words organized by categories. Figures are all other graphic forms, including graphs, charts, photographs, drawings, and diagrams. Figures that present quantitative data are divided into *charts*, typically consisting of bars, circles, points, or other shapes, and *graphs*, typically consisting of continuous lines. For a survey of common figures, see table 8.7.

In 2013, on average, men earned $50,033 a year, women $39,157, a difference of $10,876.

But if you present more than four or five numbers in a passage, readers will struggle to keep them straight, particularly if they must compare them, like this:

Between 1970 and 2010, the structure of families changed in two ways. In 1970, 85 percent of families had two parents, but by 1980 that number had declined to 77 percent, then to 73 percent by 1990, to 68 percent by 2000, and to 64 percent by 2010. The number of one-parent families rose, particularly families headed by a mother. In 1970, 11 percent of families were headed by a single mother. By 1980 that number rose to 18 percent, by 1990 to 22 percent, to 23 percent by 2000, and to 27 percent by 2010. There were some marginal changes among single fathers (headed 1 percent of families in 1970, 2 percent in 1980, 3 percent in 1990, and 4 percent in 2000 and 2010). Families with no adult in the home have remained stable at 3–4 percent.

Those data can be presented more effectively in graphic form, as in table 8.2.

8.2 Choose the Most Effective Graphic

When you graphically present data as complex as in that paragraph, you have many choices. The simplest and most common are tables, bar charts, and line graphs, each of which has a distinctive rhetorical effect.

- To emphasize specific values, use a table like table 8.2.
- To emphasize comparisons that can be seen at a glance, use a bar chart like figure 8.1.
- To emphasize trends, use a line graph like figure 8.2.

Table 8.1. Male-female salaries ($), 2013

Men	50,033
Women	39,157
Difference	10,876

Table 8.2. Changes in family structure, 1970–2010

Family type	Percentage of total families				
	1970	1980	1990	2000	2010
2 parents	85	77	73	68	64
Mother	11	18	22	23	27
Father	1	2	3	4	4
No adult	3	4	3	4	4

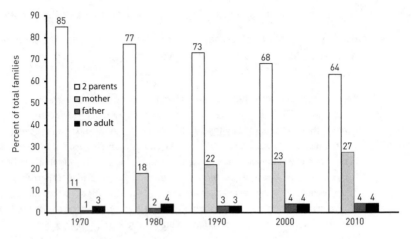

Figure 8.1. Changes in family structure, 1970–2010

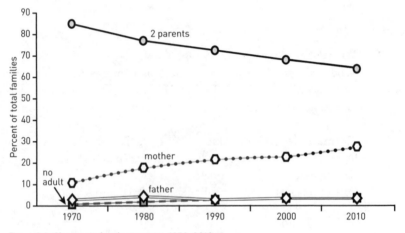

Figure 8.2. Changes in family structure, 1970–2010

While each of these forms communicates the same data, readers respond to them in different ways:

- A table seems precise and objective. It emphasizes individual numbers and forces readers to infer relationships or trends (unless you state them).
- Both charts and graphs emphasize an image that communicates values less precisely but more quickly than do the exact numbers of a table. But they differ:
    - A bar chart emphasizes comparisons among discrete items.
    - A line graph emphasizes trends, usually over time.

Choose the graphic form that best achieves the effect you intend.

Your choices also depend on your experience. If you're new to quantitative research, limit your choices to basic tables, bar charts, and line graphs. Your computer software may offer more choices, but ignore those that you aren't familiar with.

If you're doing advanced research, readers will expect you to draw from a larger range of graphics favored in your field. In that case, consult table 8.7, which describes the rhetorical uses of other common forms. You may have to consider more creative ways of representing data if you are writing a dissertation or article in a field that routinely display complex relationships in large data sets.

8.3 Design Tables and Figures

Computer programs create graphics so dazzling that you might be tempted to let your software determine their design. But readers don't care how fancy a graphic looks if it doesn't communicate your point clearly. Here are some principles for designing effective graphics. To follow them, you may have to change default settings in your graphics software. (See A.3.1.3 and A.1.3.4 on creating and inserting tables and figures in your paper.)

8.3.1 Frame Each Graphic to Help Your Readers Understand It

A graphic representing complex numbers rarely speaks for itself. You must frame it to show readers know what to see in it and how to understand its relevance to your argument.

1. Introduce tables and figures with a sentence in your text that states how the data support your point. Include in that sentence any specific number that you want readers to focus on. That number must also appear in the table or figure.
2. Label every table and figure in a way that describes its data and, if possible, their important relationships. For a table, the label is called a *title* and is set flush left above the table; for a figure, the label is called a *caption* and is set flush left below the figure. (For the forms of titles and captions, see chapter 26.) Keep titles and captions short but descriptive enough to distinguish every graphic from every other one.

   ■ Avoid making the title or caption a general topic:

   Not   Heads of households

   But   Changes in one- and two-parent heads of households, 1970–2010

- Use noun phrases; avoid relative clauses in favor of participles:

    Not   Number of families that subscribe to online streaming services

    But   Number of families subscribing to online streaming services

- Do not give background information or characterize what the data imply:

    Not   Weaker effects of counseling on depressed children before professional-ization of staff, 1995–2014

    But   Effect of counseling on depressed children, 1995–2014

- Be sure labels distinguish graphics presenting similar data:

    Not   Risk factors for high blood pressure

    But   Risk factors for high blood pressure among men in Maywood, Illinois

    Or   Risk factors for high blood pressure among men in Kingston, Jamaica

3. Insert into the table or figure information that helps readers see how the data support your point. For example, if numbers in a table show a trend and the size of the trend matters, indicate the change in a final column. If a line on a graph changes in response to an influence not mentioned on the graph, as in figure 8.3, add text to the image to explain it:

Although reading and math scores initially declined by almost 100 points following redistricting, that trend was substantially reversed by the introduction of supplemental math and reading programs.

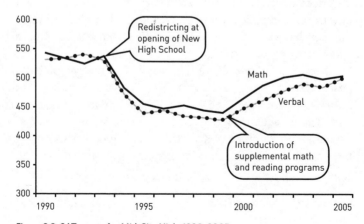

Figure 8.3. SAT scores for Mid-City High, 1990–2005

Table 8.3. Gasoline consumption

	1970	1980	1990	2000	2010
Annual miles (000)	9.5	10.3	10.5	11.7	12.2
Annual consumption (gal.)	760	760	520	533	515

Table 8.4. Per capita mileage and gasoline consumption, 1970–2010

	1970	1980	1990	2000	2010
Annual miles (000)	9.5	10.3	10.5	11.7	12.2
(% change vs. 1970)		8.4%	10.5%	23.1%	28.4%
Annual consumption (gal.)	760	760	520	533	515
(% change vs. 1970)			(31.5%)	(31.6%)	(32.2%)

4. Introduce the table or figure with a sentence that explains how to interpret it. Then highlight the part of the table or figure that you want readers to focus on, particularly any number or relationship mentioned in that introductory sentence. For example, we have to study table 8.3 to see how it supports the sentence that introduces it:

Most predictions about gasoline consumption have proved wrong.

We need another sentence explaining how the numbers support or explain the claim. We also need a more informative title and visual help that focuses us on what we should see in the table (table 8.4):

Gasoline consumption has not grown as predicted. *Though Americans drove 28 percent more miles in 2010 than in 1970, they used 32 percent less fuel.*

The added sentence tells us how to interpret the key data in table 8.4, and the highlight tells us where to find it.

8.3.2 Keep All Graphics as Simple as Their Content Allows

Some guides encourage you to put as much data as you can into a graphic. But readers want to see only the data relevant to your point, free of distractions.

■ For All Graphics
1. Include only relevant data. If you include data only for the record, label it accordingly and put it in an appendix (see A.2.3.2).
2. Keep the visual impact simple.
   ■ Box a graphic only if you group two or more figures.
   ■ Use caution in employing shading or color to convey meaning. Even if you print your paper on a color printer or submit it as a PDF, it may be printed or copied later in black and white.

▪ Do not use a three-dimensional background for a two-dimensional graphic. The added depth contributes nothing and can distort how readers judge values.

3. Use clear labels.

▪ Label rows and columns in tables and both axes in charts and graphs. (See chapter 26 for punctuation and spelling in labels.)
▪ Use tick marks and labels to indicate intervals on the vertical axis of a graph (see fig. 8.4).
▪ If possible, label lines, bar segments, and the like on the image rather than in a caption set to the side. Do so in the caption only if labels would make the image too complex to read.
▪ When specific numbers matter, add them to bars, segments or segments in charts or to dots on lines in graphs.
▪ For Tables
  ▪ Never use both horizontal and vertical lines to divide columns and rows. Use light gray lines if you want to direct your reader's eyes in one direction to compare data or if the table is unusually complex.
  ▪ For tables with many rows, lightly shading every fifth row will improve legibility.
  ▪ To ensure legibility, do not use a font size smaller than eight points.
▪ For Charts and Graphs
  ▪ Use grid lines only if the graphic is complex or readers need to see precise numbers. Make all grid lines light gray.
  ▪ Color or shade lines or bars only to show a contrast. If you do use shading, make sure it does not obscure any text, and do not use multiple shades, which might not reproduce distinctly.
  ▪ Plot data on three dimensions only when you cannot display the data in any other way and your readers are familiar with such graphs.
  ▪ Never use iconic bars (for example, images of cars to represent automobile production). They can distort how readers judge values, and they look amateurish.

8.3.3   Follow Guidelines for Tables, Bar Charts, and Line Graphs

8.3.3.1   TABLES. Tables with lots of data can seem dense, so organize them to help readers.

▪ Order the rows and columns by a principle that lets readers quickly find what you want them to see. Do not automatically choose alphabetic order.

■ Round numbers to relevant values. If differences of less than 1,000 don't matter, then 2,123,499 and 2,124,886 are irrelevantly precise.
■ Sum totals at the bottom of a column or at the end of a row, not at the top or left. Compare tables 8.5 and 8.6. Table 8.5 has a vague title and its items aren't helpfully sorted. Table 8.6 is clearer because it has an informative title and its items are organized to let us see patterns more easily.

8.3.3.2 BAR CHARTS. Bar charts communicate as much by visual impact as by specific numbers. But bars arranged in no pattern imply no point. If possible, group and arrange bars to create an image that matches your point.

For example, look at figure 8.4 in the context of the explanatory sentence before it. The items are listed alphabetically, an order that doesn't help readers see the point. In contrast, figure 8.5 supports the claim with a coherent image.

In standard bar charts, each bar represents 100 percent of a whole. But sometimes readers need to see specific values for parts of the whole. You can do that in two ways:

■ Divide the bars into proportional parts, creating a "stacked bar," as in the chart on the left in figure 8.6.

Table 8.5. Unemployment in major industrial nations, 2010–2015

	2010	2015	Change
Australia	5.2	6.2	1.0
Canada	8.0	6.9	(1.1)
France	9.7	10.7	1.0
Germany	7.1	5.2	(1.9)
Italy	8.4	11.9	3.5
Japan	5.0	3.9	(1.1)
Sweden	8.6	7.7	(0.9)
United Kingdom	7.9	6.6	(1.3)
United States	9.6	6.2	(3.4)

Table 8.6. Changes in unemployment rates of industrial nations, 2010–2015

	2010	2015	Change
United States	9.6	6.2	(3.4)
Germany	7.1	5.2	(1.9)
United Kingdom	7.9	6.6	(1.3)
Canada	8.0	6.9	(1.1)
Japan	5.0	3.9	(1.1)
Sweden	8.6	7.7	(0.9)
Australia	5.2	6.2	1.0
France	9.7	10.7	1.0
Italy	8.4	11.9	3.5

Most of the desert area in the world is concentrated in North Africa and the Middle East.

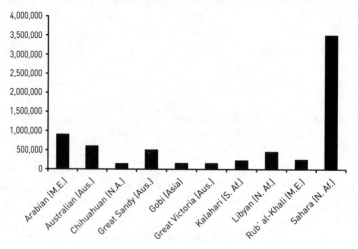

Figure 8.4. World's ten largest deserts

Most of the desert area in the world is concentrated in North Africa and the Middle East.

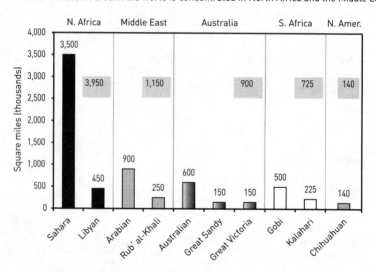

Figure 8.5. World distribution of large deserts

■ Give each part of the whole its own bar, then group the bar into clusters, as in the chart on the right in figure 8.6.

Use stacked bars only when it's more important to compare whole values than it is to compare their segments. Readers, however, can't easily gauge proportions by eye alone, so if you do use stacked bars, do this:

- Arrange segments in a logical order. If possible, put the largest segment at the bottom in the darkest shade.
- Label segments with specific numbers and connect corresponding segments with gray lines to help clarify proportions.

Figure 8.7 shows how a stacked bar chart is more readable when irrelevant segments are eliminated and those kept are logically ordered and fully labeled.

A grouped bar chart makes it easy for readers to compare parts of a whole, but difficult for them to compare different wholes because they must do mental arithmetic. If you group bars because the segments are more important than the wholes, do this:

- Arrange groups of bars in a logical order; if possible, put bars of similar size next to one another (order bars within groups in the same way).

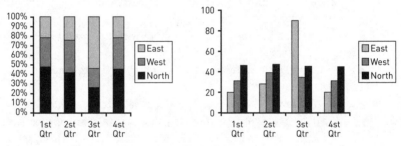

Figure 8.6. Stacked bar chart compared to grouped bar chart

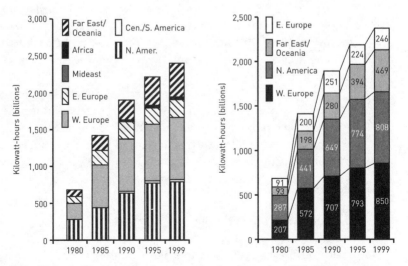

Figure 8.7. Stacked bar charts showing generators of nuclear energy, 1980–1999

■ Label groups with the number for the whole, either above each group or below the labels on the bottom.

Most data that fit a bar chart can also be represented in a pie chart. Pie charts are popular in magazines, tabloids, and annual reports, but they're harder to read than bar charts and invite misinterpretation because readers must compare proportions of segments whose sizes are often hard to judge. Most researchers avoid pie charts, especially to convey quantitative data. They use bar charts.

8.3.3.3   **LINE GRAPHS.** Because a line graph emphasizes trends, readers must see a clear image to interpret it correctly. Do the following:

■ Choose the variable that makes the line go in the direction, up or down, that supports your point. If the good news is a reduction (down) in high school dropouts, you can more effectively represent the same data as an increase in retention (up). If you want to emphasize bad news, find a way to represent your data as a falling line.

■ Plot more than six lines on one graph only if you cannot make your point in any other way.

■ Do not depend on different shades of gray to distinguish lines, as in figure 8.8.

■ If you plot fewer than ten or so values (called *data points*), indicate each with a dot, as in figure 8.9. If those values are relevant, you can add numbers above the dots. Do not add dots to lines plotted from ten or more data points.

Compare figure 8.8 and figure 8.9. Beyond its general story, figure 8.8 is harder to read because the shades of gray do not distinguish the lines well and because our eyes have to flick back and forth to connect lines with variables and their numbers. Figure 8.9 makes those connections clearer.

These different ways of showing the same data can be confusing. To cut through that confusion, test different ways of representing the same data. (Your software program will usually let you do that quickly.) Then ask someone not familiar with your data to judge the representations for their impact and clarity. Be sure to introduce your graphics with a sentence that states the claim you want the figures to support.

8.4   Communicating Data Ethically

Your graphics must be not only clear and accurate but also honest. Do not distort the image of your data to make a point. For example, the two bar charts in figure 8.10 display identical data yet send different messages.

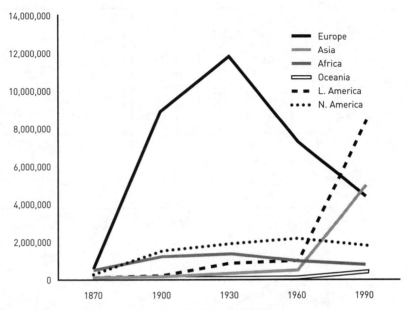

Figure 8.8. Foreign-born residents in the United States, 1870–1990

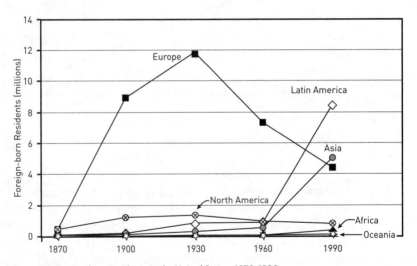

Figure 8.9. Foreign-born residents in the United States, 1870–1990

The 0–100 scale in the figure on the left creates a fairly flat slope, which makes the drop in pollution seem small. The vertical scale in the figure on the right, however, begins not at 0 but at 80. When a scale is truncated, its sharper slope exaggerates small contrasts.

Graphs can also mislead by implying false correlations. Someone

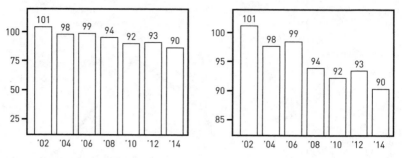

Figure 8.10. Capitol City pollution index, 2002-2014

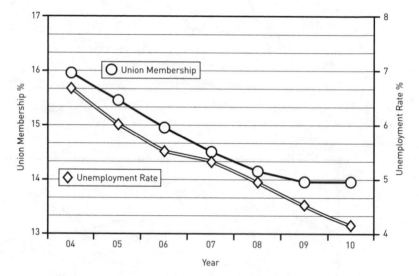

Figure 8.11. Union membership and unemployment rate, 2004-2010

claiming that unemployment goes down when union membership goes down might offer figure 8.11 as evidence. And indeed, in that graph, union membership and the unemployment rate do seem to move together so closely that a reader might infer one causes the other. But the scale for the left axis in figure 8.11 (union membership) differs from the scale for the right axis (unemployment rate). The two scales have been deliberately skewed to make it seem the two downward trends are related. They may be, but the distorted image doesn't prove it.

Graphs can also mislead when the image encourages readers to misjudge values. The two charts in figure 8.12 represent exactly the same data but seem to communicate different messages. These "stacked area" charts represent differences in values not by the *angles* of the lines but

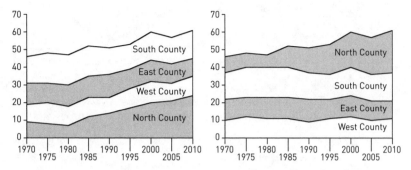

Figure 8.12. Representation of collar counties among State U. undergraduates (percentage of total)

by the areas *between* them. In both charts, the bands for south, east, and west are roughly the same width throughout, indicating little change in the values they represent. The band for the north, however, widens sharply, representing a large increase in the value it represents. In the chart on the left, readers are likely to misjudge the top three bands because they are on top of the rising north band, making those bands seem to rise as well. In the chart on the right, on the other hand, those three bands do not rise because they are on the bottom. Here only the band for the north rises.

Here are four guidelines for avoiding visual misrepresentations:

- Do not manipulate a scale to magnify or reduce a contrast.
- Do not use a figure whose image distorts values.
- Do not make a table or figure unnecessarily complex or misleadingly simple.
- If the table or figure supports a point, state it.

Table 8.7. Common graphic forms and their uses

	Data	Rhetorical uses

Bar chart

Compares the value of one variable across a series of items called *cases* (e.g., average salaries for service worker$_{variable}$ in six companies$_{cases}$).

Creates strong visual contrasts among individual cases, emphasizing comparisons. For specific values, add numbers to bars. Can show ranks or trends. Vertical bars (called *columns*) are most common, but bars can be horizontal if cases are numerous or have complex labels. See section 8.3.3.2.

Bar chart, grouped or split

Compares the value of one variable, divided into subsets, across a series of cases (e.g., average salaries$_{variable}$ for men and women service workers$_{subsets}$ in six companies$_{cases}$).

Contrasts subsets within and across individual cases; not useful for comparing total values for cases. For specific values, add numbers to bars. Grouped bars show ranking or trends poorly; useful for time series only if trends are unimportant. See section 8.3.3.2.

Bar chart, stacked

Compares the value of one variable, divided into two or more subsets, across a series of cases (e.g., harassment complaints$_{variable}$ segmented by region$_{subsets}$ in six industries$_{cases}$).

Best for comparing totals across cases and subsets *within* cases; difficult to compare subsets *across* cases (use grouped bars). For specific values, add numbers to bars and segments. Useful for time series. Can show ranks or trends for total values only. See section 8.3.3.2.

Histogram

Compares two variables, with one segmented into ranges that function like the cases in a bar graph (e.g., service workers$_{continuous}$ whose salary is $0–5,000, $5–10,000, $10–15,000, etc.$_{segmented \, variable}$).

Best for comparing segments within continuous data sets. Shows trends but emphasizes segments (e.g., a sudden spike at $5–10,000 representing part-time workers). For specific values, add numbers to bars.

Image chart

Shows value of one or more variables for cases displayed on a map, diagram, or other image (e.g., states$_{cases}$ colored red or blue to show voting patterns$_{variable}$).

Shows the distribution of the data in relation to preexisting categories; deemphasizes specific values. Best when the image is familiar, as in a map or diagram of a process.

Pie chart

Shows the proportion of a single variable for a series of cases (e.g., the budget share$_{variable}$ of US cabinet departments$_{cases}$).

Best for comparing one segment to the whole. Useful only with few segments or segments that are very different in size; otherwise comparisons among segments are difficult. For specific values, add numbers to segments. Common in popular venues, frowned on by professionals. See 8.3.3.2.

Table 8.7. (continued)

	Data	Rhetorical uses
Line graph		
	Compares continuous variables for one or more cases (e.g., temperature$_{variable}$ and viscosity$_{variable}$ in two fluids$_{cases}$).	Best for showing trends; deemphasizes specific values. Useful for time series. To show specific values, add numbers to data points. To show the significance of a trend, segment the grid (e.g., below or above average performance). See 8.3.3.3.
Area chart		
	Compares two continuous variables for one or more cases (e.g., reading test scores$_{variable}$ over time$_{variable}$ in a school district$_{case}$).	Shows trends; deemphasizes specific values. Can be used for time series. To show specific values, add numbers to data points. Areas below the lines add no information and will lead some readers to misjudge values. Confusing with multiple lines/areas.
Area chart, stacked		
	Compares two continuous variables for two or more cases (e.g., profit$_{variable}$ over time$_{variable}$ for several products$_{cases}$).	Shows the trend for the total of all cases, plus how much each case contributes to that total. Likely to mislead readers on the value or the trend for any individual case, as explained in section 8.4.
Scatterplot		
	Compares two variables at multiple data points for a single case (e.g., housing sales$_{variable}$ and distance from downtown$_{variable}$ in one city$_{case}$) or at one data point for multiple cases (e.g., brand loyalty$_{variable}$ and repair frequency$_{variable}$ for ten manufacturers$_{cases}$).	Best for showing the distribution of data, especially when there is no clear trend or when the focus is on outlying data points. If only a few data points are plotted, it allows a focus on individual values.
Bubble chart		
	Compares three variables at multiple data points for a single case (e.g., housing sales,$_{variable}$ distance from downtown,$_{variable}$ and prices$_{variable}$ in one city$_{case}$) or at one data point for multiple cases (e.g., image advertising,$_{variable}$ repair frequency,$_{variable}$ and brand loyalty$_{variable}$ for ten manufacturers$_{cases}$).	Emphasizes the relationship between the third variable (bubbles) and the first two; most useful when the question is whether the third variable is a product of the others. Readers easily misjudge relative values shown by bubbles; adding numbers mitigates that problem.

9 Revising Your Draft

Some new researchers think that once they have a draft, they're practically done. Experienced researchers know better. They write that first draft not for their readers but for themselves, to see whether they can make the case they hoped to (or even a better one). Then they revise until they think their draft meets the needs and expectations of their readers. That's hard, because we all know our own work too well to read it as others will. To revise effectively, you must know what readers look for and whether your draft helps them find it. To that end, our advice may seem mechanical. But only when you can analyze your draft objectively can you avoid reading into it what you want your readers to get out of it.

We suggest first revising overall organization, especially the "outer frame" of the introduction and conclusion; then sections, paragraphs, sentences; and finally stylistic issues such as spelling and punctuation (for guidance on these issues, see part 3). Of course no one revises so neatly. All of us fiddle with words as we move paragraphs around and reorganize as we revise a sentence. But you're likely to work best if you revise from whole to part.

Many experienced researchers find that they can edit hard copy more reliably than they can edit text on a screen. Even if you prefer to edit on a screen, consider reading at least one later draft on paper. You may catch more errors, and you'll get a better sense of your paper's overall structure than you can from the screen alone.

9.1   Check for Blind Spots in Your Argument

Completing a draft is an accomplishment, but don't move immediately to fine-tuning sentences. After the first draft, parts of your argument will likely still not stand up to a robust challenge. If you spend a lot of time polishing sentences, it can be hard to later accept that whole sections need to be rearranged or even cut. Instead, check your argument's reasoning. Have you considered the strongest relevant counterarguments? Have you looked for evidence that challenges or complicates your reasons? Have you considered alternative interpretations of your evidence? If not, now is the time. If you find it difficult to think of significant alternatives to your argument now that you have completed a draft, talk with your instructor or advisor about where your argument overlooks likely objections.

9.2   Check Your Introduction, Conclusion, and Claim

Your readers must recognize three things quickly and unambiguously:

- where your introduction ends
- where your conclusion begins
- what sentences in one or both state your claim

To make the first two clearly visible, you might insert a subhead or extra space between your introduction and body and another between the body and conclusion. (Chapter 10 discusses revising your introduction and conclusion in detail.)

9.3   Make Sure the Body of Your Paper Is Coherent

Once you frame your paper clearly, check its body. Readers will find your paper coherent when they can see the following:

- what key terms run through all of its sections
- where each section and subsection ends and the next begins
- how each section relates to the one before it
- what role each section plays in the whole
- what sentence in each section and subsection states its point
- what distinctive key terms run through each section

To ensure that your readers will see those features, check for the following:

1. Do key terms run through your whole paper?

   - Circle key terms in the claim as stated in your introduction and conclusion (review 7.3).

- Circle those same terms in the body of your paper.
- Underline other words related to concepts named by those circled terms.

If readers don't see at least one of your key terms in most paragraphs, they may think your paper wanders. Revise by working those terms into parts that lack them. If you underlined many more words than you circled, be sure that readers will recognize how the underlined words relate to the concepts named in your circled key terms. If readers might miss the connections, change some of those related words to the key terms. If that's difficult, you may have gotten off track and will need to rewrite or discard some passages.

2. Is the beginning of each section and subsection clearly signaled?

You can use headings to mark transitions from one section or subsection to the next (review 6.2.4). In a relatively short paper, rather than use headings, you might add an extra space at the major joints. If you can't decide what words to use in headings or even where to put them, your readers will likely have a problem with your paper's organization. (For styles of different levels of heads, see A.2.2.4.)

3. Does each major section begin with words that signal how that section relates to the one before it?

Readers must not only recognize where sections begin and end but also understand why they are ordered as they are (see 6.2.5–6.2.6). Signal the logic of your order with words such as *Consequently* . . . , *In contrast* . . . , *Some have objected that* . . . , or even just *First,* . . . *Second,* . . .

4. Is it clear how each section relates to the whole?

For each section, ask, *What question does this section answer?* If it doesn't help to answer one of the five questions whose answers constitute an argument (see 5.2), think about its relevance: does it create a context, explain a background concept or issue, or help readers in some other way? If you can't explain how a section relates to your claim, consider cutting it.

5. Is the point of each section stated in a sentence at the end of a brief introduction to that section (or at its end)?

If you have a choice, state the point of a section at the end of its introduction. Under no circumstances should you bury the point of a section in its middle. If a section is longer than four or five pages, you might conclude by restating your point and summarizing your argument.

6. Do the specific terms that distinguish a section run through it?

Each section and subsection needs its own key terms to unify and distinguish it from others. Repeat step 1 for each section: find the sentence that expresses its point and circle in it the key terms that distinguish that section from the others. Then check whether those terms run through that section. If you find no terms that differ from those running through the whole, then you readers might not see what distinct ideas that section contributes to the whole.

9.4 Check Your Paragraphs

Each paragraph should be relevant to the point of its section. And like sections, each paragraph should have a sentence or two introducing it, usually stating its point and including the key concepts that the rest of the paragraph develops. If the opening sentences of a paragraph don't state its point, then its last one should. Order your sentences by some principle and make them relevant to the point of the paragraph (for principles of order, see 6.2.5).

Paragraphs vary in length depending on the type of writing in which they appear. For example, they tend to be shorter in brief research reports and longer in critical essays or book chapters. If you find yourself stringing together several short paragraphs, it may mean your points are not well developed. If your paragraphs run more than a page, it may mean you are losing focus. Reserve the use of two- or three-sentence paragraphs for lists, transitions, introductions and conclusions to sections, and statements that you want to emphasize. (We use short paragraphs here so that readers can more easily skim—rarely a consideration in scholarly writing.)

9.5 Let Your Draft Cool, Then Paraphrase It

If you start your project early, you'll have time to let your revised draft cool. What seems good one day often looks different the next. When you return to your draft, don't read it straight through; skim its top-level parts: its introduction, the first paragraph of each major section, and the conclusion. Then, based only on what you have read, paraphrase it for someone who hasn't read it. Does the paraphrase hang together? Does it fairly sum up your argument? Even better, ask someone else to skim your paper by reading just its introduction and the introduction to each major section: how well that person summarizes your paper will predict how well your readers will understand it.

Finally, be receptive to feedback, especially from more experienced researchers and your teacher or advisor. You don't have to follow every suggestion, but you should consider each carefully. In chapter 12 we tell you how to get the most out of comments on writing.

10 Writing Your Final Introduction and Conclusion

Once you have a final draft and can see what you have actually written, you can write your final introduction and conclusion. These two framing parts of your paper crucially influence how readers will understand and remember the rest of it, so it's worth your time to make them as clear and compelling as you can. In chapter 2 we showed you how to develop a project around a research problem. Here we show you how to use that problem to craft an introduction likely to engage your readers and a conclusion likely to solidify their understanding and prompt new questions.

What seizes readers' attention in a research paper is not a snappy hook but a problem they think needs a solution, and what holds their attention is a promise that you've found it. As we've said, you can always work with readers who say *I don't agree.* What you can't survive are those who shrug and say *I don't care.*

Your introduction has three aims. It should do the following:

- put your research in the context of other research
- make readers understand how your paper addresses a problem they care about

- give them a framework for understanding it (which sometimes, but not always, includes announcing your claim)

Most introductions run about 10 percent of the whole (in the sciences they are often shorter).

Your conclusion also has three aims. It should do the following:

- leave readers with a clear idea of your claim
- make readers understand its importance
- suggest further research

Conclusions are usually shorter than introductions. In article-length papers, they are usually sections; in theses and dissertations, they are usually separate chapters.

10.1 Draft Your Final Introduction

Introductions to papers in different fields can seem different, but behind most of them is a pattern with the four parts described in 6.2.2:

1. Opening context or background. When this summarizes relevant research, it's called a *literature review* that puts your project in the context of other research and sets up the next step. Keep it short.
2. A statement of your research question, or your research problem's condition. This is typically a statement of what isn't known or understood or of what is flawed about the research you cited in step 1. It often begins with *but, however,* or another word signaling a qualification.
3. A statement of the significance of your question, or your research problem's consequence. This answers *So what?* It is key to motivating your readers.
4. Your claim or a promise of one. This addresses the research problem expressed in step 2. Here is an abbreviated example (each sentence could be expanded to a paragraph or more):

For centuries, risk analysts have studied risk as a problem in statistics and the rational uses of probability theory.context But risk communicators have discovered that ordinary people think about risk in ways that seem unrelated to statistically based probabilities.question/problem-condition Until we understand how nonexperts think about risk, an important aspect of human cognition will remain a puzzle.significance/problem-consequence It appears that nonexperts judge risk by visualizing worst-case scenarios, then assessing how frightening the image is.claim

10.1.1   **Establish a Context of Prior Research**

Not every paper opens with a survey of research. Some begin directly with a research question stated as something not known or understood, followed by a review of the relevant literature. This is a common strategy when the gap in knowledge or understanding is well known:

The relationship between secondhand smoke and heart disease is still contested.

But if that gap isn't well known, such an opening can feel abrupt, like this one:

Researchers do not understand how ordinary people think about risk.

As a rule, a research paper prepares readers by describing the prior research that it will extend, modify, or correct. If the paper is intended for general readers, the context it provides can be brief:

We all take risks every day—when we cross the street or eat high-fat food, and even when we take a bath. The study of risk began with games of chance, so it has long been treated mathematically. By the twentieth century, researchers used mathematical tools to study risk in many areas: investments, commercial products, even war. As a result, most researchers think that risk is a statistically quantifiable problem and that decisions about it should be rationally based.

In a paper intended for other researchers, this opening context typically describes the specific research the paper will extend or modify. It is important to represent this prior research fairly, so describe it as you think the researchers who conducted it would.

Ever since Girolamo Cardano thought about games of chance in quantitative terms in the sixteenth century (Cardano 1545), risk has been treated as a purely mathematical problem. Analyses of risk significantly improved in the seventeenth century when Pascal, Leibniz, and others developed the calculus (Bernstein 1996). In the twentieth century, researchers widened their focus to study risk in all areas of life: investments, consumer products, the environment, even war (Stimson 1990; 1998). These problems, too, have been addressed almost exclusively from a mathematical perspective. [Detailed discussion of contemporary research follows.]

Some papers, especially theses and dissertations, go on like that for pages, citing scores of books and articles only marginally relevant to the topic, usually to show how widely the researcher has read. That kind of survey can provide helpful bibliography to other researchers, especially new ones, but busy readers want to know about only the *specific* research that the researcher intends to extend, modify, or correct.

Early in your career you might not be able to write this review of prior research with much confidence, because you're unlikely to know much of it. If so, imagine your reader as someone like yourself *before* you started your research. What would you have wanted to know? What did you get wrong that your research has corrected? How has it improved your own flawed understanding? This is where you can use a working hypothesis that you rejected: *It might seem that X is so, but . . .* (see also 4.1.2).

10.1.2 Restate Your Question as Something Not Known or Fully Understood
After establishing the context, state what that prior research hasn't done or how it's incomplete, even wrong. Introduce that statement with *but, however*, or some other term indicating that you're about to modify the received knowledge and understanding that you just surveyed:

Ever since Girolamo Cardano . . . mathematical perspective.context *But risk communicators have discovered that ordinary people think about risk in ways that are irrational and unrelated to statistically realistic probabilities. What is not understood is whether such nonexpert risk assessment is based on random guesses or whether it has systematic properties.*question restated

10.1.3 State the Significance of Your Question
Now you must show your readers the *significance* of answering your research question. Imagine a reader asking *So what?*, then answer it. Frame your response as the consequence of not knowing the answer to your research question:

Ever since Girolamo Cardano . . . mathematical perspective.context But risk communicators have discovered that . . . What is not understood is whether such nonexpert risk assessment is based on random guesses or whether it has systematic properties.question restated *[So what?] Until we understand how risk is understood by nonexperts, an important aspect of human reasoning will remain a puzzle: the kind of cognitive processing that seems systematic but lies outside the range of what is called "rational thinking."*significance

Alternatively, you can phrase the consequence as a benefit:

Ever since Girolamo Cardano . . . mathematical perspective.context But risk communicators have discovered that . . . What is not understood is whether such nonexpert risk assessment is based on random guesses or whether it has systematic properties.question restated *[So what?] If we could understand how ordinary people make decisions about risks in their daily lives, we could better understand a kind of cognitive processing that seems systematic but lies outside the range of what is called "rational thinking."*significance

You may struggle to answer that *So what?* It is a problem that only experience can solve, but the fact is, even experienced researchers can be vexed by it.

10.1.4   State Your Claim

Once you state that something isn't known or understood and why it should be, readers want to see your claim, the answer to your research question (we abbreviate a good deal in what follows):

Ever since Girolamo Cardano . . . mathematical perspective._{context} But risk communicators have discovered that ordinary people think about risk in ways that are systematic but irrational and unrelated to statistically realistic probabilities._{question} [*So what?*] Until we understand how risk is understood by nonexperts, an important kind of human reasoning will remain a puzzle: the kind of cognitive processing that seems systematic but lies outside the range of what is called "rational thinking."_{significance} *It appears that nonexperts assess risk not by assigning quantitative probabilities to events that might occur but by visualizing worst-case scenarios, then assigning degrees of risk according to how vivid and frightening the image is.*_{claim}

If you have reason to withhold your claim until the end of your paper, write a sentence to conclude your introduction that uses the key terms from that claim and that frames what follows:

It appears that nonexperts assess risk not by assigning quantitative probabilities but by systematically using properties of their visual imagination._{promise of claim}

Those four steps may seem mechanical, but they constitute the introductions to most research papers in every field, both inside the academic world and out. As you read your sources, especially journal articles, watch for that four-part framework. You will not only learn a range of strategies for writing your own introductions but better understand the ones you read.

10.1.5   Draft a New First Sentence

Some writers find it so difficult to write their first sentence that they fall into clichés. Avoid these:

- Do not repeat the language of your assignment.
- Do not quote a dictionary definition: *Webster defines risk as . . .*
- Do not begin too generally: *For centuries, philosophers have debated the question of . . .* (Remember that you are not writing to everyone, only to your research community.)

If you want to begin with something livelier than prior research, try one or more of these openers (but note the warning that follows):

1. A pithy quotation:

As Dale Carnegie once said, "All life is a chance."

2. A striking fact:

Many people drive rather than fly because the vivid image of an airplane crash terrifies them, even though they are many times more likely to die in a car crash than a plane wreck.

3. A relevant anecdote:

George Miller always drove long distances to meet clients because he believed that the risk of an airplane crash was too great. Even when he broke his back in an automobile accident, he still thought he had made the right calculation. "At least I survived. The odds of surviving an airplane crash are zero!"

You can combine all three:

As Dale Carnegie once said, "All life is a chance." For example, many people drive rather than fly because the vivid image of an airplane crash terrifies them, even though they are more likely to die in a car crash than a plane wreck. George Miller always drove long distances to meet clients because he believed that the risk of an airplane crash was too great. Even after he broke his back in an automobile accident, he still thought he had made the right calculation. "At least I survived. The odds of surviving an airplane crash are zero!"

Be sure to include in these openers terms that refer to the key concepts you'll use when you write the rest of the introduction (and the rest of the paper). In this case, they include *calculating, risk, vivid image, more likely*.

Now the warning: before you write a snappy opening, be sure that others in your field use them. In some fields they're considered too journalistic for serious scholarship.

10.2 Draft Your Final Conclusion

Your conclusion sums up your argument, but just as important, it offers an opportunity to raise new questions suggested by your research. You can build your conclusion around the same elements as your introduction, only in reverse order.

10.2.1 Restate Your Claim

Restate your claim early in your conclusion, more fully than in your introduction:

Ordinary people make decisions about risk not on a rational or quantifiable basis but on the basis of at least six psychological factors that not only involve emotion but systematically draw on the power of visual imagination.

At this point you're probably sure what your claim is, but even so, take this last chance to rephrase it to make it as specific and complete as you can.

10.2.2   **Point Out a New Significance, a Practical Application, or Opportunities for Further Research (or All Three)**

After stating your claim, remind readers of its significance, or better, state a new significance or a practical application:

> These findings suggest a hitherto unsuspected aspect of human cognition, a quantitative logic independent of statistical probabilities involving degrees of precision or realism in visualization. Once we understand this imaginative but systematic assessment of risk, it should be possible for risk communicators to better explain risk in everyday life.

Finally, suggest further research. This gesture suggests how the community of researchers can continue the conversation. It mirrors the opening context:

> Although these factors improve our understanding of risk, they do not exhaust the "human" factors in judgments of it. We must also investigate the relevance of age, gender, education, and intelligence. For example, . . .

When you state what remains to do, you keep the conversation alive. So before you write your final words, imagine other researchers who are intrigued by your work and want to follow it up. What more would *you* like to know, as *their* reader? What research would you suggest they do?

10.3   **Write Your Title Last**

Your title is the first thing your readers read, but it should be the last thing you write. It should both announce your topic *and* communicate its conceptual framework, so build it out of the key terms that you earlier identified (review 9.3). Compare these three titles:

> Risk
> Thinking about Risk
> Irrational but Systematic Risk Assessment: The Role of Visual Imagination in Calculating Relative Risk

The first title is accurate but too general to give us much guidance about what is to come. The second is a bit more specific, but the third uses both a title and a subtitle to give us advance notice of the paper's key terms. When readers see the key terms from the introduction turn up throughout a paper, they are more likely to think it coheres, or holds together. Two-part titles—a main title followed by a subtitle—give you more room for key terms.

11 Revising Sentences

Your final task is to make your writing as understandable as you can for your readers, for it is their judgment of your ideas—as you have expressed them in your writing—that matters most. Readable writing, of course, depends on more than clear sentences, but clear sentences will go a long way toward making your writing readable. In this chapter, therefore, we offer some advice on how to revise your sentences so that readers will find them clear.

Sometimes you will know your writing is awkward, especially if you're writing about an unfamiliar and complex topic for intimidating readers. Other times, though, you may overestimate your writing, thinking it clear when your readers won't. You need a way to revise sentences in both of these situations: to revise those you know need help and, even more, to identify and improve those that you think are fine but that readers might not.

We can't tell you how to fix every problem in every sentence, but we can tell you how to deal with those that most often afflict writers who, in struggling to sound like "serious scholars," end up sounding merely pretentious. Here is a short example:

1a. A better understanding of student learning could achieve improvement in teaching effectiveness.

However impressive that sounds, the student who wrote it meant only this:

1b. If we better understood how students learn, we could teach them more effectively.

To diagnose 1a and revise it into 1b, you must know a few grammatical terms: *noun, verb, active verb, passive verb, whole subject, simple subject, main clause, subordinate clause*. If they're only a dim memory, skim a grammar guide before you go on.

11.1 Focus on the First Seven or Eight Words of a Sentence

Just as the key to a clearly written paper, section, or paragraph is in its first few sentences, so the key to a clearly written sentence is in its first few words. When readers grasp those first seven or eight words easily, they read what follows faster, understand it better, and remember it longer. It is the difference between these two sentences:

2a. The United Nations' insistence on acceptance by all nations of the principles of equal rights and self-determination of peoples is a product of its recognition that maintenance of stability in the world order requires that nations be guided by values beyond narrow self-interest.

2b. The United Nations insists that all nations accept the principles of equal rights and self-determination of peoples, because it recognizes that maintaining a stable world order requires that nations be guided by values beyond narrow self-interest.

To write a sentence like 2b, or to revise one like 2a into 2b, follow these seven principles:

- Get to the subject of your sentence quickly; begin sentences with long phrases and clauses only occasionally.
- Make subjects short and concrete, ideally naming the character that performs the action expressed by the verb that follows.
- Avoid separating the subject and verb with more than a word or two.
- Put key actions in verbs, not in nouns.
- Put information familiar to readers at the beginning of a sentence, new information at the end.
- Choose an active or passive verb based on which lets you best apply the preceding principles.
- Use first-person pronouns appropriately.

Those principles are not inviolable rules but guidelines you can rely on to communicate clearly with your readers. They add up to this: readers want to get past a short, concrete, familiar subject quickly and to a verb expressing a specific action. When a sentence lets them do that, the rest of the sentence will usually take care of itself. To diagnose your own writing, skim the first seven or eight words of every sentence. Look for sentences in which you don't follow our seven principles, and then revise them as follows.

11.1.1   Get to the Subject of Your Sentence Quickly

Compare these two sentences (introductory phrases are boldfaced, whole subjects italicized):

3a. **In view of claims by researchers on higher education indicating at least one change by most undergraduate students of their major field of study,** *first-year students* may need better guidance when they choose a major.

3b. *Researchers on higher education* claim that *most students* change their major field of study at least once during their undergraduate career. **If that is so,** then *first-year students* may need better guidance when they choose a major.

Most readers find 3a harder to read than 3b, because it makes them work through a twenty-four-word phrase before they reach its subject (*first-year students*). In the two sentences in 3b, readers immediately start with the subject (*Researchers on higher education*) or reach it after a very short clause (*If that is so*).

   The principle is this: start most of your sentences directly with their whole subjects. Begin only a few sentences with introductory phrases or clauses longer than ten or so words. You can usually revise long introductory phrases and subordinate clauses into separate independent sentences, as in 3b.

11.1.2   Make Subjects Short and Concrete

Readers must grasp the subject of a sentence easily, but they can't when the subject is long, complex, and abstract. Compare these two sentences (the whole subject in each is italicized; the one-word simple subject is boldfaced):

4a. *A school system's successful **adoption** of a new reading curriculum for its elementary schools* depends on the demonstration in each school of the commitment of its principal and the cooperation of teachers in setting reasonable goals.

4b. *A school **system*** will adopt a new reading curriculum for elementary schools successfully only when *each **principal*** demonstrates that *she* is committed to it and *teachers* cooperate to set reasonable goals.

In 4a, the whole subject is fourteen words long, and its simple subject is an abstraction—*adoption*. In 4b, the clearer version, the whole subject of every verb is short, and each simple subject is relatively concrete: *school system, each principal, she, teachers*. Moreover, each of those subjects performs the action in its verb: **system** *will adopt,* **principal** *demonstrates,* **she** *is committed,* **teachers** *cooperate.*

The principle is this: readers tend to judge a sentence readable when the subject of its verb names the main character in a few concrete words, ideally a character that is also the "doer" of the action expressed by the verb that follows.

But there's a complication. We are not saying that to be clear you must write only about people and concrete things. In fact, writers often tell clear stories about abstract characters:

5. *No skill* is more valued in the professional world than problem solving. *The ability to solve problems quickly* requires us to frame situations in different ways and to find more than one solution. In fact, *effective problem solving* may define general intelligence.

Few readers have trouble with those abstract subjects, because they're short and familiar: *no skill, the ability to solve problems quickly,* and *effective problem solving.* What gives readers trouble is an abstract subject that is long and unfamiliar.

To fix sentences with long, abstract subjects, revise in three steps:

- Identify the main character in the sentence.
- Find its key action, and if that is buried in an abstract noun, make it a verb.
- Make the main character the subject of that new verb.

For example, compare 6a and 6b (actions are boldfaced; verbs are capitalized):

6a. Without a means for **analyzing interactions** between social class and education in regard to the **creation** of job opportunities, success in **understanding** economic mobility will REMAIN limited.

6b. Economists do not entirely UNDERSTAND economic mobility, because they cannot ANALYZE how social class and education INTERACT to CREATE job opportunities.

In both sentences the main character is *economists*, but in 6a that character isn't the subject of any verb; in fact, it's not in the sentence at all: we must infer it from actions buried in nouns—*analyzing* and *understanding* (what economists do). We revise 6a into 6b by making the main characters, *economists, social class,* and *education,* subjects of the explicit verbs *understand, analyze, interact,* and *create.*

Readers want subjects to name the main characters in your story, ideally flesh-and-blood characters, and specific verbs to name their key actions.

11.1.3 **Avoid Separating Subjects and Verbs with More than a Word or Two**
Once past a short subject, readers want to get to a verb quickly, so avoid splitting a verb from its subject with long phrases and clauses:

7a. Some economists, because they write in a style that is impersonal and objective, do not communicate with laypeople easily.

In 7a, the *because* clause separates the subject *some economists* from the verb *do not communicate*, forcing us to mentally suspend our breath. To revise, move the interrupting clause to the beginning or end of its sentence, depending on whether it connects more closely to the sentence before or the one after. When in doubt, put it at the end (for more on this, see 11.1.5).

7b. Because some economists write in a style that is impersonal and objective, they do not communicate with laypeople easily. This inability to communicate . . .

7c. Some economists do not communicate with laypeople easily because they write in a style that is impersonal and objective. They use passive verbs and . . .

Readers manage short interruptions more easily:

8. Few economists *deliberately* write in a style that is impersonal and objective.

11.1.4 **Put Key Actions in Verbs, Not in Nouns**
Readers want to get to a verb quickly, but they also want that verb to express a key action. So avoid using an empty verb such as *have, do, make,* or *be* to introduce an action buried in an abstract noun. Make the noun a verb.

Compare these two sentences (nouns naming actions are boldfaced; verbs naming actions are capitalized; verbs expressing little action are italicized):

9a. During the early years of the First World War, the Great Powers' **attempt** at **enlisting** the United States on their side *was met* with **failure**.

9b. During the early years of the First World War, the Great Powers ATTEMPTED to ENLIST the United States on their side but FAILED.

In 9a, three important actions aren't verbs but nouns: *attempt, enlisting, failure.* Sentence 9b seems more direct because it expresses those actions in verbs: *attempted, enlist, failed.*

11.1.5   Put Information Familiar to Readers at the Beginning of a Sentence, New Information at the End

Readers understand a sentence most readily when they grasp its subject easily, and the easiest subject to grasp is not just short and concrete but also *familiar*. Compare how the second sentence in each of the following passages does or doesn't contribute to a sense of "flow":

10a. New insights into global weather patterns are emerging from recent research on the large low-pressure zones rotating above the Earth's poles, known as the polar vortices. Environmental changes that are leading temperatures at the poles to rise, this research suggests, are affecting the vortices. These temperature increases cause the vortices to deviate toward the equator, bringing with them the frigid air responsible for our recent colder winters.

10b. New insights into global weather patterns are emerging from recent research on the large low-pressure zones rotating above the Earth's poles, known as the polar vortices. The vortices, this research suggests, are being affected by environmental changes that are leading temperatures at the poles to rise. These temperature increases cause the vortices to deviate toward the equator, bringing with them the frigid air responsible for our recent colder winters.

Most readers think 10b flows better than 10a, partly because the subject of the second sentence, *The vortices*, is shorter than the longer subject of 10a: *Environmental changes that are leading temperatures at the poles to rise.* But 10b also flows better because the order of its ideas is different.

In 10a, the first words of the second sentence express new information:

10a . . . the polar vortices. Environmental changes that are leading temperatures at the poles to rise . . .

Those words about rising temperatures seem to come out of nowhere. But in 10b, the first words echo the end of the previous sentence:

10b . . . the polar vortices. The vortices . . .

Moreover, once we make that change, the end of that second sentence introduces the third more cohesively:

10b . . . leading temperatures at the poles to rise. These temperature increases . . .

Contrast 10a; the end of its second sentence doesn't flow into the beginning of the third as smoothly:

10a. . . . the vortices. These temperature increases . . .

That is why readers think that passage 10a feels choppier than 10b: the end of one sentence does not flow smoothly into the beginning of the next.

The corollary of the old-information-first principle is to put new information last, especially new technical terms. So when you introduce a new term, put it at the end of its sentence. Compare these:

11a. Calcium blockers can control muscle spasms. Sarcomeres are the small units of muscle fibers in which these drugs work. Two filaments, one thick and one thin, are in each sarcomere. The proteins actin and myosin are contained in the thin filament. When actin and myosin interact, your heart contracts.

11b. Muscle spasms can be controlled with drugs known as *calcium blockers*. They work in small units of muscle fibers called *sarcomeres*. Each sarcomere has *two filaments, one thick and one thin*. The thin filament contains *two proteins, actin and myosin*. When actin and myosin interact, your heart contracts.

In 11a, the new technical terms are *calcium blockers, sarcomeres, filaments, the proteins actin and myosin*, but they first appear early in their sentences. In contrast, in 11b those new terms first appear toward the ends of their sentences. After that, they're old information and so can appear at the beginning of the next sentences.

No principle of writing is more important than this: old before new; familiar information introduces unfamiliar information.

11.1.6　Choose Active or Passive Verbs to Reflect the Preceding Principles

You may recall advice to avoid passive verbs—good advice when a passive verb allows you to write a sentence that contradicts the principles we have discussed, as in the second sentence of this passage:

12a. Climate change may have many catastrophic effects. Tropical diseases and destructive insect life even north of the Canadian border could be increased$_{\text{passive verb}}$ by it.

That second sentence opens with an eleven-word subject conveying new information: *Tropical diseases . . . Canadian border*. It is the subject of a passive verb, *be increased*, and that verb is followed by a short, familiar bit of information from the sentence before: the concept of climate change represented by the pronoun *it*. That sentence would be clearer if its verb were active:

12b. Climate change may have many catastrophic effects. It could increase$_{\text{active verb}}$ tropical diseases and destructive insect life even north of the Canadian border.

Now the subject is familiar, and the new information in the longer phrase is at the end. In this case, the active verb is the right choice.

But if you always use active verbs, avoiding passive verbs entirely, you'll write sentences that contradict the old-new principle. We saw an example in 10a:

10a. New insights into global weather patterns are emerging from recent research on the large low-pressure zones rotating above the Earth's poles, known as the polar vortices. Environmental changes that are leading temperatures at the poles to rise, this research suggests, are affecting_{active verb} the vortices.

The verb in the second sentence is active, but the passage flows better when it's passive:

10b. New insights into global weather patterns are emerging from recent research on the large low-pressure zones rotating above the Earth's poles, known as the polar vortices. The vortices, this research suggests, are being affected_{passive verb} by environmental changes that are leading temperatures at the poles to rise.

A sentence is more readable when its subject is short, concrete, and familiar, regardless of whether its verb is active or passive. So choose active or passive voice by considering which gives you the right kind of subject: short, concrete, and familiar.

11.1.7 Use First-Person Pronouns Appropriately

Almost everyone has heard the advice to avoid using *I* or *we* in academic writing. In fact, opinions differ on this point. Some teachers tell students never to use *I*, because it makes their writing "subjective." Others encourage using *I* as a way to make writing more lively and personal.

Most instructors and editors do agree that two uses of *I* should be avoided:

- Insecure writers begin too many sentences with *I think* or *I believe* (or their equivalent, *In my opinion*). Readers assume that you think and believe what you write, so you don't have to say you do.
- Inexperienced writers too often narrate their research: *First I consulted . . . , then I examined . . .* , and so on. Readers care less about the story of your research than about its results (see 6.1).

But we believe, and most editors of scholarly journals agree, that the first person is appropriate on two occasions. That last sentence illustrates one of them: *we believe . . . that the first person . . .*

- An occasional introductory *I* (or *we*) *believe* can soften the dogmatic edge of a statement. Compare this blunter, less qualified version:

13. But ~~we believe, and most editors of scholarly journals agree, that~~ the first person is appropriate on two occasions.

The trick is not to hedge so often that you sound uncertain or so rarely that you sound smug.

■ A first-person *I* or *we* is also appropriate when it's the subject of a verb naming an action unique to you as the writer of your argument. Verbs referring to such actions typically appear in introductions (*I will show/ argue/prove/claim that X*) and in conclusions (*I have demonstrated/concluded that Y*). Since only you can show, prove, or claim what's in your argument, only you can say so with *I*:

14. In this report, I will show that social distinctions at this university are . . .

On the other hand, researchers rarely use the first person for an action that others must repeat to replicate their research. Those words include *divide, measure, weigh, examine,* and so on. Researchers rarely write sentences with active verbs like this:

15a. I *calculated* the coefficient of X.

Instead, they're likely to write in the passive, because anyone can do that:

15b. The coefficient of X *was calculated*.

Those same principles apply to *we*, if you're one of two or more authors. But many instructors and editors object to two other uses of *we*:

■ the royal *we* used to refer reflexively to the writer
■ the all-purpose *we* that refers to people in general

For example:

16. We must be careful to cite sources when we use data from them. When we read writers who fail to do that, we tend to distrust them.

In the end, though, those having authority decide. If your instructor or editor flatly forbids *I* or *we*, then so be it. When you have that authority, you can make a different choice.

Here is a final piece of advice. If you follow our seven principles, your readers will likely find your writing clear. But you can test your writing by having someone read it back to you. If that person stumbles over a passage, you can bet your readers will struggle with it too.

11.2   Diagnose What You Read

Once you understand how readers judge what they read, you know not only how to write clear prose but also why so much of what you must read seems so dense. You might struggle with some writing because its content is difficult. But you may also struggle because the writer didn't write clearly. This next passage, for example, is by no means the thickest ever written:

15a. Recognition of the fact that grammars differ from one language to another can serve as the basis for serious consideration of the problems confronting translators of the great works of world literature originally written in a language other than English.

But in half as many words, it means only this:

15b. Once we recognize that languages have different grammars, we can consider the problems of those who translate great works of literature into English.

So when you struggle to understand some academic writing (and you will), don't blame yourself, at least not first. Diagnose its sentences. If they have long subjects stuffed with abstract nouns expressing new information, the fault is probably not yours.

Unfortunately, the more experience you get reading unclear academic prose, the greater your risk of imitating it. In fact, that risk is common to all professions, academic or not. So remain aware of it as you grow in expertise.

11.3 Choose the Right Word

Another bit of standard advice is *Choose the right word*.

1. Choose the word with the right meaning. *Affect* doesn't mean *effect*; *elicit* doesn't mean *illicit*. Commonly confused words are listed in many handbooks. If you're an inexperienced writer, invest in one.
2. Choose the word with the right level of usage. If you draft quickly, you risk choosing words that might mean roughly what you think they do but are too casual for a formal paper. Someone can *criticize* another writer or *knock* him; a risk can seem *frightening* or *scary*. Those pairs have similar meanings, but most readers would judge the second in each pair to be a bit loose for academic writing.

   On the other hand, if you try too hard to sound like a real "academic," you risk using words that are too formal. You can *think* or *cogitate*, *drink* or *imbibe*. Those pairs are close in meaning, but the second in each is too fancy for a paper written in ordinary English. Whenever you're tempted to use a word that you think is especially fine, look for a more familiar one.

   The obvious advice is to look up words you're not sure of. But they're not the problem; the problem is the ones you *are* sure of. Worse, no dictionary tells you that a word like *visage* or *perambulate* is too fancy for just about any context. The short-term solution is to ask someone to read your paper before you turn it in (but be cautious before accepting too many suggestions; see 7.10). The long-term solution is to read a lot, write a lot, endure a lot of criticism, and learn from it.

11.4 Polish It Up

Before you submit your paper, read it one last time to fix errors in grammar, spelling, and punctuation. Many experienced writers read from the last sentence back to the first to keep from getting caught up in the flow of their ideas and missing the words. Do not rely solely on your word-processing program's spelling and grammar checker. It will sometimes miss words that are spelled correctly but used incorrectly—*their/there/they're, it's/its, too/to, accept/except, affect/effect, already/all ready, complement/compliment, principal/principle, discrete/discreet*, and so on—and it will flag constructions like the passive voice when they may be the best choice. (See chapter 20 for more on spelling.)

If you have used a lot of non-English words, numbers, abbreviations, and so on, check the relevant chapters in part 3 of this manual.

Finally, if your paper has a table of contents that lists titles and numbers for chapters and sections, be certain that they *exactly* match the corresponding wording and numbering in your paper's body. If in your text you refer back or forward to other sections or chapters, be sure the references are accurate.

Some students think they have to worry about the quality of their writing only in English courses. That's not true. Instructors in every discipline appreciate clear and coherent writing, and every course in which you write is an opportunity for you to practice writing better.

11.5 Give It Up and Turn It In

If one thing is harder than starting to write, it's stopping. We all want another day to get the organization right, another hour to tweak the opening paragraph, another minute to . . . (you get the idea). Experienced researchers know that nothing they write will ever be perfect and that the benefit of getting the last 1 percent or even 5 percent exactly right is rarely worth the cost. Less experienced researchers should take this lesson to heart. Dissertation students in particular agonize over reaching a standard of perfection that exists largely in their own minds. No thesis or dissertation has to be utterly perfect; what it has to be is *done*. At some point, enough is enough.

Page through it one last time to be sure that it looks the way you want it to: look at page breaks, spacing in margins, positions of tables and figures, and so on. Then give it up and turn it in.

12 Learning from Comments on Your Paper

Whether you're a beginner or an advanced researcher, you can learn much from the feedback of careful readers. But to get the most benefit from such comments—whether they are on a draft of a final version— you need to know how to use them.

As you develop as a writer and researcher, you will receive feedback from many different readers, some (like teachers and editors) having authority over you and others being people whose responses you seek out. Experienced writers know that nothing is more valuable than comments from a trusted reader. None of us can accurately judge the way readers will respond to our writing, for the simple reason that we know too much about it. We need readers to show us, through their responses, what we got right and where we went wrong.

12.1   Two Kinds of Feedback: Advice and Data

Commenting on a paper is hard (even if a reader is being paid to do it). When giving feedback, that reader's responsibility is to be honest and to try to be helpful. Your responsibility as a writer is to make the most of the comments you receive.

To do that, you must decide whether to treat a reader's comments as *advice*—observations about what you could do (or should have done) to make the paper better—or as *data* documenting a particular reader's response. When you treat comments as advice, you must decide whether to accept or reject them. Good advice, especially from a trusted reader, can be invaluable to new and experienced researchers alike. Sometimes you might feel a strong obligation to accept a reader's advice, such as when it comes from teacher, advisor, or editor. But even in those instances, you are not obligated to accept it wholesale: as a writer, you are responsible not only for your ideas but also for the choices you make in expressing them.

When you treat comments as *data*, you don't accept or reject them; you analyze them to understand why your reader responded to your paper as she did. And when you understand that, you can revise the paper or make a different decision the next time. You might know what you wanted your paper to *say*, but only your reader can tell you what it in fact *said*—at least to her. Again, the writer is ultimately responsible: if a careful reader misunderstood your paper, you should not blame her for that misunderstanding but use the data of her feedback to figure out how and why that misunderstanding occurred.

In this sense, bad advice can be great data. Even the most dedicated and careful reader is not infallible. She might misunderstand your intentions or argument, or give you wrongheaded advice (even if she is a teacher). In such cases, ignore the advice but ask yourself, *What about my paper created that misunderstanding? How did I lead my reader astray?* If you can answer those questions, you can still improve your paper, or the next one.

Here are some tips for making the most of the comments you receive, however you choose to interpret them.

12.2 Find General Principles in Specific Comments

When you review your reader's comments, focus on those that you can apply to your next project.

- Look for a pattern of errors in spelling, punctuation, and grammar. If you see one, you know what to work on.
- If your reader says you made factual errors, check your notes: Did you take bad notes or misreport them? Were you misled by an unreliable source? Whatever you find, you know what to do in your next project.
- If your reader reports only her judgments of your writing, look for what causes them. If she says your writing is choppy, dense, or awkward, check your sentences using the steps in chapter 11. If she says it's disorganized or wandering, check it against chapter 9. You won't always find what caused the complaints, but when you do you'll know what to work on next time.

12.3   Talk with Your Reader

If you receive comments that include words like *disorganized*, *illogical*, and *unsupported* but cannot find what triggered them, make an appointment with your reader to ask. Such words are not descriptions of your paper but descriptions of the reader's impressions of it. You need to find out what it is in the paper itself that is provoking those impressions. Following these guidelines will help that conversation go well:

■ If your reader marked up your spelling, punctuation, and grammar, correct those errors *before* your meeting to show that you took her comments seriously. You might also jot responses to more substantive comments, so that you can discuss them.

■ If your reader is your teacher, don't complain about your grade. Be clear that you want to understand the comments so that you can do better next time.

■ Prioritize: focus on those comments that address the most important issues, like your paper's argument and organization. It's tempting to zero in on local concerns that can be quickly corrected, especially if your reader has done a lot of line editing, or to quibble over minor points of disagreement.

■ Rehearse your questions so that they'll seem amiable: not "You say this is disorganized but you don't say why," but rather "Can you help me see where I went wrong with my organization so I can do better next time?"

■ Ask your reader to point to passages that illustrate her judgments and to explain what those passages should have looked like. Don't ask "What didn't you like?" but rather "Where exactly did I go wrong and what could I have done to fix it?"

A final word for students: you might think that meeting with your teacher is helpful only when a paper or yours receives a low grade. But that would be wrong. Even after a high grade, it's useful to know how you earned it. Your next project will likely be more challenging, so it's good to know what successful practices you can build on. Of course, in that new project you might again feel like a beginner. That's the way it goes with research.

13 Presenting Research in Alternative Forums

It may be too early in your career to think about publishing your work, but it's not too early to present. Researchers at all stages communicate their work to others in *oral presentations* to a class or at a conference or through *research posters*, a form especially common in the sciences. Increasingly, undergraduate researchers share their work with audiences beyond the classroom by participating in local research fairs or symposia. Experienced researchers also present their work to colleagues before publishing it in professional journals. Indeed, the ability to stand up and talk about your work clearly and confidently is a crucial skill for any career.

In this chapter we show you how to use your plan for a written text to prepare a talk. We also discuss the research poster, which combines elements of speech and writing. Finally, we discuss how to prepare a *conference proposal* as a first step, often, in presenting your research.

13.1   Plan Your Oral Presentation

An oral presentation may be easier to prepare than a written paper, but to benefit from the experience of delivering it, you must plan just as carefully. In giving a talk, you get immediate feedback that can be very help-ful if you are testing new ideas or new data. You want to design your presentation to elicit responses that help you refine your arguments and your analysis.

13.1.1 Narrow Your Focus

Typically, a talk delivered at a conference runs about twenty minutes (or about eight to ten double-spaced pages for text read aloud). This is not much time to communicate your ideas, so you must boil down your work to its essence or present just a part of it. Here are three common options:

- *Problem statement with a sketch of your argument.* If your problem is new, focus on its originality. Start with a short introduction (review chapter 10), then explain your reasons, summarizing your evidence for each.
- *Summary of a subargument.* If your argument is too big, focus on a key sub-argument. Mention your larger problem in your introduction and conclu-sion, but be clear that you're addressing only part of it.
- *Methodology or data report.* If you offer a new methodology or source of data, explain why it matters. Start with a brief problem statement, then focus on how your new methods or data solve it.

13.1.2 Understand the Difference between Listeners and Readers

Unless you know and respect the difference between listening and read-ing, your audience will find your presentation tedious or hard to follow. When we read, we can pause to reflect and puzzle over difficult passages. To keep on track, we can look at headings and even paragraph indenta-tions. If we wander, we can reread. But as listeners in an audience, we can do none of these things. We must be motivated to pay attention, and we need help to follow a complicated line of thought. If we lose its thread, we may drift off into our own thoughts.

That's why it's important to not simply read your paper with little or no eye contact or, if using slides, merely introduce them and repeat their content. You must engage your audience as in a conversation but with extra care for what listeners need. You have to be explicit about your purpose and your organization. Further, you have to make your sentence structure far simpler than in a written paper. So favor shorter sentences with consistent subjects (see 11.1.2). Use "I," "we," and "you" a lot. What seems clumsily repetitive to readers is usually welcomed by listeners.

13.2 Design Your Presentation to Be Listened To

To hold your listeners' attention, you must seem to be not lecturing *at* but conversing *with* them. This is a skill that does not come easily, since few of us can write as we would speak and most of us need notes to stay on track. If you do read your paper, read no faster than about 150 words per minute. That's about two minutes per page. This is faster than you speak ordinarily, so time yourself. Inexperienced presenters tend to read more quickly than their listeners can comfortably hear and digest.

It's important that your audience see you and not just the top of your head, so build in moments when you look straight out at your audience, especially when saying something important. Do so at least once or twice per page, ideally at the end of a paragraph.

Remember as well that a paper delivered orally differs in style from a written one. For one, effective sentences tend to be much shorter and use consistent subjects (see 11.1.2). Overall, you need more repetition than you would use in writing to help your listeners stay on track with you.

It is far better to talk from notes than just to read aloud, but to do that well you need to prepare and practice. In the next section we give advice on how to structure your talk and notes for this kind of delivery.

13.2.1 Sketch Your Introduction

For a twenty-minute talk, you get one shot at motivating your audience before they tune out, so prepare your introduction more carefully than any other part of your talk. Base it on the four-part problem statement described in section 10.1, plus a road map. (The times in parentheses in the list below are rough estimates.)

Use your notes only to remind yourself of the four parts, not as a word-for-word script. If you can't remember the content, you're not ready to give your talk. Sketch enough in your notes to *remind* yourself of the following:

1. What research you extend, modify, or correct (no more than a minute).
2. What question your research addresses—the gap in knowledge or understanding (thirty seconds or less).
3. Why your research matters—an answer to *So what?* (thirty seconds).

Those three steps are crucial in motivating your listeners. If your question is new or controversial, give it more time. If your listeners know its significance, mention it quickly and go on.

4. Your claim, the answer to your research question (thirty seconds or less). Listeners want to know your answer up front even more than

readers do, so state at least its gist, unless you have a compelling reason to wait for the end. If you do choose to wait to give your answer,
at least forecast it.

5. A forecast of the structure of your presentation (ten to twenty seconds). The most useful forecast is an oral table of contents: "First I will
discuss . . ." That can seem clumsy in print, but listeners need more
help than readers do. Repeat that structure as you work through the
body of your talk.

Rehearse your introduction, not only to get it right but also so you can
look your audience in the eye as you give it. You can look down at notes
later.

All told, spend no more than three minutes or so on your introduction.

13.2.2 Design Notes You Can Understand at a Glance

Do not write your notes as complete sentences (much less paragraphs)
that you read aloud; notes should help you see at a glance the structure
of your talk and cue what to say at crucial points. So *do not cut and paste
sentences from a written text; create your notes from scratch.*

Use a separate page for each main point. On each page, write out your
main point not as a topic but as claims, either in shortened form or (if
you must) in complete sentences. Above each point, you might add an explicit transition as the oral equivalent of a subhead: "The first issue is . . ."

Visually highlight those main points so that you spot them instantly.
Under them, list the evidence that supports them. If your evidence consists of numbers or quotations, you'll probably have to write them out.
Otherwise, know your evidence well enough to be able to talk about it
directly to your audience.

Organize your points so that you cover the most important ones first.
If you run long (most of us do), you can skip a later section or even jump
to your conclusion without losing anything crucial to your argument.
Never build up to a climax that you might not reach. If you must skip
something, use the question-and-answer period to return to it.

13.2.3 Model Your Conclusion on Your Introduction

As in a written paper, your conclusion is your last opportunity to communicate your claim and its significance (see 10.2). Make your conclusion
memorable, because listeners will repeat it when asked, *What did Jones
say?* Learn it well enough to present it looking at your audience, without
reading from notes. It should have these three parts:

■ your claim, in more detail than in your introduction (if listeners are
mostly interested in your reasons or data, summarize them as well)

- your answer to *So what?* (you can restate an answer from your introduction, but try to add a new one, even if it's speculative)
- suggestions for more research, what's still to be done

Rehearse your conclusion so that you know exactly how long it takes (no more than a minute or two). Then when you have that much time remaining, conclude, even if you haven't finished your last (relatively unimportant) points. If you had to skip one or two points, work them into an answer during the question-and-answer period. If your talk runs short, don't ad lib. If another speaker follows you, make her a gift of your unused time.

13.2.4 Anticipate Questions

If you're lucky, you'll get questions after your talk, so prepare answers for predictable ones. Expect questions about data or sources, especially if you didn't cover them much in your talk. If you address matters associated with well-known researchers or schools of research, be ready to expand on how your work relates to theirs, especially if you contradict or complicate their results or approach. Also be ready to answer questions about a source you never heard of. The best policy is to acknowledge that you haven't seen it but that you'll check it out. If the question seems friendly, ask why the source is relevant. Don't prepare only defensive answers. Use answers to questions to reemphasize your main points or cover matters that you may have left out.

Listen to every question carefully; then, to be sure you understand the question, *pause before you respond and think about it for a moment*. If you don't understand the question, ask the questioner to rephrase it. Don't snap back an answer reflexively and defensively. Good questions are invaluable, even when they seem hostile. Use them to refine your thinking.

13.2.5 Create Handouts

You can read short quotations or important data aloud for your listeners, but if you have many, create a handout. If you use slides, pass out printed copies. You can also hand out an outline of your main points, with white space for notes.

13.3 Plan Your Poster Presentation

A poster is a large board on which you lay out a summary of your research along with your most relevant evidence. It is a cross between a talk delivered orally and a written paper. In a poster presentation you can go into more detail than you can in a twenty-minute talk. But a poster is not just a research paper transferred to a larger canvas. It's a selection of key elements of a research project (question, claim, data, significance) designed to welcome an audience of individuals who choose to stop and visit.

Poster sessions are usually held in hallways or in a large room filled with many presenters. People move from poster to poster, reading as their interests dictate but also asking questions of the presenters, who typically stand by their posters at designated times ready to discuss their research. In this sense, a good poster can turn your imagined conversation with your research community (see chapter 1) into a real one. Posters combine the advantages of writing and speaking. While posters, like written reports, should be self-explanatory, they also encourage presenters and their audiences (typically fellow researchers) to interact one on one. Those who read your poster have more control than a listener, and they can rely on prominent visual signals that you use to organize your material—boxes, lines, colors, and larger and smaller titles.

You can design your poster using available software and templates that produce a serviceable final product. For the text of the poster itself, however, follow the guidelines for a paper to be read aloud, with two additional considerations:

1. Layer your argument. Present your argument visually in three levels of detail:

   - Highlight an abstract or a problem statement and summary at the top of the poster (box it, use larger type, etc.).
   - Under that introductory material, list your reasons as subheads in a section that summarizes your argument.
   - Under that section, restate your reasons and group your evidence under them.

2. Explain all graphs and tables. In addition to providing a caption for each graphic, add a sentence or two explaining what is important in the data and how they support your reason and claim (review 7.7 and 8.3.1).

13.4   Plan Your Conference Proposal

Conferences are good opportunities to share your work, but to be invited to speak, you usually have to submit a proposal. Write it not as a paragraph-by-paragraph summary of your work but as a thirty-second "elevator story"—what you would tell someone who asked, as you both stepped into an elevator on the way to your talk, *What are you saying today?* In fact, a carefully prepared and rehearsed elevator story is very useful for any conversation about your work, particularly interviews.

An elevator story has three parts:

- a problem statement that highlights an answer to *So what?*
- a sketch of your claim and major reasons
- a summary of your most important evidence

Conference reviewers are less interested in your exact words than in why anyone should want to listen to them. Your aims are to pose your research question and to answer the reviewer's *So what?* So focus on how your claim contributes to your field of research, especially on what's novel or controversial about it. If you address a question established by previous research, mention it, then focus on your new data or your new claim, depending on which is more original. Be aware that reviewers will often know less about your topic than you do and may need help to see the significance of your question.

Besides gaining acceptance to the conference, a conference proposal has one other objective. Its title and often its abstract (or even the full proposal) are used to attract an audience to the session in which the proposed talk will be scheduled. A good conference proposal thus has a clear and substantive title (see 10.3), one that lets an audience know what to expect.

14 On the Spirit of Research

As we've said, we can reach good conclusions in many ways other than research. But the truths we reach in those ways are personal. We can't present our intuitions and feelings as evidence to convince others of our claims; we can ask only that they take our report of our inner experience—and our claims—on faith.

In contrast, the truths of research and how we reached them must be available for public scrutiny. We base research claims on evidence available to everyone and on principles of reasoning that, we hope, our readers accept as sound. And then those readers test all of that in all the ways that they and others can imagine. That may be a high standard, but it must be if we expect others to base their understanding and actions, even their lives, on what we ask them to believe.

When you accept the principles that shape public, evidence-based belief, you accept two more that can be hard to live by. One concerns our relationship to authority. No more than five centuries ago, the search for better understanding based on evidence was often regarded as a threat. Among the powerful, many believed that all the important truths were already known and that the scholar's job was to preserve and transmit them, certainly not to challenge them. If new facts cast doubt on an old belief, the belief usually trumped the facts. Many who dared to follow evidence to conclusions that challenged authority were banished, imprisoned, or even killed.

Even today, those who reason from evidence can elicit anger among those who hold a cherished belief. For example, most historians hold, based on the sum of the evidence, that Thomas Jefferson fathered several if not all of his slave Sally Hemings's children. Others disagree, not because they have better counterevidence but because of a fiercely held belief: *a person of Jefferson's stature couldn't do such a thing* (see 5.5). But in the world of research, both academic and professional, good evidence and sound reasoning trump belief every time, or at least they should.

In some parts of the world it's still considered more important to guard settled beliefs than to test them. But in places informed by the values of research, we think differently: we believe not only that we *may* question settled beliefs but that we *must*, no matter how much authority cherishes them—so long as we support our answers with sound reasons based on reliable evidence.

But that principle requires another. When we make a claim, we must expect, even encourage, others to question not just our claim but how we reached it—to ask, *Why do you believe that?* It's often hard to welcome such questions, but we're obliged to listen with goodwill to objections, reservations, and qualifications that collectively imply *I don't agree, at least not yet.* And the more we challenge old ideas, the more we must be ready to acknowledge and answer those questions, because we may be asking others to give up deeply held beliefs.

When some students encounter these values, they find it difficult, even painful, to live by them. Some feel that a challenge to what they believe isn't a lively search for truth but a personal attack on their deepest values. Others retreat to a cynical skepticism, doubting everything and believing nothing. Others fall into mindless relativism: *We're all entitled to our own beliefs, and so all beliefs are right for those who hold them!* Many turn away from an active life of the mind, rejecting not only answers that might disturb their settled beliefs but even the questions that inspired them.

But in our worlds of work, scholarship, civic action, and even politics, we can't replace tested knowledge and hard-won understanding with personal opinion, cynicism, a relativistic view of truth, or the comfortable, settled knowledge of "authority."

That does not mean we reject long-held and time-tested beliefs lightly. We replace them only after we're persuaded by sound arguments backed by good reasons based on the best evidence available, and after an amiable but searching give-and-take that tests those arguments as severely as we can. In short, we become *responsible* believers when we can make our own sound arguments that test and evaluate those of others.

You may find it difficult to see all of this at work in a paper written for a class. But despite its cold type, a research paper written for any audience is a conversation, imagined to be sure, but still a cooperative yet rigorous inquiry into what we should and should not believe.

Part II | Source Citation

15 General Introduction to Citation Practices

Your first duty as a researcher is to get the facts right. Your second duty is to tell readers where the facts came from. To that end, you must cite the sources of the facts, ideas, or words that you use in your paper.

15.1 Reasons for Citing Your Sources

There at least four reasons to cite your sources:

1. *To give credit.* Research is hard work. Doing it well can bring rewards—good grades and a degree and, later, money and promotions. But no less important is recognition, the pride and prestige of seeing your name associated with knowledge that others value and use. In fact, for some researchers that is the only reward. So when you cite the work of others, you give them the recognition they have earned.

2. *To reassure readers about the accuracy of your facts.* Researchers cite sources to be fair to other researchers but also to earn their readers' trust. It is not enough to get the facts right. You must also tell readers

the source of the facts so that they can judge their reliability and check them if they wish. Readers do not trust a source they do not know and cannot find. If they do not trust your sources, they will not trust your facts; and if they do not trust your facts, they will not trust your argument. You establish the first link in that chain of trust by citing your sources fully, accurately, and appropriately.

3. *To show readers the research tradition that informs your work.* Researchers cite sources whose data they use, but they also cite work that they extend, support, contradict, or correct. These citations help readers not only understand your specific project but connect it to other research in your field.

4. *To help readers follow or extend your research.* Many readers use sources cited in a research paper not to check its reliability but to pursue their own work. So your citations help others not only to follow your footsteps but to strike out in new directions.

You must never appear to take credit for work that is not your own (see 7.9), and proper citation guards against the charge of plagiarism. But it also strengthens your argument and assists others who want to build on your work.

15.2   The Requirements of Citation

To fulfill the requirements of citation, you need to know when to include a source citation in your paper and what information about the source to include.

15.2.1   Situations Requiring Citations

Chapter 7, particularly 7.9, discusses in depth when you should cite materials from other sources. Briefly, you should always provide a citation in the following situations:

- when you *quote exact words* from a source (see also chapter 25 on quotations)
- when you *paraphrase ideas* that are associated with a specific source, even if you don't quote exact words from it
- when you use any ideas, data, or methods attributable to any source you consulted

As noted in 15.1, you may also use citations to *point readers to sources* that are relevant to a particular portion of your argument but not quoted or paraphrased. Such citations demonstrate that you are familiar with these sources, even if they present claims at odds with your own.

15.2.2 Information Required in Citations

Over the long tradition of citing sources, as researchers in different fields began to write in different ways, they also developed distinctive ways of citing and documenting their sources. When citation methods became standardized, researchers had to choose from not just one or two standards but many.

Citation styles differ in the elements included and in the format of these elements, but they have the same aim: to give readers the information they need to identify and find a source. For most sources, including books, articles, and other written material, that information must answer these questions:

- Who wrote, edited, or translated the text (sometimes all three)? In other words, who created it?
- What data identify the text? This includes the title and subtitle of the work; volume number, edition number, or other identifying information; and page numbers or other locating information if the reference is to a specific part of a larger text.
- Who published the text and in what context? This includes the name of the publisher, journal, or other entity responsible for making the text available and, in some cases, the title of any collection or series in which the work appears.
- When was the text published? This will consist of a year of publication and sometimes a season, month, or specific day (and sometimes a time).
- Where can the text be found? Most printed sources can be found in a library or bookstore, information that does not need to be mentioned in a citation. For a source consulted online, a link to the work (in the form of a URL) or the name of a commercial database will help readers find it. For a physical document from a one-of-a-kind collection, data will include the place where the collection is housed.

Details vary for other types of sources, such as sound and video recordings, but they answer the same five questions: Who was responsible for creating the source? What title or other data identify it? Who published it? When? Where can it be found?

Your readers will expect you to use the citation style appropriate to their particular field, not just because they are familiar with this style but because when you use it, you show them that you understand their values and practices. The details may seem trivial: Quotation marks or italics? Capitals or lowercase? Periods or commas (or parentheses and colons)? But if you do not get these small matters right, at least some of your readers will question whether they can trust you on the bigger ones. Fortunately, you don't have to memorize all these details. Instead, you can learn the forms of the citations you use most so that you do not need to look them up repeatedly. The latest citation management tools can help, especially for more common source types. For sources that are less common or have unusual elements, and for double-checking your final draft, you can consult a book like this one.

15.3   Two Citation Styles

This book covers the two most common citation forms: *notes-bibliography style*, or simply *notes style* (used widely in the humanities and in some social sciences), and *author-date style* (used in most social sciences and in the natural and physical sciences). (Together, these two styles are often referred to as the Turabian or Chicago systems of source citation.) If you are not certain which style to use, consult your instructor.

You may be asked to use different styles in different settings (for example, an art history course and a political science course). Within a given paper, however, always follow a single style consistently.

If you are new to research, read this section for a brief description of how the two citation styles work. Then, if you are using notes style, read chapter 16 for an overview of this style, and refer to chapter 17 for detailed guidelines and examples that show how to cite most types of sources, including the ones you are most likely to consult. If you are using author-date style, the overview and detailed guidelines are in chapters 18 and 19, respectively.

15.3.1   Notes Style

In notes-style citations, you signal that you have used a source by placing a superscript number at the end of the sentence in which you quote it or refer to it:

By 1911, according to one expert, an Amazon was "any woman rebel—which, to a lot of people, meant any girl who left home and went to college."[1]

You then cite the source of that quotation in a correspondingly numbered *note* that provides information about the source (author, title, and facts of publication) plus relevant page numbers. Notes are placed at the bottom of the page (called *footnotes*) or in a list collected at the end of your paper or the end of each chapter (called *endnotes*). All notes have the same general form:

N: 1. Jill Lepore, *The Secret History of Wonder Woman* (New York: Vintage Books, 2015), 17.

If you cite the same text again, you can shorten subsequent notes:

N: 2. Lepore, *Wonder Woman*, 28–29.

In most cases, you also list sources at the end of the paper in a *bibli-ography*. That list normally includes every source you cited in a note and sometimes others you consulted but did not cite. Each bibliography entry includes the same information contained in a full note, but in a slightly different form:

B: Lepore, Jill. *The Secret History of Wonder Woman.* New York: Vintage Books, 2015.

15.3.2 Author-Date Style

In author-date citations, you signal that you have used a source by plac-ing a *parenthetical citation* (including author, date, and relevant page num-bers) next to your reference to it:

By 1911, according to one expert, an Amazon was "any woman rebel—which, to a lot of people, meant any girl who left home and went to college" (Lepore 2015, 17).

At the end of the paper, you list all sources in a *reference list*. That list normally includes every source you cited in a parenthetical citation and sometimes others you consulted but did not cite. Each reference list entry includes complete bibliographical information for a source. The publica-tion date immediately follows the name of the author, making it easy to follow a parenthetical citation to its corresponding entry in the refer-ence list:

R: Lepore, Jill. 2015. *The Secret History of Wonder Woman.* New York: Vintage Books.

15.4 Electronic Sources

The standard citation forms evolved in the age of print, but researchers now not only find their sources online but also increasingly consult them online and in a variety of electronic formats. These sources have been used long enough for researchers to have created standard citation forms adapted to their special characteristics.

15.4.1 Sources Consulted Online

15.4.1.1 INFORMATION IN CITATIONS. When you cite sources consulted online, you include many of the same pieces of information as you would for print sources. For some types of sources, such as published books and journal articles, it makes little difference what format you consult. Readers will be able to follow your citations and find the same sources in the same formats. But other types of sources can be difficult to find or subject to change, or disappear without notice. These factors may make you question the authority and reliability of a source.

- A lot of content found online has no identifiable author, publisher, or sponsor. This makes it the equivalent of any other anonymous source, unlikely to be authoritative or reliable enough to use without serious qualification (see 3.3.2).
- Online content can be revised without notice, and though some websites are meticulous about documenting revisions, many are not. Further, a revision date on one site may indicate correction of a spelling error while on another it may mark changes in factual data or claims.
- Online content may be simultaneously available from more than one site, some more reliable than others.
- Most online sources are located through a URL (uniform resource locator) or a search, but URLs come and go, and search results vary over time. You cannot always be certain that a given source will be available at the same URL months, weeks, or even days later, and its disappearance could make it difficult or impossible for you or your readers to find the content you originally consulted.

Choose online sources carefully. When information is available from multiple websites or in multiple media (print and online), consult the most reliable version available, and always cite the version you consulted. As you do your research, save a screenshot or other permanent copy of any source that is likely to change or disappear.

15.4.1.2 TWO CATEGORIES OF SOURCES. Online sources fall into two categories.

1. Many online sources are like print sources in everything except medium—for example, an article published in an online journal instead of in a printed journal. Other sources of this type include online books, newspaper and magazine articles, and public documents. To cite these, begin with the standard facts of publication (author's name, title, date, and so forth). At the end of the citation, add the URL (see 15.4.1.3) or the name of the database through which you accessed the source (see 15.4.1.4). You can find examples of how to cite such items under the relevant type of source in chapter 17 (for notes style) and chapter 19 (for author-date style).

2. Other types of online sources, such as institutional or personal websites and social media, are unique to the medium and must be cited accordingly. In addition to recording each of the details relevant to the particular source, add a URL and, for undated content, an access date

(see 15.4.1.5). Examples of how to cite these items appear in 17.5 (for notes style) and 19.5 (for author-date style).

15.4.1.3 **URLS.** For any source you consult online, you must always cite the full facts of publication in addition to a URL. If the URL changes, interested readers will often be able to find your source by searching for the author, title, and other facts of publication.

Copy the URL exactly as it appears with the source. Do not make any adjustments to capitalization. If the URL ends in a slash, include it. Do not enclose the URL in brackets. It is best not to break a URL at the end of a line, but if you need to do so, see 20.4.2 for some guidelines.

Sometimes you can find a shorter version of a very long URL. If a "permalink" or other preferred form of the URL is included along with the citation data for a source, use that rather than the URL in your browser's address bar. Some sources are identified by a DOI (digital object identifier). URLs based on DOIs are more reliable (and often shorter) than most other types of URLs. To cite a source that includes a DOI, append the DOI to https://doi.org/ in your citation. For examples, see the sections on journal articles in figure 16.1 (for notes style) or figure 18.1 (for author-date style) and in chapters 17 and 19.

15.4.1.4 **COMMERCIAL DATABASES.** Many online sources, including certain books as well as articles in journals and other types of periodicals, are accessible only through a commercial database with restricted access (often through a university or other major library). If such a database lists a recommended URL along with the source, use that one instead of the one in your address bar. A URL based on a DOI, if available, is the best option (see 15.4.1.3). If no suitably short and direct URL exists, however, you may substitute the name of the database for the URL (e.g., LexisNexis Academic). For examples, see 17.1.10 and 17.4.2 (notes style) and 19.1.10 and 19.4.2 (author-date style).

15.4.1.5 **ACCESS DATES.** Most sources found online list either a date of publication or posting or the date the source was last modified or updated, but many do not. For those that do not, your citation must include the date that you accessed or retrieved the content in addition to the URL. An access date stands in for the date of publication and helps readers assess the source. For examples of cited access dates, see 17.5.1 and 17.9.1 (for notes style) or 19.5.1 and 19.9.1 (for author-date style). Note that some instructors in some fields may require access dates even for sources that include a date of publication or revision (check with your instructor). For this reason, it is generally a good idea to record access dates as part of your research. Citation management tools can help to automate this task.

15.4.2 Other Electronic Media

Sources consulted in other electronic media—for example, a book downloaded for a specific app or device, or a reference work published on disk—can usually be cited similarly to a source consulted online, but with the addition of information about the format rather than a URL. For examples, see 17.1.10 and 17.9.1 (for notes style) or 19.1.10 and 19.9.1 (for author-date style).

If a source is available in more than one format, consult the most reliable and authoritative version (see 3.3), and always cite the version you consulted.

15.5 Preparation of Citations

You can ease the process of preparing and checking citations if you anticipate what you will need.

- Use the most authoritative sources, in their most reliable version. If you find second- or thirdhand information, track down the original source.
- If a source is available in multiple versions, always cite the one you actually consulted. There may be small but important differences between the versions that could affect the accuracy of your quotations or other references to the source.
- Record all bibliographical information for your sources as you consult them and before you take notes. See figure 16.1 (for notes style) or figure 18.1 (for author-date style) for templates showing what information is needed for several common types of sources.
- Record the page number(s) for every quotation and paraphrase.
- As you draft, clearly indicate every place where you may need to cite a source. It is much easier to remove an unnecessary citation when you revise than to remember where you may have relied on someone else's ideas.
- When your draft is in its final form, consult chapter 17 or 19 to ensure that each citation is in the correct form and includes all the required data.
- You can assemble your bibliography or reference list either as you consult your sources or as you draft and revise. Be sure to check each detail carefully.

Getting each citation right can be tedious, even with the help of the latest tools. But as with every other phase of research, if you anticipate what you'll need and manage the process from the beginning, you can complete even this least exciting part of research faster, more easily, and more reliably.

15.6 Citation Management Tools

As you do your research, you may want to consider using one of a number of available citation management tools to collect data about your sources. Most sources available online or listed in a library catalog or other database include bibliographic information that can be used as the basis of your source citations. Programs like EndNote, RefWorks, and Zotero are designed to help you by capturing this information and adding it to a library of citations, where it is filtered by source type and can be further organized by research topic or paper. You can also add sources and edit information manually. Then citations can be plugged directly into your paper as needed in one of the citation styles described in this manual (and referred to in most programs as either "Turabian" or "Chicago" notes or author-date style). A few things to keep in mind:

- *Double-check your data.* As you build your library, check each field against the actual source as soon as you acquire the data for it. Make sure that authors' names, titles of works, dates, and so forth are accurate and that they are entered in the appropriate fields. Check also for missing or redundant data. (It is okay, however, to collect more data than you will use in your citations.) You will need to do this whether you entered the data yourself or exported the citation from a library catalog or other database.
- *Double-check your citations.* Once they've been inserted in your paper, make sure your citations are correctly formatted according to the citation style you've chosen. Things to look for include errant punctuation or capitalization and, more important, missing or superfluous data. Enter corrections in the citation management program (or adjust its settings, as applicable) and double-check the results. Review your final draft with extra care. These tools do make errors, and it remains your responsibility to ensure that your citations are accurate. For examples of notes-style citations, see chapters 16 and 17; for author-date style, see chapters 18 and 19.
- *Always keep at least two copies of your citations library.* If your school lets you keep a copy on its server, make sure you also have a copy on a local drive. Such backups might be needed in the event your paper must be resubmitted for any reason or if you plan to do research in the same subject area after graduation.

Citation management tools work best for papers that cite only a few types of the most common sources. Articles in academic journals, especially, are easy to work with. If you cite many different types of sources, expect to spend extra time making adjustments to your citations library and editing your final paper.

16 Notes-Bibliography Style: *The Basic Form*

A citation style used widely in the humanities and in some social sciences is the *notes-bibliography style*, or *notes style* for short (also known as Turabian or Chicago notes-bibliography or notes style). This chapter presents an overview of the basic pattern for citations in notes style, including bibliography entries, full notes, shortened notes, and parenthetical notes. Examples of notes are identified with an N; examples of bibliography entries are identified with a B.

In notes style, you signal that you have used a source by placing a superscript number at the end of the sentence in which you quote or otherwise refer to that source:

According to one scholar, "The railroads had made Chicago the most important meeting place between East and West."[1]

You then cite the source of that information in a correspondingly numbered *note* that provides information about the source (author, title, and facts of publication) plus relevant page numbers. Notes are placed at the bottom of the page (called *footnotes*) or in a list collected at the end of your paper or the end of each chapter (called *endnotes*). All notes have the same general form:

N: 1. William Cronon, *Nature's Metropolis: Chicago and the Great West* (New York: W. W. Norton, 1991), 92–93.

If you cite the same source again, you can refer to it in a shortened form:

N: 2. Cronon, *Nature's Metropolis*, 383.

In most cases, you also list sources at the end of the paper in a *bibliography*. That list normally includes every source you cited in a note and sometimes others you consulted but did not cite. Each bibliography entry includes the same information contained in a full note, but in a slightly different form:

B: Cronon, William. *Nature's Metropolis: Chicago and the Great West.* New York: W. W. Norton, 1991.

Readers expect you to follow all the rules for correctly citing your sources. These rules cover not only what data you must include and in what order but also punctuation, capitalization, italics, and so on. To get your citations exactly right, you must pay close attention to the kinds of details that few researchers can easily remember and that even the best citation management tools can help with only part of the way. Read this chapter for an overview. Then use chapter 17 to look up the details.

16.1 Basic Patterns

Although sources and their citations come in almost endless variety, you are likely to use only a few kinds. While you may need to look up details to cite some unusual sources, you can easily learn the basic patterns for the few kinds you will use most often. This will help you to record accurate and reliable bibliographical data quickly and efficiently as you do your research.

The rest of this section describes the basic patterns, and figure 16.1 provides templates for and examples of several common types of sources.

Figure 16.1. Templates for notes and bibliography entries

The following templates show what elements should be included in what order when citing several common types of sources in notes *(N)* and bibliographies *(B)*. They also show punctuation, capitalization of titles, and when to use italics or quotation marks. Gray shading shows abbreviations (or their spelled-out versions) and other terms as they would actually appear in a citation. ## stands in for footnote number. *XX* stands in for page number(s) actually cited, *YY–YY* for a full span of page numbers for an article or a chapter.

For further examples, explanations, and variations, see chapter 17. For templates of shortened note forms, see figure 16.2.

Books

1. Single Author or Editor

N: ##. Author's First and Last Names, *Title of Book: Subtitle of Book* (Place of Publication: Publisher's Name, Date of Publication), XX.

> 1. Angela Duckworth, Grit: *The Power of Passion and Perseverance* (New York: Scribner, 2016), 82.

B: Author's Last Name, Author's First Name. *Title of Book: Subtitle of Book*. Place of Publication: Publisher's Name, Date of Publication.

> Duckworth, Angela. Grit: *The Power of Passion and Perseverance*. New York: Scribner, 2016.

For a book with an editor instead of an author, adapt the pattern as follows:

N: ##. Editor's First and Last Names, ed., Title of Book . . .

> 2. Gyan Prakash, ed., *Noir Urbanisms* . . .

B: Editor's Last Name, Editor's First Name, ed. Title of Book . . .

> Prakash, Gyan. ed. *Noir Urbanisms* . . .

For more than one editor, adapt the examples in template 2 and use *eds*.

2. Multiple Authors

For a book with two authors, use the following pattern:

N: ##. Author #1's First and Last Names and Author #2's First and Last Names, *Title of Book: Subtitle of Book* (Place of Publication: Publisher's Name, Date of Publication), XX.

> 3. Susanne Y. P. Choi and Yinni Peng, *Masculine Promise: Migration, Family, and Gender in China* (Oakland: University of California Press, 2016), 111–12.

B: Author #1's Last Name, Author #1's First Name, and Author #2's First and Last Names. *Title of Book: Subtitle of Book*. Place of Publication: Publisher's Name, Date of Publication.

> Choi, Susanne Y. P., and Yinni Peng. *Masculine Promise: Migration, Family, and Gender in China*. Oakland: University of California Press, 2016.

For a book with three authors, adapt the pattern as follows:

N: ##. Author #1's First and Last Names, Author #2's First and Last Names, and Author #3's First and Last Names, *Title of Book* . . .

> 4. Karen White, Beatriz Williams, and Lauren Willig, *The Forgotten Room* . . .

Figure 16.1. Templates for notes and bibliography entries (continued)

B: Author #1's Last Name, Author #1's First Name, Author #2's First and Last Names, and Author #3's First and Last Names. *Title of Book* . . .

White, Karen, Beatriz Williams, and Lauren Willig. *The Forgotten Room* . . .

For a book with four or more authors, adapt the note pattern only, as follows:

N: ##. Author #1's First and Last Names et al., *Title of Book* . . .

5. Barry Eichengreen et al., *The Korean Economy* . . .

3. Author Plus Editor or Translator

For a book with an author plus an editor, use the following pattern:

N: ##. Author's First and Last Names, *Title of Book: Subtitle of Book*, ed. Editor's First and Last Names (Place of Publication: Publisher's Name, Date of Publication), XX.

6. Jane Austen, *Mansfield Park: An Annotated Edition*, ed. Deidre Shauna Lynch (Cambridge, MA: Belknap Press of Harvard University Press, 2016), 223–24.

If a book has more than one editor in addition to the author, use *ed.* (not *eds.*) in the note.

B: Author's Last Name, Author's First Name. *Title of Book: Subtitle of Book*. Edited by Editor's First and Last Names. Place of Publication: Publisher's Name, Date of Publication.

Austen, Jane. *Mansfield Park: An Annotated Edition*. Edited by Deidre Shauna Lynch. Cambridge, MA: Belknap Press of Harvard University Press, 2016.

If a book has a translator instead of an editor, substitute the words *trans.* and *Translated by* and the translator's name for the editor data.

4. Edition Number

N: ##. Author's First and Last Names, *Title of Book: Subtitle of Book*, Edition Number ed. (Place of Publication: Publisher's Name, Date of Publication), XX.

7. Mary Kinzie, *A Poet's Guide to Poetry*, 2nd ed. (Chicago: University of Chicago Press, 2013), 83.

B: Author's Last Name, Author's First Name. *Title of Book: Subtitle of Book*. Edition Number ed. Place of Publication: Publisher's Name, Date of Publication.

Kinzie, Mary. *A Poet's Guide to Poetry*. 2nd ed. Chicago: University of Chicago Press, 2013.

5. Single Chapter in an Edited Book

N: ##. Chapter Author's First and Last Names, "Title of Chapter: Subtitle of Chapter," in *Title of Book: Subtitle of Book*, ed. Editor's First and Last Names (Place of Publication: Publisher's Name, Date of Publication), XX.

8. Kelly Gillespie, "Before the Commission: Ethnography as Public Testimony," in *If Truth Be Told: The Politics of Public Ethnography*, ed. Didier Fassin (Durham, NC: Duke University Press, 2017), 72.

Figure 16.1. Templates for notes and bibliography entries (continued)

B: Chapter Author's Last Name, Chapter Author's First Name. "Title of Chapter: Subtitle of Chapter." In *Title of Book: Subtitle of Book*, edited by Editor's First and Last Names, YY–YY. Place of Publication: Publisher's Name, Date of Publication.

Gillespie, Kelly. "Before the Commission: Ethnography as Public Testimony." In *If Truth Be Told: The Politics of Public Ethnography*, edited by Didier Fassin, 69–95. Durham, NC: Duke University Press, 2017.

Journal Articles

6. Journal Article—Basic Format

N: ##. Author's First and Last Names, "Title of Article: Subtitle of Article," *Title of Journal* Volume Number, Issue Number (Date of Publication): XX.

9. Ben Mercer, "Specters of Fascism: The Rhetoric of Historical Analogy in 1968," *Journal of Modern History* 88, no. 1 (March 2016): 98.

B: Author's Last Name, Author's First Name. "Title of Article: Subtitle of Article." *Title of Journal* Volume Number, Issue Number (Date of Publication): YY–YY.

Mercer, Ben. "Specters of Fascism: The Rhetoric of Historical Analogy in 1968." *Journal of Modern History* 88, no. 1 (March 2016): 96–129.

For an article with multiple authors, follow the relevant pattern for authors' names in template 2.

7. Journal Article Online

For a journal article consulted online, include a URL. For articles that include a DOI, form the URL by appending the DOI to https://doi.org/ rather than using the URL in your address bar. The DOI for the Fernandez article in the example below is 10.1086/685998.

N: ##. Author's First and Last Names, "Title of Article: Subtitle of Article," *Title of Journal* Volume Number, Issue Number (Date of Publication): XX, URL.

10. Patricio A. Fernandez, "Practical Reasoning: Where the Action Is," *Ethics* 126, no. 4 (July 2016): 872, https://doi.org/10.1086/685998.

B: Author's Last Name, Author's First Name. "Title of Article: Subtitle of Article." *Title of Journal* Volume Number, Issue Number (Date of Publication): YY–YY. URL.

Fernandez, Patricio A. "Practical Reasoning: Where the Action Is." *Ethics* 126, no. 4 (July 2016): 869–900. https://doi.org/10.1086/685998.

See 15.4.1 for more details.

Chapter 17 includes examples of a wide range of sources, including exceptions to the patterns discussed here.

16.1.1 Order of Elements

The elements in notes and bibliography entries follow the same general order for all types of sources: author, title, facts of publication. However, notes present authors' names in standard order (first name first), while bibliography entries present them in inverted order (last name first) for alphabetical listing. Notes citing specific passages usually include page numbers or other locating information; bibliography entries do not, though they do include a full span of page numbers for a source that is part of a larger work, such as an article in a periodical or a chapter in a book.

16.1.2 Punctuation

In notes, separate most elements with commas; in bibliography entries, separate them with periods. In notes, enclose facts of publication in parentheses; in bibliography entries, do not. The styles are different because a note is intended to be read like text, where a period might signal the end of a citation. Bibliographies are designed as lists in which each source has its own entry, so periods can be used without confusion to separate such elements as author, title, and publication data.

16.1.3 Capitalization

Most titles can be capitalized using headline style. But for titles in languages other than English, use sentence style. (See 22.3.1 for both styles.) Capitalize proper nouns in the usual way (see chapter 22).

16.1.4 Italics and Quotation Marks

Use italics for titles of larger entities (books, journals); for titles of smaller entities (chapters, articles), use roman type and quotation marks. Also use roman type and quotation marks for titles of works that have not been formally published (such as manuscripts or dissertations), even if they are book length. See also 22.3.2.

16.1.5 Numbers

In titles, any numbers are spelled out or given in numerals exactly as they are in the original. Use lowercase roman numerals to refer to page numbers that are in roman numerals in the original. References to all other numbers (such as chapter numbers or figure numbers) are given in arabic numerals, even if in the original they are in roman numerals or spelled out.

16.1.6 Abbreviations

In notes, abbreviate terms such as *editor* or *edited by* (*ed.*) and *translator* or *translated by* (*trans.*). In bibliography entries, these terms are often spelled out when they introduce a name (*Edited by*) but abbreviated when they follow it (*ed.*). The plural of a noun form is usually formed by adding *s* (*eds.*) unless the abbreviation ends in an *s* (use *trans.* for both singular and plural). Abbreviations for *edited by* (*ed.*) and the like are never plural. Terms such as *volume*, *edition*, and *number* (*vol.*, *ed.*, and *no.*) are always abbreviated.

16.1.7 Indentation

Notes are indented like other paragraphs in the text: the first line of each note is indented, and anything that runs over to a new line is flush left. Bibliography entries have hanging indents: the first line of each entry is flush left, and anything that runs over is indented.

16.2 Bibliographies

Papers that use the notes-bibliography citation style typically include both notes and a bibliography that lists all sources cited in the notes. Although the same information appears in both notes and bibliography, readers need it in both places because they use notes and bibliographies differently. Notes let readers quickly check the source for a particular reference without disrupting the flow of their reading. A bibliography shows readers the extent of your research and its relationship to prior work. A bibliography also helps readers use your sources in their own research. So unless you have only a handful of sources or your instructor tells you otherwise, always include both notes and a bibliography in your papers. If you do not include a bibliography, make sure that your notes present complete information for each source, at least the first time you cite it.

16.2.1 Types of Bibliographies

In most cases, your bibliography should include every work you cite in your text. (For exceptions, see 16.2.3.) You may also include works that were important to your thinking but that you did not specifically mention in the text. Label this kind *Bibliography* or *Sources Consulted*. See figure A.15 in the appendix for a sample page of a bibliography.

There are other options:

- *Selected bibliography*. Some bibliographies do not include all works cited in notes, either to save space or to omit minor references unlikely to interest readers. You may use a selected bibliography if you have good reasons and your instructor or advisor approves. Label it *Selected Bibliography* and add a headnote that explains your principle of selection.

■ *Single-author bibliography.* Some writers list works by one person, usually as a separate list in addition to a standard bibliography, but sometimes as the only bibliography in a single-author study with few other sources. Label such a list *Works of [Author's Name]* or use a more descriptive title (*Published Works of, Writings of,* or whatever is appropriate). You can arrange it chronologically or alphabetically by title. If your list is chronological, titles published in the same year are listed alphabetically.

■ *Annotated bibliography.* Some writers annotate each bibliography entry with a brief description of the work's contents or relevance to their research. In most cases, if you annotate one entry you should annotate them all. But researchers sometimes annotate only the most important works or those whose relevance to their research may not be evident. If your annotations are brief phrases, add them in brackets after the publication data (note that there is no period within or after the bracketed entry):

B: Toulmin, Stephen. *The Uses of Argument.* Cambridge: Cambridge University Press, 1958. [a seminal text describing argument in nonsymbolic language]

You may also add full-sentence annotations on a new line indented from the left margin:

B: Toulmin, Stephen. *The Uses of Argument.* Cambridge: Cambridge University Press, 1958. This is the seminal text describing the structure of an argument in nonsymbolic language.

16.2.2 Arrangement of Entries

16.2.2.1 ALPHABETICAL BY AUTHOR. A bibliography is normally a single list of all sources arranged alphabetically by the last name of the author, editor, or whoever is first in each entry. (For alphabetizing names from languages other than English, compound names, and other special cases, see 16.2.2.2.) Most word processors and citation management tools can sort entries alphabetically. For all but the simplest of lists, however, the results will typically need some adjusting. If you are writing a thesis or dissertation, your department or university may specify that you should alphabetize the entries letter by letter or word by word; see 16.58–61 of *The Chicago Manual of Style,* 17th edition (2017), for an explanation of these two systems.

If your bibliography includes two or more works written, edited, or translated by the same individual, arrange the entries alphabetically by title (ignoring articles such as *a* and *the*). For all entries after the first, replace the individual's name with a long dash, called a 3-em dash (see

21.7.3). For edited or translated works, put a comma and the appropriate designation (*ed.*, *trans.*, or the like) after the dash. List all such works before any that the individual coauthored or coedited. Successive entries by two or more authors in which only the first author's name is the same are alphabetized according to the coauthors' last names. Note that it is best to make all these adjustments manually—*after* you have sorted your complete bibliography alphabetically by name.

B: Gates, Henry Louis, Jr. *America behind the Color Line: Dialogues with African Americans.* New York: Warner Books, 2004.

———. *Black in Latin America.* New York: New York University Press, 2011.

———, ed. *The Classic Slave Narratives.* New York: Penguin Putnam, 2002.

———. *The Signifying Monkey: A Theory of African-American Literary Criticism.* New York: Oxford University Press, 1988.

———. *Tradition and the Black Atlantic: Critical Theory in the African Diaspora.* New York: BasicCivitas, 2010.

Gates, Henry Louis, Jr., and Cornel West. *The African-American Century: How Black Americans Have Shaped Our Country.* New York: Free Press, 2000.

Gates, Henry Louis, Jr., and Donald Yacovone. *The African Americans: Many Rivers to Cross.* Carlsbad, CA: SmileyBooks, 2013.

The same principles apply to works by a single group of authors named in the same order.

B: Marty, Martin E., and R. Scott Appleby, eds. *Accounting for Fundamentalisms.* Chicago: University of Chicago Press, 2004.

———. *The Glory and the Power: The Fundamentalist Challenge to the Modern World.* Boston: Beacon Press, 1992.

Marty, Martin E., and Micah Marty. *When True Simplicity Is Gained: Finding Spiritual Clarity in a Complex World.* Grand Rapids, MI: William B. Eerdmans, 1998.

If a source does not have a named author or editor, alphabetize it based on the first element of the citation, generally a title. Ignore articles such as *a* and *the*.

B: *Account of the Operations of the Great Trigonometrical Survey of India.* 22 vols. Dehra Dun: Survey of India, 1870–1910.

"The Great Trigonometrical Survey of India." *Calcutta Review* 38 (1863): 26–62.

"State and Prospects of Asia." *Quarterly Review* 63, no. 126 (March 1839): 369–402.

16.2.2.2 SPECIAL TYPES OF NAMES. Some authors' names consist of more than a readily identifiable "first name" and "last name." In many cases you can determine the correct order by consulting your library's catalog. For historical names, the biographical entries at Merriam-Webster.com can be helpful. This section outlines some general principles for alphabetizing such names in your bibliography. In shortened or parenthetical notes, use the last name exactly as inverted (shown below in bold). If your paper involves names from languages other than English, follow the conventions for those languages.

- *Compound names.* Alphabetize compound last names, including hyphenated names, by the first part of the compound. If a woman uses both her own family name and her husband's but does not hyphenate them, generally alphabetize by the second surname. While many languages have predictable patterns for compound names (see below), others—such as French and German—do not.

  Hine, Darlene Clark   **Mies van der Rohe**, Ludwig
  Kessler-Harris, Alice   **Teilhard de Chardin**, Pierre

- *Names with particles.* Depending on the language, particles such as *de, di, D',* and *van* may or may not be considered the first part of a last name for alphabetizing. Consult one of the resources noted above if you are unsure about a particular name. Note that particles may be either lowercased or capitalized, and some are followed by an apostrophe.

  Beauvoir, Simone de   **Kooning**, Willem de
  de Gaulle, Charles   **Medici, Lorenzo de'**
  di Leonardo, Micaela   **Van Rensselaer**, Stephen

- *Names beginning with "Mac," "Saint," or "O'."* Names that begin with *Mac, Saint,* or *O'* can have many variations in abbreviation (*Mc, St.*), spelling (*Sainte, San*), capitalization (*Macmillan, McAllister*), and hyphenation or apostrophes (*O'Neill* or *Odell; Saint-Gaudens* or *St. Denis*). Alphabetize all such names based on the letters actually present; do not group them because they are similar.
- *Spanish names.* Many Spanish last names are compound names consisting of an individual's paternal and maternal family names, sometimes joined by the conjunction *y*. Alphabetize such names under the first part.

  Ortega y Gasset, José   **Sánchez Mendoza**, Juana

- *Arabic names.* Alphabetize Arabic last names that begin with the particle *al-* or *el-* (the) under the element following the particle. Names that begin with *Abu, Abd,* and *Ibn,* like English names beginning with *Mac* or *Saint,* should be alphabetized under these terms.

  Abu Zafar Nadvi, Syed   **Ibn Saud**, Aziz
  Hakim, Tawfiq al-   **Jamal**, Muhammad Hamid al-

- *Chinese, Japanese, and Korean names.* If an author with a Chinese, Japanese, or Korean name follows traditional usage (family name followed by given name), do not invert the name or insert a comma between the "first" and "last" names. If the author follows Westernized usage (given name followed by family name), treat the name as you would an English name.

Traditional usage	Westernized usage
Chao Wu-chi	**Kurosawa**, Noriaki
Kim Dae-jung	**Lee**, Chang-rae
Yoshida Shigeru	**Tsou**, Tang

16.2.2.3 OTHER THAN ALPHABETICAL. Occasionally readers will find an order other than alphabetical more useful. Single-author bibliographies are often more usefully arranged chronologically, as are specialized listings such as newspaper articles, archival records, and so on. You may also find it useful to invent an order for a specific purpose—for example, a list of topographical maps arranged by state or region. If you do use an order other than alphabetical or chronological, explain your choice in a headnote.

16.2.2.4 CATEGORIZED LISTINGS. You may organize a longer bibliography into categories to help readers see related sources as a group. Common ways of categorizing longer bibliographies into sections include these:

- By *format*. You can create separate lists for manuscripts, archival collections, recordings, and so on.
- By *primacy*. You can separate primary sources from secondary and tertiary ones, as in a single-author bibliography.
- By *field*. You can group sources by field, either because your readers will have different interests (as in the bibliography to this book) or because you mix work from fields not usually combined. For example, a work on the theory and psychology of comic literature might categorize sources as follows: *Theory of Comedy, Psychological Studies, Literary Criticism, Comic Works.*

If you categorize sources, present them either in separate bibliographies or in a single bibliography divided into sections. Introduce each separate bibliography or section with a subheading and, if necessary, a headnote. In a single bibliography, use the same principle of order within each section (usually alphabetical), and do not list a source in more than one section unless it clearly could be categorized in two or more ways. If you use different principles of order, create separate bibliographies, each with its own explanatory heading.

16.2.3 Sources That May Be Omitted

By convention, you may omit the following types of sources from a bibliography:

- brief published items, such as abstracts (17.2.8), pamphlets and reports (17.7.3), and reviews of published works or performances (17.9.2)
- newspaper articles (see 17.4)
- blog posts and comments (17.5.2), postings to social media (17.5.3) or to online forums or mailing lists (17.5.4), and interviews and personal communications (17.6)
- individual documents in manuscript collections (17.7.4 and 17.7.5)
- classical, medieval, and early English literary works (17.8.1) and (in some cases) well-known English-language plays (17.10.4.2)
- the Bible and other sacred works (17.8.2)
- well-known reference works, such as major dictionaries and encyclopedias (17.9.1)
- some sources in the visual and performing arts, including artworks (17.10.1) and live performances (17.10.2)
- the US Constitution (17.11.5), legal cases (17.11.7), and some other types of public documents (17.11.2.5)

You may choose to include in your bibliography a specific item from one of these categories that is critical to your argument or frequently cited.

If you use many such sources from a single larger entity—for example, several documents from a single manuscript collection—you may cite the larger entity, as discussed in the relevant sections of chapter 17.

16.3 Notes

Writers use several different kinds of notes, depending on their field, their readers, and the nature of their project. This section explains your options and how to choose among them.

16.3.1 Footnotes versus Endnotes

Your department may specify whether you should use footnotes or endnotes, especially for a thesis or dissertation. If not, you should generally choose footnotes, which are easier to read. Endnotes force readers to flip to the back of the paper or of each chapter to check every citation. If you include substantive comments in endnotes (see 16.3.5), readers may ignore them because they cannot tell without turning to the back which notes are substantive and which only cite sources.

On the other hand, choose endnotes when your footnotes are so long or numerous that they take up too much space on the page, making your report unattractive and difficult to read. Also, endnotes better accommodate tables, quoted poetry, and anything else that requires a lot of room or complex formatting.

If you use endnotes and include only a few substantive notes, you can reduce the risk that readers will miss them by separating substantive notes from source notes. Number source notes and present them as endnotes. Signal substantive notes with asterisks and other symbols (see 16.3.3) and present them as footnotes.

16.3.2 Referencing Notes in Text

Whenever you refer to or otherwise use material from a source, you must insert into your text a superscript number that directs your reader to a note that gives bibliographical information about that source. Put the number at the end of the sentence or clause containing the quotation or other material (see also 25.2). Normally the note number should follow any mark of punctuation, including a closing parenthesis.

Magic was a staple of the Kinahan charm.[1]

"This," wrote George Templeton Strong, "is what our tailors can do."[2]

(In an earlier book he had said quite the opposite.)[3]

If, however, the note refers to material before a dash, put the reference number before the dash:

The bias surfaced in the Shotwell series[4]—though not obviously.

Do not include more than one reference number at the same location (such as [5,6]). Instead, use one number and include all citations or comments in a single note (see 16.3.5).

Avoid putting a note number inside or at the end of a chapter title or subtitle. If your note applies to the entire chapter, omit the number and put an unnumbered footnote on the first page, before any numbered notes. You may, on the other hand, attach a note number to a subhead.

16.3.3 Numbering Notes

Number notes consecutively, beginning with 1. If your paper has separate chapters, restart each chapter with note 1. Do not skip a number or use numbers such as 5a.

If you use endnotes for source citations but footnotes for substantive comments (see 16.3.1), do not number the footnotes. Instead label the first footnote on a page with an asterisk (*). If you have more than one footnote on a page, use superscript symbols in the sequence * † ‡ §.

For notes to tables, see 26.2.7.

16.3.4   Formatting Notes

Use regular paragraph indents for both footnotes and endnotes. Begin each note with its reference number, formatted not as a superscript but as regular text. Put a period and a space between the number and the text of the note. For notes labeled with symbols (see 16.3.3), a space but not a period should appear between the symbol and the text of the note.

If your local guidelines allow it, you may instead use superscripts for reference numbers and symbols in notes. (By default, word processors typically apply identical formatting to the number or symbol in the text and its corresponding number or symbol in the note, making this the easier option.) You should then begin the text of each note with an intervening space but no period.

16.3.4.1   FOOTNOTES. Begin every footnote on the page on which you reference it. Put a short rule between the last line of text and the first footnote on each page, including any notes that run over from previous pages (your word processor should do this automatically). If a footnote runs over to the next page, it is best if it breaks in midsentence, so that readers do not think the note is finished and overlook the part on the next page. Single-space each footnote. If you have more than one footnote on a page, put a blank line between notes. See figure A.10 for a sample page of text with footnotes.

16.3.4.2   ENDNOTES. Endnotes should be listed together after the end of the text and any appendixes but before the bibliography. Single-space each note, and put a blank line between notes. Label the list *Notes*. If you restart numbering for each chapter, add a subheading before the first note to each chapter: "Chapter 1" and so forth. See figure A.14 for a sample page of endnotes.

16.3.5   Complex Notes

16.3.5.1   CITATIONS. If you cite several sources to make a single point, group them into a single note to avoid cluttering your text with reference numbers. List the citations in the same order in which the references appear in the text; separate citations with semicolons.

Only when we gather the work of several scholars—Walter Sutton's explications of some of Whitman's shorter poems; Paul Fussell's careful study of structure in "Cradle"; S. K. Coffman's close readings of "Crossing Brooklyn Ferry" and "Passage to India"— do we begin to get a sense of both the extent and the specificity of Whitman's forms.[1]

N: 1. Sutton, "The Analysis of Free Verse Form, Illustrated by a Reading of Whitman," *Journal of Aesthetics and Art Criticism* 18, no. 2 (December 1959): 241–54; Fussell, "Whitman's Curious Warble: Reminiscence and Reconciliation," in *The Presence of Whitman*, ed. R. W. B. Lewis (New York: Columbia University Press, 1962), 28–51; Coffman, " 'Crossing Brooklyn Ferry': A Note on the Catalogue Technique in Whitman's Poetry," *Modern Philology* 51, no. 4 (May 1954): 225–32; Coffman, "Form and Meaning in Whitman's 'Passage to India,' " *PMLA* 70, no. 3 (June 1955): 337–49.

It is also useful to group citations when you refer readers to a number of additional sources (called a "string cite"):

N: 2. On activists, school reforms, and school protests, see Ray Santana and Mario Esparza, "East Los Angeles Blowouts," in *Parameters of Institutional Change: Chicano Experiences in Education*, ed. Armando Valdéz (Hayward, CA: Southwest Network, 1974), 1–9; Mario T. García and Sal Castro, *Blow Out! Sal Castro and the Chicano Struggle for Educational Justice* (Durham: University of North Carolina Press, 2011); and Henry J. Gutierrez, "The Chicano Education Rights Movement and School Segregation, Los Angeles, 1962–1970" (PhD diss., University of California, Irvine, 1990).

16.3.5.2 CITATIONS AND COMMENTS. If a note includes both a citation and a substantive comment, put the citation first with a period after it, followed by the comment in a separate sentence.

To come to Paris was to experience the simultaneous pleasures of the best contemporary art and the most vibrant art center.[1]

N: 1. Natt, "Paris Art Schools," 269. Gilded Age American artists traveled to other European art centers, most notably Munich, but Paris surpassed all others in size and importance.

When you include a quotation in a note, put the citation after the terminal punctuation of the quotation.

Property qualifications dropped out of US practice for petit juries gradually during the nineteenth century but remained in force for grand juries in some jurisdictions until the mid-twentieth century.[2]

N: 2. "A grand jury inquires into complaints and accusations brought before it and, based on evidence presented by the state, issues bills of indictment." Kermit Hall, *The Magic Mirror: Law in American History* (New York: Oxford University Press, 1989), 172.

Be judicious in your use of substantive comments in notes. If a point is critical to your argument, include it in the text. If it is peripheral, think carefully about whether it is important enough to mention in a note.

16.4 Short Forms for Notes

In some fields, your instructor may expect you to give full bibliographical data in each note, but in most you can give a complete citation the first time you cite a work and a shortened one in subsequent notes. In a few fields, writers use a shortened form for all citations, with complete data listed only in the bibliography.

If you don't know the practice common in your field, consult your local guidelines.

16.4.1 Shortened Notes

A shortened note should include enough information for readers to find the full citation in your bibliography or in an earlier note. The two main choices are *author-only* notes and *author-title* notes. In some fields, writers use the author-title form for all shortened notes; in others, writers use the author-only form for most shortened notes, but the author-title form when they cite more than one work by the same author. (Unless your local guidelines specify otherwise, prefer the author-title form.) If a source does not have an author (or editor), you can use a *title-only* note. Figure 16.2 provides templates for each type of shortened note.

An author-only note includes the author's last name and page numbers (or other locator), separated by a comma and followed by a period. If the work has an editor rather than an author, use the editor's last name but do not add *ed.* An author-title note adds a shortened title composed of up to four distinctive words from the full title. Use a comma to separate the author and the shortened title, and put the title in italics or quotation marks as you would in a full note.

N: 1. Dana Velasco Murillo, *Urban Indians in a Silver City: Zacatecas, Mexico, 1546–1810* (Stanford, CA: Stanford University Press, 2016), 140.

     2. Velasco Murillo, *Urban Indians,* 142.

or

     2. Velasco Murillo, 142.

     3. Charles W. Collier, "The Death of Gun Control: An American Tragedy," *Critical Inquiry* 41, no. 1 (2014): 102.

     4. Collier, "Gun Control," 127–28.

or

     4. Collier, 127–28.

     5. Hasan Kwame Jeffries, "Remaking History: Barack Obama, Political Cartoons, and the Civil Rights Movement," in *Civil Rights History from the Ground Up: Local Struggles, a National Movement,* ed. Emilye Crosby (Athens: University of Georgia Press, 2011), 260.

     6. Jeffries, "Remaking History," 261–62.

or

     6. Jeffries, 261–62.

Figure 16.2. Templates for shortened notes

The following templates show what elements should be included in what order in the three types of shortened notes (see 16.4.1 for when to use each type). They also show punctuation, capitalization of titles, and typography of the elements. Gray shading shows terms as they would actually appear in a citation. ## stands in for note number; *XX* stands in for page numbers cited.

Author-Only Notes

1. Single Author

N: ##. Author's Last Name, XX.

        1. Duckworth, 88.

For a work cited by editor or translator instead of author (see 17.1.1), use the editor or translator in place of the author. Do not add *ed.* or *trans.*, as in a full note.

N: ##. Editor's or Translator's Last Name, XX.

        2. Prakash, 41–42.

If two or more authors have the same last name, distinguish them by adding first names or initials.

2. Two or Three Authors

N: ##. Author #1's Last Name and Author #2's Last Name, XX.

        3. Choi and Peng, 140.

N: ##. Author #1's Last Name, Author #2's Last Name, and Author #3's Last Name, XX.

        4. White, Williams, and Willig, 122.

3. Four or More Authors

N: ##. Author #1's Last Name et al., XX.

        5. Eichengreen et al., 215.

Author-Title Notes

4. Books

N: ##. Author's Last Name, *Shortened Title*, XX.

        6. Duckworth, *Grit*, 88.

For books by more than one author, follow the pattern for authors' names in templates 2 and 3.

Figure 16.2. Templates for shortened notes (continued)

---

5. Articles

N: ##. Author's Last Name, "Shortened Title," XX.

   7. Fernandez, "Practical Reasoning," 880–81.

For articles by more than one author, follow the pattern for authors' names in templates 2 and 3.

Title-Only Notes

6. Books without an Author

N: ##. *Shortened Title,* XX.

   8. *Account of Operations, 252.*

7. Articles without an Author

N: ##. "Shortened Title," XX.

   9. "Great Trigonometrical Survey," 26–27.

For multiple authors or editors, list the last names in the same order in which they appear in a full note.

N: 7. Ellen G. Friedman and Miriam Fuchs, eds., *Breaking the Sequence: Women's Experimental Fiction* (Princeton, NJ: Princeton University Press, 2014), 312.

   8. Friedman and Fuchs, *Women's Experimental Fiction,* 320.

or

   8. Friedman and Fuchs, 320.

16.4.2 *Ibid.*

At one time, writers shortened citations in notes by using Latin terms and abbreviations: *idem,* "the same"; *op.* cit., for *opere citato,* "in the work cited"; and *loc.* cit., for *loco citato,* "in the place cited." This practice has fallen out of favor, so avoid all Latin citation terms except one—*ibid.,* from *ibidem* or "in the same place." Some writers still use *ibid.* to shorten a citation to a work cited in the immediately preceding note.

N: 1. Buchan, *Advice to Mothers,* 71.
   2. Ibid., 95.
   3. Ibid.

In notes, *ibid.* should not be italicized; at the start of a note, it should be capitalized. Since *ibid.* is an abbreviation, it must end with a period; if the citation includes a page number, put a comma after *ibid.* If the page number of a reference is the same as in the previous note, do not include a page number after *ibid.* Do not use *ibid.* after a note that contains more than one citation, and avoid using *ibid.* to refer to footnotes that do not appear on the same page.

Unless your local guidelines require the use of *ibid.*, you may instead use one of the shortened forms discussed in 16.4.1 to refer to an immediately preceding note.

16.4.3 Parenthetical Notes

16.4.3.1 PARENTHETICAL NOTES VERSUS FOOTNOTES OR ENDNOTES. You may want to use parenthetical notes if you are discussing a particular work at length and need to cite it frequently. Such in-text references can make your text easier to follow. The first time you cite the work, provide full bibliographical data in a footnote or endnote; for subsequent references, use parenthetical notes instead of shortened notes (see 16.4.1). For examples, see 16.4.3.2.

You may also use parenthetical notes for certain types of sources that readers can identify with only a few elements, such as a newspaper article (see 17.4), a legal case (17.11.7), an older literary work (17.8.1), a biblical or other sacred work (17.8.2), or a source in the visual and performing arts (17.10). These sources can often be omitted from your bibliography (see 16.2.3).

In studies of language and literature, parenthetical notes have generally replaced footnotes or endnotes for most source citations, including the first reference to each work.

16.4.3.2 FORMATTING PARENTHETICAL NOTES. Insert a parenthetical note where you would place a reference number for a note: at the end of a quotation, sentence, or clause. The note comes before rather than after any comma, period, or other punctuation mark when the quotation is run into the text. With a block quotation, the note follows the terminal punctuation mark (not shown here; see 25.2.2.1 for an example).

The fullest parenthetical note includes the same information as the author-title form of a shortened note, with the elements separated by commas. (Note that both the elements and the punctuation are slightly different from those used in parenthetical citations in author-date style, described in chapters 18 and 19; do not confuse or combine the two styles.)

"What on introspection seems to happen immediately and without effort is often a complex symphony of processes that take time to complete" (LeDoux, *Synaptic Self*, 116).

According to one expert, the norms of friendship are different in the workplace (Little, "Norms of Collegiality," 330).

For most types of sources, you will have three additional options for shortening parenthetical notes, as follows:

- *Page numbers only.* You may include in the parentheses only the page number(s) or other locator if readers can readily identify the specific source from your text, either because it is a main object of your study (as in the first example below referring to a particular edition of Harriet Beecher Stowe's *Uncle Tom's Cabin*) or because you mention the author or title in your text. Either way, you must provide full bibliographic information elsewhere.

  "Poor John!" interposes Stowe's narrative voice, "It *was* rather natural; and the tears that fell, as he spoke, came as naturally as if he had been a white man" (169).

  Ernst Cassirer notes this in *Language and Myth* (59–60).

- *Author and page number.* You should include the author and page number(s) or other locator if readers cannot readily identify the source from your text, as long as you cite only one work by that author.

  While one school claims that "material culture may be the most objective source of information we have concerning America's past" (Deetz, 259), others disagree.

- *Title and page number.* You should include a shortened title and page number(s) or other locator if readers can readily identify the author from your text but you cite more than one work by that author.

  According to Furet, "the Second World War completed what the First had begun—the domination of the great political religions over European public opinion" (*Passing of an Illusion*, 360).

If you cite a work often, you can abbreviate the title. If the abbreviation is not obvious, you may specify it in the note for its first citation. (If you use more than five such abbreviations in your citations, list them in a separate section of your paper; see A.2.1.11.)

N: 1. François Furet, *The Passing of an Illusion: The Idea of Communism in the Twentieth Century,* trans. Deborah Furet (Chicago: University of Chicago Press, 1999), 368 (cited in text as *PI*).

According to Furet, "the Second World War completed what the First had begun—the domination of the great political religions over European public opinion" (*PI*, 360).

For newspaper articles and other types of sources in which author, title, and page number are not the key identifying elements (see 16.4.3.1 and the relevant sections of chapter 17), modify the parenthetical note style as needed. For an example, see 17.4.3.

17 Notes-Bibliography Style: *Citing Specific Types of Sources*

Chapter 16 presents an overview of the basic pattern for citations in the notes-bibliography style, including bibliography entries, full notes, shortened notes, and parenthetical notes. If you are not familiar with this citation style, read that chapter before consulting this one.

This chapter provides detailed information on the form of notes and bibliography entries for a wide range of sources. It starts with the most commonly cited sources—books and journal articles—before addressing a wide variety of other sources. The sections on books (17.1) and journal articles (17.2) discuss variations in such elements as authors' names and titles of works in greater depth than sections on less common sources.

Examples of sources consulted online are included alongside most other types of examples. Electronic book formats are discussed at 17.1.10. For some general considerations, especially if you are new to research, see 15.4. For tips related to citation management tools, see 15.6.

Examples of notes are identified with an N and bibliography entries with a B. In some cases, the examples show the same work cited in both forms to illustrate the similarities and differences between them; in other cases, they show different works to illustrate variations in elements even within a specific type of source. For shortened forms of notes, see 16.4.

If you cannot find an example in this chapter, consult chapter 14 of *The Chicago Manual of Style*, 17th edition (2017). You may also create your own style, adapted from the principles and examples given here. Most instructors, departments, and universities accept such adaptations as long as you apply them consistently.

17.1 Books

Citations of books may include a wide range of elements. Many of the variations in elements discussed in this section are also relevant to other types of sources.

17.1.1 Author's Name

Give the name of each author (and editor, translator, or other contributor) exactly as it appears on the title page, and in the same order. If a name includes more than one initial, use spaces between them (see 24.2.1). For multiple authors, see figure 16.1.

In notes, list authors' names in standard order (first name first):

N: 1. Ankhi Mukherjee, *What Is a Classic? Postcolonial Rewriting and Invention of the Canon* (Stanford, CA: Stanford University Press, 2013), 184–85.

2. G. J. Barker-Benfield, *Abigail and John Adams: The Americanization of Sensibility* (Chicago: University of Chicago Press, 2010), 499.

3. Donald R. Kinder and Allison Dale-Riddle, *The End of Race? Obama, 2008, and Racial Politics in America* (New Haven, CT: Yale University Press, 2012), 47.

In bibliography entries, put the first-listed author's name in inverted order (last name first), except for some non-English names and other cases explained in 16.2.2.2. Names of any additional authors should follow but should not be inverted.

B: Barker-Benfield, G. J. *Abigail and John Adams: The Americanization of Sensibility*. Chicago: University of Chicago Press, 2010.

Kinder, Donald R., and Allison Dale-Riddle. *The End of Race? Obama, 2008, and Racial Politics in America*. New Haven, CT: Yale University Press, 2012.

Mukherjee, Ankhi. *What Is a Classic? Postcolonial Rewriting and Invention of the Canon.* Stanford, CA: Stanford University Press, 2013.

17.1.1.1   EDITOR OR TRANSLATOR IN ADDITION TO AN AUTHOR. If a title page lists an editor or a translator in addition to an author, treat the author's name as described above. Add the editor or translator's name after the book's title. If there is a translator as well as an editor, list the names in the same order as on the title page of the original. If the author's name appears in the title, you may omit it from the note but not from the bibliography entry.

In notes, insert the abbreviation *ed.* (never *eds.*, since in this context it means "edited by" rather than "editor") or *trans.* before the editor's or translator's name.

N: 1. Elizabeth I, *Collected Works*, ed. Leah S. Marcus, Janel Mueller, and Mary Beth Rose (Chicago: University of Chicago Press, 2000), 102–4.

2. Georg Wilhelm Friedrich Hegel, *The Science of Logic*, ed. and trans. George di Giovanni (Cambridge: Cambridge University Press, 2010), 642–43.

3. *The Noé Jitrik Reader: Selected Essays on Latin American Literature*, ed. Daniel Balderston, trans. Susan E. Benner (Durham, NC: Duke University Press, 2005), 189.

In bibliography entries, insert the phrase *Edited by* or *Translated by* before the editor's or translator's name.

B: Elizabeth I. *Collected Works*. Edited by Leah S. Marcus, Janel Mueller, and Mary Beth Rose. Chicago: University of Chicago Press, 2000.

Hegel, Georg Wilhelm Friedrich. *The Science of Logic*. Edited and translated by George di Giovanni. Cambridge: Cambridge University Press, 2010.

Jitrik, Noé. *The Noé Jitrik Reader: Selected Essays on Latin American Literature*. Edited by Daniel Balderston. Translated by Susan E. Benner. Durham, NC: Duke University Press, 2005.

When a title page identifies an editor or translator with a complicated description, such as "Edited with an Introduction and Notes by" or "Translated with a Foreword by," you can simplify this phrase to *edited by* or *translated by* and follow the above examples. In general, if a foreword or an introduction is written by someone other than the author, you need not mention that person unless you cite that part specifically (see 17.1.8).

17.1.1.2   EDITOR OR TRANSLATOR IN PLACE OF AN AUTHOR. When an editor or a translator is listed on a book's title page instead of an author, use that person's name in the author's slot. Treat it as you would an author's name (see the beginning of this section), but add the abbreviation *ed.* or *trans.* following the name. If there are multiple editors or translators, use *eds.* or *trans.* (singular and plural) and follow the principles for multiple authors shown in figure 16.1.

N: 1. Seamus Heaney, trans., *Beowulf: A New Verse Translation* (New York: W. W. Norton, 2000), 55.

   2. María del Mar Logroño Narbona, Paulo G. Pinto, and John Tofik Karam, eds., *Crescent over Another Horizon: Islam in Latin America, the Caribbean, and Latino USA* (Austin: University of Texas Press, 2015), 140–41.

B: Heaney, Seamus, trans. *Beowulf: A New Verse Translation.* New York: W. W. Norton, 2000.

   Logroño Narbona, María del Mar, Paulo G. Pinto, and John Tofik Karam, eds. *Crescent over Another Horizon: Islam in Latin America, the Caribbean, and Latino USA.* Austin: University of Texas Press, 2015.

17.1.1.3   ORGANIZATION AS AUTHOR. If a publication issued by an organization, association, commission, or corporation has no personal author's name on the title page, list the organization itself as author in the bibliography, even if it is also given as publisher. For public documents, see 17.11.

B: American Bar Association. *The 2016 Federal Rules Book.* Chicago: American Bar Association, 2016.

   National Commission on Terrorist Attacks upon the United States. *The 9/11 Commission Report.* New York: W. W. Norton, 2004.

17.1.1.4   PSEUDONYM. Treat a widely recognized pseudonym as if it were the author's real name. If the name listed as the author's is known to be a pseudonym but the real name is unknown, add *pseud.* in brackets after the pseudonym.

N: 1. Mark Twain, *The Prince and the Pauper: A Tale for Young People of All Ages* (New York: Harper and Brothers, 1899), 34.

B: Centinel [pseud.]. "Letters." In *The Complete Anti-Federalist*, edited by Herbert J. Storing. Chicago: University of Chicago Press, 1981.

17.1.1.5   ANONYMOUS AUTHOR. If the authorship is known or guessed at but omitted from the book's title page, include the name in brackets (with a question mark if there is uncertainty). If the author or editor is unknown, avoid the use of *Anonymous* in place of a name (but see below), and begin the note or bibliography entry with the title.

N: 1. [James Hawkes?], *A Retrospect of the Boston Tea-Party, with a Memoir of George R. T. Hewes,* by a Citizen of New-York (New-York, 1834), 128–29.

   2. *A True and Sincere Declaration of the Purpose and Ends of the Plantation Begun in Virginia, of the Degrees Which It Hath Received, and Means by Which It Hath Been Advanced* (London, 1610), 17.

B: [Hawkes, James?]. *A Retrospect of the Boston Tea-Party, with a Memoir of George R. T. Hewes.* By a Citizen of New-York. New-York, 1834.

A True and Sincere Declaration of the Purpose and Ends of the Plantation Begun in Virginia, of the Degrees Which It Hath Received, and Means by Which It Hath Been Advanced. London, 1610.

If the author is explicitly listed as "Anonymous" on the title page, cite the book accordingly.

B: Anonymous. *The Secret Lives of Teachers.* Chicago: University of Chicago Press, 2015.

17.1.2   Title

List complete book titles and subtitles. Italicize both, and separate the title from the subtitle with a colon. (In the rare case of two subtitles, either follow the punctuation in the original or use a colon before the first and a semicolon before the second.)

N: 1. Philip Marsden, *Rising Ground: A Search for the Spirit of Place* (Chicago: University of Chicago Press, 2016), 113–14.

Capitalize most titles and subtitles headline-style; that is, capitalize the first letter of the first and last words of the title and subtitle and all major words. For titles in languages other than English, use sentence-style capitalization—that is, capitalize only the first letter of the first word of the title and subtitle and any proper nouns or other terms that would be capitalized under the conventions of the original language (in some Romance languages, proper adjectives and some proper nouns are not capitalized). (See 22.3.1 for a more detailed discussion of the two styles.)

(headline style) *How to Do It: Guides to Good Living for Renaissance Italians*

(sentence style) *A quoi rêvent les algorithmes: Nos vies à l'heure des big data*

Preserve the spelling, hyphenation, and punctuation of the original title, with two exceptions: change words in full capitals (except for initialisms or acronyms; see chapter 24) to upper- and lowercase, and change an ampersand (&) to *and.* Spell out numbers or give them as numerals according to the original (*Twelfth Century* or *12th Century*) unless there is a good reason to make them consistent with other titles in the list.

For titles of chapters and other parts of a book, see 17.1.8.

17.1.2.1 SPECIAL ELEMENTS IN TITLES. Several elements in titles require special treatment.

■ *Dates.* Use a comma to set off dates at the end of a title or subtitle, even if there is no punctuation in the original source. But if the source introduces the dates with a preposition (for example, "from 1920 to 1945") or a colon, do not add a comma.

N: 1. Romain Hayes, *Subhas Chandra Bose in Nazi Germany: Politics, Intelligence, and Propaganda, 1941–43* (New York: Columbia University Press, 2011), 151–52.

B: Sorenson, John L., and Carl L. Johannessen. *World Trade and Biological Exchanges before 1492*. Bloomington, IN: iUniverse, 2009.

■ *Titles within titles.* When the title of a work that would normally be italicized appears *within* the italicized title of another, enclose the quoted title in quotation marks. (If the title-within-a-title would normally be enclosed in quotation marks, keep the quotation marks.)

N: 2. Elisabeth Ladenson, *Dirt for Art's Sake: Books on Trial from "Madame Bovary" to "Lolita"* (Ithaca, NY: Cornell University Press, 2007), 17.

B: McHugh, Roland. *Annotations to "Finnegans Wake."* 2nd ed. Baltimore: Johns Hopkins University Press, 1991.

However, when the entire main title of a book consists of a title within a title, do not add quotation marks (but keep any quotation marks used in the source).

N: 3. Alan Light, *Let's Go Crazy: Prince and the Making of "Purple Rain"* (New York: Atria Books, 2014), 88.

B: Wilde, Oscar. *The Picture of Dorian Gray: An Annotated, Uncensored Edition*. Edited by Nicholas Frankel. Cambridge, MA: Harvard University Press, 2011.

■ *Italicized terms.* When an italicized title includes terms normally italicized in text, such as species names or names of ships, set the terms in roman type.

N: 4. T. Hugh Pennington, *When Food Kills: BSE,* E. coli, *and Disaster Science* (New York: Oxford University Press, 2003), 15.

B: Lech, Raymond B. *The Tragic Fate of the* U.S.S. Indianapolis: *The U.S. Navy's Worst Disaster at Sea*. New York: Cooper Square Press, 2001.

■ *Question marks and exclamation points.* When a title or a subtitle ends with a question mark or an exclamation point, no other punctuation normally follows. One exception: if the title would normally be followed by a comma, as in a shortened note (see 16.4.1), keep the comma. See also 21.12.1.

N: 5. Jafari S. Allen, *¡Venceremos? The Erotics of Black Self-Making in Cuba* (Durham, NC: Duke University Press, 2011), 210–11.
           6. Allen, *¡Venceremos?*, 212.

B: Wolpert, Stanley. *India and Pakistan: Continued Conflict or Cooperation?* Berkeley: University of California Press, 2010.

17.1.2.2   OLDER TITLES. For titles of works published in the eighteenth century or earlier, retain the original punctuation and spelling. Also retain the original capitalization, even if it does not follow headline style. Words in all capital letters, however, should be given in upper- and lowercase. If the title is very long, you may shorten it, but provide enough information for readers to find the full title in a library or publisher's catalog. Indicate omissions in such titles by three ellipsis dots. Put the dots in square brackets to show that they are not part of the original title. (Square brackets are also used in the first example to show that the place of publication is known but did not appear with the source.) If the omission comes at the end of a title in a bibliography entry, add a period after the bracketed dots.

N: 1. John Ray, *Observations Topographical, Moral, and Physiological: Made in a Journey Through part of the Low-Countries, Germany, Italy, and France: with A Catalogue of Plants not Native of England* [. . .] *Whereunto is added A Brief Account of Francis Willughby, Esq., his Voyage through a great part of Spain* ([London], 1673), 15.

B: Escalante, Bernardino. *A Discourse of the Navigation which the Portugales doe make to the Realmes and Provinces of the East Partes of the Worlde* [. . .]. Translated by John Frampton. London, 1579.

17.1.2.3   NON-ENGLISH TITLES. Use sentence-style capitalization for non-English titles, following the capitalization principles for proper nouns and other terms within the relevant language. If you are unfamiliar with these principles, consult a reliable source.

N: 1. José Reveles, *Échale la culpa a la heroína: De Iguala a Chicago* (New York: Vintage Español, 2016), 94.
   2. Ljiljana Piletić Stojanović, ed. *Gutfreund i češki kubizam* (Belgrade: Muzej savremene umetnosti, 1971), 54–55.

B: Kelek, Necla. *Die fremde Braut: Ein Bericht aus dem Inneren des türkischen Lebens in Deutschland.* Munich: Goldmann Verlag, 2006.

If you add the English translation of a title, place it after the original. Enclose it in brackets, without italics or quotation marks, and capitalize it sentence-style.

N: 3. Henryk Wereszycki, *Koniec sojuszu trzech cesarzy* [The end of the Three Emperors' League] (Warsaw: PWN, 1977), 5.

B: Yu Guoming. *Zhongguo chuan mei fa zhan qian yan tan suo* [New perspectives on news and communication]. Beijing: Xin hua chu ban she, 2011.

If you need to cite both the original and a translation, use one of the following forms, depending on whether you want to focus readers on the original or the translation.

B: Furet, François. *Le passé d'une illusion*. Paris: Éditions Robert Laffont, 1995. Translated by Deborah Furet as *The Passing of an Illusion* (Chicago: University of Chicago Press, 1999).

or

Furet, François. *The Passing of an Illusion*. Translated by Deborah Furet. Chicago: University of Chicago Press, 1999. Originally published as *Le passé d'une illusion* (Paris: Éditions Robert Laffont, 1995).

17.1.3 Edition

Some works are published in more than one edition. Each edition differs in content or format or both. Always include information about the edition you actually consulted (unless it is a first edition, which is usually not labeled as such).

17.1.3.1 REVISED EDITIONS. When a book is reissued with significant content changes, it may be called a "revised" edition or a "second" (or subsequent) edition. This information usually appears on the book's title page and is repeated, along with the date of the edition, on the copyright page.

When you cite an edition other than the first, include the number or description of the edition after the title. Abbreviate such wording as "Second Edition, Revised and Enlarged" as *2nd ed.*; abbreviate "Revised Edition" as *rev. ed.* Include the publication date only of the edition you are citing, not of any previous editions (see 17.1.6).

N: 1. Paul J. Bolt, Damon V. Coletta, and Collins G. Shackelford Jr., eds., *American Defense Policy*, 8th ed. (Baltimore: Johns Hopkins University Press, 2005), 157–58.

B: Foley, Douglas E. *Learning Capitalist Culture: Deep in the Heart of Tejas*. 2nd ed. Philadelphia: University of Pennsylvania Press, 2010.
Levitt, Steven D., and Stephen J. Dubner. *Freakonomics: A Rogue Economist Explores the Hidden Side of Everything*. Rev. ed. New York: HarperCollins, 2006.

17.1.3.2 REPRINT EDITIONS. Many books are reissued or published in more than one format—for example, in a paperback edition (by the original publisher or a different publisher) or in electronic form (see 17.1.10). Always record the facts of publication for the version you consulted. If the edition you consulted was published more than a year or two after the original edition or is a modern printing of a classic work, you may include the publication dates of both the original and the edition you are citing (see 17.1.6.3).

N: 1. Randall Jarrell, *Pictures from an Institution: A Comedy* (1954; repr., Chicago: University of Chicago Press, 2010), 79–80.

B: Dickens, Charles. *Pictures from Italy*. 1846. Reprint, Cambridge: Cambridge University Press, 2011.

17.1.4   Volume

If a book is part of a multivolume work, include this information in your citations.

17.1.4.1   SPECIFIC VOLUME. To cite a specific volume that carries its own title, list the title for the multivolume work as a whole, followed by the volume number and title of the specific volume. Give the publication date of the individual volume. Abbreviate *vol.* and use arabic numbers for volume numbers.

N: 1. Hamid Naficy, *A Social History of Iranian Cinema*, vol. 4, *The Globalizing Era, 1984–2010* (Durham, NC: Duke University Press, 2012), 44.

B: Naficy, Hamid. *A Social History of Iranian Cinema*. Vol. 4, *The Globalizing Era, 1984–2010*. Durham, NC: Duke University Press, 2012.

If the volumes are not individually titled, list each volume that you cite in the bibliography (see also 17.1.4.2). In a note, put the specific volume number (without *vol.*) immediately before the page number, separated by a colon and no intervening space.

N: 2. Muriel St. Clare Byrne, ed., *The Lisle Letters* (Chicago: University of Chicago Press, 1981), 4:243.

B: Byrne, Muriel St. Clare, ed. *The Lisle Letters*. Vols. 1 and 4. Chicago: University of Chicago Press, 1981.

Some multivolume works have both a general editor and editors or authors for each volume. When citing a specific volume in such a work, include information about the volume editor(s) or author(s) (see 17.1.1) as well as information about the editor(s) of the multivolume work as a whole. The example from *The History of Cartography* shows not only how to cite an individual contribution to such a work (see 17.1.9) but also how to cite a volume published in more than one physical part (*vol. 2, bk. 3*). The examples from *The Papers of Martin Luther King, Jr.* show how to cite a specific volume under the editor(s) of the work as a whole (useful when citing more than one volume from the same work; see also 17.1.4.2) or under the editor(s) of an individual volume.

N: 3. Barbara E. Mundy, "Mesoamerican Cartography," in *The History of Cartography*, ed. J. Brian Harley and David Woodward, vol. 2, bk. 3, *Cartography in the Traditional African, American, Arctic, Australian, and Pacific Societies*, ed. David Woodward and G. Malcolm Lewis (Chicago: University of Chicago Press, 1998), 233.

B: Carson, Clayborne, ed. *The Papers of Martin Luther King, Jr.* Vol. 7, *To Save the Soul of America, January 1961–August 1962*, edited by Tenisha Armstrong. Berkeley: University of California Press, 2014.

or

Armstrong, Tenisha, ed. *To Save the Soul of America, January 1961–August 1962*. Vol. 7 of *The Papers of Martin Luther King, Jr.*, edited by Clayborne Carson. Berkeley: University of California Press, 1992–.

17.1.4.2 MULTIVOLUME WORK AS A WHOLE. To cite a multivolume work as a whole, give the title, the total number of volumes, and, if the volumes have been published over several years, the full span of publication dates.

B: Aristotle. *Complete Works of Aristotle: The Revised Oxford Translation*. Edited by J. Barnes. 2 vols. Princeton, NJ: Princeton University Press, 1983.
Tillich, Paul. *Systematic Theology*. 3 vols. Chicago: University of Chicago Press, 1951–63.

For works that include individual volume titles or volume editors (see 17.1.4.1), it is usually best to cite the volumes individually.

17.1.5 Series

If a book belongs to a series, you may choose to include information about the series to help readers locate the source and understand the context in which it was published. Place the series information after the title (and any volume or edition number or editor's name) and before the facts of publication.

Put the series title in roman type with headline-style capitalization, omitting any initial *The*. If the volumes in the series are numbered, include the number of the work cited following the series title. The name of the series editor is often omitted, but you may include it after the series title. If you include both an editor and a volume number, the number is preceded by *vol.*

N: 1. Blake M. Hausman, *Riding the Trail of Tears*, Native Storiers: A Series of American Narratives (Lincoln: University of Nebraska Press, 2011), 25.

B: Lunning, Frenchy, ed. *World Renewal*. Mechademia 10. Minneapolis: University of Minnesota Press, 2014.
Stein, Gertrude. *Selections*. Edited by Joan Retallack. Poets for the Millennium, edited by Pierre Joris and Jerome Rothenberg, vol. 6. Berkeley: University of California Press, 2008.

17.1.6 Facts of Publication

The facts of publication usually include three elements: the place (city) of publication, the publisher's name, and the date (year) of publication.

In notes these elements are enclosed in parentheses; in bibliography entries they are not.

N: 1. Ta-Nehisi Coates, *Between the World and Me* (New York: Spiegel & Grau, 2015), 122–23.

B: Coates, Ta-Nehisi. *Between the World and Me.* New York: Spiegel & Grau, 2015.

For books published before the twentieth century, you may omit the publisher's name.

N: 2. Charles Darwin, *The Descent of Man, and Selection in Relation to Sex* (London, 1871), 1:16–17.

B: Darwin, Charles. *The Descent of Man, and Selection in Relation to Sex.* 2 vols. London, 1871.

17.1.6.1   **PLACE OF PUBLICATION.** The place of publication is the city where the book publisher's main editorial offices are located. If you do not see it listed on the title page, look for it on the copyright page instead. Where two or more cities are given ("Chicago and London," for example), include only the first.

Los Angeles: Getty Publications
New York: Columbia University Press

If the city of publication might be unknown to readers or confused with another city of the same name, add the abbreviation of the state (see 24.3.1), province, or (if necessary) country. When the publisher's name includes the state name, no state abbreviation is needed.

Cheshire, CT: Graphics Press
Harmondsworth, UK: Penguin Books
Cambridge, MA: MIT Press
Chapel Hill: University of North Carolina Press

Prefer current, commonly used English names for cities whenever such forms exist. (When in doubt about which form to use, record the name of the city as it appears with the source.)

Belgrade (*not* Beograd)   Milan (*not* Milano)

When the place of publication is not known (an uncommon occurrence for older works, which typically specify a city of publication), you may use the abbreviation *n.p.* in a note (or *N.p.* in a bibliography entry) before the publisher's name. If the place can be guessed, include it in brackets and add a question mark to indicate uncertainty.

(n.p.: Windsor, 1910)
[Lake Bluff, IL?]: Vliet and Edwards, 1920

It is common for books published more recently through modern self-publishing platforms not to list a place of publication. If you cite such a source, the place of publication can usually be omitted (see 17.1.6.2 for an example).

17.1.6.2 PUBLISHER'S NAME. Give the publisher's name for each book exactly as it appears on the title page, even if you know that the name has since changed or appears in a different form for other books in your bibliography.

Harcourt Brace and World
Harcourt Brace Jovanovich
Harcourt, Brace

You may, however, omit an initial *The* and such abbreviations as *Inc.*, *Ltd.*, *S.A.*, *Co.*, *& Co.*, and *Publishing Co.* (and the spelled-out forms of such corporate abbreviations).

University of Texas Press	*instead of*	The University of Texas Press
Houghton Mifflin	*instead of*	Houghton Mifflin Co.
Little, Brown	*instead of*	Little, Brown & Co.

For non-English publishers, do not translate or abbreviate any part of the publisher's name, but give the city name in its English form (as noted in 17.1.6.1). When the publisher is unknown, use just the place (if known) and date of publication. If a book has been self-published, however, this fact may be noted (see also 17.1.6.1).

B: Albin, Eleazar. *A Natural History of Birds: Illustrated with a Hundred and One Copper Plates, Engraven from the Life.* London: printed by the author, 1738.
Rai, Alisha. *Serving Pleasure.* Self-published, CreateSpace, 2015.

17.1.6.3 DATE OF PUBLICATION. The publication date for a book consists only of a year, not a month or day, and is usually identical to the copyright date. It generally appears on the copyright page and sometimes on the title page.

Revised editions and reprints may include more than one copyright date. In this case, the most recent indicates the publication date—for example, 2017 in the string "© 2003, 2010, 2017." See 17.1.3 for citing publication dates in such works.

If you cannot determine the publication date of a printed work, use the abbreviation *n.d.* in place of the year. If no date is provided but you believe you know it, you may add it in brackets, with a question mark to indicate uncertainty.

B: Agnew, John. *A Book of Virtues.* Edinburgh, n.d.
Miller, Samuel. *Another Book of Virtues.* Boston, [1750?].

If a book is under contract with a publisher and is already titled but the date of publication is not yet known, use *forthcoming* in place of the date. Treat any book not yet under contract as an unpublished manuscript (see 17.7.4).

N: 1. Jane Q. Author, *Book Title* (Place of Publication: Publisher's Name, forthcoming).

17.1.7   Page Numbers and Other Locators

Page numbers and other information used to identify the location of a cited passage or element generally appear in notes but not in bibliographies. One exception: if you cite a chapter or other section of a book in a bibliography, give the page range for that chapter or section (see 17.1.8 for examples).

For guidelines on expressing a span of numbers, see 23.2.4. For page numbers and other locators in e-book formats, see 17.1.10.

17.1.7.1   PAGE, CHAPTER, AND DIVISION NUMBERS. The locator is usually the last item in a note. Before page numbers, the word *page* or the abbreviation *p.* or *pp.* is generally omitted. Use arabic numbers except for pages numbered with roman numerals in the original.

N: 1. Richard Arum and Josipa Roksa, *Academically Adrift: Limited Learning on College Campuses* (Chicago: University of Chicago Press, 2011), 145–46.
2. Jacqueline Jones, preface to the new edition of *Labor of Love, Labor of Sorrow: Black Women, Work, and the Family, from Slavery to the Present*, rev. ed. (New York: Basic Books, 2010), xiv–xv.

Sometimes you may want to refer to a full chapter (abbreviated *chap.*), part (*pt.*), book (*bk.*), or section (*sec.*) instead of a span of page numbers.

N: 3. Srikant M. Datar, David A. Garvin, and Patrick G. Cullen, *Rethinking the MBA: Business Education at a Crossroads* (Boston: Harvard Business Press, 2010), pt. 2.

Some books printed before 1800 do not carry page numbers but are divided into signatures and then into leaves or folios, each with a front side (*recto*, or *r*) and a back side (*verso*, or *v*). To cite such pages, include the relevant string of numbers and identifiers, run together without spaces or italics: for example, G6v, 176r, 232r–v, or (if you are citing entire folios) fol. 49.

17.1.7.2   OTHER TYPES OF LOCATORS. Sometimes you will want to cite a specific note, a figure or table, or a numbered line (as in some works of poetry).

- *Note numbers.* Use the abbreviation *n* (plural *nn*) to cite notes. If the note cited is the only footnote on its page or is an unnumbered footnote, add *n* after the page number (with no intervening space or punctuation). If there are other footnotes or endnotes on the same page as the note cited, list the page number followed by *n* or (if two or more consecutive notes are cited) *nn* and the note number(s).

N: 1. Anthony Grafton, *The Footnote: A Curious History* (Cambridge, MA: Harvard University Press, 1997), 72n.

2. Dwight Bolinger, *Language: The Loaded Weapon* (London: Longman, 1980), 192n23, 192n30, 199n14, 201nn16–17.

- *Illustration and table numbers.* Use the abbreviation *fig.* for *figure*, but spell out *table*, *map*, *plate*, and names of other types of illustrations. Give the page number before the illustration number.

N: 3. Richard Sobel, *Public Opinion in U.S. Foreign Policy: The Controversy over Contra Aid* (Boston: Rowman and Littlefield, 1993), 87, table 5.3.

- *Line numbers.* For poetry and other works best identified by line number, avoid the abbreviations l. (line) and ll. (lines); they are too easily confused with the numerals 1 and 11. Use *line* or *lines*, or use numbers alone where you have made it clear that you are referring to lines.

N: 4. Ogden Nash, "Song for Ditherers," lines 1–4.

17.1.8 Chapters and Other Parts of a Book

In most cases you can cite the main title of any book that offers a continuous argument, narrative, or theme, even if you actually use only a section of it. But sometimes you will want to cite an independent essay or chapter if that is the part most relevant to your research. By doing so, you help readers see how the source fits into your project.

B: Nishizaki, Yoshinori. "Big Is Good: The Banharn-Jaemsai Observatory Tower in Suphanburi." In *A Sarong for Clio: Essays on the Intellectual and Cultural History of Thailand—Inspired by Craig J. Reynolds*, edited by Maurizio Peleggi, 143–62. Ithaca, NY: Cornell University Press, 2015.

instead of

Peleggi, Maurizio, ed. *A Sarong for Clio: Essays on the Intellectual and Cultural History of Thailand—Inspired by Craig J. Reynolds*. Ithaca, NY: Cornell University Press, 2015.

17.1.8.1 **PARTS OF SINGLE-AUTHOR BOOKS.** If you cite a chapter or other titled part of a single-author book, include the title of the part first, in roman type and enclosed in quotation marks. After the designation *in*, give the book title. In a bibliography entry, include the full span of page numbers for that part following the book title; in a note, give the page number(s) for a specific reference as you would for any other quotation.

N: 1. Roxane Gay, "The Careless Language of Sexual Violence," in *Bad Feminist* (New York: Harper Perennial, 2014), 130.

B: Gay, Roxane. "The Careless Language of Sexual Violence." In *Bad Feminist*, 128–36. New York: Harper Perennial, 2014.

If you cite a part with a generic title such as *introduction, preface,* or *afterword,* add that term before the title of the book in roman type without quotation marks. If the part is written by someone other than the main author of the book, give the part author's name first and the book author's name after the title.

N: 2. Grant H. Kester, preface to the 2013 edition of *Conversation Pieces: Community and Communication in Modern Art,* updated ed. (Berkeley: University of California Press, 2013), xii.
       3. Craig Calhoun, foreword to *Multicultural Politics: Racism, Ethnicity, and Muslims in Britain,* by Tariq Modood (Minneapolis: University of Minnesota Press, 2005), xii.

If the author of the generic part is the same as the author of the book, cite the book as a whole in the bibliography, not just the part.

B: Calhoun, Craig. Foreword to *Multicultural Politics: Racism, Ethnicity, and Muslims in Britain,* by Tariq Modood, ix–xv. Minneapolis: University of Minnesota Press, 2005.
       Kester, Grant H. *Conversation Pieces: Community and Communication in Modern Art.* Updated ed. Berkeley: University of California Press, 2013.

17.1.8.2 **PARTS OF EDITED COLLECTIONS.** If you cite part of an edited collection with contributions by multiple authors, list the part author and title (in roman type, enclosed in quotation marks) first. After the designation *in,* give the book title and the name of the editor. In a bibliography entry, include the full span of page numbers for that part following the book title; in a note, give the page number(s) for a specific reference as you would for any other quotation.

N: 1. Cameron Binkley, "Saving Redwoods: Clubwomen and Conservation, 1900–1925," in *California Women and Politics: From the Gold Rush to the Great Depression,* ed. Robert W. Cherny, Mary Ann Irwin, and Ann Marie Wilson (Lincoln: University of Nebraska Press, 2011), 155.

B: Binkley, Cameron. "Saving Redwoods: Clubwomen and Conservation, 1900–1925." In *California Women and Politics: From the Gold Rush to the Great Depression,* edited by Robert W. Cherny, Mary Ann Irwin, and Ann Marie Wilson, 151–74. Lincoln: University of Nebraska Press, 2011.

If you cite two or more contributions to the same edited collection, you may use one of the space-saving shortened forms discussed in 16.4.1. The first time you cite any part from the book in a note, give full bibliographical information about both the part and the book as a whole. Thereafter, if you cite another part from the book, provide the full author's name and title of the part, but give the information about the book in shortened form. Subsequent notes for individual parts follow one of the shortened note forms (author-only, shown here, or author-title).

N: 2. Robert Bruegmann, "Built Environment of the Chicago Region," in *Chicago Neighborhoods and Suburbs: A Historical Guide,* ed. Ann Durkin Keating (Chicago: University of Chicago Press, 2008), 259.

3. Janice L. Reiff, "Contested Spaces," in Keating, 55.

4. Bruegmann, 299–300.

5. Reiff, 57.

In your bibliography, provide a full citation for the whole book and a variation on the shortened note form for individual parts.

B: Bruegmann, Robert. "Built Environment of the Chicago Region." In Keating, 76–314.

Keating, Ann Durkin, ed. *Chicago Neighborhoods and Suburbs: A Historical Guide.* Chicago: University of Chicago Press, 2008.

Reiff, Janice, L. "Contested Spaces." In Keating, 55–63.

17.1.8.3 WORKS IN ANTHOLOGIES. Cite a short story, poem, essay, or other work published in an anthology in the same way you would a contribution to an edited collection with multiple authors. Give the titles of most works published in anthologies in roman type, enclosed in quotation marks. An exception is a book-length poem or prose work that is anthologized in full or in part; its title should be italicized (see 22.3.2).

N: 1. Isabel Allende, "The Spirits Were Willing," in *The Oxford Book of Latin American Essays,* ed. Ilan Stavans (New York: Oxford University Press, 1997), 463–64.

B: Wigglesworth, Michael. Excerpt from *The Day of Doom.* In *The New Anthology of American Poetry,* vol. 1, *Traditions and Revolutions, Beginnings to 1900,* edited by Steven Gould Axelrod, Camille Roman, and Thomas Travisano, 68–74. New Brunswick, NJ: Rutgers University Press, 2003.

If the original publication date of a work is important in the context of your paper, include it after the title of the work and before the title of the anthology in both your notes and your bibliography.

N: 2. Isabel Allende, "The Spirits Were Willing" (1984), in *The Oxford Book...*

B: Wigglesworth, Michael. Excerpt from *The Day of Doom.* 1662. In *The New Anthology...*

17.1.9 Letters and Other Communications in Published Collections

To cite a letter, memorandum, or other such item collected in a book, give the names of the sender and recipient followed by the date of the correspondence. (For unpublished personal communications, see 17.6.2; for unpublished letters in manuscript collections, see 17.7.4.) The word *letter* is unnecessary, but label other forms, such as a report or memorandum. Give the title and other data for the collection in the usual form for an edited book. Subsequent notes to the same item can be shortened to the names of the sender and recipient (plus a date if necessary).

N: 1. Henry James to Edith Wharton, November 8, 1905, in *Letters*, ed. Leon Edel, vol. 4, *1895–1916* (Cambridge, MA: Belknap Press of Harvard University Press, 1984), 373.

2. James to Wharton, 375.

3. E. B. White to Harold Ross, memorandum, May 2, 1946, in *Letters of E. B. White*, ed. Dorothy Lobrano Guth (New York: Harper and Row, 1976), 273.

In the bibliography, cite the whole collection.

B: James, Henry. *Letters*. Edited by Leon Edel. Vol. 4, *1895–1916*. Cambridge, MA: Belknap Press of Harvard University Press, 1984.

White, E. B. *Letters of E. B. White*. Edited by Dorothy Lobrano Guth. New York: Harper and Row, 1976.

17.1.10 Electronic Books

Electronic books, or e-books, are cited just like print books, as discussed throughout 17.1. In addition, you will need to include information about the format you consulted. If you read the book online, include a URL. If you consulted the book in a commercial database, you can instead give the name of the database. See 15.4.1 for more details.

On the other hand, if you downloaded a book from Amazon or Apple or the like in a format that requires a specific app or device, include that information instead.

Many e-book formats lack fixed page numbers. Avoid citing app- or device-specific screen or location numbers, which may not be the same for others even if they consult the same format. Instead, cite by chapter or section number (see 17.1.7.1) or, if these are unnumbered, by the name of the chapter or section (see 17.1.8). Especially for a frequently cited source, it may be better simply to consult a version that reproduces the pagination of a printed edition. In the Dostoevsky example below, the page images from the Internet Archive are easier to cite than the reflowable Project Gutenberg text, and because they reproduce the original text exactly, they are also more authoritative.

N: 1. Janet M. Davis, *The Gospel of Kindness: Animal Welfare and the Making of Modern America* (Oxford: Oxford University Press, 2016), 144–45, https://doi.org/10.1093/acprof:oso/9780199733156.001.0001.

2. Eric Schlosser, *Fast Food Nation: The Dark Side of the American Meal* (Boston: Houghton Mifflin, 2001), 88, ProQuest Ebrary.

3. Jessa Crispin, *The Dead Ladies Project: Exiles, Expats, and Ex-Countries* (Chicago: University of Chicago Press, 2015), 100–101, Adobe Digital Editions PDF.

4. Malcolm Gladwell, *Outliers: The Story of Success* (Boston: Little, Brown, 2008), chap. 1, sec. 4, Kindle.

5. Harper Lee, *Go Set a Watchman* (New York: Harper, 2015), chap. 19, iBooks.

6. Fyodor Dostoevsky, *Crime and Punishment*, trans. Constance Garnett (Project Gutenberg, last updated November 5, 2012), pt. 6, chap. 1, http://gutenberg.org/files/2554/2554-h/2554-h.htm.

or, better,

6. Fyodor Dostoevsky, *Crime and Punishment*, trans. Constance Garnett, ed. William Allan Neilson (New York: P. F. Collier & Son, 1917), 444, https://archive.org/details/crimepunishmentoodostuoft.

B: Crispin, Jessa. *The Dead Ladies Project: Exiles, Expats, and Ex-Countries*. Chicago: University of Chicago Press, 2015. Adobe Digital Editions PDF.

Davis, Janet M. *The Gospel of Kindness: Animal Welfare and the Making of Modern America*. Oxford: Oxford University Press, 2016. https://doi.org/10.1093/acprof:oso/9780199733156.001.0001.

Dostoevsky, Fyodor. *Crime and Punishment*. Translated by Constance Garnett. Edited by William Allan Neilson. New York: P. F. Collier, 1917. https://archive.org/details/crimepunishmentoodostuoft.

Gladwell, Malcolm. *Outliers: The Story of Success*. Boston: Little, Brown, 2008. Kindle.

Lee, Harper. *Go Set a Watchman*. New York: Harper, 2015. iBooks.

Schlosser, Eric. *Fast Food Nation: The Dark Side of the American Meal*. Boston: Houghton Mifflin, 2001. ProQuest Ebrary.

17.2 Journal Articles

Journals are scholarly or professional periodicals available primarily in academic libraries and by subscription. They often include the word *journal* in their title (*Journal of Modern History*), but not always (*Signs*). Journals are not the same as magazines, which are usually intended for a more general readership. This distinction is important because journal articles and magazine articles are cited differently (see 17.3). If you are unsure whether a periodical is a journal or a magazine, see whether its articles include citations; if so, treat it as a journal.

Many journal articles are available online, often through your school's library website or from a commercial database. To cite an article that you read online, include a URL. If a URL is listed along with the article, use that instead of the one in your browser's address bar. If a DOI is listed, append the DOI to https://doi.org/ to form the URL. If you consulted the article in a commercial database, you may give the name of the database instead of a URL. See 15.4.1 for more details.

17.2.1   Author's Name

Give authors' names exactly as they appear at the heads of their articles. Names in the notes are listed in standard order (first name first). In the bibliography, the name of the first-listed author is inverted. For some special cases, see 16.2.2.2.

17.2.2   Article Title

List complete article titles and subtitles. Use roman type, separate the title from the subtitle with a colon, and enclose both in quotation marks. Use headline-style capitalization (see 22.3.1).

N: 1. Quentin Taylor, "The Mask of Publius: Alexander Hamilton and the Politics of Expediency," *American Political Thought* 5, no. 1 (Winter 2016): 63, https://doi.org/10.1086/684559.

B: Taylor, Quentin. "The Mask of Publius: Alexander Hamilton and the Politics of Expediency." *American Political Thought* 5, no. 1 (Winter 2016): 55–79. https://doi.org/10.1086/684559.

Terms normally italicized in text, such as species names and book titles, remain italicized within an article title; terms quoted in the title are enclosed in single quotation marks because the title itself is within double quotation marks. Do not add either a colon or a period after a title or subtitle that ends in a question mark or an exclamation point. If the title would normally be followed by a comma, as in the shortened note example below (see 16.4.1), use both marks. See also 21.12.1.

N: 2. Lisa A. Twomey, "Taboo or Tolerable? Hemingway's *For Whom the Bell Tolls* in Postwar Spain," *Hemingway Review* 30, no. 2 (Spring 2011): 55.
3. Twomey, "Taboo or Tolerable?," 56.

B: Lewis, Judith. " 'Tis a Misfortune to Be a Great Ladie': Maternal Mortality in the British Aristocracy, 1558–1959." *Journal of British Studies* 37, no. 1 (January 1998): 26–53. http://www.jstor.org/stable/176034.

Titles in languages other than English should generally be capitalized sentence-style (see 22.3.1) according to the conventions of the particular language. If you add an English translation, enclose it in brackets, without quotation marks.

N: 4. Antonio Carreño-Rodríguez, "Modernidad en la literatura gauchesca: Carnavalización y parodia en el *Fausto* de Estanislao del Campo," *Hispania* 92, no. 1 (March 2009): 13–14, http://www.jstor.org/stable/40648253.

B: Kern, W. "Waar verzamelde Pigafetta zijn Maleise woorden?" [Where did Pigafetta collect his Malaysian words?]. *Tijdschrift voor Indische taal-, land-en volkenkunde* 78 (1938): 271–73.

17.2.3 Journal Title

After the article title, list the journal title in italics, with headline-style capitalization (see 22.3.1). Give the title exactly as it appears on the title page or on the journal website; do not use abbreviations, although you can omit an initial *The* (see also 22.3.2.1). If the official title is an initialism such as *PMLA*, do not expand it. For non-English journal titles, you may use either headline-style or sentence-style capitalization, but retain all initial articles (*Der Spiegel*).

17.2.4 Issue Information

Most journal citations include volume number, issue number, month or season, and year. Readers may not need all of these elements to locate an article, but including them all guards against a possible error in one of them.

17.2.4.1 VOLUME AND ISSUE NUMBERS. The volume number follows the journal title without intervening punctuation and is not italicized. Use arabic numerals even if the journal itself uses roman numerals. If there is an issue number, it follows the volume number, separated by a comma and preceded by *no.*

N: 1. Campbell Brown, "Consequentialize This," *Ethics* 121, no. 4 (July 2011): 752, https://doi.org/10.1086/660696.

B: Ionescu, Felicia. "Risky Human Capital and Alternative Bankruptcy Regimes for Student Loans." *Journal of Human Capital* 5, no. 2 (Summer 2011): 153–206. https://doi.org/10.1086/661744.

When a journal uses issue numbers only, without volume numbers, a comma follows the journal title.

B: Beattie, J. M. "The Pattern of Crime in England, 1660–1800." *Past and Present*, no. 62 (February 1974): 47–95.

17.2.4.2 DATE OF PUBLICATION. The date of publication appears in parentheses after the volume number and issue information. Follow the practice of the journal regarding date information; it must include the year and may include a season, a month, or an exact day. Capitalize seasons in journal citations, even though they are not capitalized in text.

N: 1. Marjorie Garber, "Over the Influence," *Critical Inquiry* 42, no. 4 (Summer 2016): 735, https://doi.org/10.1086/686960.

B: Bartfeld, Judi, and Myoung Kim. "Participation in the School Breakfast Program: New Evidence from the ECLS-K." *Social Service Review* 84, no. 4 (December 2010): 541–62. https://doi.org/10.1086/657109.

If an article has been accepted for publication but has not yet appeared, use *forthcoming* in place of the date and page numbers. Treat any article not yet accepted for publication as an unpublished manuscript (see 17.7.4).

N: 2. Margaret M. Author, "Article Title," *Journal Name* 98 (forthcoming).

B: Author, Margaret M. "Article Title." *Journal Name* 98 (forthcoming).

17.2.5 Page Numbers

If you cite a particular passage in a note, give only the specific page(s) cited. For a bibliography entry or a note that cites the entire article, give the full span of page numbers for the article (see 23.2.4). By convention, page numbers of journal articles follow colons rather than commas.

N: 1. Tim Hitchcock, "Begging on the Streets of Eighteenth-Century London," *Journal of British Studies* 44, no. 3 (July 2005): 478, https://doi.org/10.1086/429704.

B: Wang, ShiPu. "We Are Scottsboro Boys: Hideo Noda's Visual Rhetoric of Transracial Solidarity." *American Art* 30, no. 1 (Spring 2016): 16–20. https://doi.org/10.1086/686545.

17.2.6 Special Issues and Supplements

A journal issue devoted to a single theme is known as a *special issue*. It carries a normal volume and issue number. If a special issue has a title and an editor of its own, include both in the citations. The title is given in roman type and enclosed in quotation marks.

N: 1. Rajeswari Sunder Rajan, "Zeitgeist and the Literary Text: India, 1947, in Qurratulain Hyder's *My Temples, Too* and Salman Rushdie's *Midnight's Children*," in "Around 1948: Interdisciplinary Approaches to Global Transformation," ed. Leela Gandhi and Deborah L. Nelson, special issue, *Critical Inquiry* 40, no. 4 (Summer 2014): 440–41, https://doi.org/10.1086/676415.

B: Sunder Rajan, Rajeswari. "Zeitgeist and the Literary Text: India, 1947, in Qurratulain Hyder's *My Temples, Too* and Salman Rushdie's *Midnight's Children*." In "Around 1948: Interdisciplinary Approaches to Global Transformation," edited by Leela Gandhi and Deborah L. Nelson. Special issue, *Critical Inquiry* 40, no. 4 (Summer 2014): 439–65. https://doi.org/10.1086/676415.

If you need to cite the issue as a whole, omit the article information.

B: Gandhi, Leela, and Deborah L. Nelson, eds. "Around 1948: Interdisciplinary Approaches to Global Transformation." Special issue, *Critical Inquiry* 40, no. 4 (Summer 2014).

A journal *supplement* may also have a title and an author or editor of its own. Unlike a special issue, it is numbered separately from the regular issues of the journal, often with S as part of its page numbers. Use a comma between the volume number and the supplement number.

N: 2. Ivar Ekeland, James J. Heckman, and Lars Nesheim, "Identification and Estimation of Hedonic Models," in "Papers in Honor of Sherwin Rosen," *Journal of Political Economy* 112, S1 (February 2004): S72, https://doi.org/10.1086/379947.

B: Ekeland, Ivar, James J. Heckman, and Lars Nesheim. "Identification and Estimation of Hedonic Models." In "Papers in Honor of Sherwin Rosen," *Journal of Political Economy* 112, S1 (February 2004): S60–S109. https://doi.org/10.1086/379947.

17.2.7 Abstracts

You can cite information in the abstract of a journal article or other work in a note. Include the full citation for the journal article (or other work, such as a dissertation) and insert the word *abstract* within the citation, following the title.

N: 1. Campbell Brown, "Consequentialize This," abstract, *Ethics* 121, no. 4 (July 2011): 749.

In your bibliography, cite the full article (or other work) and not the abstract.

17.3 Magazine Articles

Articles in magazines are cited much like journal articles (see 17.2), but dates and page numbers are treated differently.

Cite magazines by date only, even if they are numbered by volume and issue. Do not enclose the date in parentheses. If you cite a specific passage in a note, include its page number. But you may omit the article's inclusive page numbers in a bibliography entry, since magazine articles often span many pages that include extraneous material. If you include page numbers, use a comma rather than a colon to separate them from the date of issue. As with journals, you can omit an initial *The* from the magazine title (see also 22.3.2.1).

N: 1. Jill Lepore, "The Woman Card," *New Yorker*, June 27, 2016, 23.

B: Lepore, Jill. "The Woman Card." *New Yorker*, June 27, 2016.

If you cite a department or column that appears regularly, capitalize it headline-style and do not enclose it in quotation marks.

N: 2. Barbara Wallraff, Word Court, *Atlantic Monthly*, June 2005, 128.

Magazine articles consulted online should include a URL (see 15.4.1.3) or the name of a commercial database (see 15.4.1.4). Typically there will be no page numbers to cite.

N: 3. Gabriel Roth, "Old England's Overthrow," *Slate*, June 24, 2016, http://www.slate.com /articles/news_and_politics/politics/2016/06/the_british_establishment_conspired _with_voters_to_destroy_itself.html.

4. Michael K. Williams, interview by Eliana Dockterman, *Time*, July 25, 2016, EBSCO-host.

B: Lukianoff, Greg, and Jonathan Haidt. "The Coddling of the American Mind." *Atlantic*, September 2015. http://www.theatlantic.com/magazine/archive/2015/09/the-coddling -of-the-american-mind/399356/.

Magazine articles published online sometimes include readers' comments. These are cited like comments on blog posts (see 17.5.2).

17.4   Newspaper Articles

17.4.1   Name of Newspaper

You can usually omit an initial *The* from the name of an English-language newspaper (see also 22.3.2.1). If the name of a local newspaper does not include a city, it may be added to the official title. If a name is shared by many cities or is obscure, you may add the state or province in parentheses (for abbreviations, see 24.3.1); for national papers, you may need to identify the country. For non-English newspapers, you may use headline-style capitalization, but retain an initial article if it is formally part of the name; add city or other information after titles for clarity, if necessary.

Chicago Tribune	*Le Monde*
New York Times	*La Crónica de Hoy* (Mexico City)
Hackensack (NJ) Record	*Al-Akhbar* (Beirut)
Saint Paul (Alberta or *AB) Journal*	*Times* (UK)

The name of a news website can usually be treated in a similar way, except that a location will rarely be necessary.

Huffington Post	*Vox*

For blogs, which are treated similarly, see 17.5.2. For websites, see 17.5.1.

17.4.2   Citing Newspapers in Notes

In most cases, cite articles and other pieces from newspapers (or news websites) only in notes. Include a specific article in your bibliography only if it is critical to your argument or frequently cited.

Follow the general pattern for citation of articles in magazines (see 17.3). Omit page numbers, even for a printed edition, because a newspaper may have several editions in which items may appear on different pages or may even be dropped. You may clarify which edition you consulted by adding *final edition*, *Midwest edition*, or whatever applies. Articles read online should include a URL. For articles obtained through a commercial database, you may give the name of the database instead. See 15.4.1 for more details.

N: 1. "Residency Ruling: State Supreme Court Guts Local Control," *Milwaukee Journal Sentinel*, editorial, June 24, 2016.

2. Fergus McIntosh, letter to the editor, *New York Times*, June 24, 2016.

3. John Pareles, obituary for David Bowie, *New York Times*, January 26, 2016, New York edition.

4. Saif al-Islam Gaddafi, interview by Simon Denyer, *Washington Post*, April 17, 2011.

5. Rob Pegoraro, "Apple's iPhone Is Sleek, Smart and Simple," *Washington Post*, July 5, 2007, LexisNexis Academic.

6. Associated Press, "Ex UConn Student Applies for Probation over Mac and Cheese Meltdown," *USA Today College*, November 23, 2015, http://college.usatoday.com/2015/11/23/mac-and-cheese-uconn-probation/.

7. Erin Anderssen, "Through the Eyes of Generation Z," *Globe and Mail* (Toronto), June 25, 2016, http://www.theglobeandmail.com/news/national/through-the-eyes-of-generation-z/article30571914/.

8. Dara Lind, "Moving to Canada, Explained," *Vox*, September 15, 2016, http://www.vox.com/2016/5/9/11608830/move-to-canada-how.

B: Svrluga, Susan. "Harvard Law School Will No Longer Require LSAT for Admission." *Washington Post*, March 9, 2017. https://www.washingtonpost.com/news/grade-point/wp/2017/03/08/harvard-law-school-will-no-longer-require-the-lsat-for-admission/.

To cite a comment, refer to a shortened form of the article (which must be cited or mentioned in full elsewhere). See also 17.5.2.

N: 9. Lauren K., March 9, 2017, comment on Svrluga, "Harvard Law School."

Articles from Sunday "magazine" supplements or other special sections should be treated as you would magazine articles (see 17.3).

17.4.3 Citing Newspapers in Text

Often you will be able to cite an article by weaving several key elements into your text. At a minimum, include the name and date of the paper and the author of the article (if any). Some of this information can appear in parentheses, even if it does not follow the form for parenthetical notes described in 16.4.3.

In his op-ed in support of a challenge by students over the use of Woodrow Wilson's name at Princeton (*New York Times*, November 24, 2015), Davis traces the negative impact of Wilson's policies on his paternal grandfather's career at the Government Printing Office.

17.5   Websites, Blogs, and Social Media

17.5.1   Website Content

Cite web pages and related content by identifying the following elements: author, title of the page (in roman type, enclosed in quotation marks), title (or description) of the site (usually in roman type; see 22.3.2.3), the owner or sponsor of the site (if not the same as the title), and a publication or revision date. Include a URL as the final element (see 15.4.1.3).

For a frequently updated source (such as a wiki), you can record a time stamp if the source includes one. If no date can be determined from the source, include an access date (see 15.4.1.5). Cite website content in the notes; include a specific item in your bibliography only if it is critical to your argument or frequently cited.

N: 1. "Privacy Policy," Privacy & Terms, Google, last modified March 25, 2016, http://www.google.com/policies/privacy/.

2. "Balkan Romani," Endangered Languages, Alliance for Linguistic Diversity, accessed June 10, 2016, http://www.endangeredlanguages.com/lang/5342.

3. "Wikipedia: Manual of Style," Wikimedia Foundation, last modified June 27, 2016, 09:57, http://en.wikipedia.org/wiki/Wikipedia:Manual_of_Style.

4. Susan B. Higgins, "High School Students Explore Key Issues Facing American Indian Communities," News at Princeton, Princeton University, June 23, 2016, https://www.princeton.edu/main/news/archive/S46/66/02A46/.

5. "History," Columbia University, accessed July 1, 2016, http://www.columbia.edu/content/history.html.

In a bibliography, list a source that doesn't include an author under the title of the website or the name of its owner or sponsor.

B: Google. "Privacy Policy." Privacy & Terms. Last modified March 25, 2016. http://www.google.com/intl/en/privacypolicy.html.

Articles from news websites can usually be cited like articles in newspapers (see 17.4). For blogs, see 17.5.2.

17.5.2   Blog Posts

Blog posts (also called entries) are similar to articles in magazines and newspapers and can be cited in much the same way (see 17.3 and 17.4). Put the title of the post in quotation marks and the title of the blog in italics (you can indicate "blog" in parentheses if it is not clear from the title). If the blog is part of a larger publication such as a newspaper or website, give the name of the publication after the title of the blog. Citations of blog posts can usually be limited to notes. Include a specific item in your bibliography only if it is critical to your argument or frequently cited; if you cite multiple posts from the same blog, you may choose to cite the blog as a whole in the bibliography.

N: 1. Sharon Jayson, "Is Selfie Culture Making Our Kids Selfish?," *Well* (blog), *New York Times*, June 23, 2016, http://well.blogs.nytimes.com/2016/06/23/is-selfie-culture -making-our-kids-selfish/.

2. Lindy West, "Sweden Introduces New Gender-Neutral Pronoun, Makes Being a Man ILLEGAL," *Jezebel*, April 11, 2013, http://jezebel.com/sweden-introduces-new -gender-neutral-pronoun-makes-bei-472492079.

3. William Germano, "Futurist Shock," *Lingua Franca* (blog), *Chronicle of Higher Education*, February 15, 2017, http://www.chronicle.com/blogs/linguafranca/2017/02/15 /futurist-shock/.

B: Germano, William. "Futurist Shock." *Lingua Franca* (blog). *Chronicle of Higher Education*, February 15, 2017, http://www.chronicle.com/blogs/linguafranca/2017/02/15/futurist -shock/.

or

Lingua Franca (blog). *Chronicle of Higher Education*. http://www.chronicle.com/blogs /linguafranca/.

Comments can be cited in terms of a shortened form of the original post (which must be cited or mentioned in full elsewhere). Cite the name exactly as it appears, along with any identifying information in parentheses. List the date of the comment rather than the date of the post (though they may be the same).

N: 4. Muberra (Istanbul), June 26, 2016, comment on Jayson, "Selfie Culture."

17.5.3 Social Media

Social media content is normally cited in the text or notes but not in the bibliography. Include a specific item in your bibliography only if it is critical to your argument or frequently cited. To cite direct messages and other personal or private content, follow the guidelines for citing personal communications (see 17.6.2). For publicly posted content, model your citations on the examples shown here. Include the following elements:

1. The author of the post. List a screen name in addition to the name of the person or group on the account, if known. Otherwise, just use the screen name.

2. In place of a title, the text of the post. Quote up to the first 160 characters (enough to capture the typical text message), capitalized as in the original. (If you quoted the post in your text, there is no need to repeat it in a note.)

3. The type of post. This can include a description (*photo*, *video*, etc.).
4. The date, including month, day, and year. You can also include a time stamp to help differentiate a post from others on the same day.
5. A URL. A URL can often be found via the date stamp for the item.

Comments are cited in reference to a shortened form of the original post, which must be cited in full elsewhere. Like newspaper articles or blog posts, social media can often be cited in the text, as in the first example. If it is especially important to link back to the original post, use a note instead.

Conan O'Brien's tweet was characteristically deadpan: "In honor of Earth Day, I'm recycling my tweets" (@ConanOBrien, April 22, 2015).

N: 1. Junot Díaz, "Always surprises my students when I tell them that the 'real' medieval was more diverse than the fake ones most of us consume," Facebook, February 24, 2016, https://www.facebook.com/junotdiaz.writer/posts/972495572815454.

2. Conan O'Brien (@ConanOBrien), "In honor of Earth Day, I'm recycling my tweets," Twitter, April 22, 2015, 11:10 a.m., https://twitter.com/ConanOBrien/status/590940792967016448.

3. Chicago Manual of Style, "Is the world ready for singular they? We thought so back in 1993," Facebook, April 17, 2015, https://www.facebook.com/ChicagoManual/posts/10152906193679151.

4. Pete Souza (@petesouza), "President Obama bids farewell to President Xi of China at the conclusion of the Nuclear Security Summit," Instagram photo, April 1, 2016, https://www.instagram.com/p/BDrmfXTtNCt/.

5. Kristaps Licis, February 24, 2016, comment on Díaz, "Always surprises."

6. Michele Truty, April 17, 2015, comment on Chicago Manual of Style, "singular they."

B: Chicago Manual of Style. "Is the world ready for singular they? We thought so back in 1993." Facebook, April 17, 2015. https://www.facebook.com/ChicagoManual/posts/10152906193679151.

Items shared on social media tend to disappear; always keep a screenshot of whatever you cite in case you need to refer to it later (see also 15.4.1.1).

17.5.4   Online Forums and Mailing Lists

To cite material from an online forum or mailing list, include the name of the correspondent, the title of the subject or thread (in quotation marks and capitalized as in the original), the name of the forum or list, and the date and time of the post or message. Omit email addresses. (Posts on private forums or lists should be cited as personal communications; see 17.6.2.) Include a URL (see 15.4.1.3). As with social media (see 17.5.3), such items should normally be cited in a note but may instead be incorporated into the text.

N: 1. Caroline Braun, reply to "How did the 'cool kids' from high school turn out?," Quora, August 9, 2016, https://www.quora.com/How-did-the-cool-kids-from-high-school-turn -out/.

2. Sharon Naylor, "Removing a Thesis," email to Educ. & Behavior Science ALA Discussion List, August 23, 2011 (1:47:54 p.m. ET), http://listserv.uncc.edu/archives/ebss-1 .html.

or

Sharon Naylor, in her email of August 23, 2011, to the Educ. & Behavior Science ALA Discussion List (http://listserv.uncc.edu/archives/ebss-1.html), pointed out that . . .

17.6   Interviews and Personal Communications

17.6.1   Interviews

Unpublished interviews (including those you have conducted yourself) should usually be cited only in notes. Include a specific interview in your bibliography only if it is critical to your argument or frequently cited. Begin the note with the names of the person interviewed and the interviewer; also include the place and date of the interview (if known) and the location of any recordings or transcripts (if available). Notice the form for a shortened note, which differs from the usual pattern (see 16.4.1).

N: 1. David Shields, interview by author, Seattle, July 22, 2016.

2. Benjamin Spock, interview by Milton J. E. Senn, November 20, 1974, interview 67A, transcript, Senn Oral History Collection, National Library of Medicine, Bethesda, MD.

3. Shields, interview; Spock, interview.

If you cannot reveal the name of the person interviewed, cite it in a form appropriate to the context. Explain the absence of a name ("All interviews were confidential; the names of interviewees are withheld by mutual agreement") in a note or a preface.

N: 4. Interview with a home health aide, July 31, 2017.

Cite a published interview according to the rules for that type of publication, with one difference: the interviewee is treated as author. If the identity of the interviewee is clear from the title, it need not be repeated in a note but should be listed in a bibliography.

N.   5. "Edward Snowden Explains How to Reclaim Your Privacy," interview by Micah Lee, *The Intercept*, November 12, 2015, https://theintercept.com/2015/11/12/edward-snowden -explains-how-to-reclaim-your-privacy/.

B.   Snowden, Edward. "Edward Snowden Explains How to Reclaim Your Privacy." Interview by Micah Lee. *The Intercept*, November 12, 2015. https://theintercept.com/2015/11/12 /edward-snowden-explains-how-to-reclaim-your-privacy/.

For more examples, see 17.3 (magazine), 17.4.2 (newspaper), 17.10.3.6 (video). See also 22.3.2.1.

17.6.2 Personal Communications

Cite conversations, letters, email or text messages, and direct or private messages shared through social media only in notes. The key elements are the name of the other person, the type of communication, and the date of the communication. In many cases, you may be able to use a parenthetical note (see 16.4.3) or include some or all of this information in the text. Omit email addresses. To cite content shared publicly through social media, see 17.5.3; for online forums and mailing lists, see 17.5.4. To cite letters in published collections, see 17.1.9. For items in manuscript collections, see 17.7.4.

In a conversation with me on March 1, 2017, Carla C. Ramirez confirmed that . . .

A copy of the postcard, postmarked San Diego, March 7, 1965 (Emma Fenton to author, Instagram direct message, March 25, 2017), . . .

N: 1. Roland J. Zuckerman, email message to author, June 1, 2017.

17.7   Papers, Lectures, and Manuscript Collections

17.7.1 Theses and Dissertations

Theses and dissertations are cited much like books except for the title, which is in roman type and enclosed in quotation marks. After the author and title, list the kind of paper, the academic institution, and the date. Like the publication data for a book, these are enclosed in parentheses in a note but not in a bibliography. Abbreviate *dissertation* as *diss.* If you've consulted the paper online, include a URL. If you consulted the paper in an institutional repository or commercial database, you can list the name of the repository or database instead. See 15.4.1 for more details.

N: 1. Karen Leigh Culcasi, "Cartographic Representations of Kurdistan in the Print Media" (master's thesis, Syracuse University, 2003), 15.

2. Dana S. Levin, "Let's Talk about Sex . . . Education: Exploring Youth Perspectives, Implicit Messages, and Unexamined Implications of Sex Education in Schools" (PhD diss., University of Michigan, 2010), 101–2, http://hdl.handle.net/2027.42/75809.

3. Guadalupe Navarro-Garcia, "Integrating Social Justice Values in Educational Leadership: A Study of African American and Black University Presidents" (PhD diss., University of California, Los Angeles, 2016), 44, ProQuest Dissertations & Theses Global.

B: Navarro-Garcia, Guadalupe. "Integrating Social Justice Values in Educational Leadership: A Study of African American and Black University Presidents." PhD diss., University of California, Los Angeles, 2016. ProQuest Dissertations & Theses Global.

17.7.2 Lectures and Papers Presented at Meetings

Cite a lecture or a paper presented at a meeting by the name of the speaker or presenter and the title of the speech or presentation (in quotation marks), followed by the sponsorship and location of the meeting and the date of the speech or presentation. Information about the meeting is enclosed in parentheses in a note but not in a bibliography. If you consulted a text or transcript of the lecture or paper online, include a URL (see 15.4.1.3). If you watched or listened to the presentation online, adapt the examples here to the advice at 17.10.3.3.

N: 1. Viviana Hong, "Censorship in Children's Literature during Argentina's Dirty War (1976–1983)" (lecture, University of Chicago, Chicago, IL, April 30, 2015).

2. Julie Leininger Pycior, "Trailblazers and Harbingers: Mexicans in New York before 1970" (paper presented at the 130th annual meeting of the American Historical Society, Atlanta, GA, January 8, 2016).

B: Carvalho Filho, Irineu de, and Renato P. Colistete. "Education Performance: Was It All Determined 100 Years Ago? Evidence from São Paulo, Brazil." Paper presented at the 70th annual meeting of the Economic History Association, Evanston, IL, September 24-26, 2010. http://mpra.ub.uni-muenchen.de/24494/1/MPRA_paper _24494.pdf.

17.7.3 Pamphlets and Reports

Cite a pamphlet, corporate report, brochure, or similar freestanding publication as you would a book. If you lack data for some of the usual elements, such as author and publisher, give enough other information to identify the document. Such sources should usually be cited only in notes. Include such an item in your bibliography only if it is critical to your argument or frequently cited. Sources consulted online should include a URL (see 15.4.1.3).

N: 1. Hazel V. Clark, *Mesopotamia: Between Two Rivers* (Mesopotamia, OH: Trumbull County Historical Society, 1957).

2. Elisabeth Hirschhorn Donahue, ed., *Woodrow Wilson School of Public and International Affairs: Annual Report 2014-15* (Princeton, NJ: Princeton University, 2015), http://wws.princeton.edu/about-wws/wws-annual-report.

17.7.4 Manuscript Collections

Documents from physical collections of unpublished manuscripts involve more complicated and varied elements than published sources. In your citations, include as much identifying information as you can, format the elements consistently, and adapt the general patterns outlined here as needed.

17.7.4.1 **ELEMENTS TO INCLUDE AND THEIR ORDER.** If possible, identify the author and date of each item, the title or type of document, the name of the collection, and the name of the depository. In a note, begin with the author's name; if a document has a title but no author, or the title is more important than the author, list the title first.

N: 1. George Creel to Colonel House, September 25, 1918, Edward M. House Papers, Yale University Library, New Haven, CT.

2. James Oglethorpe to the Trustees, January 13, 1733, Phillipps Collection of Egmont Manuscripts, 14200:13, University of Georgia Library, Athens (hereafter cited as Egmont MSS).

3. Burton to Merriam, telegram, January 26, 1923, box 26, folder 17, Charles E. Merriam Papers, University of Chicago Library.

4. Minutes of the Committee for Improving the Condition of Free Blacks, Pennsylvania Abolition Society, 1790–1803, Papers of the Pennsylvania Society for the Abolition of Slavery, Historical Society of Pennsylvania, Philadelphia (hereafter cited as Minutes, Pennsylvania Society).

5. Memorandum by Alvin Johnson, 1937, file 36, Horace Kallen Papers, YIVO Institute, New York.

6. Joseph Purcell, "A Map of the Southern Indian District of North America" [ca. 1772], MS 228, Ayer Collection, Newberry Library, Chicago.

For shortened notes, adapt the usual pattern of elements (see 16.4.1) to accommodate the available information and identify the document unambiguously.

N: 7. R. S. Baker to House, November 1, 1919, House Papers.

8. Minutes, April 15, 1795, Pennsylvania Society.

If you cite only one document from a collection and it is critical to your argument or frequently cited within your paper, you may choose to include it in your bibliography. Begin the entry with the author's name; if a document has a title but no author, or the title is more important than the author, list the title first.

B: Dinkel, Joseph. Description of Louis Agassiz written at the request of Elizabeth Cary Agassiz. 1869. Agassiz Papers. Houghton Library, Harvard University, Cambridge, MA.

If you cite multiple documents from a collection, list the collection as a whole in your bibliography, under the name of the collection, the author(s) of the items in the collection, or the depository. For similar types of unpublished material that have not been placed in archives, replace information about the collection with such wording as "in the author's possession" or "private collection," and do not mention the location.

B: Egmont Manuscripts. Phillipps Collection. University of Georgia Library, Athens.

House, Edward M., Papers. Yale University Library, New Haven, CT.

Pennsylvania Society for the Abolition of Slavery. Papers. Historical Society of Pennsylvania, Philadelphia.

Strother, French, and Edward Lowry. Undated correspondence. Herbert Hoover Presidential Library, West Branch, IA.

Women's Organization for National Prohibition Reform. Papers. Alice Belin du Pont files, Pierre S. du Pont Papers. Eleutherian Mills Historical Library, Wilmington, DE.

17.7.4.2 HOW TO FORMAT THE ELEMENTS. Here are some special formatting recommendations for documents in manuscript collections.

- *Specific versus generic titles.* Use quotation marks for specific titles of documents but not for generic terms such as *report* and *minutes.* Capitalize generic names of this kind only if they are part of a formal heading in the manuscript, not if they are merely descriptive.
- *Locating information.* Although some manuscripts may include page numbers that can be included in notes, many will have other types of locators, or none at all. Older manuscripts are usually numbered by signatures only or by folios (*fol., fols.*) rather than by page. Some manuscript collections have identifying series or file numbers that you can include in a citation. Items on microfilm may have roll (or sheet) and frame numbers.
- *Papers and manuscripts.* In titles of manuscript collections the terms *papers* and *manuscripts* are synonymous. Both are acceptable, as are the abbreviations *MS* and *MSS* (plural).
- *Letters.* To cite a letter in a note, start with the name of the letter writer, followed by *to* and the name of the recipient. You may omit first names if the identities of the sender and the recipient are clear from the text. Omit the word *letter,* which is understood, but for other forms of communication, specify the type (telegram, memorandum). For letters in published collections, see 17.1.9.

17.7.5 **Online Collections**

Some manuscript collections have been scanned and organized for consultation online. Cite such items by adapting the rules for manuscript collections in 17.7.4. Include a URL for the item or items cited (see also 15.4.1.3).

N: 1. Daily Expenses, July 1787, images 7–8, George Washington Papers, Series 5: Financial Papers, 1750–96, Library of Congress, Washington, DC, http://memory.loc.gov/ammem/gwhtml/gwseries5.html.

B: Washington, George, Papers. Series 5: Financial Papers, 1750–96. Library of Congress, Washington, DC. http://memory.loc.gov/ammem/gwhtml/gwseries5.html.

17.8 Older Works and Sacred Works

17.8.1 Classical, Medieval, and Early English Literary Works

Literary works produced in classical Greece and Rome, medieval Europe, and Renaissance England are cited differently from modern literary works. These sources are often organized into numbered sections (books, lines, stanzas, and so forth) that are generally cited in place of page numbers. Because such works have been published in so many versions and translations over the centuries, the facts of publication for modern editions are generally less important than in other types of citations.

For this reason, classical, medieval, and early English literary works should usually be cited only in footnotes or, for frequently cited works, in parenthetical notes (see 16.4.3), as in the first example below. Include the author's name, the title, and the section number (given in arabic numerals). See below regarding differences in punctuation, abbreviations, and numbers among different types of works.

The eighty days of inactivity reported by Thucydides (8.44.4) for the Peloponnesian fleet at Rhodes, terminating before the end of winter (8.60.2–3), suggests . . .

N: 1. Ovid, *Amores* 1.7.27.
  2. *Beowulf*, lines 2401–7.
  3. Spenser, *The Faerie Queene*, bk. 2, canto 8, st. 14.

If your paper is in literary studies or another field concerned with close analysis of texts, or if differences in translations are relevant, include such works in your bibliography. Follow the rules for other translated and edited books in 17.1.1.1.

N: 4. Propertius, *Elegies*, ed. and trans. G. P. Goold, Loeb Classical Library 18 (Cambridge, MA: Harvard University Press, 1990), 45.

B: Aristotle. *Complete Works of Aristotle: The Revised Oxford Translation*. Edited by J. Barnes. 2 vols. Princeton, NJ: Princeton University Press, 1983.

17.8.1.1   CLASSICAL WORKS. In addition to the general principles listed above, the following rules apply to citations of classical works.

Use no punctuation between the title of a work and a line or section number. Numerical divisions are separated by periods without spaces. Use arabic numerals (and lowercase letters, if needed) for section numbers. Put commas between two or more citations of the same source and semicolons between citations of different sources.

N: 1. Aristophanes, *Frogs* 1019–30.
  2. Cicero, *In Verrem* 2.1.21, 2.3.120; Tacitus, *Germania* 10.2–3.
  3. Aristotle, *Metaphysics* 3.2.996b5–8; Plato, *Republic* 360e–361b.

You can abbreviate the names of authors, works, collections, and so forth. The most widely accepted abbreviations appear in the *Oxford Classical Dictionary*. Use these abbreviations rather than *ibid.* in succeeding references to the same work. In the first example, the author (Thucydides) stands in for the title so no comma is needed.

N: 4. Thuc. 2.40.2–3.
5. Pindar, *Isthm.* 7.43–45.

17.8.1.2   MEDIEVAL WORKS. The form for classical references works equally well for medieval works written in languages other than English.

N: 1. Augustine, *De civitate Dei* 20.2.
2. Abelard, *Epistle 17 to Heloïse* (Migne, *PL* 180.375c–378a).

17.8.1.3   EARLY ENGLISH WORKS. In addition to the general principles listed above, the following rules apply to citations of early English literary works.

Cite poems and plays by book, canto, and stanza; stanza and line; act, scene, and line; or similar divisions.

N: 1. Chaucer, "Wife of Bath's Prologue," *Canterbury Tales,* lines 105–14.
2. Milton, *Paradise Lost,* book 1, lines 83–86.

You may shorten numbered divisions by omitting words such as *act* and *line*, using a system similar to the one for classical references (see 17.8.1.1). Be sure to explain your system in the first note.

N: 3. Milton, *Paradise Lost* 1.83–86 (references are to book and line numbers).

If editions differ in wording, line numbering, and even scene division—common in works of Shakespeare—include the work in your bibliography, with edition specified. If you do not have a bibliography, specify the edition in the first note.

B: Shakespeare, William. *Hamlet.* Edited by Ann Thompson and Neil Taylor. Arden Shakespeare 3. London: Arden Shakespeare, 2006.

17.8.2   The Bible and Other Sacred Works

Cite the Bible and sacred works of other religious traditions in footnotes, endnotes, or parenthetical notes (see 16.4.3). You do not need to include these works in your bibliography.

For citations from the Bible, include the abbreviated name of the book, the chapter number, and the verse number—never a page number. Depending on the context, you may use either traditional or shorter abbreviations for the names of books (see 24.6); consult your instructor if you are unsure which form is appropriate. Use arabic numerals for chapter and verse numbers (with a colon between them) and for numbered books.

Traditional abbreviations:

N: 1. 1 Thess. 4:11, 5:2–5, 5:14.

Shorter abbreviations:

N: 2. 2 Sm 11:1–17, 11:26–27; 1 Chr 10:13–14.

Since books and numbering differ among versions of the scriptures, identify the version you are using in your first citation with either the spelled-out name or an accepted abbreviation (see 24.6.4).

N: 3. 2 Kings 11:8 (New Revised Standard Version).
4. 1 Cor. 6:1–10 (NAB).

For citations from the sacred works of other religious traditions, adapt the general pattern for biblical citations as appropriate (see 24.6.5).

17.9   Reference Works and Secondary Citations

17.9.1   Reference Works

Well-known reference works, such as major dictionaries and encyclopedias, should usually be cited only in notes. You generally need not include them in your bibliography, although you may choose to include a specific work that is critical to your argument or frequently cited. Within the note, you may omit the facts of publication, but you must specify the edition (if not the first, or unless no edition is specified). Items consulted online will require a URL (see 15.4.1.3); for undated items, include an access date (see 15.4.1.5). For a work arranged by key terms such as a dictionary or encyclopedia, cite the item (not the volume or page number) preceded by s.v. (*sub verbo*, "under the word"; pl. *s.vv.*).

N: 1. *Oxford English Dictionary*, s.v. "ROFL," accessed March 9, 2017, http://www.oed.com/view/Entry/156942#eid1211161030.
2. *Encyclopaedia Britannica*, s.v. "Dame Margaret Drabble," accessed June 26, 2016, http://www.britannica.com/biography/Margaret-Drabble.

Reference works on disk should include information about the medium.

B: *Oxford English Dictionary*. 2nd ed. New York: Oxford University Press, 2009. CD-ROM, version 4.0.

For reference works that are more specialized or less well known, include the publication details in your notes, and list the work in your bibliography.

N: 3. *MLA Handbook*, 8th ed. (New York: Modern Language Association of America, 2016), 3.3.2.

B: Aulestia, Gorka. *Basque–English Dictionary*. Reno: University of Nevada Press, 1989.

An individual entry by a named author can be cited like a chapter in a book (see 17.1.8).

17.9.2   Reviews

Reviews of books, performances, and so forth may appear in a variety of periodicals and other sources and should usually be cited only in a note. Include a specific review in your bibliography only if it is critical to your argument or frequently cited.

Include the name of the reviewer; the words *review of*, followed by the name of the work reviewed and its author (or composer, director, or the like); any other pertinent information (such as film studio or location of a performance); and, finally, the periodical or other source in which the review appeared. If the review was consulted online, include a URL (see 15.4.1.3).

N: 1. Richard Williams, review of Bob Dylan in concert at the Royal Albert Hall, London, UK, *Guardian*, October 22, 2015, https://www.theguardian.com/music/2015/oct/22/bob-dylan-review-royal-albert-hall-london.

2. Richard Brody, review of *Gravity*, directed by Alfonso Cuarón, Warner Bros. Pictures, *New Yorker*, October 4, 2013.

B: Cox, Katharine. Review of *Covered in Ink: Tattoos, Women, and the Politics of the Body*, by Beverly Yuen Thompson. *Journal of Gender Studies* 25, no. 3 (2016): 349–50. https://doi.org/10.1080/09589236.2016.1171889.

17.9.3   One Source Quoted in Another

Responsible researchers avoid repeating quotations that they have not actually seen in the original. If one source includes a useful quotation from another source, readers expect you to obtain the original to verify not only that the quotation is accurate but also that it fairly represents what the original meant.

If the original source is unavailable, however, cite it as "quoted in" the secondary source in your note. For the bibliography entry, adapt the "quoted in" format as needed.

N: 1. Louis Zukofsky, "Sincerity and Objectification," *Poetry* 37 (February 1931): 269, quoted in Bonnie Costello, *Marianne Moore: Imaginary Possessions* (Cambridge, MA: Harvard University Press, 1981), 78.

B: Zukofsky, Louis. "Sincerity and Objectification." *Poetry* 37 (February 1931): 269. Quoted in Bonnie Costello, *Marianne Moore: Imaginary Possessions* (Cambridge, MA: Harvard University Press, 1981).

The same situation may arise with a quotation you find in a secondary source drawn from a primary source (see 3.1). Often you will not be able to consult the primary source, especially if it is in an unpublished manuscript collection. In this case, follow the principles outlined above.

If, however, you consult a primary document or other work exhibited by the holding institution as part of an online collection (as opposed to a copy posted by someone else), such a source can usually be considered primary for the purposes of research. See 17.7.5 and 17.10.1.1 for examples.

17.10 Sources in the Visual and Performing Arts

The visual and performing arts generate a variety of sources, including artworks, live performances, broadcasts and streams, recordings in various media, and texts. Citing these sources involves determining which elements are needed to fully identify them, formatting the elements consistently, and adapting the general patterns outlined here as needed.

Some of the sources covered in this section, where noted, can be cited in notes only or by weaving the key elements into your text, although you may choose to include a specific item in your bibliography that is critical to your argument or frequently cited. If your paper is for a course in the arts, media studies, or a similar field, consult your instructor.

17.10.1 Artworks and Graphics

17.10.1.1 PAINTINGS, SCULPTURES, AND PHOTOGRAPHS. Cite paintings, sculptures, photographs, drawings, and the like only in notes. Include the name of the artist, the title of the artwork (in italics) and date of its creation (preceded by "ca." [circa] if approximate), and the name of the institution that houses it (if any), including location. You may also include the medium and related information, if relevant. For images consulted online, include a URL (see also 15.4.1.3). Whenever possible, consult the item through the website of the institution at which the item is physically located.

N: 1. Georgia O'Keeffe, *The Cliff Chimneys*, 1938, oil on canvas, Milwaukee Art Museum, http://collection.mam.org/details.php?id=11207.

2. Michelangelo, *David*, 1501–4, Galleria dell'Accademia, Florence.

3. Ansel Adams, *North Dome, Basket Dome, Mount Hoffman, Yosemite*, ca. 1935, silver print, 16.5 × 21.9 cm, Smithsonian American Art Museum, Renwick Gallery, Washington, DC, http://edan.si.edu/saam/id/object/1994.91.1.

4. Erich Buchholz, *Untitled*, 1920, gouache on paper, Museum of Modern Art, New York, http://www.moma.org/collection/works/38187.

Instead of using a note, you can sometimes cite artworks by weaving the elements into your text. Some of the elements can appear in parentheses, even if they do not follow the form for parenthetical notes described in 16.4.3.

O'Keeffe first demonstrated this technique in *The Cliff Chimneys* (1938, Milwaukee Art Museum).

If you viewed the artwork in the context of another work such as a book and your local guidelines require you to identify this source, give the publication information in place of the institutional name and location.

N: 5. Georgia O'Keeffe, *The Cliff Chimneys*, 1938, in Barbara Buhler Lynes, Lesley Poling-Kempes, and Frederick W. Turner, *Georgia O'Keeffe and New Mexico: A Sense of Place* (Princeton, NJ: Princeton University Press, 2004), 25.

17.10.1.2 GRAPHIC ARTS. Cite graphic sources such as print advertisements, maps, cartoons, and so forth only in notes, adapting the basic patterns for artworks and giving as much information as possible. Give any title or caption in roman type, enclosed in quotation marks, and identify the type of graphic, in parentheses, if it is unclear from the title. For items consulted online, include a URL (see 15.4.1.3); for undated sources, also include an access date (see 15.4.1.5).

N: 1. Apple Inc., "Shot on iPhone 6S by Anh N.," full-page advertisement, *New Yorker*, July 4, 2016, back cover.

2. *Yu ji tu* [Map of the tracks of Yu], AD 1136, Forest of Stone Steles Museum, Xi'an, China, stone rubbing, 1933?, 84 × 82 cm, Library of Congress, http://www.loc.gov/item /gm71005080/.

3. Chrissy Teigen crying at the 2015 Golden Globe Awards, animated GIF, GIPHY, accessed July 3, 2016, http://giphy.com/gifs/girl-lol-crying-P2kEMJjHosUUg.

4. Evan Brown, "The 10 Commandments of Typography," infographic, DesignMantic, April 11, 2014. http://www.designmantic.com/blog/infographics/ten-commandments-of -typography/.

17.10.2 Live Performances

Cite live theatrical, musical, or dance performances only in notes. Include the title of the work performed, the author, any key contributors or performers and an indication of their roles, the venue and its location, and the date. Italicize the titles of plays and long musical compositions, but set the titles of shorter works in roman type, enclosed in quotation marks except for musical works referred to by genre (see 22.3.2.3).

N: 1. *Hamilton*, music and lyrics by Lin-Manuel Miranda, directed by Thomas Kail, choreographed by Andy Blakenbuehler, Richard Rodgers Theatre, New York, NY, February 2, 2016.

2. Simone Dinnerstein, pianist, Intermezzo in A, op. 118, no. 2, by Johannes Brahms, Portland Center for the Performing Arts, Portland, OR, January 15, 2012.

Instead of using a note, you may be able to weave the elements into your text. Some of the elements can appear in parentheses, even if they do not follow the form for parenthetical notes described in 16.4.3.

Simone Dinnerstein's performance of Brahms's Intermezzo in A, op. 118, no. 2 (January 15, 2012, at Portland Center for the Performing Arts), was anything but intermediate . . .

To cite recordings and broadcasts of live performances, add information about the medium. See 17.10.3 for similar types of examples.

N: 3. Artur Rubinstein, pianist, "Spinning Song," by Felix Mendelssohn, Ambassador College, Pasadena, CA, January 15, 1975, on *The Last Recital for Israel* (BMG Classics, 1992), VHS.

17.10.3 Multimedia

Citations of movies, television and radio programs, recorded music, and other works in multimedia formats will vary depending on the type of source. At a minimum, identify the title of the work, the date it was created or published or otherwise made available, the name of the studio or other entity responsible for producing or distributing the work, and information about the medium in which you consulted it. If you consulted the source online, include a URL (see 15.4.1.3).

17.10.3.1 MOVIES. In the notes, list the title of the movie (in italics) followed by the name of the director, the name of the company that produced or distributed the movie, and year the movie was released or created or otherwise made available. (You may also include a publication date for the recording.) Include information about writers, actors, producers, and so forth if it is relevant to your discussion. Finish with any relevant information about the medium (including timings as displayed with the source). If you watched online, include a URL (see 15.4.1.3).

N: 1. *Dr. Strangelove, or: How I Learned to Stop Worrying and Love the Bomb*, directed by Stanley Kubrick, featuring Peter Sellers, George C. Scott, and Sterling Hayden (Columbia, 1964), 0:11:43 to 0:14:54, https://www.amazon.com/dp/B000P407K4.

2. *Gravity*, directed by Alfonso Cuarón (2013; Warner Bros. Pictures, 2014), Blu-ray Disc, 1080p HD.

3. *Dope*, directed by Rick Famuyiwa (Open Road Films, 2015), https://www.netflix .com/watch/80037759.

4. A. E. Weed, *At the Foot of the Flatiron* (American Mutoscope and Biograph, 1903), 35mm film, from Library of Congress, *The Life of a City: Early Films of New York, 1898–1906*, MPEG video, 2:19 at 15 fps, https://www.loc.gov/item/00694378.

In the bibliography, you can list the movie either under the name of the director or under the title.

B: *Dope*. Directed by Rick Famuyiwa. Open Road Films, 2015. 1 hr., 43 min. https://www .netflix.com/watch/80037759.

or

Famuyiwa, Rick, director. *Dope*. Open Road Films, 2015. 1 hr., 43 min. https://www.netflix .com/watch/80037759.

Information about ancillary material included with the movie should be woven into the text.

In a special feature titled "Complete Silence," Cuarón acknowledges a tension between realism and audience expectations . . .

17.10.3.2 **TELEVISION AND RADIO PROGRAMS.** To cite a television or radio program include, at a minimum, the title of the program, the name of the episode or segment, the date on which it was first aired or made available, and the entity that produced or broadcast the work. You may also include an episode number, the name of the director or author of the episode or segment, and (if relevant to your discussion) the names of key performers. Italicize the titles of programs, but put the titles of episodes or segments in roman type, enclosed in quotation marks. Finish with any relevant information about the medium. If you watched online, include a URL (see 15.4.1.3).

N: 1. "Pen-Pal Passion Is Revived In Broadway's 'She Loves Me,' " hosted by David Bianculli, *Fresh Air*, on NPR, June 24, 2016, http://www.npr.org/2016/06/23/483245382 /pen-pal-passion-is-revived-in-broadways-she-loves-me.

2. *Mad Men*, season 1, episode 12, "Nixon vs. Kennedy," directed by Alan Taylor, featuring Jon Hamm, Elisabeth Moss, and Vincent Kartheiser, aired October 11, 2007, on AMC (Lions Gate Television, 2007), DVD, disc 4.

3. *Jane the Virgin*, season 2, chapter 36, directed by Uta Briesewitz, aired March 7, 2016, on the CW Television Network.

4. *American Crime Story: The People v. O. J. Simpson*, episode 6, "Marcia, Marcia, Marcia," directed by Ryan Murphy, written by D. V. DeVincentis, featuring Sterling K. Brown,

Kenneth Choi, and Sarah Paulson, aired March 8, 2016, on FX, https://www.amazon
.com/dp/Bo1ARVPCOA/.

5. *The Brady Bunch*, season 3, episode 10, "Her Sister's Shadow," directed by Russ
Mayberry, aired November 19, 1971, on ABC, https://www.hulu.com/the-brady-bunch.

Instead of using a note, you can often cite such programs by weaving
the key elements into your text, especially if some or all of the additional
elements are not relevant to the citation.

By alluding to *The Brady Bunch* (specifically "Her Sister's Shadow," from 1971), the title
of episode 6 ("Marcia, Marcia, Marcia," March 8, 2016) not only calls attention to the
central role of television in the trial but also . . .

In the bibliography, radio and television programs are normally cited
by the title of the program or series.

B: *Brady Bunch, The*. Season 3, episode 10, "Her Sister's Shadow." Directed by Russ Mayberry. Aired November 19, 1971, on ABC. https://www.hulu.com/the-brady-bunch.

17.10.3.3 **VIDEOS AND PODCASTS.** To cite videos other than movies (17.10.3.1) or
television programs (17.10.3.2), adapt the examples in those sections accordingly. To cite a podcast, adapt the example for citing a radio program
at 17.10.3.2.

N: 1. Beyoncé, "Sorry," directed by Kahlil Joseph and Beyoncé Knowles, June 22, 2016,
music video, 4:25, https://youtu.be/QxsmWxxoulM.

2. Fred Donner, "How Islam Began," Alumni Weekend 2011, University of Chicago,
June 3, 2011, video of lecture, https://youtu.be/5RFK5u51khA.

3. Mike Danforth and Ian Chillag, "F-Bombs, Chicken, and Exclamation Points,"
April 21, 2015, in *How to Do Everything*, produced by Gillian Donovan, podcast, MP3 audio, 18:46, http://www.npr.org/podcasts/510303/how-to-do-everything.

4. Aaron M. Kessler, "The Driverless Now," produced by Poh Si Teng and Jessica
Naudziunas, *New York Times*, May 2, 2015, video, 2:01, http://www.nytimes.com/video
/business/100000003662208/the-driverless-now.html.

Citations of videos and podcasts can normally be limited to the notes
or, like citations of newspaper articles, woven into the text (see 17.4.3).
If a source is critical to your paper or frequently cited, however, you may
include it in your bibliography.

B: Lyiscott, Jamila. "3 Ways to Speak English." Filmed February 2014 in New York, NY. TED
video, 4:29. https://www.ted.com/talks/jamila_lyiscott_3_ways_to_speak_english.

17.10.3.4 **SOUND RECORDINGS.** To cite recorded music and the like, include as much
information as you can to distinguish it from similar recordings, including the date of the recording, the name of the recording company, the

identifying number of the recording, the copyright date (if different from the year of the recording), and any relevant information about the medium. Titles of albums should be in italics; individual selections should be in quotation marks except for musical works referred to by genre (see 22.3.2.3). Abbreviate *compact disc* as CD. Recordings consulted online should include a URL (see 15.4.1.3); in some cases the name of a music service can stand in for a URL.

N: 1. Billie Holiday, vocalist, "I'm a Fool to Want You," by Joel Herron, Frank Sinatra, and Jack Wolf, recorded February 20, 1958, with Ray Ellis, track 1 on *Lady in Satin*, Columbia CL 1157, 33⅓ rpm.

2. Rihanna, "Umbrella," featuring Jay-Z, track 1 on *Good Girl Gone Bad*, Island Def Jam, 2007, Spotify streaming audio, 320 kbps.

3. Richard Strauss, *Don Quixote*, with Emanuel Feuermann (violoncello) and the Philadelphia Orchestra, conducted by Eugene Ormandy, recorded February 24, 1940, Biddulph LAB 042, 1991, CD.

4. Pink Floyd, "Atom Heart Mother," recorded April 29, 1970, Fillmore West, San Francisco, Concert Vault streaming audio, http://www.concertvault.com/pink-floyd/fillmore-west-april-29-1970.html.

In the bibliography you can list the recording under the name of the composer or the performer, depending on which is more relevant to your discussion.

B: Rubinstein, Artur, pianist. *The Chopin Collection*. Recorded 1946, 1958–67. RCA Victor/ BMG 60822-2-RG, 1991. 11 CDs.

Shostakovich, Dmitri. Symphony no. 5 / Symphony no. 9. Conducted by Leonard Bernstein. Recorded with the New York Philharmonic, October 20, 1959 (no. 5), and October 19, 1965 (no. 9). Sony SMK 61841, 1999. CD.

Treat recordings of drama, prose or poetry readings, lectures, and the like as you would musical recordings.

N: 5. Dylan Thomas, *Under Milk Wood*, performed by Dylan Thomas et al., recorded May 14, 1953, on *Dylan Thomas: The Caedmon Collection*, Caedmon, 2002, 11 CDs, discs 9–10.

B: Strayed, Cheryl. *Wild: From Lost to Found on the Pacific Crest Trail*. Read by Bernadette Dunne. New York: Random House Audio, 2012. Audible audio ed., 13 hr., 6 min.

17.10.3.5 **VIDEO GAMES AND APPS.** To cite video games and apps, adapt the examples included throughout this section on multimedia as needed. Titles of video games, like titles of movies, can be italicized. Include a version number and information about the device or operating system required to run the game or app. In the first bibliography entry example, the publishing information for *Gems and Gemstones* is in parentheses because such annotations are styled like notes.

N: 1. *Gems and Jewels*, iPad ed., v. 1.01 (Touchpress, 2011), adapted from Lance Grande and Allison Augustyn, *Gems and Gemstones: Timeless Natural Beauty of the Mineral World* (Chicago: University of Chicago Press, 2009).

2. *Angry Birds Transformers*, v. 1.4.25 (Rovio Entertainment, 2014), Android 4.0 or later. Soundtrack by Vince DiCola and Kenny Meriedeth.

B: Grande, Lance, and Allison Augustyn. *Gems and Jewels*. iPad ed., v. 1.01. Touchpress, 2011. Adapted from Lance Grande and Allison Augustyn, *Gems and Gemstones: Timeless Natural Beauty of the Mineral World* (Chicago: University of Chicago Press, 2009).

Rovio Entertainment. *Angry Birds Transformers*. V. 1.4.25. Rovio Entertainment, 2014. Android 4.0 or later. Soundtrack by Vince DiCola and Kenny Meriedeth.

17.10.3.6   INTERVIEWS. To cite interviews in multimedia formats, treat the person interviewed as the author, and identify the interviewer in the context of the citation. Also include the program or publication and date of the interview (or publication or air date). Interviews are normally cited only in the notes. List the interview in your bibliography only if it is critical to your paper or frequently cited. For unpublished interviews and interviews in other types of published sources, see 17.6.1.

N: 1. Bernie Sanders, interview by Rachel Maddow, *The Rachel Maddow Show*, September 18, 2015, on MSNBC, video, 19:51, https://youtu.be/8jV4sv9waBo.

17.10.3.7   ADVERTISEMENTS. Cite advertisements from television, radio, and the like only in notes or by weaving the elements into your text.

N: 1. Fitbit, "Dualities," advertisement, aired February 7, 2016, during Super Bowl 50 on CBS, 30 sec., http://www.superbowlcommercials2016.org/fitbit/.

As with television shows (17.10.3.2), you can often cite advertisements by weaving the key elements into your text rather than using a note, especially if some or all of the additional elements are not available or relevant to the citation.

Fitbit's "Duality," a thirty-second spot that aired during the third quarter of Super Bowl 50 (CBS, February 7, 2016) . . .

17.10.4   Texts in the Visual and Performing Arts

17.10.4.1   ART EXHIBITION CATALOGS. Cite an art exhibition catalog as you would a book. In the bibliography entry only, include information about the exhibition following the publication data.

N: 1. Jennifer Y. Chi, ed., *The Eye of the Shah: Qajar Court Photography and the Persian Past* (Princeton, NJ: Princeton University Press, 2015), 33.

B: Chi, Jennifer Y., ed. *The Eye of the Shah: Qajar Court Photography and the Persian Past*. Princeton, NJ: Princeton University Press, 2015. Published in conjunction with an exhibition of the same name at New York University's Institute for the Study of the Ancient World, October 22, 2015–January 17, 2016.

17.10.4.2 PLAYS. In some cases you can cite well-known English-language plays in notes only. (See also 17.8.1.) Omit publication data, and cite passages by act and scene (or other division) instead of by page number.

N: 1. Eugene O'Neill, *Long Day's Journey into Night,* act 2, scene 1.

If your paper is in literary studies or another field concerned with close analysis of texts, or if you are citing a translation or an obscure work, cite every play as you would a book, and include each in your bibliography. Cite passages either by division or by page, according to your local guidelines.

N: 2. Enid Bagnold, *The Chalk Garden* (New York: Random House, 1956), 8–9.

B: Anouilh, Jean. *Becket, or The Honor of God.* Translated by Lucienne Hill. New York: Riverhead Books, 1996.

17.10.4.3 MUSICAL SCORES. Cite a published musical score as you would a book.

N: 1. Giuseppe Verdi, *Giovanna d'Arco, dramma lirico* in four acts, libretto by Temistocle Solera, ed. Alberto Rizzuti, 2 vols., Works of Giuseppe Verdi, ser. 1, Operas (Chicago: University of Chicago Press; Milan: G. Ricordi, 2008).

B: Mozart, Wolfgang Amadeus. *Sonatas and Fantasies for the Piano.* Prepared from the autographs and earliest printed sources by Nathan Broder. Rev. ed. Bryn Mawr, PA: Theodore Presser, 1960.

Cite an unpublished score as you would unpublished material in a manuscript collection.

N: 2. Ralph Shapey, "Partita for Violin and Thirteen Players," score, 1966, Special Collections, Joseph Regenstein Library, University of Chicago.

17.11 Public Documents

Public documents include a wide array of sources produced by governments at all levels throughout the world. This section presents basic principles for some common types of public documents available in English; if you need to cite other types, adapt the closest model.

Such documents involve more complicated and varied elements than most types of published sources. In your citations, include as much identifying information as you can, format the elements consistently, and adapt the general patterns outlined here as needed.

The bulk of this section is concerned with documents published by US governmental bodies and agencies. For documents published by the governments of Canada and the United Kingdom and by international bodies, see 17.11.9–11. For unpublished government documents, see 17.11.12.

17.11.1   Elements to Include, Their Order, and How to Format Them

In your citations, include as many of the following elements as you can:

- name of the government (country, state, city, county, or other division) and government body (legislative body, executive department, court bureau, board, commission, or committee) that issued the document
- title, if any, of the document or collection
- name of individual author, editor, or compiler, if given
- report number or other identifying information (such as place of publication and publisher, for certain freestanding publications or for items in secondary sources)
- date of publication
- page numbers or other locators, if relevant
- a URL, or the name of the database, for sources consulted online (see 15.4.1 and, for examples, 17.11.2.2, 17.11.3, 17.11.7, and 17.11.11)

In general, list the relevant elements in the order given above. Certain elements may be left out of the notes but should be included in the bibliography. Other types of exceptions are explained in the following sections of 17.11.

N: 1. Select Committee on Homeland Security, Homeland Security Act of 2002, 107th Cong., 2d sess., 2002, HR Rep. 107-609, pt. 1, 11-12.

B: US Congress, House of Representatives, Select Committee on Homeland Security. Homeland Security Act of 2002. 107th Cong., 2d sess., 2002. HR Rep. 107-609, pt. 1.

Note that, by convention, ordinals in public documents end in *d* instead of *nd* (*2d* instead of *2nd*).

17.11.2   Congressional Publications

For congressional publications, bibliography entries usually begin with the designation *US Congress*, followed by *Senate* or *House of Representatives* (or *House*). (You may also simplify this to *US Senate* or *US House*.) In notes, US is usually omitted. Other common elements include committee and subcommittee, if any; title of document; number of the Congress and session (abbreviated *Cong.* and *sess.* respectively in this position); date of publication; and number and description of the document (for example, H. Doc. 487), if available.

17.11.2.1 DEBATES. Since 1873, congressional debates have been published by the government in the *Congressional Record* (in notes, often abbreviated as *Cong. Rec.*). Whenever possible, cite the permanent volumes, which often reflect changes from the daily editions of the *Record*. (For citations of the daily House or Senate edition, retain the *H* or *S* in page numbers.)

N: 1. *Cong. Rec.*, 110th Cong., 1st sess., 2008, vol. 153, pt. 8: 11629–30.

B: US Congress. *Congressional Record.* 110th Cong., 1st sess., 2008. Vol. 153, pt. 8.

Occasionally you may need to identify a speaker in a debate, the subject, and a date in a note.

N: 2. Senator Kennedy of Massachusetts, speaking for the Joint Resolution on Nuclear Weapons Freeze and Reductions, on March 10, 1982, to the Committee on Foreign Relations, SJ Res. 163, 97th Cong., 1st sess., *Cong. Rec.* 128, pt. 3: 3832–34.

Before 1874, congressional debates were published in *Annals of the Congress of the United States* (also known by other names and covering the years 1789–1824), *Register of Debates* (1824–37), and *Congressional Globe* (1833–73). Cite these works similarly to the *Congressional Record*.

17.11.2.2 REPORTS AND DOCUMENTS. When you cite reports and documents of the Senate (abbreviated S.) and the House (*H.* or *HR*), include both the Congress and session numbers and, if possible, the series number. Notice the form for a shortened note, which differs from the usual pattern (see 16.4.1). The bibliography example was consulted online using an official government resource (the US Government Publishing Office). See also 15.4.1.3.

N: 1. Select Committee on Homeland Security, Homeland Security Act of 2002, 107th Cong., 2d sess., 2002, HR Rep. 107–609, pt. 1, 11–12.
   2. Declarations of a State of War with Japan, Germany, and Italy, 77th Cong., 1st sess., 1941, S. Doc. 148, serial 10575, 2–5.
   3. Select Committee, Homeland Security Act, 11.
   4. Reorganization of the Federal Judiciary, 75th Cong., 1st sess., 1937, S. Rep. 711.

B: US Congress, House. Blocking Property and Suspending Entry of Certain Persons Engaging in Significant Malicious Cyber-Enabled Activities. 114th Cong., 1st sess., 2015. H. Doc. 114–22. https://www.gpo.gov/fdsys/pkg/CDOC-114hdoc22.

17.11.2.3 BILLS AND RESOLUTIONS. Congressional bills (proposed laws) and resolutions are published in pamphlet form. In citations, bills and resolutions originating in the House of Representatives are abbreviated *HR* or *H. Res.*, and those originating in the Senate *S.* or *S. Res.* Include publication details in the *Congressional Record* (if available). If a bill has been enacted, cite it as a statute (see 17.11.2.5).

N: 1. Email Privacy Act, H. Res. 699, 114th Cong., 2d sess., *Congressional Record* 162, no. 65, daily ed. (April 27, 2016): H2022.

B: US Congress, House. Email Privacy Act. H. Res. 699. 114th Cong., 2d sess. *Congressional Record* 162, no. 65, daily ed. (April 27, 2016): H2022-28.

17.11.2.4 HEARINGS. Records of testimony given before congressional committees are usually published with formal titles, which should be included in citations (in italics). The relevant committee is normally listed as part of the title. Notice the form for a shortened note, which differs from the usual pattern (see 16.4.1).

N: 1. *Hearing before the Select Committee on Homeland Security*, HR 5005, Homeland Security Act of 2002, day 3, 107th Cong., 2d sess., July 17, 2002, 119-20.
   2. HR 5005, *Hearing*, 203.

B: US Congress, Senate. *Famine in Africa: Hearing before the Committee on Foreign Relations*. 99th Cong., 1st sess., January 17, 1985.

17.11.2.5 STATUTES. Statutes, which are bills or resolutions that have been passed into law, are first published separately and then collected in the annual bound volumes of the *United States Statutes at Large*, which began publication in 1874. Later they are incorporated into the *United States Code*. Cite *US Statutes*, the *US Code*, or both. Section numbers in the *Code* are preceded by a section symbol (§; use §§ and *et seq.* to indicate more than one section).

   Cite statutes in notes only; you do not need to include them in your bibliography. Notice the form for a shortened note, which differs from the usual pattern (see 16.4.1).

N: 1. Atomic Energy Act of 1946, Public Law 585, 79th Cong., 2d sess. (August 1, 1946), 12, 19.
   2. Fair Credit Reporting Act of 1970, *US Code* 15 (2000), §§ 1681 et seq.
   3. Homeland Security Act of 2002, Public Law 107-296, *US Statutes at Large* 116 (2002): 2163-64, codified at *US Code* 6 (2002), §§ 101 et seq.
   4. Homeland Security Act, 2165.

Before 1874, laws were published in the seventeen-volume *Statutes at Large of the United States of America, 1789–1873*. Citations of this collection include the volume number and its publication date.

17.11.3 Presidential Publications

Presidential proclamations, executive orders, vetoes, addresses, and the like are published in the *Weekly Compilation of Presidential Documents* and in *Public Papers of the Presidents of the United States*. Proclamations and executive orders are also carried in the daily *Federal Register* and then published in title 3 of the *Code of Federal Regulations*. Once they have been published in the *Code*, use that as your source. Put individual titles in quotation marks. The example of a proclamation was consulted online from an official government resource (see also 15.4.1.3).

N: 1. Barack Obama, Proclamation 9465, "Establishment of the Stonewall National Monument," *Federal Register* 81, no. 125 (June 29, 2016): 42215, https://federalregister.gov/a/2016-15536.

2. William J. Clinton, Executive Order 13067, "Blocking Sudanese Government Property and Prohibiting Transactions with Sudan," *Code of Federal Regulations*, title 3 (1997 comp.): 230.

B: US President. Proclamation 9465. "Establishment of the Stonewall National Monument." *Federal Register* 81, no. 125 (June 29, 2016): 42215-20. https://federalregister.gov/a/2016-15536.

The public papers of US presidents are collected in two multivolume works: *Compilation of the Messages and Papers of the Presidents, 1789–1897* and, starting with the Hoover administration, *Public Papers of the Presidents of the United States*. (Papers not covered by either of these works are published elsewhere.) To cite items in these collections, follow the recommendations for multivolume books (see 17.1.4).

17.11.4 Publications of Government Departments and Agencies

Executive departments, bureaus, and agencies issue reports, bulletins, circulars, and other materials. Italicize the title, and include the name of any identified author(s) after the title.

N: 1. US Department of the Treasury, *Report of the Secretary of the Treasury Transmitting a Report from the Register of the Treasury of the Commerce and Navigation of the United States for the Year Ending the 30th of June, 1850*, 31st Cong., 2d sess., House Executive Document 8 (Washington, DC, 1850-51).

B: US Department of the Interior, Minerals Management Service, Environmental Division. *Oil-Spill Risk Analysis: Gulf of Mexico Outer Continental Shelf (OCS) Lease Sales, Central Planning Area and Western Planning Area, 2007-2012, and Gulfwide OCS Program, 2007-2046*, by Zhen-Gang Ji, Walter R. Johnson, and Charles F. Marshall. Edited by Eileen M. Lear. MMS 2007-040, June 2007.

17.11.5 US Constitution

The US Constitution should be cited only in notes; you need not include it in your bibliography. Include the article or amendment, section, and, if relevant, clause. Use arabic numerals and, if you prefer, abbreviations for terms such as *amendment* and *section*.

N: 1. US Constitution, art. 2, sec. 1, cl. 3.
           2. US Constitution, amend. 14, sec. 2.

In many cases you can use a parenthetical note (see 16.4.3) or even include the identifying information in your text. Spell out the part designations in text. Capitalize the names of specific amendments when used in place of numbers.

The US Constitution, in article 1, section 9, forbids suspension of the writ "unless when in Cases of Rebellion or Invasion the public Safety may require it."

The First Amendment protects the right of free speech.

17.11.6 Treaties

The texts of treaties signed before 1950 are published in *United States Statutes at Large*; the unofficial citation is to the *Treaty Series* (TS) or the *Executive Agreement Series* (EAS). Those signed in 1950 or later appear in *United States Treaties and Other International Agreements* (UST, 1950–) or *Treaties and Other International Acts Series* (TIAS, 1945–). Treaties involving more than two nations may be found in the *United Nations Treaty Series* (UNTS, 1946–) or, from 1920 to 1946, in the *League of Nations Treaty Series* (LNTS).

Italicize titles of the publications mentioned above and their abbreviated forms. Unless they are named in the title of the treaty, list the parties subject to the agreement, separated by hyphens. An exact date indicates the date of signing and is therefore preferable to a year alone, which may differ from the year the treaty was published. Notice the form for a shortened note, which differs from the usual pattern (see 16.4.1).

N: 1. Treaty Banning Nuclear Weapon Tests in the Atmosphere, in Outer Space, and Under Water, US-UK-USSR, August 5, 1963, *UST* 14, pt. 2, 1313.
           2. Convention concerning Military Service, Denmark-Italy, July 15, 1954, *TIAS* 250, no. 3516, 45.
           3. Nuclear Test Ban Treaty, 1317–18.

B: United States. Naval Armament Limitation Treaty with the British Empire, France, Italy, and Japan. February 6, 1922. *US Statutes at Large* 43, pt. 2.

17.11.7 Legal Cases

Citations of legal cases generally take the same form for courts at all levels. In notes, give the full case name (including the abbreviation *v.*)

in italics. Include the volume number (arabic), name of the reporter (abbreviated; see below), ordinal series number (if applicable), opening page number of the decision, abbreviated name of the court and date (together in parentheses), and other relevant information, such as the name of the state or local court (if not identified by the series title). Actual pages cited follow the opening page number, separated by a comma.

Cite cases in notes only; you do not need to include them in your bibliography.

N: 1. *United States v. Christmas*, 222 F.3d 141, 145 (4th Cir. 2000).

       2. *Profit Sharing Plan v. MBank Dallas, N.A.*, 683 F. Supp. 592 (ND Tex. 1988).

A shortened note may consist of the case name and, if needed, a page number.

N: 3. *Christmas,* 146.

The one element that depends on the level of the court is the name of the reporter. The most common ones are as follows.

▪ *US Supreme Court.* For Supreme Court decisions, cite *United States Supreme Court Reports* (abbreviated US) or, if not yet published there, *Supreme Court Reporter* (abbreviated S. Ct.).

N: 4. *AT&T Corp. v. Iowa Utilities Bd.*, 525 US 366 (1999).

       5. *Brendlin v. California*, 127 S. Ct. 2400 (2007).

▪ *Lower federal courts.* For lower federal-court decisions, cite *Federal Reporter* (F.) or *Federal Supplement* (F. Supp.).

N: 6. *United States v. Dennis*, 183 F. 201 (2d Cir. 1950).

       7. *Eaton v. IBM Corp.*, 925 F. Supp. 487 (SD Tex. 1996).

▪ *State and local courts.* For state and local court decisions, cite official state reporters whenever possible. If you use a commercial reporter, cite it as in the second example below. If the reporter does not identify the court's name, include it before the date, within the parentheses.

N: 8. *Williams v. Davis*, 27 Cal. 2d 746 (1946).

       9. *Bivens v. Mobley*, 724 So. 2d 458, 465 (Miss. Ct. App. 1998).

Cases consulted online should normally be cited to the appropriate reporter(s) as described above. A URL that points directly to an official resource may be added as the final element (see also 15.4.1.3).

N: 10. *State v. Griffin*, 211 W. Va. 508, 566 S.E.2d 645 (2002), http://www.courtswv.gov/supreme-court/docs/spring2002/30433.htm.

Many researchers use Lexis or Westlaw to research court cases and other legal materials. To cite a case in one of those databases, add any identifying date and number supplied by the database (see also 15.4.1.4). Page or screen numbers are typically preceded by an asterisk.

N: 11. *Family Service Association of Steubenville v. Wells Township*, 2015 US Dist. LEXIS 75017, *7 (SD Ohio, June 10, 2015), LexisNexis Academic.

17.11.8   State and Local Government Documents

Cite state and local government documents as you would federal documents. Use roman type (no quotation marks) for state laws and municipal ordinances; use italics for codes (compilations) and the titles of freestanding publications.

N: 1. Illinois Institute for Environmental Quality (IIEQ), *Review and Synopsis of Public Participation regarding Sulfur Dioxide and Particulate Emissions*, by Sidney M. Marder, IIEQ Document 77/21 (Chicago, 1977), 44–45.

   2. Methamphetamine Control and Community Protection Act, *Illinois Compiled Statutes*, chap. 720, no. 646, sec. 10 (2005).

   3. *Page's Ohio Revised Code Annotated*, title 35, sec. 3599.01 (2011).

   4. New Mexico Constitution, art. 4, sec. 7.

B: Illinois Institute for Environmental Quality (IIEQ). *Review and Synopsis of Public Participation regarding Sulfur Dioxide and Particulate Emissions*, by Sidney M. Marder. IIEQ Document 77/21. Chicago, 1977.

17.11.9   Canadian Government Documents

Cite Canadian government documents similarly to US public documents. End citations with the word *Canada* (in parentheses) unless it is obvious from the context.

Canadian statutes appeared through 1985 in the *Revised Statutes of Canada*, a consolidation that was published every fifteen to thirty years; federal statutes enacted since then are cited as session laws in the annual *Statutes of Canada*. Identify the statute by title, reporter, year of compilation, chapter, and section.

N: 1. Canada Wildlife Act, *Revised Statutes of Canada* 1985, chap. W-9, sec. 1.

   2. Assisted Human Reproduction Act, *Statutes of Canada* 2004, chap. 2, sec. 2.

Canadian Supreme Court cases since 1876 are published in *Supreme Court Reports* (SCR). Federal Court cases are published in *Federal Courts Reports* (FC, 1971–2003; FCR, 2004–) or *Exchequer Court Reports* (Ex. CR, 1875–1971). Cases not found in any of these sources may be found in *Dominion Law Reports* (DLR). Include the name of the case (in italics), followed by the date (in parentheses), the volume number (if any), the abbreviated name of the reporter, and the opening page of the decision.

N: 3. *Robertson v. Thomson Corp.,* (2006) 2 SCR 363 (Canada).

            4. *Canada v. CBC/Radio-Canada,* (2014) 1 FCR 142.

17.11.10 British Government Documents

Cite British government documents similarly to US public documents. End citations with the phrase *United Kingdom* (in parentheses) unless it is obvious from the context.

Acts of Parliament should usually be cited only in a note. Include a specific act in your bibliography only if it is critical to your argument or frequently cited. Identify acts by title, date, and chapter number (arabic numeral for national number, lowercase roman for local). Acts from before 1963 are cited by regnal year and monarch's name (abbreviated) and ordinal (arabic numeral).

N: 1. Act of Settlement, 1701, 12 & 13 Will. 3, chap. 2.

            2. Consolidated Fund Act, 1963, chap. 1 (United Kingdom).

            3. Manchester Corporation Act, 1967, chap. xl.

Most British legal cases can be found in the applicable report in the *Law Reports,* among these the Appeal Cases (AC), Queen's (King's) Bench (QB, KB), Chancery (Ch.), Family (Fam.), and Probate (P.) reports. Until recently the courts of highest appeal in the United Kingdom (except for criminal cases in Scotland) had been the House of Lords (HL) and the Judicial Committee of the Privy Council (PC). In 2005 the Supreme Court of the United Kingdom (UKSC) was established.

Include the name of the case, in italics (cases involving the Crown refer to *Rex* or *Regina*); the date, in parentheses; the volume number (if any) and abbreviated name of the reporter; and the opening page of the decision. If the court is not apparent from the name of the reporter, or if the jurisdiction is not clear from context, include either or both, as necessary, in parentheses.

N: 4. *Regina v. Dudley and Stephens,* (1884) 14 QBD 273 (DC).

            5. *Regal (Hastings) Ltd. v. Gulliver,* (1967) 2 AC 134 (HL) (appeal taken from Eng.).

            6. *NML Capital Limited (Appellant) v. Republic of Argentina (Respondent),* (2011) UKSC 31.

17.11.11 Publications of International Bodies

Documents published by international bodies such as the United Nations can be cited much like books. Identify the authorizing body (and any author or editor), the title or topic of the document, the publisher or place of publication (or both), and the date, followed by a page reference in the notes. Also include any series or other identifying publication information. For documents consulted online, include a URL (see 15.4.1.3).

N: 1. League of Arab States and United Nations, *The Third Arab Report on the Millennium Development Goals 2010 and the Impact of the Global Economic Crises* (Beirut: Economic and Social Commission for Western Asia, 2010), 82.

B: United Nations Security Council. Resolution 2222, Protection of Civilians in Armed Conflict. S/RES/2222. New York: UN, May 27, 2015. http://www.un.org/en/sc/documents/resolutions/2015.shtml.

17.11.12 Unpublished Government Documents

If you cite unpublished government documents, follow the patterns given for unpublished manuscripts in 17.7.4.

Most unpublished documents of the US government are housed in the National Archives and Records Administration (NARA) in Washington, DC, or in one of its branches, and cataloged online. Cite them all, including films, photographs, and sound recordings as well as written materials, by record group (RG) number.

The comparable institution for unpublished Canadian government documents is the Library and Archives Canada (LAC) in Ottawa, Ontario. The United Kingdom has a number of depositories of unpublished government documents, most notably the National Archives (NA) and the British Library (BL), both in London. Each of these resources has been cataloged online.

18 Author-Date Style: *The Basic Form*

A citation style used widely in most social sciences and in the natural and physical sciences is the *author-date style,* so called because the author's name and the date of publication are the critical elements for identifying sources. This chapter presents an overview of the basic pattern for citations in author-date style, including both reference list entries and parenthetical citations. (The citation style presented in this chapter is also known as the Turabian or Chicago author-date or reference list style.) Examples of parenthetical citations are identified with a P; examples of reference list entries are identified with an R.

In author-date style, you signal that you have used a source by placing a *parenthetical citation* (including author, date, and relevant page numbers) next to your reference to that source:

According to one scholar, "The railroads had made Chicago the most important meeting place between East and West" (Cronon 1991, 92–93).

At the end of the paper, you list all sources in a *reference list*. That list normally includes every source you cited in a parenthetical citation and sometimes others you consulted but did not cite. Since parenthetical citations do not include complete bibliographical information for a source, you must include that information in your reference list. All reference list entries have the same general form:

R: Cronon, William. 1991. *Nature's Metropolis: Chicago and the Great West.* New York: W. W. Norton.

Readers expect you to follow all the rules for correctly citing your sources. These rules cover not only what data you must include and in what order but also punctuation, capitalization, italics, and so on. To get your citations exactly right, you must pay close attention to the kinds of details that few researchers can easily remember and that even the best citation management tools can help with only part of the way. Read this chapter for an overview. Then use chapter 19 to look up the details.

18.1 Basic Patterns

Although sources and their citations come in almost endless variety, you are likely to use only a few kinds. While you may need to look up details to cite some unusual sources, you can easily learn the basic patterns for the few kinds you will use most often. This will help you to record accurate and reliable bibliographical data quickly and efficiently as you do your research.

The rest of this section describes the basic patterns, and figure 18.1 provides templates for several common types of sources. Chapter 19 includes examples of a wide range of sources, including exceptions to the patterns discussed here.

18.1.1 Order of Elements

The order of elements in reference list entries follows the same general pattern for all types of sources: author, date (year) of publication, title, other facts of publication. Parenthetical citations include only the first two of these elements. If they cite specific passages, they also include page numbers or other locating information; reference list entries do not, though they do include a full span of page numbers for a source that is part of a larger work, such as an article in a periodical or a chapter in a book.

Figure 18.1. Templates for reference list entries and parenthetical citations

The following templates show what elements should be included in what order when citing several common types of sources in reference lists (R) and parenthetical citations (P). They also show punctuation, capitalization of titles, and when to use italics or quotation marks. Gray shading shows abbreviations (or their spelled-out versions) and other terms as they would actually appear in a citation. XX stands in for page number(s) actually cited, YY–YY for a full span of page numbers for an article or a chapter.

For further examples, explanations, and variations, see chapter 19.

Books

1. Single Author or Editor

R: Author's Last Name, Author's First Name. Year of Publication. *Title of Book: Subtitle of Book*. Place of Publication: Publisher's Name.

Duckworth, Angela. 2016. Grit: *The Power of Passion and Perseverance*. New York: Scribner.

P: (Author's Last Name Year of Publication, XX)

(Duckworth 2016, 82)

For a book with an editor instead of an author, adapt the pattern as follows:

R: Editor's Last Name, Editor's First Name, ed. Year of Publication . . .

Prakash, Gyan, ed. 2010 . . .

P: (Editor's Last Name Year of Publication, XX)

(Prakash 2010, 89–90)

For more than one editor, adapt the examples in template 2 and use *eds*.

2. Multiple Authors

For a book with two authors, use the following pattern:

R: Author #1's Last Name, Author #1's First Name, and Author #2's First and Last Names. Year of Publication. *Title of Book: Subtitle of Book*. Place of Publication: Publisher's Name.

Choi, Susanne Y. P., and Yinni Peng. 2016. *Masculine Promise: Migration, Family, and Gender in China*. Oakland: University of California Press.

P: (Author #1's Last Name and Author #2's Last Name Year of Publication, XX)

(Choi and Peng, 111–12)

For a book with three authors, adapt the pattern as follows:

R: Author #1's Last Name, Author #1's First Name, Author #2's First and Last Names, and Author #3's First and Last Names. Year of Publication . . .

White, Karen, Beatriz Williams, and Lauren Willig. 2016 . . .

P: (Author #1's Last Name, Author #2's Last Name, and Author #3's Last Name Year of Publication, XX)

(White, Williams, and Willig 2016, 6–7)

For a book with four or more authors, adapt the parenthetical citation pattern only, as follows:

P: (Author #1's Last Name et al. Year of Publication, XX)

(Eichengreen et al. 2015, 120)

3. Author Plus Editor or Translator

For a book with an author plus an editor, use the following pattern:

R: Author's Last Name, Author's First Name. Year of Publication. *Title of Book: Subtitle of Book.* Edited by Editor's First and Last Names. Place of Publication: Publisher's Name.

Austen, Jane. 2016. *Mansfield Park: An Annotated Edition.* Edited by Deidre Shauna Lynch. Cambridge, MA: Belknap Press of Harvard University Press.

P: (Author's Last Name Year of Publication, XX)

(Austen 2016, 223–24)

If a book has a translator instead of an editor, substitute the phrase *Translated by* and the translator's name for the editor data in the reference list entry.

4. Edition Number

R: Author's Last Name, Author's First Name. Year of Publication. *Title of Book: Subtitle of Book.* Edition Number ed. Place of Publication: Publisher's Name.

Kinzie, Mary. 2013. *A Poet's Guide to Poetry.* 2nd ed. Chicago: University of Chicago Press.

P: (Author's Last Name Year of Publication, XX)

(Kinzie 2013, 83)

5. Single Chapter in an Edited Book

R: Chapter Author's Last Name, Chapter Author's First Name. Year of Publication. "Title of Chapter: Subtitle of Chapter." In *Title of Book: Subtitle of Book,* edited by Editor's First and Last Names, YY–YY. Place of Publication: Publisher's Name.

Gillespie, Kelly. 2017. "Before the Commission: Ethnography as Public Testimony." In *If Truth Be Told: The Politics of Public Ethnography*, edited by Didier Fassin, 69–95. Durham, NC: Duke University Press.

P: (Chapter Author's Last Name Year of Publication, XX)

(Gillespie 2017, 72)

Figure 18.1. Templates for reference list entries and parenthetical citations (continued)

Journal Articles

6. Journal Article—Basic Format

R: Author's Last Name, Author's First Name. Year of Publication. "Title of Article: Subtitle of Article." *Title of Journal* Volume Number, Issue Number (Additional Date Information): YY–YY.

> Mercer, Ben. 2016. "Specters of Fascism: The Rhetoric of Historical Analogy in 1968." *Journal of Modern History* 88, no. 1 (March): 96–129.

P: (Author's Last Name Year of Publication, XX)

> (Mercer 2016, 98)

For an article with multiple authors, follow the relevant pattern for authors' names in template 2.

7. Journal Article Online

For a journal article consulted online, include a URL. For articles that include a DOI, form the URL by appending the DOI to https://doi.org/ rather than using the URL in your address bar. The DOI for the Fernandez article in the example below is 10.1086/685998.

R: Author's Last Name, Author's First Name. Year of Publication. "Title of Article: Subtitle of Article." *Title of Journal* Volume Number, Issue Number (Additional Date Information): YY–YY. URL.

> Fernandez, Patricio A. 2016. "Practical Reasoning: Where the Action Is." *Ethics* 126, no. 4 (July): 869–900. https://doi.org/10.1086/685998.

P: (Author's Last Name Year of Publication, XX)

> (Fernandez 2016, 872)

See 15.4.1 for more details.

18.1.2 Punctuation

In reference list entries, separate most elements with periods; in parenthetical citations, do not use a punctuation mark between the author and the date, but separate the date from a page number with a comma.

18.1.3 Capitalization

Most titles can be capitalized using headline style. But for titles in languages other than English, use sentence style. (See 22.3.1 for both styles.) Capitalize proper nouns in the usual way (see chapter 22). In some fields, you may be required to use sentence style for most titles except for titles of journals, magazines, and newspapers; check your local guidelines.

18.1.4   Italics and Quotation Marks

Use italics for titles of larger entities (books, journals); for titles of smaller entities (chapters, articles), use roman type and quotation marks. Also use roman type and quotation marks for titles of works that have not been formally published (such as manuscripts or dissertations), even if they are book length. See also 22.3.2.

18.1.5   Numbers

In titles, any numbers are spelled out or given in numerals exactly as they are in the original. Use lowercase roman numerals to refer to page numbers that are in roman numerals in the original. References to all other numbers (such as chapter numbers or figure numbers) are given in arabic numerals, even if in the original they are in roman numerals or spelled out.

18.1.6   Abbreviations

Abbreviate terms such as *editor* and *translator* (*ed.* and *trans.*) when they come after a name, but spell them out when they introduce it (*Edited by*). The plural is usually formed by adding *s* (*eds.*) unless the abbreviation ends in an *s* (use *trans.* for both singular and plural). Terms such as *volume, edition,* and *number* (*vol., ed.,* and *no.*) are always abbreviated.

18.1.7   Indentation

Reference list entries have hanging indents: the first line of each entry is flush left, and anything that runs over to a new line is indented. Parenthetical citations are placed within the text and are not indented.

18.2   Reference Lists

In papers that use author-date style, the reference list presents full bibliographical information for all the sources cited in parenthetical citations (other than a few special types of sources; see 18.2.2). You may also include works that were important to your thinking but that you did not specifically mention in the text. In addition to providing bibliographical information, a reference list shows readers the extent of your research and its relationship to prior work, and it helps readers use your sources in their own research. If you use the author-date citation style, you must include a reference list in your paper.

Label the list *References*. See figure A.16 in the appendix for a sample page of a reference list.

18.2.1 Arrangement of Entries

18.2.1.1 ALPHABETICAL AND CHRONOLOGICAL BY AUTHOR. A reference list is normally a single list of all sources arranged alphabetically by the last name of the author, editor, or whoever is first in each entry. (For alphabetizing names from languages other than English, compound names, and other special cases, see 18.2.1.2.) Most word processors and citation management tools can sort entries alphabetically. For all but the simplest of lists, however, the results will typically need some adjusting. If you are writing a thesis or dissertation, your department or university may specify that you should alphabetize the entries letter by letter or word by word; see 16.58–61 of *The Chicago Manual of Style*, 17th edition (2017), for an explanation of these two systems.

If your reference list includes two or more works written, edited, or translated by the same individual, arrange the entries chronologically by publication date. For all entries after the first, replace the individual's name with a long dash, called a 3-em dash (see 21.7.3). For edited or translated works, put a comma and the appropriate designation (*ed.*, *trans.*, or the like) after the dash. List all such works before any that the individual coauthored or coedited. Successive entries by two or more authors in which only the first author's name is the same are alphabetized according to the coauthors' last names. Note that it is best to make all these adjustments manually—*after* you have sorted your complete reference list alphabetically by name.

R: Gates, Henry Louis, Jr. 1988. *The Signifying Monkey: A Theory of African-American Literary Criticism.* New York: Oxford University Press.

———, ed. 2002. *The Classic Slave Narratives.* New York: Penguin Putnam.

———. 2004. *America behind the Color Line: Dialogues with African Americans.* New York: Warner Books.

———. 2010. *Tradition and the Black Atlantic: Critical Theory in the African Diaspora.* New York: BasicCivitas.

———. 2011. *Black in Latin America.* New York: New York University Press.

Gates, Henry Louis, Jr., and Cornel West. 2000. *The African-American Century: How Black Americans Have Shaped Our Country.* New York: Free Press.

Gates, Henry Louis, Jr., and Donald Yacovone. 2013. *The African Americans: Many Rivers to Cross.* Carlsbad, CA: SmileyBooks.

The same principles apply to works by a single group of authors named in the same order.

R: Marty, Martin E., and R. Scott Appleby. 1992. *The Glory and the Power: The Fundamentalist Challenge to the Modern World.* Boston: Beacon Press.

———, eds. 2004. *Accounting for Fundamentalisms.* Chicago: University of Chicago Press.

Marty, Martin E., and Micah Marty. 1998. *When True Simplicity Is Gained: Finding Spiritual Clarity in a Complex World.* Grand Rapids, MI: William B. Eerdmans.

If your reference list includes more than one work published in the same year by an author or group of authors named in the same order, arrange the entries alphabetically by title (ignoring articles such as *a* and *the*). Add the letters *a, b, c,* and so forth to the year, in roman type without an intervening space. Your parenthetical citations to these works should include the letters (see 18.3.2).

R: Fogel, Robert William. 2004a. *The Escape from Hunger and Premature Death, 1700–2100: Europe, America, and the Third World.* New York: Cambridge University Press.
———. 2004b. "Technophysio Evolution and the Measurement of Economic Growth." *Journal of Evolutionary Economics* 14, no. 2: 217–21.

If a book or journal article does not have an author or editor (or other named compiler, such as a translator), put the title first in your reference list entry and alphabetize based on it, ignoring articles such as *a* and *the*.

R: *Account of the Operations of the Great Trigonometrical Survey of India.* 1870–1910. 22 vols. Dehra Dun: Survey of India.
"The Great Trigonometrical Survey of India." 1863. *Calcutta Review* 38:26–62.
"State and Prospects of Asia." 1839. *Quarterly Review* 63, no. 126 (March): 369–402.

For magazine and newspaper articles without authors, use the title of the magazine or newspaper in place of the author (see 19.3 and 19.4). For other types of sources, see the relevant section in chapter 19 for guidance; if not stated otherwise, use a title in this position.

18.2.1.2 SPECIAL TYPES OF NAMES. Some authors' names consist of more than a readily identifiable "first name" and "last name." In many cases you can determine the correct order by consulting your library's catalog. For historical names, the biographical entries at Merriam-Webster.com can be helpful. This section outlines some general principles for alphabetizing such names in your reference list. In shortened or parenthetical notes, use the last name exactly as inverted (shown below in bold). If your paper involves names from languages other than English, follow the conventions for those languages.

■ *Compound names.* Alphabetize compound last names, including hyphenated names, by the first part of the compound. If a woman uses both her own family name and her husband's but does not hyphenate them, generally alphabetize by the second surname. While many languages have predictable patterns for compound names (see below), others—such as French and German—do not.

Hine, Darlene Clark	**Mies van der Rohe**, Ludwig
Kessler-Harris, Alice	**Teilhard de Chardin**, Pierre

- *Names with particles.* Depending on the language, particles such as *de, di, D,'* and *van* may or may not be considered the first part of a last name for alphabetizing. Consult one of the resources noted above if you are unsure about a particular name. Note that particles may be either lowercased or capitalized, and some are followed by an apostrophe.

Beauvoir, Simone de	**Kooning**, Willem de
de Gaulle, Charles	**Medici**, Lorenzo de'
di Leonardo, Micaela	**Van Rensselaer**, Stephen

- *Names beginning with "Mac," "Saint," or "O'."* Names that begin with *Mac, Saint,* or *O'* can have many variations in abbreviation (*Mc, St.*), spelling (*Sainte, San*), capitalization (*Macmillan, McAllister*), and hyphenation or apostrophes (*O'Neill* or *Odell; Saint-Gaudens* or *St. Denis*). Alphabetize all such names based on the letters actually present; do not group them because they are similar.
- *Spanish names.* Many Spanish last names are compound names consisting of an individual's paternal and maternal family names, sometimes joined by the conjunction *y.* Alphabetize such names under the first part.

Ortega y Gasset, José	**Sánchez Mendoza**, Juana

- *Arabic names.* Alphabetize Arabic last names that begin with the particle *al-* or *el-* (the) under the element following the particle. Names that begin with *Abu, Abd,* and *Ibn,* like English names beginning with *Mac* or *Saint,* should be alphabetized under these terms.

Abu Zafar Nadvi, Syed	**Ibn Saud**, Aziz
Hakim, Tawfiq al-	**Jamal**, Muhammad Hamid al-

- *Chinese, Japanese, and Korean names.* If an author with a Chinese, Japanese, or Korean name follows traditional usage (family name followed by given name), do not invert the name or insert a comma between the "first" and "last" names. If the author follows Westernized usage (given name followed by family name), treat the name as you would an English name.

Traditional usage	*Westernized usage*
Chao Wu-chi	**Kurosawa**, Noriaki
Kim Dae-jung	**Lee**, Chang-rae
Yoshida Shigeru	**Tsou**, Tang

18.2.1.3 CATEGORIZED LISTINGS. Because readers following a parenthetical citation will have only an author and a date to help them identify the relevant reference list entry, organize the list as described above except in rare cases. Under the following circumstances, you may consider dividing the list into separate categories:

- If you have more than three or four entries for a special type of source, such as manuscripts, archival collections, recordings, and so on, list them separately from the rest of your entries.
- If it is critical to distinguish primary sources from secondary and tertiary ones, list the entries in separate sections.

If you categorize sources, introduce each separate section with a subheading and, if necessary, a headnote. Order the entries within each section according to the principles given above, and do not list a source in more than one section unless it clearly could be categorized in two or more ways.

18.2.2   Sources That May Be Omitted

By convention, you may omit the following types of sources from a reference list:

- comments on online magazine or newspaper articles and blog posts (19.3, 19.4.2, 19.5.2), postings to social media (19.5.3) or to online forums or mailing lists (19.5.4), and anonymous unpublished interviews and personal communications (19.6)
- classical, medieval, and early English literary works (19.8.1) and (in some cases) well-known English-language plays (19.10.4.2)
- the Bible and other sacred works (19.8.2)
- well-known reference works, such as major dictionaries and encyclopedias (19.9.1)
- some sources in the visual and performing arts, including artworks (19.10.1) and live performances (19.10.2)
- certain types of public documents (19.11), including the US Constitution (19.11.5)

You may choose to include in your reference list a specific item from one of these categories that is critical to your argument or frequently cited.

18.3   Parenthetical Citations

Parenthetical citations include enough information for readers to find the full citation in your reference list—usually the author's name, the date of publication, and (if you are citing a specific passage), a page number or other locating information. The name and date must match those in the relevant reference list entry exactly. (Note that both the elements and the punctuation in parenthetical citations are slightly different from those used in notes-style parenthetical notes, which are described in 16.4.3; do not confuse or combine the two styles.)

18.3.1 Placement in Text

Whenever you refer to or otherwise use material from a source, you must insert into your text a parenthetical citation with basic identifying information about that source. Normally the parenthetical citation should be placed at the end of the sentence or clause containing the quotation or other material. But if the author's name is mentioned in the text, put the rest of the citation (in parentheses) immediately after the author's name. The closing parenthesis precedes a comma, period, or other punctuation mark when the quotation is run into the text. See also 25.2.

"What on introspection seems to happen immediately and without effort is often a complex symphony of processes that take time to complete" (LeDoux 2003, 116).

While one school claims that "material culture may be the most objective source of information we have concerning America's past" (Deetz 1996, 259), others disagree.

The color blue became more prominent in the eighteenth century (Pastoureau 2001, 124).

According to Gould (2007, 428), the song "spreads a deadpan Liverpudlian irony over the most clichéd sentiment in all of popular music."

With a block quotation, however, the parenthetical citation follows the terminal punctuation mark.

He concludes with the following observation:

> The new society that I sought to depict and that I wish to judge is only being born. Time has not yet fixed its form; the great revolution that created it still endures, and in what is happening in our day it is almost impossible to discern what will pass away with the revolution itself and what will remain after it. (Tocqueville 2000, 673)

See figure A.11 for a sample page of text with parenthetical citations.

18.3.2 Special Elements and Format Issues

The basic pattern for parenthetical citations is described in 18.1, and templates for several common types of sources appear in figure 18.1. This section covers special elements that may need to be included and special format issues that may arise in parenthetical citations of all types.

In the following situations, treat the name of an editor, translator, or other compiler of a work as you would an author's name, unless otherwise specified.

18.3.2.1 **AUTHORS WITH SAME LAST NAME.** If you cite works by more than one author with the same last name, add the author's first initial to each parenthetical citation, even if the dates are different. If the initials are the same, spell out the first names.

(J. Smith 2011, 140)   (Howard Bloom 2005, 15)
(T. Smith 2008, 25–26)   (Harold Bloom 2010, 270)

18.3.2.2 **WORKS WITH SAME AUTHOR AND DATE.** If you cite more than one work published in the same year by an author or group of authors named in the same order, arrange the entries alphabetically by title in your reference list and add the letters *a*, *b*, *c*, and so forth to the year (see 18.2.1.1). Use the same designations in your parenthetical citations (letters in roman type, without an intervening space after the date).

(Hsu 2017a, 74)   (Hsu 2017b, 59–60)

18.3.2.3 **NO AUTHOR.** If you cite a book or journal article without an author, use the title in place of the author in your reference list (see 18.2.1). In parenthetical citations, use a shortened title composed of up to the first four words from the full title (though you can usually omit *a*, *an*, or *the*), and put the title in italics or roman as in the reference list.

(*Account of Operations* 1870–1910)
("Great Trigonometrical Survey" 1863, 26)

For magazine and newspaper articles without authors, use the title of the magazine or newspaper in place of the author in both locations (see 19.3 and 19.4). For other types of sources, see the relevant section in chapter 19 for guidance; if not stated otherwise, use a shortened title in this position.

18.3.2.4 **NO DATE.** If you cite a published work without a date, use the designation *n.d.* (no date) in place of the date in both your reference list and parenthetical citations. Use roman type and lowercase letters.

(Smith n.d., 5)

For other types of sources, see the relevant section in chapter 19 for guidance.

18.3.2.5 **MORE THAN ONE WORK CITED.** If you cite several sources to make a single point, group them into a single parenthetical citation. List them alphabetically, chronologically, or in order of importance (depending on the context), and separate them with semicolons.

Several theorists disagreed strongly with this position (Armstrong and Malacinski 2003; Pickett and White 2009; Beigl 2010).

Additional works by the same author can be cited by date only.

(Wiens 1989a; 1989b)

18.3.3 Footnotes and Parenthetical Citations

If you wish to make substantive comments on the text, use footnotes instead of parenthetical citations. See 16.3.2–16.3.4 for note placement, numbering, and format. To cite a source within a footnote, use the normal parenthetical citation form.

N: 1. As Jill Lepore (2015, 228) observed, "Marston wanted the kids who read his comics to imagine a woman as president of the United States."

19 Author-Date Style: *Citing Specific Types of Sources*

Chapter 18 presents an overview of the basic pattern for citations in the author-date style, including both reference list entries and parenthetical citations. If you are not familiar with this citation style, read that chapter before consulting this one.

This chapter provides detailed information on the form of reference list entries (and, to a lesser extent, parenthetical citations) for a wide range of sources. It starts with the most commonly cited sources—books and journal articles—before addressing a wide variety of other sources. The sections on books (19.1) and journal articles (19.2) discuss variations in such elements as authors' names and titles of works in greater depth than sections on less common sources.

Examples of sources consulted online are included alongside most other types of examples. Electronic book formats are discussed at 19.1.10. For some general considerations, especially if you are new to research, see 15.4. For tips related to citation management tools, see 15.6.

Most sections include guidelines and examples for reference list entries (identified with an R). Since most parenthetical citations follow the basic pattern described in chapter 18, they are discussed here (and identified with a P) only for clarification or if unusual elements might cause confusion in preparing a parenthetical citation (for example, when a work has no author).

If you cannot find an example in this chapter, consult chapter 15 of *The Chicago Manual of Style*, 17th edition (2017). You may also create your own style, adapted from the principles and examples given here. Most instructors, departments, and universities accept such adaptations, as long as you apply them consistently.

19.1   Books

Citations of books may include a wide range of elements. Many of the variations in elements discussed in this section are also relevant to other types of sources.

19.1.1   Author's Name

In your reference list, give the name of each author (and editor, translator, or other contributor) exactly as it appears on the title page, and in the same order. If a name includes more than one initial, use spaces between them (see 24.2.1). Put the first-listed author's name in inverted order (last name first), except for some non-English names and other cases explained in 18.2.1.2. Names of any additional authors should follow but should not be inverted.

R: Barker-Benfield, G. J. 2010. *Abigail and John Adams: The Americanization of Sensibility*. Chicago: University of Chicago Press.

Kinder, Donald R., and Allison Dale-Riddle. 2012. *The End of Race? Obama, 2008, and Racial Politics in America*. New Haven, CT: Yale University Press.

Mukherjee, Ankhi. 2013. *What Is a Classic? Postcolonial Rewriting and Invention of the Canon*. Stanford, CA: Stanford University Press.

In parenthetical citations, use only the author's last name, exactly as given in the reference list. For works with three or more authors, see figure 18.1.

P: (Barker-Benfield 2010, 499)

(Kinder and Dale-Riddle 2010, 47)

(Mukherjee 2013, 184–85)

19.1.1.1 **EDITOR OR TRANSLATOR IN ADDITION TO AN AUTHOR.** If a title page lists an editor or a translator in addition to an author, treat the author's name as described above. Add the editor or translator's name after the book's title. If there is a translator as well as an editor, list the names in the same order as on the title page of the original.

In reference list entries, insert the phrase *Edited by* or *Translated by* before the editor's or translator's name.

R: Elizabeth I. 2000. *Collected Works.* Edited by Leah S. Marcus, Janel Mueller, and Mary Beth Rose. Chicago: University of Chicago Press.

Hegel, Georg Wilhelm Friedrich. 2010. *The Science of Logic.* Edited and translated by George di Giovanni. Cambridge: Cambridge University Press.

Jitrik, Noé. 2005. *The Noé Jitrik Reader: Selected Essays on Latin American Literature.* Edited by Daniel Balderston. Translated by Susan E. Benner. Durham, NC: Duke University Press.

When a title page identifies an editor or translator with a complicated description, such as "Edited with an Introduction and Notes by" or "Translated with a Foreword by," you can simplify this phrase to *edited by* or *translated by* and follow the above examples. In general, if a foreword or an introduction is written by someone other than the author, you need not mention that person unless you cite that part specifically (see 19.1.9).

In parenthetical citations, do not include the name of an editor or translator if the work appears in your reference list under the author's name.

P: (Elizabeth I 2000, 102–4)

(Hegel 2010, 642–43)

(Jitrik 2005, 189)

19.1.1.2 **EDITOR OR TRANSLATOR IN PLACE OF AN AUTHOR.** When an editor or a translator is listed on a book's title page instead of an author, use that person's name in the author's slot. Treat it as you would an author's name (see the beginning of this section), but in the reference list, add the abbreviation *ed.* or *trans.* following the name. If there are multiple editors or translators, use *eds.* or *trans.* (singular and plural) and follow the principles for multiple authors shown in figure 18.1.

R: Heaney, Seamus, trans. 2000. *Beowulf: A New Verse Translation.* New York: W. W. Norton.

Logroño Narbona, María del Mar, Paulo G. Pinto, and John Tofik Karam, eds. 2015. *Crescent over Another Horizon: Islam in Latin America, the Caribbean, and Latino USA*. Austin: University of Texas Press.

P: (Heaney 2000, 55)

(Logroño Narbona, Pinto, and Karam 2015, 140–41)

19.1.1.3   **ORGANIZATION AS AUTHOR.** If a publication issued by an organization, association, commission, or corporation has no personal author's name on the title page, list the organization itself as author, even if it is also given as publisher. For public documents, see 19.9.

R: American Bar Association. 2016. *The 2016 Federal Rules Book*. Chicago: American Bar Association.

P: (American Bar Association 2016, 192)

19.1.1.4   **PSEUDONYM.** Treat a widely recognized pseudonym as if it were the author's real name. If the name listed as the author's is known to be a pseudonym but the real name is unknown, add *pseud.* in brackets after the pseudonym in a reference list entry, though not in a parenthetical citation.

R: Centinel [pseud.]. 1981. "Letters." In *The Complete Anti-Federalist*, edited by Herbert J. Storing. Chicago: University of Chicago Press.

Twain, Mark. 1899. *The Prince and the Pauper: A Tale for Young People of All Ages*. New York: Harper and Brothers.

P: (Twain 1899, 34)

(Centinel 1981, 2)

19.1.1.5   **ANONYMOUS AUTHOR.** If the authorship is known or guessed at but omitted from the book's title page, include the name in brackets (with a question mark if there is uncertainty). If the author or editor is unknown, avoid the use of *Anonymous* in place of a name (but see below), and begin the reference list entry with the title. In parenthetical citations, use a shortened title (see 18.3.2).

R: [Hawkes, James?]. 1834. *A Retrospect of the Boston Tea-Party, with a Memoir of George R. T. Hewes*. By a Citizen of New-York. New-York.

A True and Sincere Declaration of the Purpose and Ends of the Plantation Begun in Virginia, of the Degrees Which It Hath Received, and Means by Which It Hath Been Advanced. 1610. London.

P: ([Hawkes, James?] 1834, 128–29)

(*True and Sincere Declaration* 1610, 17)

If the author is explicitly listed as "Anonymous" on the title page, cite the book accordingly.

B: Anonymous. 2015. *The Secret Lives of Teachers*. Chicago: University of Chicago Press.

P: (Anonymous 2015, 202)

19.1.2 Date of Publication

The publication date for a book consists only of a year, not a month or day, and is usually identical to the copyright date. It generally appears on the copyright page and sometimes on the title page.

In a reference list entry, set off the date as its own element with periods. In a parenthetical citation, put it after the author's name without intervening punctuation.

R: Chen, Cheng. 2016. *The Return of Ideology: The Search for Regime Identities in Post-communist Russia and China*. Ann Arbor: University of Michigan Press.

P: (Chen 2016, 34–35)

Revised editions and reprints may include more than one copyright date. In this case, the most recent indicates the publication date—for example, 2017 in the string "© 2003, 2010, 2017." See 19.1.4 for citing publication dates in such works.

If you cannot determine the publication date of a printed work, use the abbreviation *n.d.* in place of the year. If no date is provided but you believe you know it, you may add it in brackets, with a question mark to indicate uncertainty. (For the use of access dates for undated sources consulted online, see 19.5.1.)

R: Agnew, John. n.d. *A Book of Virtues*. Edinburgh.
Miller, Samuel. [1750?]. *Another Book of Virtues*. Boston.

P: (Agnew n.d., 5)
(Miller [1750?], 5)

If a book is under contract with a publisher and is already titled but the date of publication is not yet known, use *forthcoming* in place of the date. To avoid confusion, include a comma after the author's name in a parenthetical citation of this type. Treat any book not yet under contract as an unpublished manuscript (see 19.6).

R: Author, Jane Q. Forthcoming. *Book Title*. Place of Publication: Publisher's Name.

P: (Author, forthcoming, 16)

19.1.3   Title

List complete book titles and subtitles in reference list entries. Italicize both, and separate the title from the subtitle with a colon. (In the rare case of two subtitles, either follow the punctuation in the original or use a colon before the first and a semicolon before the second.)

R: Marsden, Philip. 2016. *Rising Ground: A Search for the Spirit of Place.* Chicago: University of Chicago Press.

Capitalize all titles and subtitles headline-style; that is, capitalize the first letter of the first and last words of the title and subtitle and all major words. For titles in languages other than English, use sentence-style capitalization—that is, capitalize only the first letter of the first word of the title and subtitle and any proper nouns or other terms that would be capitalized under the conventions of the original language (in some Romance languages, proper adjectives and some proper nouns are not capitalized). (See 22.3.1 for a more detailed discussion of the two styles.)

(headline style) *How to Do It: Guides to Good Living for Renaissance Italians*

(sentence style) *A quoi rêvent les algorithmes: Nos vies à l'heure des big data*

Preserve the spelling, hyphenation, and punctuation of the original title, with two exceptions: change words in full capitals (except for initialisms or acronyms; see chapter 24) to upper- and lowercase, and change an ampersand (&) to *and*. Spell out numbers or give them as numerals according to the original (*twelfth century* or *12th century*) unless there is a good reason to make them consistent with other titles in the list.

For titles of chapters and other parts of a book, see 19.1.9.

19.1.3.1   SPECIAL ELEMENTS IN TITLES.   Several elements in titles require special treatment.

■ *Dates.* Use a comma to set off dates at the end of a title or subtitle, even if there is no punctuation in the original source. But if the source introduces the dates with a preposition (for example, "from 1920 to 1945") or a colon, do not add a comma.

R: Hayes, Romain. 2011. *Subhas Chandra Bose in Nazi Germany: Politics, Intelligence, and Propaganda, 1941–43.* New York: Columbia University Press.
     Sorenson, John L., and Carl L. Johannessen. 2009. *World Trade and Biological Exchanges before 1492.* Bloomington, IN: iUniverse.

■ *Titles within titles.* When the title of a work that would normally be italicized appears *within* the italicized title of another, enclose the quoted title in quotation marks. (If the title-within-a-title would normally be enclosed in quotation marks, keep the quotation marks.)

R: Ladenson, Elisabeth. 2007. *Dirt for Art's Sake: Books on Trial from "Madame Bovary" to "Lolita."* Ithaca, NY: Cornell University Press.

McHugh, Roland. 1991. *Annotations to "Finnegans Wake."* 2nd ed. Baltimore: Johns Hopkins University Press.

However, when the entire main title of a book consists of a title within a title, do not add quotation marks (but keep any quotation marks used in the source).

R: Light, Alan. 2014. *Let's Go Crazy: Prince and the Making of "Purple Rain."* New York: Atria Books.

Wilde, Oscar. 2011. *The Picture of Dorian Gray: An Annotated, Uncensored Edition.* Edited by Nicholas Frankel. Cambridge, MA: Harvard University Press.

■ *Italicized terms.* When an italicized title includes terms normally italicized in text, such as species names or names of ships, set the terms in roman type.

R: Pennington, T. Hugh. 2003. *When Food Kills: BSE,* E. coli, *and Disaster Science.* New York: Oxford University Press.

Lech, Raymond B. 2001. *The Tragic Fate of the* U.S.S. Indianapolis: *The U.S. Navy's Worst Disaster at Sea.* New York: Cooper Square Press.

■ *Question marks and exclamation points.* When a title or a subtitle ends with a question mark or an exclamation point, no other punctuation normally follows (but see 21.12.1).

R: Allen, Jafari S. 2011. *¡Venceremos? The Erotics of Black Self-Making in Cuba.* Durham, NC: Duke University Press.

Wolpert, Stanley. 2010. *India and Pakistan: Continued Conflict or Cooperation?* Berkeley: University of California Press.

19.1.3.2 **OLDER TITLES.** For titles of works published in the eighteenth century or earlier, retain the original punctuation and spelling. Also retain the original capitalization, even if it does not follow headline style. Words in all capital letters, however, should be given in upper- and lowercase. If the title is very long, you may shorten it, but provide enough information for readers to find the full title in a library or publisher's catalog. Indicate omissions in such titles by three ellipsis dots. Put the dots in square brackets to show that they are not part of the original title. (Square brackets are also used in the second example to show that the place of publication is known but did not appear with the source.) If the omission comes at the end of a title, add a period after the bracketed dots.

R: Escalante, Bernardino. 1579. *A Discourse of the Navigation which the Portugales doe make to the Realmes and Provinces of the East Partes of the Worlde* [. . .]. Translated by John Frampton. London.

Ray, John. 1673. *Observations Topographical, Moral, and Physiological: Made in a Journey Through part of the Low-Countries, Germany, Italy, and France: with A Catalogue of Plants not Native of England* [. . .] *Whereunto is added A Brief Account of Francis Willughby, Esq., his Voyage through a great part of Spain.* [London].

19.1.3.3   **NON-ENGLISH TITLES.** Use sentence-style capitalization for non-English titles, following the capitalization principles for proper nouns and other terms within the relevant language. If you are unfamiliar with these principles, consult a reliable source.

R: Kelek, Necla. 2006. *Die fremde Braut: Ein Bericht aus dem Inneren des türkischen Lebens in Deutschland.* Munich: Goldmann Verlag.

Piletić Stojanović, Ljiljana, ed. 1971. *Gutfreund i češki kubizam.* Belgrade: Muzej savremene umetnosti.

Reveles, José. 2016. *Échale la culpa a la heroína: De Iguala a Chicago.* New York: Vintage Español.

If you add the English translation of a title, place it after the original. Enclose it in brackets, without italics or quotation marks, and capitalize it sentence-style.

R: Wereszycki, Henryk. 1977. *Koniec sojuszu trzech cesarzy* [The end of the Three Emperors' League]. Warsaw: PWN.

Yu Guoming. 2011. *Zhongguo chuan mei fa zhan qian yan tan suo* [New perspectives on news and communication]. Beijing: Xin hua chu ban she.

If you need to cite both the original and a translation, use one of the following forms, depending on whether you want to focus readers on the original or the translation.

R: Furet, François. 1995. *Le passé d'une illusion.* Paris: Éditions Robert Laffont. Translated by Deborah Furet as *The Passing of an Illusion* (Chicago: University of Chicago Press, 1999).

or

Furet, François. 1999. *The Passing of an Illusion.* Translated by Deborah Furet. Chicago: University of Chicago Press. Originally published as *Le passé d'une illusion* (Paris: Éditions Robert Laffont, 1995).

19.1.4   Edition

Some works are published in more than one edition. Each edition differs in content or format or both. Always include information about the edition you actually consulted (unless it is a first edition, which is usually not labeled as such).

19.1.4.1 REVISED EDITIONS. When a book is reissued with significant content changes, it may be called a "revised" edition or a "second" (or subsequent) edition. This information usually appears on the book's title page and is repeated, along with the date of the edition, on the copyright page.

When you cite an edition other than the first, include the number or description of the edition after the title. Abbreviate such wording as "Second Edition, Revised and Enlarged" as *2nd ed.*; abbreviate "Revised Edition" as *Rev. ed.* Include the publication date only of the edition you are citing, not of any previous editions (see 19.1.2).

R: Foley, Douglas E. 2010. *Learning Capitalist Culture: Deep in the Heart of Tejas.* 2nd ed. Philadelphia: University of Pennsylvania Press.

Levitt, Steven D., and Stephen J. Dubner. 2006. *Freakonomics: A Rogue Economist Explores the Hidden Side of Everything.* Rev. ed. New York: HarperCollins.

19.1.4.2 REPRINT EDITIONS. Many books are reissued or published in more than one format—for example, in a paperback edition (by the original publisher or a different publisher) or in electronic form (see 19.1.10). Always record the facts of publication for the version you consulted. If the edition you consulted was published more than a year or two after the original edition, you may include the date of the original (see 19.1.2) in parentheses in the reference list entry.

R: Jarrell, Randall. 2010. *Pictures from an Institution: A Comedy.* Chicago: University of Chicago Press. (Orig. pub. 1954.)

P: (Jarrell 2010, 79–80)

If the reprint is a modern printing of a classic work, you should still cite the reprint edition, but if the original publication date is important in the context of your paper, include it in brackets before the reprint date in both your reference list and your parenthetical citations.

R: Dickens, Charles. 2011. *Pictures from Italy.* Cambridge: Cambridge University Press. (Orig. pub. 1846.)

P: (Dickens 2011, 10)

or

R: Dickens, Charles. [1846] 2011. *Pictures from Italy.* Cambridge: Cambridge University Press.

P: (Dickens [1846] 2011, 10)

19.1.5   Volume

If a book is part of a multivolume work, include this information in your citations.

19.1.5.1   SPECIFIC VOLUME. To cite a specific volume that carries its own title, list the title for the multivolume work as a whole, followed by the volume number and title of the specific volume. Use the publication date of the individual volume. Abbreviate *vol.* and use arabic numbers for volume numbers. See also 18.2.1.

R: Naficy, Hamid. 2011. *A Social History of Iranian Cinema.* Vol. 2, *The Industrializing Years, 1941–1978.* Durham, NC: Duke University Press.

———. 2012. *A Social History of Iranian Cinema.* Vol. 4, *The Globalizing Era, 1984–2010.* Durham, NC: Duke University Press.

P: (Hamid 2011, 119)

(Hamid 2012, 44)

If the volumes are not individually titled, list each volume that you cite in the reference list (see also 19.1.5.2). In a parenthetical citation, put the specific volume number immediately before the page number, separated by a colon and no intervening space.

R: Byrne, Muriel St. Clare, ed. 1981. *The Lisle Letters.* Vols. 1 and 4. Chicago: University of Chicago Press.

P: (Byrne 1981, 4:243)

Some multivolume works have both a general editor and editors or authors for each volume. When citing a specific volume in such a work, include information about the volume editor(s) or author(s) (see 19.1.1) as well as information about the editor(s) of the multivolume work as a whole. The example from *The History of Cartography* shows not only how to cite an individual contribution to such a work (see 19.1.9) but also how to cite a volume published in more than one physical part (*vol.* 2, *bk.* 3).

R: Armstrong, Tenisha, ed. 2014. *To Save the Soul of America, January 1961–August 1962.* Vol. 7 of *The Papers of Martin Luther King, Jr.,* edited by Clayborne Carson. Berkeley: University of California Press.

Mundy, Barbara E. 1998. "Mesoamerican Cartography." In *The History of Cartography,* edited by J. Brian Harley and David Woodward, vol. 2, bk. 3, *Cartography in the Traditional African, American, Arctic, Australian, and Pacific Societies,* edited by David Woodward and G. Malcolm Lewis, 183–256. Chicago: University of Chicago Press.

P: (Armstrong 2014, 182)

(Mundy 1998, 233)

19.1.5.2 MULTIVOLUME WORK AS A WHOLE. To cite a multivolume work as a whole, give the title and the total number of volumes. If the volumes have been published over several years, list the full span of publication dates in both your reference list and your parenthetical citations.

R: Aristotle. 1983. *Complete Works of Aristotle: The Revised Oxford Translation.* Edited by J. Barnes. 2 vols. Princeton, NJ: Princeton University Press.
Tillich, Paul. 1951–63. *Systematic Theology.* 3 vols. Chicago: University of Chicago Press.

P: (Tillich 1951–63, 2:41)

For works that include individual volume titles or volume editors (see 19.1.5.1), it is usually best to cite each volume in the reference list individually.

19.1.6 Series

If a book belongs to a series, you may choose to include information about the series to help readers locate the source and understand the context in which it was published. Place the series information after the title (and any volume or edition number or editor's name) and before the facts of publication.

Put the series title in roman type with headline-style capitalization, omitting any initial *The.* If the volumes in the series are numbered, include the number of the work cited following the series title. The name of the series editor is often omitted, but you may include it after the series title. If you include both an editor and a volume number, the number is preceded by *vol.*

R: Hausman, Blake M. 2011. *Riding the Trail of Tears.* Native Storiers: A Series of American Narratives. Lincoln: University of Nebraska Press.
Lunning, Frenchy, ed. 2014. *World Renewal.* Mechademia 10. Minneapolis: University of Minnesota Press.
Stein, Gertrude. 2008. *Selections.* Edited by Joan Retallack. Poets for the Millennium, edited by Pierre Joris and Jerome Rothenberg, vol. 6. Berkeley: University of California Press.

19.1.7 Facts of Publication

The facts of publication usually include two elements: the place (city) of publication and the publisher's name. (A third fact of publication, the date, appears as a separate element following the author's name in this citation style; see 19.1.2.)

R: Coates, Ta-Nehisi. 2015. *Between the World and Me.* New York: Spiegel & Grau.

For books published before the twentieth century, you may omit the publisher's name.

R: Darwin, Charles. 1871. *The Descent of Man, and Selection in Relation to Sex.* 2 vols. London.

19.1.7.1   **PLACE OF PUBLICATION.** The place of publication is the city where the book publisher's main editorial offices are located. If you do not see it listed on the title page, look for it on the copyright page instead. Where two or more cities are given ("Chicago and London," for example), include only the first.

Los Angeles: Getty Publications
New York: Columbia University Press

If the city of publication might be unknown to readers or confused with another city of the same name, add the abbreviation of the state (see 24.3.1), province, or (if necessary) country. When the publisher's name includes the state name, no state abbreviation is needed.

Cheshire, CT: Graphics Press
Harmondsworth, UK: Penguin Books
Cambridge, MA: MIT Press
Chapel Hill: University of North Carolina Press

Prefer current, commonly used English names for cities whenever such forms exist. (When in doubt about which form to use, record the name of the city as it appears with the source.)

Belgrade (*not* Beograd)   Milan (*not* Milano)

When the place of publication is not known (an uncommon occurrence for older works, which typically specify a city of publication), you may use the abbreviation *N.p.* before the publisher's name. If the place can be guessed, include it in brackets and add a question mark to indicate uncertainty.

N.p.: Windsor.
[Lake Bluff, IL?]: Vliet and Edwards.

It is common for books published more recently through modern self-publishing platforms not to list a place of publication. If you cite such a source, the place of publication can usually be omitted (see 19.1.7.2 for an example).

19.1.7.2   **PUBLISHER'S NAME.** Give the publisher's name for each book exactly as it appears on the title page, even if you know that the name has since changed or appears in a different form for other books in your reference list.

Harcourt Brace and World
Harcourt Brace Jovanovich
Harcourt, Brace

You may, however, omit an initial *The* and such abbreviations as *Inc.*, *Ltd.*, *S.A.*, *Co.*, *& Co.*, and *Publishing Co.* (and the spelled-out forms of such corporate abbreviations).

University of Texas Press	*instead of*	The University of Texas Press
Houghton Mifflin	*instead of*	Houghton Mifflin Co.
Little, Brown	*instead of*	Little, Brown & Co.

For non-English publishers, do not translate or abbreviate any part of the publisher's name, but give the city name in its English form (as noted in 19.1.7.1). When the publisher is unknown, use just the place (if known). If a book has been self-published, however, this fact may be noted (see also 17.1.7.1).

R: Albin, Eleazar. 1738. *A Natural History of Birds: Illustrated with a Hundred and One Copper Plates, Engraven from the Life*. London: printed by the author.
Rai, Alisha. 2015. *Serving Pleasure*. Self-published, CreateSpace.

19.1.8   Page Numbers and Other Locators
Page numbers and other information used to identify the location of a cited passage or element generally appear in parenthetical citations but not in reference lists. One exception: if you cite a chapter or other section of a book in a reference list, give the page range for that chapter or section (see 19.1.9 for examples).

For guidelines for expressing a span of numbers, see 23.2.4. For page numbers and other locators in e-book formats, see 19.1.10.

19.1.8.1   PAGE, CHAPTER, AND DIVISION NUMBERS.   The locator is usually the last item in a parenthetical citation. Before page numbers, the word *page* or the abbreviation *p.* or *pp.* is generally omitted. Use arabic numbers except for pages numbered with roman numerals in the original.

P: (Arum and Roksa 2011, 145–46)
(Jones 2010, xiv–xv)

Sometimes you may want to refer to a full chapter (abbreviated *chap.*), part (*pt.*), book (*bk.*), or section (*sec.*) instead of a span of page numbers.

P: (Datar, Garvin, and Cullen 2010, pt. 2)

Some books printed before 1800 do not carry page numbers but are divided into signatures and then into leaves or folios, each with a front side (*recto*, or *r*) and a back side (*verso*, or *v*). To cite such pages, include the relevant string of numbers and identifiers, run together without spaces or italics: for example, G6v, 176r, 232r–v, or (if you are citing entire folios) fol. 49.

19.1.8.2 OTHER TYPES OF LOCATORS. Sometimes you will want to cite a specific note, a figure or table, or a numbered line (as in some works of poetry).

- *Note numbers.* Use the abbreviation *n* (plural *nn*) to cite notes. If the note cited is the only footnote on its page or is an unnumbered footnote, add *n* after the page number (with no intervening space or punctuation). If there are other footnotes or endnotes on the same page as the note cited, list the page number followed by *n* or (if two or more consecutive notes are cited) *nn* and the note number(s).

P: (Grafton 1997, 72n)
    (Bolinger 1980, 192n23, 192n30, 199n14, 201nn16–17)

- *Illustration and table numbers.* Use the abbreviation *fig.* for *figure*, but spell out *table*, *map*, *plate*, and names of other types of illustrations. Give the page number before the illustration number.

P: (Sobel 1993, 87, table 5.3)

- *Line numbers.* For poetry and other works best identified by line number, avoid the abbreviations *l.* (line) and *ll.* (lines); they are too easily confused with the numerals 1 and 11. Use *line* or *lines*, or use numbers alone where you have made it clear that you are referring to lines.

P: (Nash 1945, lines 1–4)

19.1.9 Chapters and Other Parts of a Book

In most cases you can cite the main title of any book that offers a continuous argument, narrative, or theme, even if you actually use only a section of it. But sometimes you will want to cite an independent essay or chapter if that is the part most relevant to your research. By doing so, you help readers see how the source fits into your project.

R: Nishizaki, Yoshinori. 2015. "Big Is Good: The Banharn-Jaemsai Observatory Tower in Suphanburi." In *A Sarong for Clio: Essays on the Intellectual and Cultural History of Thailand—Inspired by Craig J. Reynolds,* edited by Maurizio Peleggi, 143–62. Ithaca, NY: Cornell University Press.

P: (Nishizaki 2015, 143)

instead of

R: Peleggi, Maurizio, ed. 2015. *A Sarong for Clio: Essays on the Intellectual and Cultural History of Thailand—Inspired by Craig J. Reynolds*. Ithaca, NY: Cornell University Press.

P: (Peleggi 2015, 143)

19.1.9.1 PARTS OF SINGLE-AUTHOR BOOKS. If you cite a chapter or other titled part of a single-author book, the reference list should include the title of the part first, in roman type and enclosed in quotation marks. After the designation *In*, give the book title, followed by the full span of page numbers for that part.

R: Gay, Roxane. 2014. "The Careless Language of Sexual Violence." In *Bad Feminist*, 128–136. New York: Harper Perennial.

Some books attributed to a single author include a separately authored part with a generic title such as *preface* or *afterword*. To cite such a part, add that term before the title of the book in roman type without quotation marks, and capitalize the first word only. Parenthetical citations mention only the part author's name.

R: Calhoun, Craig. 2005. Foreword to *Multicultural Politics: Racism, Ethnicity, and Muslims in Britain*, by Tariq Modood, ix–xv. Minneapolis: University of Minnesota Press.

P: (Calhoun 2005, xii)

If the author of the generic part is the same as the author of the book, however, cite the book as a whole in the reference list, not just the part (the part, if relevant, can be mentioned in the text).

19.1.9.2 PARTS OF EDITED COLLECTIONS. In a reference list, if you cite part of an edited collection with contributions by multiple authors, first list the part author, the date, and the part title (in roman type, enclosed in quotation marks). After the designation *In*, give the book title, the name of the editor, and the full span of page numbers for that part. Parenthetical citations mention only the part author's name.

R: Binkley, Cameron. 2011. "Saving Redwoods: Clubwomen and Conservation, 1900–1925." In *California Women and Politics: From the Gold Rush to the Great Depression*, edited by Robert W. Cherny, Mary Ann Irwin, and Ann Marie Wilson, 151–74. Lincoln: University of Nebraska Press.

P: (Binkley 2011, 155)

If you cite two or more contributions to the same edited collection, you may use a space-saving shortened form. In your reference list, provide a full citation for the whole book and shortened citations for each individual part. For the latter, provide the full author's name, the publication date, and the full title of the part; after the designation *In*, add the shortened name of the book's editor, the publication date, and the full span of page numbers for that part.

R: Bruegmann, Robert. 2008. "Built Environment of the Chicago Region." In Keating 2008, 76–314.

Keating, Ann Durkin, ed. 2008. *Chicago Neighborhoods and Suburbs: A Historical Guide.* Chicago: University of Chicago Press.

Reiff, Janice, L. 2008. "Contested Spaces." In Keating 2008, 55–63.

If you use this form, your parenthetical citations should refer to the parts only, not to the book as a whole.

P: (Bruegmann 2008, 299–300)   *not*   (Keating 2008, 299–300)

  (Reiff 2008, 57)   *not*   (Keating 2008, 57)

19.1.9.3 **WORKS IN ANTHOLOGIES.** Cite a short story, poem, essay, or other work published in an anthology in the same way you would a contribution to an edited collection with multiple authors. Give the titles of most works published in anthologies in roman type, enclosed in quotation marks. An exception is a book-length poem or prose work that is anthologized in full or in part; its title should be italicized (see 22.3.2).

R: Allende, Isabel. 1997. "The Spirits Were Willing." In *The Oxford Book of Latin American Essays,* edited by Ilan Stavans, 461–67. New York: Oxford University Press.

Wigglesworth, Michael. 2003. Excerpt from *The Day of Doom.* In *The New Anthology of American Poetry,* vol. 1, *Traditions and Revolutions, Beginnings to 1900,* edited by Steven Gould Axelrod, Camille Roman, and Thomas Travisano, 68–74. New Brunswick, NJ: Rutgers University Press.

P: (Allende 1997, 463–64)

  (Wigglesworth 2003, 68)

If the original publication date of a work is important in the context of your paper, include it in brackets before the anthology's publication date in both your reference list and your parenthetical citations.

R: Wigglesworth, Michael. [1662] 2003. Excerpt from . . .

P: (Wigglesworth [1662] 2003, 68)

19.1.9.4 **LETTERS AND OTHER COMMUNICATIONS IN PUBLISHED COLLECTIONS.** Cite a letter, memorandum, or other such item in a published collection by the date of the collection. (For unpublished personal communications, see 19.6.2; for unpublished letters in manuscript collections, see 19.7.4.)

The word *letter* is unnecessary, but label other forms, such as a report or memorandum. Give the title and other data for the collection in the usual form for an edited book. The dates of individual correspondence should be woven into the text.

R: James, Henry. 1984. *Letters*. Edited by Leon Edel. Vol. 4, *1895–1916*. Cambridge, MA: Belknap Press of Harvard University Press.

White, E. B. 1976. *Letters of E. B. White*. Edited by Dorothy Lobrano Guth. New York: Harper & Row.

In a letter to Edith Wharton on November 8, 1905 (James 1984, 373), James wrote . . .

White (1976, 273) sent Ross an interoffice memo on May 2, 1946, pointing out that . . .

19.1.10 Electronic Books

Electronic books, or e-books, are cited just like print books, as discussed throughout 19.1. In addition, you will need to include information about the format you consulted. If you read the book online, include a URL. If you consulted the book in a commercial database, you can instead give the name of the database. See 15.4.1 for more details.

On the other hand, if you downloaded a book from Amazon or Apple or the like in a format that requires a specific app or device, include that information instead.

Many e-book formats lack fixed page numbers. Avoid citing app- or device-specific screen or location numbers, which may not be the same for others even if they consult the same format. Instead, cite by chapter or section number (see 19.1.8.1) or, if these are unnumbered, by the name of the chapter or section (see 19.1.9). Especially for a frequently cited source, it may be better simply to consult a version that reproduces the pagination of a printed edition. In the Dostoevsky example below, the page images from the Internet Archive are easier to cite than the reflowable Project Gutenberg text, and because they reproduce the original text exactly, they are also more authoritative.

R: Crispin, Jessa. 2015. *The Dead Ladies Project: Exiles, Expats, and Ex-Countries*. Chicago: University of Chicago Press, Adobe Digital Editions PDF.

Davis, Janet M. 2016. *The Gospel of Kindness: Animal Welfare and the Making of Modern America*. Oxford: Oxford University Press. https://doi.org/10.1093/acprof:oso/9780199733156.001.0001.

Dostoevsky, Fyodor. 2012. *Crime and Punishment/* Translated by Constance Garnett. Project Gutenberg. Last updated November 5, 2012. http://gutenberg.org/files/2554/2554-h/2554-h.htm.

or, better,

Dostoevsky, Fyodor. 1917. *Crime and Punishment*. Translated by Constance Garnett. Edited by William Allan Neilson. New York: P. F. Collier & Son. https://archive.org/details /crimepunishmentoodostuoft.

Gladwell, Malcolm. 2008. *Outliers: The Story of Success*. Boston: Little, Brown, 2008. Kindle.

Lee, Harper. 2015. *Go Set a Watchman*. New York: Harper. iBooks.

Schlosser, Eric. 2001. *Fast Food Nation: The Dark Side of the American Meal*. Boston: Houghton Mifflin. ProQuest Ebrary.

P: (Crispin 2015, 100–101)
(Davis 2016, 144–45)
(Dostoevsky 2012, pt. 6, chap. 1)

or, better,

(Dostoevsky 1917, 444)
(Gladwell 2008, 193)
(Lee 2015, chap. 19)
(Schlosser 2001, 88)

19.2   Journal Articles

Journals are scholarly or professional periodicals available primarily in academic libraries and by subscription. They often include the word *journal* in their title (*Journal of Modern History*) but not always (*Signs*). Journals are not the same as magazines, which are usually intended for a more general readership. This distinction is important because journal articles and magazine articles are cited differently (see 19.3). If you are unsure whether a periodical is a journal or a magazine, see whether its articles include citations; if so, treat it as a journal.

Many journal articles are available online, often through your school's library website or from a commercial database. To cite an article that you read online, include a URL. If a URL is listed along with the article, use that instead of the one in your browser's address bar. If a DOI is listed, append the DOI to https://doi.org/ to form the URL. If you consulted the article in a commercial database, you may give the name of the database instead of a URL. See 15.4.1 for more details.

19.2.1   Author's Name

Give authors' names exactly as they appear at the heads of their articles. Use last names in parenthetical citations. In the reference list, the name of the first-listed author is inverted. For some special cases, see 18.2.1.2.

19.2.2 Date of Publication

The main date of publication for a journal article consists only of a year. In a reference list entry, set it off as its own element with periods following the author's name. In a parenthetical citation, put it after the author's name without intervening punctuation.

R: Bartfeld, Judi, and Myoung Kim. 2010. "Participation in the School Breakfast Program: New Evidence from the ECLS-K." *Social Service Review* 84, no. 4 (December): 541–62. https://doi.org/10.1086/657109.

Garber, Marjorie. 2016. "Over the Influence," *Critical Inquiry* 42, no. 4 (Summer): 731–59. https://doi.org/10.1086/686960.

P: (Bartfeld and Kim 2010, 550–51)

(Garber 2016, 735)

Notice that additional date information appears in parentheses later in a reference list entry, after the volume number and issue information (see 19.2.5).

If an article has been accepted for publication but has not yet appeared, use *forthcoming* in place of the date (and page numbers). To avoid confusion, include a comma after the author's name in a parenthetical citation of this type. Treat any article not yet accepted for publication as an unpublished manuscript (see 19.6).

R: Author, Margaret M. Forthcoming. "Article Title." *Journal Name* 98.

P: (Author, forthcoming)

19.2.3 Article Title

List complete article titles and subtitles. Use roman type, separate the title from the subtitle with a colon, and enclose both in quotation marks. Use headline-style capitalization (see 22.3.1).

R: Taylor, Quentin. 2016. "The Mask of Publius: Alexander Hamilton and the Politics of Expediency." *American Political Thought* 5, no. 1 (Winter): 55–79. https://doi.org/10.1086/684559.

Terms normally italicized in text, such as species names and book titles, remain italicized within an article title; terms quoted in the title are enclosed in single quotation marks because the title itself is within double quotation marks. Do not add either a colon or a period after a title or subtitle that ends in a question mark or an exclamation point. But see 21.12.1.

R: Lewis, Judith. 1998. " 'Tis a Misfortune to Be a Great Ladie': Maternal Mortality in the British Aristocracy, 1558–1959." *Journal of British Studies* 37, no 1 (January): 26–40. http://www.jstor.org/stable/176034.

Twomey, Lisa A. 2011. "Taboo or Tolerable? Hemingway's *For Whom the Bell Tolls* in Postwar Spain." *Hemingway Review* 30, no. 2 (Spring): 54–72.

Titles in languages other than English should generally be capitalized sentence-style (see 22.3.1) according to the conventions of the particular language. If you add an English translation, enclose it in brackets, without quotation marks.

R: Carreño-Rodríguez, Antonio. 2009. "Modernidad en la literatura gauchesca: Carnavalización y parodia en el *Fausto* de Estanislao del Campo." *Hispania* 92, no. 1 (March): 12–24. http://www .jstor .org /stable /40648253.

Kern, W. 1938. "Waar verzamelde Pigafetta zijn Maleise woorden?" [Where did Pigafetta collect his Malaysian words?]. *Tijdschrift voor Indische taal-, land-en volkenkunde* 78:271–73.

19.2.4 Journal Title

After the article title, list the journal title in italics, with headline-style capitalization (see 22.3.1). Give the title exactly as it appears on the title page or on the journal website; do not use abbreviations, although you can omit an initial *The* (see also 22.3.2.1). If the official title is an initialism such as *PMLA*, do not expand it. For non-English journal titles, you may use either headline-style or sentence-style capitalization, but retain all initial articles (*Der Spiegel*).

19.2.5 Issue Information

In addition to a date of publication, most reference list entries include volume number, issue number, and month or season. Readers may not need all of these elements to locate an article, but including them all guards against a possible error in one of them.

The volume number follows the journal title without intervening punctuation and is not italicized. Use arabic numerals even if the journal itself uses roman numerals. If there is an issue number, it follows the volume number, separated by a comma and preceded by *no.*

Include additional date information beyond the year of publication (see 19.2.2) in parentheses after the volume and issue number. Follow the practice of the journal regarding such information; it may include a season, a month, or an exact day. Capitalize seasons in journal citations, even though they are not capitalized in text.

R: Brown, Campbell. 2011. "Consequentialize This." *Ethics* 121, no. 4 (July): 749–71. https://doi.org/10.1086/660696.

Ionescu, Felicia. 2011. "Risky Human Capital and Alternative Bankruptcy Regimes for Student Loans." *Journal of Human Capital* 5, no. 2 (Summer): 153–206. https://doi.org /10.1086/661744.

When a journal uses issue numbers only, without volume numbers, a comma follows the journal title.

R: Beattie, J. M. 1974. "The Pattern of Crime in England, 1660–1800." *Past and Present,* no. 62 (February): 47–95.

19.2.6 Page Numbers

For a reference list entry, give the full span of page numbers for the article (see 23.2.4). By convention, page numbers of journal articles in reference lists follow colons rather than commas.

R: Hitchcock, Tim. 2005. "Begging on the Streets of Eighteenth-Century London." *Journal of British Studies* 44, no. 3 (July): 478–98. https://doi.org/10.1086/429704.
Wang, ShiPu. 2016. "We Are Scottsboro Boys: Hideo Noda's Visual Rhetoric of Transracial Solidarity." *American Art* 30, no. 1 (Spring): 16–20. https://doi.org/10.1086/686545.

If you cite a particular passage in a parenthetical citation, give only the specific page(s) cited, preceded by a comma (not a colon).

P: (Hitchcock 2005, 478)
(Wang 2016, 16–17)

19.2.7 Special Issues and Supplements

A journal issue devoted to a single theme is known as a *special issue.* It carries a normal volume and issue number. If a special issue has a title and an editor of its own, include both in a reference list entry. The title is given in roman type and enclosed in quotation marks. In a parenthetical citation, give only the author of the part cited.

R: Sunder Rajan, Rajeswari. 2014. "Zeitgeist and the Literary Text: India, 1947, in Qurratulain Hyder's *My Temples, Too* and Salman Rushdie's *Midnight's Children.*" In "Around 1948: Interdisciplinary Approaches to Global Transformation," edited by Leela Gandhi and Deborah L. Nelson. Special issue, *Critical Inquiry* 40, no. 4 (Summer): 439–65. https://doi.org/10.1086/676415.

P: (Sunder Rajan 2014, 440–41)

If you need to cite the issue as a whole, omit the article information.

R: Gandhi, Leela, and Deborah L. Nelson, eds. 2014. "Around 1948: Interdisciplinary Approaches to Global Transformation." Special issue, *Critical Inquiry* 40, no. 4 (Summer).

A journal *supplement* may also have a title and an author or editor of its own. Unlike a special issue, it is numbered separately from the regular issues of the journal, often with S as part of its page numbers. Use a comma between the volume number and the supplement number.

R: Ekeland, Ivar, James J. Heckman, and Lars Nesheim. 2004. "Identification and Estimation of Hedonic Models." In "Papers in Honor of Sherwin Rosen," *Journal of Political Economy* 112, S1 (February): S60–S109. https://doi.org/10.1086/379947.

19.2.8 Abstracts

You can cite information in the abstract of a journal article or other work in a parenthetical citation. In the reference list, include the full citation for the journal article (or other work, such as a dissertation). In the parenthetical citation, insert the word *abstract*, set off by commas, after the year of publication and before any page number.

R: Brown, Campbell. 2011. "Consequentialize This." *Ethics* 121, no. 4 (July): 749–71.

P: (Brown 2011, abstract, 749)

19.3 Magazine Articles

Articles in magazines are cited much like journal articles (see 19.2), but dates and page numbers are treated differently.

Cite magazines by date only, even if they are numbered by volume and issue. In reference list entries, put the year in the usual position and the month and day (if specified) after the magazine title (but not in parentheses). You can repeat the year with the month and day in the reference list entry to avoid any confusion regarding the exact date. If you cite a specific passage in a parenthetical citation, include its page number. But you may omit the article's inclusive page numbers in a reference list entry, since magazine articles often span many pages that include extraneous material. (If you do include page numbers, use a comma rather than a colon to separate them from the date of issue.) As with journals, you can omit an initial *The* from the magazine title (see also 22.3.2.1).

R: Lepore, Jill. 2016. "The Woman Card." *New Yorker*, June 27, 2016.

P: (Lepore 2016, 23)

If you cite a department or column that appears regularly, capitalize it headline-style and do not enclose it in quotation marks.

R: Walraff, Barbara. 2005. Word Court. *Atlantic Monthly*, June 2005.

P: (Walraff 2005, 128)

Magazine articles consulted online should include in the reference list entry a URL (see also 15.4.1.3) or the name of a commercial database (see 15.4.1.4). Typically there will be no page numbers to cite.

R: Lukianoff, Greg, and Jonathan Haidt. 2015. "The Coddling of the American Mind." *Atlantic*, September 2015. http://www.theatlantic.com/magazine/archive/2015/09/the -coddling-of-the-american-mind/399356/.

Williams, Michael K. 2016. Interview by Eliana Dockterman. *Time*, July 25, 2016. EBSCOhost.

P: (Lukianoff and Haidt 2015)

(Williams 2016)

Magazine articles published online sometimes include readers' comments. These are cited like comments on blog posts (see 19.5.2).

19.4 Newspaper Articles

19.4.1 Name of Newspaper

You can usually omit an initial *The* from the name of an English-language newspaper (see also 22.3.2.1). If the name of a local newspaper does not include a city, it may be added to the official title. If a name is shared by many cities or is obscure, you may add the state or province in parentheses (for abbreviations, see 24.3.1); for national papers, you may need to identify the country. For non-English newspapers, you may use headline-style capitalization, but retain an initial article if it is formally part of the name; add city or other information after titles for clarity, if necessary.

Chicago Tribune	*Le Monde*
New York Times	*La Crónica de Hoy* (Mexico City)
Hackensack (NJ) Record	*Al-Akhbar* (Beirut)
Saint Paul (Alberta or AB) Journal	*Times* (UK)

The name of a news website can usually be treated in a similar way, except that a location will rarely be necessary.

Huffington Post	*Vox*

For blogs, which are treated similarly, see 19.5.2. For websites, see 19.5.1.

19.4.2 Citing Newspapers in Reference Lists and Parentheses

In your reference list, cite articles and other pieces from newspapers (or news websites) generally as you would articles in magazines (see 19.3). As with magazine articles, you can repeat the year with the month and day in the reference list entry to avoid any confusion regarding the exact date. For an unsigned article, use the name of the newspaper in place of the author. Because a newspaper may have several editions with slightly different contents, you may clarify which edition you consulted by adding *final edi-*

tion, *Midwest edition*, or some such identifier. Articles read online should include a URL. For articles obtained through a commercial database, you may give the name of the database instead. See 15.4.1 for more details.

R: Anderssen, Erin. 2016. "Through the Eyes of Generation Z." *Globe and Mail* (Toronto), June 25, 2016. http://www.theglobeandmail.com/news/national/through-the-eyes -of-generation-z/article30571914/.

Associated Press. 2015. "Ex UConn Student Applies for Probation over Mac and Cheese Meltdown." *USA Today College*, November 23, 2015. http://college.usatoday.com /2015/11/23/mac-and-cheese-uconn-probation/.

Gaddafi, Saif al-Islam. 2011. Interview by Simon Denyer. *Washington Post*, April 17, 2011.

Lind, Dara. 2016. "Moving to Canada, Explained." *Vox.* September 15, 2016. http://www .vox.com/2016/5/9/11608830/move-to-canada-how.

McIntosh, Fergus. 2016. Letter to the editor, *New York Times*, June 24, 2016.

Milwaukee Journal Sentinel. 2016. "Residency Ruling: State Supreme Court Guts Local Control." Editorial. June 24, 2016.

Pareles, John. 2016. Obituary for David Bowie. *New York Times*, January 26, 2016. New York edition.

Pegoraro, Rob. 2007. "Apple's iPhone Is Sleek, Smart and Simple." *Washington Post*, July 5, 2007. LexisNexis Academic.

Svrluga, Susan. 2017. "Harvard Law School Will No Longer Require LSAT for Admission." *Washington Post*, March 9, 2017. https://www.washingtonpost.com/news /grade-point/wp/2017/03/08/harvard-law-school-will-no-longer-require-the-lsat -for-admission/.

Omit page numbers in parenthetical citations because the item may appear on different pages or may even be dropped in different editions of the newspaper.

P: (Anderssen 2016)

(Associated Press 2015)

(Gaddafi 2011)

(Lind 2016)

(McIntosh 2016)

(*Milwaukee Journal Sentinel* 2016)

(Pareles 2016)

(Pegoraro 2007)

(Svrluga 2017)

Comments to online articles are cited in the text in reference to the article, which must be cited in the reference list or elsewhere in the text. See also 19.4.3 and 19.5.2.

. . . according to a comment by Lauren K. (Svrluga 2017).

Articles from Sunday "magazine" supplements or other special sections should be treated as you would magazine articles (see 19.3).

19.4.3 Citing Newspapers in Text

Instead of using a standard parenthetical citation, you can include some of the elements of the citation in your text. You should still give a full citation to the article in your reference list.

In his op-ed in support of a challenge by students over the use of Woodrow Wilson's name at Princeton (*New York Times*, November 24, 2015), Davis traces the negative impact of Wilson's policies on his paternal grandfather's career at the Government Printing Office.

19.5 Websites, Blogs, and Social Media

19.5.1 Website Content

Cite web pages and related content by identifying the following elements in your reference list entries: author, publication or revision date, title of the page (in roman type, enclosed in quotation marks), title (or description) of the site (usually in roman type; see 22.3.2.3), and the owner or sponsor of the site (if not the same as the title). Include a URL as the final element (see 15.4.1.3).

If there is no author, the source should be listed under the name of the owner or sponsor of the site or its title. For a frequently updated source (such as a wiki), you can record a time stamp if the source includes one. You can repeat the year with the month and day in the reference list entry to avoid any confusion regarding the exact date. If no date can be determined from the source, use *n.d.* (see 19.1.2) and include an access date (see 15.4.1.5).

R: Alliance for Linguistic Diversity. n.d. "Balkan Romani." Endangered Languages. Accessed June 10, 2016. http://www.endangeredlanguages.com/lang/5342.

Columbia University. n.d. "History." Accessed July 1, 2016. http://www.columbia.edu /content/history.html.

Google. 2016. "Privacy Policy." Privacy & Terms. Last modified March 25, 2016. http:// www.google.com/intl/en/privacypolicy.html.

Higgins, Susan B. 2016. "High School Students Explore Key Issues Facing American Indian Communities." News at Princeton, Princeton University, June 23, 2016. https://www .princeton.edu/main/news/archive/S46/66/02A46/.

Wikipedia. 2016. "Wikipedia: Manual of Style." Wikimedia Foundation. Last modified June 27, 2016, 09:57. http://en.wikipedia.org/wiki/Wikipedia:Manual_of_Style.

P: (Alliance for Linguistic Diversity n.d.)

(Columbia University n.d.)

(Google 2016)

(Higgins 2016)

(Wikipedia 2016)

Articles from news websites can usually be cited like articles in newspapers (see 19.4). For blogs, see 19.5.2.

19.5.2   Blog Posts

Blog posts (also called entries) are similar to articles in magazines and newspapers and can be cited in much the same way (see 19.3 and 19.4). In the reference list, put the title of the post in quotation marks and the title of the blog in italics (you can indicate "blog" in parentheses if it is not clear from the title). If the blog is part of a larger publication such as a newspaper or website, give the name of the publication after the title of the blog. You can repeat the year with the month and day in the reference list entry to avoid any confusion regarding the exact date.

R: Germano, William. 2017. "Futurist Shock." *Lingua Franca* (blog). *Chronicle of Higher Education*, February 15, 2017, http://www.chronicle.com/blogs/linguafranca/2017/02/15 /futurist-shock/.

Jayson, Sharon. 2016. "Is Selfie Culture Making Our Kids Selfish?" *Well* (blog). *New York Times*, June 23, 2016. http://well.blogs.nytimes.com/2016/06/23/is-selfie-culture -making-our-kids-selfish/.

West, Lindy. 2013. "Sweden Introduces New Gender-Neutral Pronoun, Makes Being a Man ILLEGAL." *Jezebel*, April 11, 2013. http://jezebel.com/sweden-introduces-new -gender-neutral-pronoun-makes-bei-472492079.

P: (Germano 2017)

(Jayson 2016)

(West 2013)

Comments are cited in the text, in reference to the original post, which must be cited in the reference list or elsewhere in the text. Identify the commenter and the date of the comment. Cite the name exactly as it appears, along with any identifying information. You can include the information either parenthetically or directly in the text.

P: (Muberra [Istanbul], June 26, 2016, comment on Jayson 2016)

According to a comment on June 26, 2016, by Muberra of Istanbul (Jayson 2016), . . .

References to an entire blog should also be made in the text rather than in a reference list. The URL can be listed in parentheses.

Lingua Franca, a blog published by the *Chronicle of Higher Education* (http://www .chronicle.com/blogs/linguafranca/), . . .

19.5.3   Social Media

Social media content can normally be cited in the text or in parenthetical citations. Include a specific item in your reference list only if it is critical to your argument or frequently cited. To cite direct messages and other personal or private content, follow the guidelines for citing personal communications (see 19.6.2). For publicly posted content, model your citations on the examples shown here. Include the following elements:

1. The author of the post. List a screen name in addition to the name of the person or group on the account, if known. Otherwise just use the screen name.
2. The year of the post. List the year after the author's name to facilitate parenthetical citations.
3. In place of a title, the text of the post. Quote up to the first 160 characters (enough to capture the typical text message), capitalized as in the original.
4. The type of post. This can include a description (*photo, video,* etc.).
5. The exact date of the post, including month and day. You can repeat the year with the month and day in the reference list entry to avoid any confusion regarding the exact date. You can also include a time stamp to help differentiate a post from others on the same day.
6. A URL. A URL can often be found via the date stamp for the item.

Social media can often be cited in the text, as in the first example. (If it is especially important to link back to the original post and there is no reference list entry to refer to, add the URL in parentheses, after the date.)

Conan O'Brien's tweet was characteristically deadpan: "In honor of Earth Day, I'm recycling my tweets" (@ConanOBrien, April 22, 2015).

R: Chicago Manual of Style. 2015. "Is the world ready for singular they? We thought so back in 1993." Facebook, April 17, 2015. https://www.facebook.com/ChicagoManual/posts/10152906193679151.

Díaz, Junot. 2016. "Always surprises my students when I tell them that the 'real' medieval was more diverse than the fake ones most of us consume." Facebook, February 24, 2016. https://www.facebook.com/junotdiaz.writer/posts/972495572815454.

O'Brien, Conan [@ConanOBrien]. 2015. "In honor of Earth Day, I'm recycling my tweets." Twitter, April 22, 2015, 11:10 a.m. https://twitter.com/ConanOBrien/status/590940792967016448.

Souza, Pete [@petesouza]. 2016. "President Obama bids farewell to President Xi of China at the conclusion of the Nuclear Security Summit." Instagram photo, April 1, 2016. https://www.instagram.com/p/BDrmfXTtNCt/.

P: (Chicago Manual of Style 2015)
(Díaz 2016)
(O'Brien 2015)
(Souza 2016)

Comments are cited in the text, in reference to the original post, which must be cited in the reference list or elsewhere in the text.

Michele Truty agreed, saying that "we do need a gender-neutral pronoun" (April 17, 2015, comment on Chicago Manual of Style 2015).

Items shared on social media tend to disappear; always keep a screen-shot of whatever you cite in case you need to refer to it later (see also 15.4.1.1).

19.5.4   Online Forums and Mailing Lists

Material posted or sent to an online forum or mailing list should nor-mally be cited only in the text. Include the name of the correspondent, the title of the subject or thread (in quotation marks and capitalized as in the original), the name of the forum or list, and the date and time of the post or message. Omit email addresses. (Posts on private forums or lists should be cited as personal communications; see 19.6.2.) Include a URL (see 15.4.1.3).

As with newspaper articles (see 19.4.3), you may choose to weave much of this information into the text. Be sure to preserve enough infor-mation to allow readers to identify the source.

P: (Caroline Braun, reply to "How did the 'cool kids' from high school turn out?," Quora, August 9, 2016, https://www.quora.com/How-did-the-cool-kids-from-high-school -turn-out/)

Sharon Naylor, in her email of August 23, 2011, to the Educ. & Behavior Science ALA Discussion List (http://listserv.uncc.edu/archives/ebss-1.html), pointed out that . . .

If you cite several items from a particular group or list, you may choose to include a particular thread or subject as a whole in your reference list. For the date, use the year (or span of years) for the posts cited in the text.

R: Quora. 2016. "How did the 'cool kids' of high school turn out?" https://www.quora.com /How-did-the-cool-kids-from-high-school-turn-out/.

19.6   Interviews and Personal Communications

19.6.1   Interviews

To cite an unpublished interview (including one you have conducted yourself), begin a reference list entry with the name of the person in-terviewed, followed by the date and the name of the interviewer. Also include the place and specific day of the interview (if known) and the location of any recordings or transcripts (if available). (You can repeat the year with the month and day in the reference list entry to avoid any confusion regarding the exact date.)

R: Shields, David. 2016. Interview by author. Seattle. July 22, 2016.

Spock, Benjamin. 1974. Interview by Milton J. E. Senn. November 20, 1974. Interview 67A, transcript, Senn Oral History Collection, National Library of Medicine, Bethesda, MD.

In parenthetical citations, use the name of the person interviewed, not that of the interviewer.

P: (Shields 2016)

(Spock 1974)

If you cannot reveal the name of the person interviewed, use only a parenthetical citation or weave the information into the text; you do not need to include the interview in your reference list. Explain the absence of a name ("All interviews were confidential; the names of interviewees are withheld by mutual agreement") in a footnote or a preface.

P: (interview with a home health aide, July 31, 2017)

Cite a published interview according to the rules for that type of publication, with one difference: the interviewee is treated as author.

R. Snowden, Edward. 2015. "Edward Snowden Explains How to Reclaim Your Privacy." Interview by Micah Lee. *The Intercept*, November 12, 2015. https://theintercept.com/2015/11/12/edward-snowden-explains-how-to-reclaim-your-privacy/.

P: (Snowden 2015)

For more examples, see 19.3 (magazine), 19.4.2 (newspaper), 19.10.3.6 (video). See also 22.3.2.1.

19.6.2 Personal Communications

Cite conversations, letters, email or text messages, and direct or private messages shared through social media only in parenthetical citations. The key elements, which should be separated with commas, are the name of the other person, the date, and the type of communication. In many cases you may be able to include some or all of this information in the text. Omit email addresses. To cite content shared publicly through social media, see 19.5.3; for online forums and mailing lists, see 19.5.4. To cite letters in published collections, see 19.1.9.4. For items in manuscript collections, see 19.7.4.

P: (Roland J. Zuckerman, email message to author, June 1, 2017)

In a conversation with me on March 1, 2017, Carla C. Ramirez confirmed that . . .

A copy of the postcard, postmarked San Diego, March 7, 1965 (Emma Fenton to author, Instagram direct message, March 25, 2017), . . .

19.7 Papers, Lectures, and Manuscript Collections

19.7.1 Theses and Dissertations

Theses and dissertations are cited much like books except for the title, which is in roman type and enclosed in quotation marks. After the author, date, and title, list the kind of paper and the academic institution. Abbreviate *dissertation* as *diss.* If you've consulted the paper online, include a URL. If you consulted the document in an institutional repository or commercial database, you can list the name of the repository or database instead. See 15.4.1 for more details.

R: Culcasi, Karen Leigh. 2003. "Cartographic Representations of Kurdistan in the Print Media." Master's thesis, Syracuse University.

Levin, Dana S. 2010. "Let's Talk about Sex . . . Education: Exploring Youth Perspectives, Implicit Messages, and Unexamined Implications of Sex Education in Schools." PhD diss., University of Michigan. http://hdl.handle.net/2027.42/75809.

Navarro-Garcia, Guadalupe. 2016. "Integrating Social Justice Values in Educational Leadership: A Study of African American and Black University Presidents." PhD diss., University of California, Los Angeles. ProQuest Dissertations & Theses Global.

19.7.2 Lectures and Papers Presented at Meetings

After the author, date, and title of the lecture or paper, list the sponsorship, location of the meeting, and the specific date(s) of the meeting at which it was given. (You can repeat the year with the month and day in the reference list entry to avoid any confusion regarding the exact date.) If you consulted a text or transcript of the lecture or paper online, include a URL (see 15.4.1.3). If you watched or listened to the presentation online, adapt the examples here to the advice at 19.10.3.3.

R: Carvalho Filho, Irineu de, and Renato P. Colistete. 2010. "Education Performance: Was It All Determined 100 Years Ago? Evidence from São Paulo, Brazil." Paper presented at the 70th annual meeting of the Economic History Association, Evanston, IL, September 24–26, 2010. http://mpra.ub.uni-muenchen.de/24494/1/MPRA_paper _24494.pdf.

Hong, Viviana. 2015. "Censorship in Children's Literature during Argentina's Dirty War (1976–1983)." Lecture, University of Chicago, Chicago, IL, April 30, 2015.

Pycior, Julie Leininger. 2016. "Trailblazers and Harbingers: Mexicans in New York before 1970." Paper presented at the 130th annual meeting of the American Historical Society, Atlanta, GA, January 8, 2016.

19.7.3 Pamphlets and Reports

Cite a pamphlet, corporate report, brochure, or similar freestanding publication as you would a book. If you lack data for some of the usual elements, such as author and publisher, give enough other information to identify the document. Sources consulted online should include a URL (see 15.4.1.3).

R: Clark, Hazel V. 1957. *Mesopotamia: Between Two Rivers.* Mesopotamia, OH: Trumbull County Historical Society.

Donahue, Elisabeth Hirschhorn, ed. 2015. *Woodrow Wilson School of Public and International Affairs: Annual Report 2014–15.* Princeton, NJ: Princeton University. http://wws .princeton.edu/about-wws/wws-annual-report.

19.7.4 Manuscript Collections

Documents from physical collections of unpublished manuscripts involve more complicated and varied elements than published sources. In your citations, include as much identifying information as you can, format the elements consistently, and adapt the general patterns outlined here as needed.

19.7.4.1 ELEMENTS TO INCLUDE AND THEIR ORDER. If you cite multiple documents from a collection, list the collection as a whole in your reference list, under the name of the collection, the author(s) of the items in the collection, or the depository. For similar types of unpublished material that have not been placed in archives, replace information about the collection with such wording as "in the author's possession" or "private collection," and do not mention the location. Do not include a date, since most collections contain items from various dates.

R: Egmont Manuscripts. Phillipps Collection. University of Georgia Library, Athens. House, Edward M., Papers. Yale University Library, New Haven, CT.

Pennsylvania Society for the Abolition of Slavery. Papers. Historical Society of Pennsylvania, Philadelphia.

Strother, French, and Edward Lowry. Undated correspondence. Herbert Hoover Presidential Library, West Branch, IA.

Women's Organization for National Prohibition Reform. Papers. Alice Belin du Pont files, Pierre S. du Pont Papers. Eleutherian Mills Historical Library, Wilmington, DE.

To cite an individual document from such a collection in your text, identify the author and date, the title or type of document, and the name of the collection or the depository used in the reference list entry. Separate the elements with commas. In many cases you may be able to include some or all of this information in the text.

P: (James Oglethorpe to the trustees, January 13, 1733, Egmont Manuscripts)

In his letter of January 13, 1733, to the trustees (Egmont Manuscripts), James Oglethorpe declared . . .

If you cite only one document from a collection, list it individually in your reference list, and follow the usual pattern for parenthetical citations.

R: Dinkel, Joseph. 1869. Description of Louis Agassiz written at the request of Elizabeth Cary Agassiz. Agassiz Papers. Houghton Library, Harvard University, Cambridge, MA.

P: (Dinkel 1869)

19.7.4.2 HOW TO FORMAT THE ELEMENTS. Here are some special formatting recommendations for documents in manuscript collections.

- *Specific versus generic titles.* Use quotation marks for specific titles of documents but not for generic terms such as *report* and *minutes*. Capitalize generic names of this kind only if they are part of a formal heading in the manuscript, not if they are merely descriptive.
- *Locating information.* Although some manuscripts may include page numbers that can be included in parenthetical citations, many will have other types of locators, or none at all. Older manuscripts are usually numbered by signatures only or by folios (*fol.*, *fols.*) rather than by page. Some manuscript collections have identifying series or file numbers that you can include in a citation. Items on microfilm may have roll (or sheet) and frame numbers.
- *Papers and manuscripts.* In titles of manuscript collections the terms *papers* and *manuscripts* are synonymous. Both are acceptable, as are the abbreviations *MS* and *MSS* (plural).
- *Letters.* To cite a letter in a parenthetical citation, start with the name of the letter writer, followed by *to* and the name of the recipient. Omit the word *letter*, which is understood, but for other forms of communication, specify the type (telegram, memorandum). For letters in published collections, see 19.1.9.4.

19.7.5 Online Collections

Some manuscript collections have been scanned and organized for consultation online. Cite such items by adapting the rules for manuscript collections in 19.7.4. Include a URL for the collection in the reference list entry (see also 15.4.1.3).

R: Washington, George, Papers. 1750–96. Series 5: Financial Papers. Library of Congress, Washington, DC. http://memory.loc.gov/ammem/gwhtml/gwseries5.html.

P: (Daily Expenses, July 1787, images 7–8, Washington Papers 1750–96)

19.8 Older Works and Sacred Works

19.8.1 Classical, Medieval, and Early English Literary Works

Literary works produced in classical Greece and Rome, medieval Europe, and Renaissance England are cited differently from modern literary works. These sources are often organized into numbered sections (books, lines, stanzas, and so forth) that are generally cited in place of page numbers. Because such works have been published in so many versions and translations over the centuries, the date and other facts of publication for modern editions are generally less important than in other types of citations.

For this reason, classical, medieval, and early English literary works should usually be cited only in parenthetical citations. If the author's name and the title are not already mentioned in the surrounding text, include them along with the section number upon first reference. If subsequent citations clearly refer to the same work, list only the section number. See below regarding differences in punctuation, abbreviations, and numbers among different types of works.

The eighty days of inactivity for the Peloponnesian fleet at Rhodes (Thucydides, *The History of the Peloponnesian War* 8.44.4), terminating before the end of winter (8.60.2–3), suggests . . .

or

The eighty days of inactivity reported by Thucydides for the Peloponnesian fleet at Rhodes (*The History of the Peloponnesian War* 8.44.4), terminating before the end of winter (8.60.2–3), suggests . . .

If your paper is in literary studies or another field concerned with close analysis of texts, or if differences in translations are relevant, include such works in your reference list. Follow the rules for other translated and edited books in 19.1.1.1.

R: Propertius. 1990. *Elegies*. Edited and translated by G. P. Goold. Loeb Classical Library 18. Cambridge, MA: Harvard University Press.

Aristotle. 1983. *Complete Works of Aristotle: The Revised Oxford Translation*. Edited by J. Barnes. 2 vols. Princeton, NJ: Princeton University Press.

19.8.1.1   CLASSICAL WORKS. In addition to the general principles listed above, the following rules apply to citations of classical works.

Use no punctuation between the title of a work and a line or section number. Numerical divisions are separated by periods without spaces. Use arabic numerals (and lowercase letters, if needed) for section numbers. Put commas between two or more citations of the same source and semicolons between citations of different sources.

> P: (Aristophanes, *Frogs* 1019–30)
> (Cicero, *In Verrem* 2.1.21, 2.3.120; Tacitus, *Germania* 10.2–3)
> (Aristotle, *Metaphysics* 3.2.996b5–8; Plato, *Republic* 360e–361b)

You can abbreviate the names of authors, works, collections, and so forth. The most widely accepted abbreviations appear in the *Oxford Classical Dictionary*. Use these abbreviations rather than *ibid.* in succeeding references to the same work. In the first example, the author (Thucydides) stands in for the title so no comma is needed.

> P: (Thuc. 2.40.2–3)
> (Pindar, *Isthm.* 7.43–45)

19.8.1.2   MEDIEVAL WORKS. The form for classical references works equally well for medieval works written in languages other than English.

> P: (Augustine, *De civitate Dei* 20.2)
> (Abelard, *Epistle 17 to Heloïse*, in Migne, *PL* 180.375c–378a)

19.8.1.3   EARLY ENGLISH WORKS. In addition to the general principles listed above, the following rules apply to citations of early English literary works.

Cite poems and plays by book, canto, and stanza; stanza and line; act, scene, and line; or similar divisions. Separate the elements with commas for clarity.

> P: (Chaucer, "Wife of Bath's Prologue," *Canterbury Tales*, lines 105–14)
> (Milton, *Paradise Lost*, book 1, lines 83–86)

You may shorten numbered divisions by omitting words such as *act* and *line*, using a system similar to the one for classical references (see 19.8.1.1). Be sure to explain your system in a footnote ("References are to book and line numbers").

> P: (Milton, *Paradise Lost* 1.83–86)

If editions differ in wording, line numbering, and even scene division—common in works of Shakespeare—include the work in your reference list, with edition specified.

R: Shakespeare, William. 2006. *Hamlet*. Edited by Ann Thompson and Neil Taylor. Arden Shakespeare 3. London: Arden Shakespeare.

19.8.2 The Bible and Other Sacred Works

Cite the Bible and sacred works of other religious traditions in parenthetical citations. You do not need to include them in your reference list.

For citations from the Bible, include the abbreviated name of the book, the chapter number, and the verse number—never a page number. Depending on the context, you may use either traditional or shorter abbreviations for the names of books (see 24.6); consult your instructor if you are unsure which form is appropriate. Use arabic numerals for chapter and verse numbers (with a colon between them) and for numbered books.

Traditional abbreviations:

P: (1 Thess. 4:11, 5:2-5, 5:14)

Shorter abbreviations:

P: (2 Sm 11:1-17, 11:26-27; 1 Chr 10:13-14)

Since books and numbering differ among versions of the scriptures, identify the version you are using in brackets in your first citation with either the spelled-out name or an accepted abbreviation (see 24.6.4).

P: (2 Kings 11:8 [New Revised Standard Version])
(1 Cor. 6:1-10 [NAB])

For citations from the sacred works of other religious traditions, adapt the general pattern for biblical citations as appropriate (see 24.6.5).

19.9 Reference Works and Secondary Citations

19.9.1 Reference Works

Well-known reference works, such as major dictionaries and encyclopedias, should usually be cited only in parenthetical citations. You generally need not include them in your reference list, although you may choose to include a specific work that is critical to your argument or frequently cited. Omit the date, but specify the edition (if not the first, or unless no edition is specified). Articles consulted online will require a URL (see 15.4.1.3); for undated items, include an access date (see 15.4.1.5). For a work arranged by key terms such as a dictionary or encyclopedia, cite the item (not the volume or page number) preceded by s.v. (*sub verbo*, "under the word"; pl. *s.vv.*)

P: (*Oxford English Dictionary*, 3rd ed., s.v. "ROFL," accessed March 9, 2017, http://www.oed
.com/view/Entry/156942#eid1211161030)

(*Encyclopaedia Britannica*, s.v. "Dame Margaret Drabble," accessed June 26, 2016, http://
www.britannica.com/biography/Margaret-Drabble)

Reference works on disk should include information about the medium.

P: (*Oxford English Dictionary*, 2nd ed., CD-ROM, version 4.0, s.v. "onomatopoeia")

Treat reference works that are more specialized or less well known as
you would a book (see 19.1).

R: *MLA Handbook*. 2016. 8th ed. New York: Modern Language Association of America.
Aulestia, Gorka. 1989. *Basque–English Dictionary*. Reno: University of Nevada Press.

P: (*MLA Handbook* 2016, 6.8.2)
(Aulestia 1989, 509)

An individual entry by a named author can be cited like a chapter in a
book (see 19.1.9).

19.9.2 Reviews

Reviews of books, performances, and so forth may appear in a variety of
periodicals and other sources. In your reference list, include the name
of the reviewer; the words *review of*, followed by the name of the work
reviewed and its author (or composer, director, or the like); any other
pertinent information (such as film studio or location of a performance);
and, finally, the periodical in which the review appeared. (You can repeat
the year with the month and day in the reference list entry to avoid any
confusion regarding the exact date.) If the review was consulted online,
include a URL (see 15.4.1.3).

R: Brody, Richard. 2013. Review of *Gravity*, directed by Alfonso Cuarón. Warner Bros. Pictures. *New Yorker*, October 4, 2013.

Cox, Katharine. 2016. Review of *Covered in Ink: Tattoos, Women, and the Politics of the Body*,
by Beverly Yuen Thompson. *Journal of Gender Studies* 25, no. 3: 349–50. https://doi.org
/10.1080/09589236.2016.1171889.

Williams, Richard. 2015. Review of Bob Dylan in concert at the Royal Albert Hall, London,
UK. *Guardian*, October 22, 2015. https://www.theguardian.com/music/2015/oct/22
/bob-dylan-review-royal-albert-hall-london.

19.9.3 One Source Quoted in Another

Responsible researchers avoid repeating quotations that they have not
actually seen in the original. If one source includes a useful quotation
from another source, readers expect you to obtain the original to verify

not only that the quotation is accurate but also that it fairly represents what the original meant.

If the original source is unavailable, however, cite it as "quoted in" the secondary source in your reference list. In a parenthetical citation, give only the name of the original author.

R: Zukofsky, Louis. 1931. "Sincerity and Objectification." *Poetry* 37 (February): 269. Quoted in Bonnie Costello, *Marianne Moore: Imaginary Possessions* (Cambridge, MA: Harvard University Press, 1981).

P: (Zukofsky 1931, 269)

The same situation may arise with a quotation you find in a secondary source drawn from a primary source (see 3.1). Often you will not be able to consult the primary source, especially if it is in an unpublished manuscript collection. In this case, follow the principles outlined above.

If, however, you consult a primary document or other work exhibited by the holding institution as part of an online collection (as opposed to a copy posted by someone else), such a source can usually be considered primary for the purposes of research. See 19.7.5 and 19.10.1.1 for examples.

19.10 Sources in the Visual and Performing Arts

The visual and performing arts generate a variety of sources, including artworks, live performances, broadcasts and streams, recordings in various media, and texts. Citing these sources involves determining which elements are needed to fully identify them, formatting the elements consistently, and adapting the general patterns outlined here as needed.

Some of the sources covered in this section, where noted, can be cited in parenthetical citations only or by weaving the key elements into your text, although you may choose to include a specific item in your reference list that is critical to your argument or frequently cited. If your paper is for a course in the arts, media studies, or a similar field, consult your instructor.

19.10.1 Artworks and Graphics

19.10.1.1 PAINTINGS, SCULPTURES, AND PHOTOGRAPHS. Cite paintings, sculptures, photographs, drawings, and the like only in parenthetical citations. Include the name of the artist, the title of the artwork (in italics) and date of its creation (preceded by "ca." [circa] if approximate), and the name of the institution that houses it (if any), including location. Separate the elements with commas. You may also include the medium and related information, if relevant.

P: (Georgia O'Keeffe, *The Cliff Chimneys*, 1938, oil on canvas, Milwaukee Art Museum)

(Michelangelo, *David*, 1501–4, Galleria dell'Accademia, Florence)

(Ansel Adams, *North Dome, Basket Dome, Mount Hoffman, Yosemite*, ca. 1935, silver print, 16.5 × 21.9 cm, Smithsonian American Art Museum, Washington, DC)

(Erich Buchholz, *Untitled*, 1920, gouache on paper, Museum of Modern Art, New York)

Instead of using a parenthetical citation, you can sometimes cite artworks by weaving the elements into your text.

O'Keeffe first demonstrated this technique in *The Cliff Chimneys* (1938, Milwaukee Art Museum).

If you viewed the artwork in a published source or online and your local guidelines require you to identify this source, include it in your reference list. For images consulted online, include a URL (see also 15.4.1.3). Whenever possible, consult the item through the website of the institution at which it is physically located. In your parenthetical citation, if the source is different from the artist, give the usual author-date citation in place of the institutional name and location.

R: Buchholz, Erich. 1920. *Untitled*. Gouache on paper. Museum of Modern Art, New York. http://www.moma.org/collection/works/38187.

Lynes, Barbara Buhler, Lesley Poling-Kempes, and Frederick W. Turner. 2004. *Georgia O'Keeffe and New Mexico: A Sense of Place*. Princeton, NJ: Princeton University Press.

P: (Buchholz 1920)

(Georgia O'Keeffe, *The Cliff Chimneys*, 1938, in Lynes, Poling-Kempes, and Turner 2004, 25)

19.10.1.2 GRAPHIC ARTS.   Cite graphic sources such as print advertisements, maps, cartoons, and so forth only in parenthetical citations, adapting the basic patterns for artworks and giving as much information as possible. Give any title or caption in roman type, enclosed in quotation marks, and identify the type of graphic if it is unclear from the title. For items consulted online, include a URL (see 15.4.1.3); for undated sources, also include an access date (see 15.4.1.5).

P: (Apple Inc., "Shot on iPhone 6S by Anh N.," full-page advertisement, *New Yorker*, July 4, 2016, back cover)

(*Yu ji tu* [Map of the tracks of Yu], AD 1136, Forest of Stone Steles Museum, Xi'an, China, stone rubbing, 1933?, 84 × 82 cm, Library of Congress, http://www.loc.gov/item /gm71005080/)

(Chrissy Teigen crying at the 2015 Golden Globe Awards, animated GIF, GIPHY, accessed July 3, 2016, http://giphy.com/gifs/girl-lol-crying-P2kEMJjHosUUg)

(Evan Brown, "The 10 Commandments of Typography," infographic, DesignMantic, April 11, 2014. http://www.designmantic.com/blog/infographics/ten-commandments -of-typography/)

Any information included in the text need not be repeated in the parenthetical citation.

Apple's full-page *New Yorker* ad ("Shot on iPhone 6S by Anh N.," back cover, July 4, 2016) . . .

19.10.2 Live Performances

Cite live theatrical, musical, or dance performances only in parenthetical citations. Include the title of the work performed, the author, any key contributors or performers and an indication of their roles, the venue and its location, and the date. Italicize the titles of plays and long musical compositions, but set the titles of shorter works in roman type, enclosed in quotation marks except for musical works referred to by genre (see 22.3.2.3). If the citation is focused on an individual's performance, list that person's name before the title of the work. Separate the elements with commas.

P: (*Hamilton*, music and lyrics by Lin-Manuel Miranda, directed by Thomas Kail, choreographed by Andy Blakenbuehler, Richard Rodgers Theatre, New York, NY, February 2, 2016)

(Simone Dinnerstein, pianist, Intermezzo in A, op. 118, no. 2, by Johannes Brahms, Portland Center for the Performing Arts, Portland, OR, January 15, 2012.)

Instead of relying entirely on a parenthetical citation, you can usually weave some of the elements into your text.

Simone Dinnerstein's performance of Brahms's Intermezzo in A, op. 118, no. 2 (January 15, 2012, at Portland Center for the Performing Arts), was anything but intermediate . . .

If you viewed or listened to a live performance in a recorded medium, cite the recording in your reference list. See 19.10.3 for similar types of examples.

R: Rubinstein, Artur, pianist. 1975. "Spinning Song," by Felix Mendelssohn. Ambassador College, Pasadena, CA, January 15, 1975. On *The Last Recital for Israel*. BMG Classics, 1992. VHS.

19.10.3 Multimedia

Citations of movies, television and radio programs, recorded music, and other works in multimedia formats will vary depending on the type of source. At a minimum, identify the title of the work, the date it was created or published or otherwise made available, the name of the studio or other entity responsible for producing or distributing the work, and information about the medium in which you consulted it. If you consulted the source online, include a URL (see 15.4.1.3).

19.10.3.1 MOVIES. In the reference list, cite a movie under the name of the director. After the date (the year the movie was released or created or otherwise made available), give the title of the movie (in italics), followed by the name of the company that produced or distributed it. (You may also include a publication date for the recording.) Include information about writers, actors, producers, and so forth if it is relevant to your discussion. Finish with any relevant information about the medium. If you watched online, include a URL (see 15.4.1.3).

R: Cuarón, Alfonso, director. 2013. *Gravity*. Warner Bros. Pictures, 2014. Blu-ray Disc, 1080p HD.

Famuyiwa, Rick, director. *Dope*. Open Road Films, 2015. 1 hr., 43 min. https://www.netflix .com/watch/80037759.

Kubrick, Stanley, director. 1964. *Dr. Strangelove, or: How I Learned to Stop Worrying and Love the Bomb*. Featuring Peter Sellers, George C. Scott, and Sterling Hayden. Columbia. 1 hr., 34 min. https://www.amazon.com/dp/B000P407K4.

Weed, A. E. 1903. *At the Foot of the Flatiron*. American Mutoscope and Biograph. 35mm film. From Library of Congress, *The Life of a City: Early Films of New York, 1898–1906*. MPEG video, 2:19 at 15 fps. https://www.loc.gov/item/00694378.

In the text you can include information about timings, in the form displayed with the source.

P: (Kubrick 1964, 0:11:43 to 0:14:54)

Information about ancillary material included with the movie should be woven into the text, with the parenthetical reference referring to the movie as a whole.

In a special feature titled "Complete Silence" (Cuarón 2013), the director acknowledges a tension between realism and audience expectations . . .

19.10.3.2 TELEVISION AND RADIO PROGRAMS. To cite a television or radio program, include, at a minimum, the title of the program, the name of the episode or segment, the date on which it was first aired or made available, and the entity that produced or broadcast the work. (You can repeat the year with the month and day in the reference list entry to avoid any confusion regarding the exact date.) You may also include an episode number, the name of the director or author of the episode or segment, and (if relevant to your discussion) the names of key performers. Italicize the titles of programs, but put the titles of episodes or segments in roman type, enclosed in quotation marks. Finish with any relevant information about the medium. If you watched online, include a URL (see 15.4.1.3).

R: *American Crime Story: The People v. O. J. Simpson.* 2016. Episode 6, "Marcia, Marcia, Marcia." Directed by Ryan Murphy. Written by D. V. DeVincentis. Featuring Sterling K. Brown, Kenneth Choi, and Sarah Paulson. Aired March 8, 2016, on FX. https://www .amazon.com/dp/B01ARVPCOA/.

Brady Bunch, The. 1971. Season 3, episode 10, "Her Sister's Shadow." Directed by Russ Mayberry. Aired November 19, 1971, on ABC. https://www.hulu.com/the-brady -bunch.

Fresh Air. 2016. "Pen-Pal Passion Is Revived In Broadway's 'She Loves Me.'" Hosted by David Bianculli. NPR, June 24, 2016. http://www.npr.org/2016/06/23/483245382/pen -pal-passion-is-revived-in-broadways-she-loves-me.

Jane the Virgin. 2016. Season 2, chapter 36. Directed by Uta Briesewitz. Aired March 7, 2016, on the CW Television Network.

Mad Men. 2007. Season 1, episode 12, "Nixon vs. Kennedy." Directed by Alan Taylor. Featuring Jon Hamm, Elisabeth Moss, and Vincent Kartheiser. Aired October 11, 2007, on AMC. Lions Gate Television. DVD, disc 4.

P: (*People v. O. J. Simpson* 2016)

Instead of using a parenthetical citation, you can often cite such programs by weaving the key elements into your text, especially if some or all of the additional elements are not relevant to the citation.

By alluding to *The Brady Bunch* (specifically "Her Sister's Shadow," from 1971), the title of episode 6 ("Marcia, Marcia, Marcia," March 8, 2016) not only calls attention to the central role of television in the trial but also . . .

19.10.3.3 **VIDEOS AND PODCASTS.** To cite videos other than movies (19.10.3.1) or television programs (19.10.3.2), adapt the examples in those sections accordingly. To cite a podcast, adapt the example for citing a radio program (19.10.3.2).

R: Beyoncé. 2016. "Sorry." Directed by Kahlil Joseph and Beyoncé Knowles. June 22, 2016. Music video, 4:25. https://youtu.be/QxsmWxxouIM.

Danforth, Mike, and Ian Chillag. 2015. "F-Bombs, Chicken, and Exclamation Points." April 21, 2015. In *How to Do Everything*, produced by Gillian Donovan. Podcast, MP3 audio, 18:46. http://www.npr.org/podcasts/510303/how-to-do-everything.

Donner, Fred. 2011. "How Islam Began." Alumni Weekend 2011, University of Chicago, June 3. Video of lecture. https://youtu.be/5RFK5u51khA.

Kessler, Aaron M. 2015. "The Driverless Now." Produced by Poh Si Teng and Jessica Naudziunas. *New York Times*, May 2, 2015. Video, 2:01. http://www.nytimes.com /video/business/100000003662208/the-driverless-now.html.

If relevant, you may include the time at which the cited material appears in the file in your parenthetical citation.

P: (Beyoncé 2016, at 1:09–1:24)

19.10.3.4   SOUND RECORDINGS.   To cite recorded music and the like, include as much information as you can to distinguish it from similar recordings, including the date of the recording, the name of the recording company, the identifying number of the recording, the copyright date (if different from the year of the recording), and any relevant information about the medium. List the recording under the name of the composer or the performer, depending on which is more relevant to your discussion. Titles of albums should be in italics; individual selections should be in quotation marks except for musical works referred to by genre (see 22.3.2.3). Abbreviate *compact disc* as CD. Recordings consulted online should include a URL (see 15.4.1.3); in some cases the name of a music service can stand in for a URL. In general, cite by year of recording, but you may repeat dates to avoid any confusion.

R: Holiday, Billie, vocalist. 1958. "I'm a Fool to Want You," by Joel Herron, Frank Sinatra, and Jack Wolf. Recorded February 20, 1958, with Ray Ellis. Track 1 on *Lady in Satin*. Columbia CL 1157. 33⅓ rpm.

Pink Floyd. 1970. "Atom Heart Mother." Recorded April 29, 1970, at Fillmore West, San Francisco. Concert Vault streaming audio. http://www.concertvault.com/pink-floyd /fillmore-west-april-29-1970.html.

Rihanna. 2007. "Umbrella." Featuring Jay-Z. Track 1 on *Good Girl Gone Bad*, Island Def Jam. Spotify streaming audio, 320 kbps.

Rubinstein, Artur, pianist. 1946 and 1958–67. *The Chopin Collection*. RCA Victor/BMG 60822-2-RG, 1991. 11 CDs.

Shostakovich, Dmitri. 1959 and 1965. Symphony no. 5 / Symphony no. 9. Conducted by Leonard Bernstein. Recorded with the New York Philharmonic, October 20, 1959 (no. 5), and October 19, 1965 (no. 9). Sony SMK 61841, 1999. CD.

Strauss, Richard. 1940. Don Quixote. With Emanuel Feuermann (violoncello) and the Philadelphia Orchestra, conducted by Eugene Ormandy. Recorded February 24, 1940. Biddulph LAB 042, 1991. CD.

P: (Holiday 1958)
(Shostakovich 1959 and 1965)

Treat recordings of drama, prose or poetry readings, lectures, and the like as you would musical recordings.

R: Strayed, Cheryl. *Wild: From Lost to Found on the Pacific Crest Trail*. Read by Bernadette Dunne. New York: Random House Audio, 2012. Audible audio ed., 13 hr., 6 min.

Thomas, Dylan. 1953. *Under Milk Wood.* Performed by Dylan Thomas et al. Recorded May 14, 1953. On *Dylan Thomas: The Caedmon Collection*, discs 9–10. Caedmon, 2002. 11 CDs.

19.10.3.5 VIDEO GAMES AND APPS. To cite video games and apps, adapt the examples included throughout this section on multimedia as needed. Titles of video games, like titles of movies, can be italicized. Include a version number and information about the device or operating system required to run the game or app. In the first example, the publishing information for *Gems and Gemstones* is in parentheses because such annotations are styled like regular text.

R: Grande, Lance, and Allison Augustyn. 2011. *Gems and Jewels.* iPad ed., v. 1.01. Touch-press. Adapted from Lance Grande and Allison Augustyn, *Gems and Gemstones: Timeless Natural Beauty of the Mineral World* (Chicago: University of Chicago Press, 2009).

Rovio Entertainment. 2014. *Angry Birds Transformers.* V. 1.4.25. Rovio Entertainment. Android 4.0 or later. Soundtrack by Vince DiCola and Kenny Meriedeth.

19.10.3.6 INTERVIEWS. To cite interviews in multimedia formats, treat the person interviewed as the author, and identify the interviewer in the context of the citation. Also include the program or publication and date of the interview (or publication or air date). For unpublished interviews and interviews in other types of published sources, see 19.6.1.

R: Sanders, Bernie. 2015. Interview by Rachel Maddow. *The Rachel Maddow Show.* September 18, 2015, MSNBC. Video, 19:51. https://youtu.be/8jV4sv9waBo.

P: (Sanders 2015)

19.10.3.7 ADVERTISEMENTS. Cite advertisements from television, radio, and the like only in parenthetical citations or by weaving the elements into your text, or both.

P: (Fitbit, "Dualities," advertisement, aired February 7, 2016, during Super Bowl 50, CBS, 30 sec., http://www.superbowlcommercials2016.org/fitbit/)

As with television shows (19.10.3.2), you can often cite advertisements by weaving the key elements into your text, especially if some or all of the additional elements are not available or relevant to the citation.

Fitbit's "Duality," a thirty-second spot that aired during the third quarter of Super Bowl 50 (CBS, February 7, 2016) . . .

19.10.4 Texts in the Visual and Performing Arts

19.10.4.1 ART EXHIBITION CATALOGS. Cite an art exhibition catalog as you would a book. In your reference list, include information about the exhibition following the publication data.

R: Chi, Jennifer Y., ed. 2015. *The Eye of the Shah: Qajar Court Photography and the Persian Past*. Princeton, NJ: Princeton University Press. Published in conjunction with an exhibition of the same name at New York University's Institute for the Study of the Ancient World, October 22, 2015–January 17, 2016.

19.10.4.2 PLAYS. In some cases you can cite well-known English-language plays in parenthetical citations only. (See also 19.8.1.) Separate the elements with commas. Omit publication data, and cite passages by act and scene (or other division) instead of by page number.

P: (Eugene O'Neill, *Long Day's Journey into Night*, act 2, scene 1)

If your paper is in literary studies or another field concerned with close analysis of texts, or if you are citing a translation or an obscure work, cite every play as you would a book, and include each in your reference list. Cite passages either by division or by page, according to your local guidelines.

R: Anouilh, Jean. 1996. *Becket, or The Honor of God*. Translated by Lucienne Hill. New York: Riverhead Books.
Bagnold, Enid. 1956. *The Chalk Garden*. New York: Random House.

P: (Bagnold 1956, 8–9)
(Anouilh 1996, act 1, scene 1)

19.10.4.3 MUSICAL SCORES. Cite a published musical score as you would a book.

R: Mozart, Wolfgang Amadeus. 1960. *Sonatas and Fantasies for the Piano*. Prepared from the autographs and earliest printed sources by Nathan Broder. Rev. ed. Bryn Mawr, PA: Theodore Presser.
Verdi, Giuseppe. 2008. *Giovanna d'Arco, dramma lirico* in four acts. Libretto by Temistocle Solera. Edited by Alberto Rizzuti. 2 vols. Works of Giuseppe Verdi, ser. 1, Operas. Chicago: University of Chicago Press; Milan: G. Ricordi.

Cite an unpublished score as you would unpublished material in a manuscript collection.

R: Shapey, Ralph. 1966. "Partita for Violin and Thirteen Players." Score. Special Collections, Joseph Regenstein Library. University of Chicago.

19.11 Public Documents

Public documents include a wide array of sources produced by governments at all levels throughout the world. This section presents basic principles for some common types of public documents available in English; if you need to cite other types, adapt the closest model.

Such documents involve more complicated and varied elements than most types of published sources. In your citations, include as much identifying information as you can, format the elements consistently, and adapt the general patterns outlined here as needed.

The bulk of this section is concerned with documents published by US governmental bodies and agencies. For documents published by the governments of Canada and the United Kingdom and by international bodies, see 19.11.9–11. For unpublished government documents, see 19.11.12.

19.11.1 Elements to Include, Their Order, and How to Format Them

In your reference list, include as many of the following elements as you can:

- name of the government (country, state, city, county, or other division) and government body (legislative body, executive department, court bureau, board, commission, or committee) that issued the document
- date of publication
- title, if any, of the document or collection
- name of individual author, editor, or compiler, if given
- report number or other identifying information (such as place of publication and publisher, for certain freestanding publications or for items in secondary sources)
- page numbers or other locators, if relevant
- a URL, or the name of the database, for sources consulted online (see 15.4.1 and, for examples, 19.11.2.2, 19.11.3, 19.11.7, and 19.11.11)

In general, list the relevant elements in the order given above. Exceptions for certain types of documents are explained in the following sections of 19.11.

R: US Congress, House of Representatives, Select Committee on Homeland Security. 2002. Homeland Security Act of 2002. 107th Cong., 2d sess. HR Rep. 107–609, pt. 1.

For parenthetical citations, treat the information listed before the date in your reference list as the author. If this information is lengthy, you may shorten it, as long as you do so logically and consistently in your citations. In many cases you may be able to include some or all of this information in the text instead of a parenthetical citation.

P: (US House 2002, 81–82)

. . . as the Select Committee decreed in its report accompanying the Homeland Security Act of 2002 (81–82).

Note that, by convention, ordinals in public documents end in *d* instead if *nd* (2*d* instead of 2*d*).

19.11.2 Congressional Publications

For congressional publications, reference list entries usually begin with the designation *US Congress,* followed by *Senate* or *House of Representatives* (or *House*). (You may also simplify this to *US Senate* or *US House.*) Other common elements include committee and subcommittee, if any; date of publication; title of document; number of the Congress and session (abbreviated *Cong.* and *sess.* respectively in this position); and number and description of the document (for example, H. Doc. 487), if available.

19.11.2.1 DEBATES. Since 1873, congressional debates have been published by the government in the *Congressional Record.* Whenever possible, cite the permanent volumes, which often reflect changes from the daily editions of the *Record.* Begin parenthetical citations with the abbreviation *Cong. Rec.,* and identify the volume and part numbers as well as the page numbers. (For citations of the daily House or Senate edition, retain the *H* or *S* in page numbers.)

R: US Congress. *Congressional Record.* 2008. 110th Cong., 1st sess. Vol. 153, pt. 8.

P: (*Cong. Rec.* 2008, 153, pt. 8: 11629–30)

If you need to identify a speaker and the subject in a debate, do so in text, and include a parenthetical citation for the publication only.

Senator Kennedy of Massachusetts spoke for the Joint Resolution on Nuclear Weapons Freeze and Reductions (*Cong. Rec.* 1982, 128, pt. 3: 3832–34).

Before 1874, congressional debates were published in *Annals of the Congress of the United States* (also known by other names and covering the years 1789–1824), *Register of Debates* (1824–37), and *Congressional Globe* (1833–73). Cite these works similarly to the *Congressional Record.*

19.11.2.2 REPORTS AND DOCUMENTS. When you cite reports and documents of the Senate (abbreviated S.) and the House (*H.* or *HR*), include both the Congress and session numbers and, if possible, the series number. This example was consulted online using an official government resource (the US Government Publishing Office). See also 15.4.1.3.

R: US Congress, House. 2015. Blocking Property and Suspending Entry of Certain Persons Engaging in Significant Malicious Cyber-Enabled Activities. 114th Cong., 1st sess. H. Doc. 114-22. https://www.gpo.gov/fdsys/pkg/CDOC-114hdoc22.

P: (US House 2015, 1–2)

19.11.2.3 BILLS AND RESOLUTIONS. Congressional bills (proposed laws) and resolutions are published in pamphlet form. In citations, bills and resolutions originating in the House of Representatives are abbreviated *HR* or *H. Res.* and those originating in the Senate, *S.* or *S. Res.* Include publication details in the *Congressional Record* (if available). If a bill has been enacted, cite it as a statute (see 19.9.2.5).

R: US Congress, House. 2016. Email Privacy Act. H. Res. 699. 114th Cong., 2d sess. *Congressional Record* 162, no. 65, daily ed. (April 27): H2022-28.

P: (US House 2016, H2022)

19.11.2.4 HEARINGS. Records of testimony given before congressional committees are usually published with formal titles, which should be included in reference list entries (in italics). The relevant committee is normally listed as part of the title.

R: US Congress, House. 2002. *Hearing before the Select Committee on Homeland Security.* HR 5005, Homeland Security Act of 2002, day 3. 107th Cong., 2d sess., July 17.

P: (US House 2002, 119–20)

19.11.2.5 STATUTES. Statutes, which are bills or resolutions that have been passed into law, are first published separately and then collected in the annual bound volumes of the *United States Statutes at Large*, which began publication in 1874. Later they are incorporated into the *United States Code.* Cite *US Statutes*, the *US Code*, or both. Section numbers in the *Code* are preceded by a section symbol (§; use §§ and *et seq.* to indicate more than one section).

In a parenthetical citation, indicate the year the act was passed; in your reference list, also include the publication date of the statutory compilation, which may differ from the year of passage.

R: Atomic Energy Act of 1946. Public Law 585. 79th Cong., 2d sess. August 1.
Fair Credit Reporting Act of 1970. *US Code* 15 (2000), §§ 1681 et seq.
Homeland Security Act of 2002. Public Law 107-296. *US Statutes at Large* 116 (2002): 2135-321. Codified at *US Code* 6 (2002), §§ 101 et seq.

P: (Atomic Energy Act of 1946, 12, 19)
(Fair Credit Reporting Act of 1970)
(Homeland Security Act of 2002, 2163–64)

Before 1874, laws were published in the seventeen-volume *Statutes at Large of the United States of America, 1789–1873*. Citations of this collection include the volume number and its publication date.

19.11.3 Presidential Publications

Presidential proclamations, executive orders, vetoes, addresses, and the like are published in the *Weekly Compilation of Presidential Documents* and in *Public Papers of the Presidents of the United States*. Proclamations and executive orders are also carried in the daily *Federal Register* and then published in title 3 of the *Code of Federal Regulations*. Once they have been published in the *Code*, use that as your source. Put individual titles in quotation marks. The example of a proclamation was consulted online from an official government resource (see also 15.4.1.3).

R: US President. 1997. Executive Order 13067. "Blocking Sudanese Government Property and Prohibiting Transactions with Sudan." *Code of Federal Regulations*, title 3 (1997 comp.): 230–31.

US President. 2016. Proclamation 9465. "Establishment of the Stonewall National Monument." *Federal Register* 81, no. 125 (June 29): 42215–20. https://federalregister.gov/a/2016-15536.

P: (US President 1997)

(US President 2016)

The public papers of US presidents are collected in two multivolume works: *Compilation of the Messages and Papers of the Presidents, 1789–1897* and, starting with the Hoover administration, *Public Papers of the Presidents of the United States*. (Papers not covered by either of these works are published elsewhere.) To cite items in these collections, follow the recommendations for multivolume books (see 19.1.5).

19.11.4 Publications of Government Departments and Agencies

Executive departments, bureaus, and agencies issue reports, bulletins, circulars, and other materials. Italicize the title, and include the name of any identified author(s) after the title.

R: US Department of the Interior, Minerals Management Service, Environmental Division. 2007. *Oil-Spill Risk Analysis: Gulf of Mexico Outer Continental Shelf (OCS) Lease Sales, Central Planning Area and Western Planning Area, 2007–2012, and Gulfwide OCS Program, 2007–2046*, by Zhen-Gang Ji, Walter R. Johnson, and Charles F. Marshall. Edited by Eileen M. Lear. MMS 2007–040, June 2007.

US Department of the Treasury. 1850–51. *Report of the Secretary of the Treasury Transmitting a Report from the Register of the Treasury of the Commerce and Navigation of the United States for the Year Ending the 30th of June, 1850*. 31st Cong., 2d sess. House Executive Document 8. Washington, DC.

P: (US Department of the Interior 2007, 23)

(US Department of the Treasury 1850–51, 15–16)

19.11.5 US Constitution

The US Constitution should be cited only in parenthetical citations; you need not include it in your reference list. Include the article or amendment, section, and, if relevant, clause. Use arabic numerals and, if you prefer, abbreviations for terms such as *amendment* and *section*.

P: (US Constitution, art. 2, sec. 1, cl. 3)

(US Constitution, amend. 14, sec. 2)

In many cases you can include the identifying information in your text, but spell out the part designations. Capitalize the names of specific amendments when used in place of numbers.

The US Constitution, in article 1, section 9, forbids suspension of the writ "unless when in Cases of Rebellion or Invasion the public Safety may require it."

The First Amendment protects the right of free speech.

19.11.6 Treaties

The texts of treaties signed before 1950 are published in *United States Statutes at Large*; the unofficial citation is to the *Treaty Series* (TS) or the *Executive Agreement Series* (EAS). Those signed in 1950 or later appear in *United States Treaties and Other International Agreements* (UST, 1950–) or *Treaties and Other International Acts Series* (TIAS, 1945–). Treaties involving more than two nations may be found in the *United Nations Treaty Series* (UNTS, 1946–) or, from 1920 to 1946, in the *League of Nations Treaty Series* (LNTS).

Italicize titles of the publications mentioned above and their abbreviated forms. Unless they are named in the title of the treaty, list the parties subject to the agreement, separated by hyphens. An exact date indicates the date of signing and may be included in addition to the year the treaty was published. (You can repeat the year with the month and day in the reference list entry to avoid any confusion regarding the exact date.)

R: United States. 1922. Naval Armament Limitation Treaty with the British Empire, France, Italy, and Japan. February 6, 1922. *US Statutes at Large* 43, pt. 2.

US Department of State. 1963. Treaty Banning Nuclear Weapon Tests in the Atmosphere, in Outer Space, and Under Water. US-UK-USSR. August 5, 1963. *UST* 14, pt. 2.

P: (United States 1922)

(US Department of State 1963, 1313)

19.11.7 Legal Cases

Citations of legal cases generally take the same form for courts at all levels. In your reference list, italicize the full case name (including the abbreviation *v.*). Include the volume number (arabic), name of the reporter (abbreviated; see below), ordinal series number (if applicable), opening page number of the decision, abbreviated name of the court and date (together in parentheses), and other relevant information, such as the name of the state or local court (if not identified by the reporter title).

R: *Profit Sharing Plan v. Mbank Dallas, N.A.* 683 F. Supp. 592 (N.D. Tex. 1988).
 United States v. Christmas. 222 F.3d 141 (4th Cir. 2000).

The one element that depends on the level of the court is the name of the reporter. The most common ones are as follows.

■ *US Supreme Court.* For Supreme Court decisions, cite *United States Supreme Court Reports* (abbreviated US) or, if not yet published there, *Supreme Court Reporter* (abbreviated S. Ct.).

R: *AT&T Corp. v. Iowa Utilities Bd.* 525 US 366 (1999).
 Brendlin v. California. 127 S. Ct. 2400 (2007).

■ *Lower federal courts.* For lower federal-court decisions, cite *Federal Reporter* (F.) or *Federal Supplement* (F. Supp.).

R: *Eaton v. IBM Corp.* 925 F. Supp. 487 (S.D. Tex. 1996).
 United States v. Dennis. 183 F. 201 (2d Cir. 1950).

■ *State and local courts.* For state and local court decisions, cite official state reporters whenever possible. If you use a commercial reporter, cite it as in the first example below. If the reporter does not identify the court's name, include it before the date, within parentheses.

R: *Bivens v. Mobley.* 724 So. 2d 458 (Miss. Ct. App. 1998).
 Williams v. Davis. 27 Cal. 2d 746 (1946).

To cite a legal case in your text, give the name of the case and the date (if citing specific language, provide the page number as well). In many instances you may be able to include either or both elements in the text.

P: (*United States v. Christmas* 2000)

  . . . this principle was best exemplified by *United States v. Christmas* (2000).

Cases consulted online should normally be cited to the appropriate reporter(s) as described above. A URL that points directly to an official resource may be added as the final element (see also 15.4.1.3).

R: *State v. Griffin.* 211 W. Va. 508, 566 S.E.2d 645 (2002). http://www.courtswv.gov/supreme
 -court/docs/spring2002/30433.htm.

Many researchers use Lexis or Westlaw to research court cases and other legal materials. To cite a case in one of those databases, add any identifying date and number supplied by the database (see also 15.4.1.4). Page or screen numbers are typically preceded by an asterisk.

R: *Family Service Association of Steubenville v. Wells Township.* 2015 US Dist. LEXIS 75017, *7 (SD Ohio, June 10, 2015). LexisNexis Academic.

19.11.8 State and Local Government Documents

Cite state and local government documents as you would federal documents. Use roman type (no quotation marks) for state laws and municipal ordinances; use italics for codes (compilations) and the titles of freestanding publications. State constitutions are cited only in parenthetical citations or in the text (see also 19.11.5).

R: Illinois Institute for Environmental Quality (IIEQ). 1977. *Review and Synopsis of Public Participation regarding Sulfur Dioxide and Particulate Emissions.* By Sidney M. Marder. IIEQ Document 77/21. Chicago.
Methamphetamine Control and Community Protection Act. 2005. *Illinois Compiled Statutes,* chap. 720, no. 646 (2005).
Page's Ohio Revised Code Annotated. 2011. Title 35, Elections.

P: (IIEQ 1977, 44–45)
(Methamphetamine Control and Community Protection Act 2005, sec. 10)
(*Page's Ohio Revised Code Annotated* 2011, sec. 3599.01)
(New Mexico Constitution, art. 4, sec. 7)

19.11.9 Canadian Government Documents

Cite Canadian government documents similarly to US public documents. End citations with the word *Canada* (in parentheses) unless it is obvious from the context.

Canadian statutes appeared through 1985 in the *Revised Statutes of Canada,* a consolidation that was published every fifteen to thirty years; federal statutes enacted since then are cited as session laws in the annual *Statutes of Canada.* Identify the statute by title, reporter, year of compilation, chapter, and section.

R: Assisted Human Reproduction Act. *Statutes of Canada* 2004, chap. 2, sec. 2.
Canada Wildlife Act. *Revised Statutes of Canada* 1985, chap. W-9, sec. 1.

P: (Canada Wildlife Act 1985)

Canadian Supreme Court cases since 1876 are published in *Supreme Court Reports* (SCR). Federal Court cases are published in *Federal Courts Reports* (FC, 1971–2003; FCR, 2004–) or *Exchequer Court Reports* (Ex. CR, 1875–1971). Cases not found in any of these sources may be found in *Dominion Law Reports* (DLR). Include the name of the case (in italics), followed by the date (in parentheses), the volume number (if any), the abbreviated name of the reporter, and the opening page of the decision.

R: *Canada v. CBC/Radio-Canada.* (2014) 1 FCR 142.
Robertson v. Thomson Corp. (2006) 2 SCR 363 (Canada).

19.11.10 British Government Documents

Cite British government documents similarly to US public documents. End citations with the phrase *United Kingdom* (in parentheses or brackets) unless it is obvious from the context.

Acts of Parliament should usually be cited only in parenthetical citations or in the text. Include a specific act in your reference list only if it is critical to your argument or frequently cited. Identify acts by title, date, and chapter number (arabic numeral for national number, lowercase roman for local). Acts from before 1963 are cited by regnal year and monarch's name (abbreviated) and ordinal (arabic numeral).

P: (Act of Settlement 1701, 12 & 13 Will. 3, c. 2)
(Consolidated Fund Act 1963, chap. 1 [United Kingdom])
(Manchester Corporation Act 1967, chap. xl)

Most British legal cases can be found in the applicable report in the *Law Reports*, among these the Appeal Cases (AC), Queen's (King's) Bench (QB, KB), Chancery (Ch.), Family (Fam.), and Probate (P.) reports. Until recently the courts of highest appeal in the United Kingdom (except for criminal cases in Scotland) had been the House of Lords (HL) and the Judicial Committee of the Privy Council (PC). In 2005 the Supreme Court of the United Kingdom (UKSC) was established.

Include the name of the case, in italics (cases involving the Crown refer to *Rex* or *Regina*); the date, in parentheses; the volume number (if any) and abbreviated name of the reporter; and the opening page of the decision. If the court is not apparent from the name of the reporter, or if the jurisdiction is not clear from context, include either or both, as necessary, in parentheses.

R: *NML Capital Limited (Appellant) v. Republic of Argentina (Respondent).* (2011) UKSC 31.
Regal (Hastings) Ltd. v. Gulliver. (1967) 2 AC 134 (HL) (appeal taken from Eng.).
Regina v. Dudley and Stephens. (1884) 14 QBD 273 (DC).

19.11.11 Publications of International Bodies

Documents published by international bodies such as the United Nations can be cited much like books. Identify the authorizing body (and any author or editor), the date, the title or topic of the document, and the publisher or place of publication (or both). Also include any series or other identifying publication information. For documents consulted online, include a URL (see 15.4.1.3).

R: League of Arab States and United Nations. 2010. *The Third Arab Report on the Millennium Development Goals 2010 and the Impact of the Global Economic Crises.* Beirut: Economic and Social Commission for Western Asia.

United Nations Security Council. 2015. Resolution 2222, Protection of Civilians in Armed Conflict. S/RES/2222. New York: UN, May 27. http://www.un.org/en/sc/documents /resolutions/2015.shtml.

P: League of Arab States and United Nations 2010, 82)
(UN General Assembly 2015)

19.11.12 Unpublished Government Documents

If you cite unpublished government documents, follow the patterns given for unpublished manuscripts in 19.7.4.

Most unpublished documents of the US government are housed in the National Archives and Records Administration (NARA) in Washington, DC, or in one of its branches, and cataloged online. Cite them all, including films, photographs, and sound recordings as well as written materials, by record group (RG) number.

The comparable institution for unpublished Canadian government documents is the Library and Archives Canada (LAC) in Ottawa, Ontario. The United Kingdom has a number of depositories of unpublished government documents, most notably the National Archives (NA) and the British Library (BL), both in London. Each of these resources has been cataloged online.

Part III | Style

20 Spelling

Model your spelling on American usage and be consistent, except in quotations, where you should usually follow the original spelling exactly (see chapter 25). When in doubt, consult a dictionary. Be aware, however, that dictionaries may differ on how to spell the same word and that some are more accurate and up-to-date than others.

The most reliable authority for spelling is Merriam-Webster. Both *Merriam-Webster's Collegiate Dictionary* and a larger, unabridged dictionary are available from Merriam-Webster.com (the unabridged version is available only online). For the names of people and places, consult the biographical and geographical listings in either of those resources or in *Encyclopaedia Britannica*.

Where Merriam-Webster offers a choice between spellings, use the following principles to select one: Where variants are separated by *or*, choose either one and use it consistently; where variants are separated by *also*, use the first. If the preferred spelling in Merriam-Webster differs from the conventional one in your discipline, follow the spelling of the discipline. For style guides in various disciplines, see the bibliography.

The spell-checking feature in most word processors can catch certain spelling errors but not others. It will normally fail to recognize, for example, that you typed *lead* when you meant *led*, or *quite* instead of *quiet*. It won't always help with proper nouns or terms from other languages, and it may lead you to make global spelling changes that in some cases are inaccurate. A spell-checker is not a substitute for a good dictionary and careful proofreading.

This chapter offers general guidelines for spellings not found in most dictionaries. If you are writing a thesis or dissertation, your department or university may have specific requirements for spelling (including use of particular dictionaries). Those requirements are usually available from the office of theses and dissertations. If you are writing a class paper, your instructor may also ask you to follow certain principles of spelling. Review these requirements before you prepare your paper. They take precedence over the guidelines suggested here.

20.1   Plurals

20.1.1   General Rule

For most common nouns, form the plural by adding *s* (or *es* for words ending in *ch, j, s, sh, x,* or *z*). Most dictionaries give plural forms only for words that do not follow the general rule.

The general rule applies to the names of persons and to other proper nouns. If a proper noun ends in *y*, however, do not change the *y* to *ie*, as required for many common nouns. (Do not confuse plural forms with possessives, which are described in 20.2.)

the Costellos   the Rodriguezes
the Frys (*not* the Fries)   the two Germanys

20.1.2   Special Cases

20.1.2.1   COMPOUND WORDS. For compound words consisting of two nouns, make the last noun plural (usually by adding *s* or *es*).

bookkeepers   district attorneys   actor-singers

When the compound consists of a noun followed by a prepositional phrase or adjective, make the main noun plural.

sisters-in-law   attorneys general   men-of-war

20.1.2.2 LETTERS AND NUMERALS. In most cases, form the plurals of capital letters and numerals by adding s alone (not 's).

three As, one B, and two Cs   the 1950s   767s

With lowercase letters, however, an s without an apostrophe can seem to create a different word (*is*) or an abbreviation (*ms*), so add an apostrophe. The apostrophe and s are roman even if the letter is italic (see 22.2.2).

x's and *y*'s

20.1.2.3 ABBREVIATIONS. Form plurals of abbreviations without internal periods by adding s alone. If the singular form of the abbreviation ends in a period, put the s before the period. (See 24.1.3 on the punctuation of abbreviations. For academic degrees, see 24.2.3.)

URLs   vols.
DVDs   eds.
PhDs

A few abbreviations have irregular plurals (see also 24.7).

pp. (plural of p., page)   nn. (plural of n., note)

If you are writing in the sciences and using abbreviations for units of measure (see 24.5), use the same abbreviation for both the singular and the plural.

6 kg   37 m²

20.1.2.4 TERMS IN ITALICS AND QUOTATION MARKS. Form the plural of a term in italics by adding s alone (not 's) in roman type. Form the plural of a term in quotation marks by adding s—or, better, rephrase the sentence.

two *Chicago Tribune*s

. . . included many "To be continued"s

or, better,

. . . included many instances of "To be continued"

20.2 Possessives

20.2.1 General Rule

Form the possessive of most singular common and proper nouns, including those that end in s, x, or z, by adding an apostrophe and s. This rule also applies to letters and numerals used as singular nouns, and to abbreviations. It also applies to proper names ending in s (whether or not the s is pronounced), as in the last three examples. (Do not confuse possessives with plural forms, which are described in 20.1.) For special cases, see 20.2.2.

an argument's effects	the phalanx's advance	Russ's suggestion
the horse's mouth	the waltz's tempo	Descartes's *Discourse on Method*
2018's economic outlook	JFK's speech	Aristophanes's plays

Inanimate nouns—except for references to time—rarely take the possessive form.

a day's length	*but not*	the house's door

Form the possessive of most plural common and proper nouns by adding only an apostrophe. For special cases, see 20.2.2.

politicians' votes	*not*	politicians's votes
the Rodriguezes' house	*not*	the Rodriguezes's house

For irregular plurals that do not end in s, add s after the apostrophe.

the mice's nest	children's literature

20.2.2 Special Cases

20.2.2.1 SINGULAR NOUNS ENDING IN "S." Form the possessive of the following types of nouns with only an apostrophe:

- nouns that name a group or collective entity but are treated as grammatically singular

politics' true meaning	the United States' role

- nouns in a few traditional *For . . . sake* expressions that end in an s or an s sound

for goodness' sake	for righteousness' sake

but

for appearance's sake

To avoid an awkward result, rephrasing is sometimes the better option. (For use of the abbreviation *US* in a case like the first one below, see 24.3.1.)

the role of the United States	*instead of*	the United States' role
for the sake of appearance	*instead of*	for appearance's sake

20.2.2.2 COMPOUND WORDS. Form the possessives of singular compound words by adding an apostrophe and s to the last word, even if the main noun is first.

his sister-in-law's business   the attorney general's decision

Form the possessives of plural compounds in the usual way (by adding an apostrophe alone), unless the plural part comes first (see 20.1.2). In that case, rephrase.

district attorneys' decisions

but

decisions of the attorneys general

not

attorneys' general decisions

and not

attorneys general's decisions

20.2.2.3 MULTIPLE NOUNS. If a possessive indicates that two or more entities each possess something separately, make all the nouns possessive.

New York's and Chicago's teams   historians' and economists' methods

If a possessive indicates that two or more entities possess something jointly, make only the last noun possessive.

Minneapolis and St. Paul's teams   historians and economists' data

20.2.2.4 TERMS IN ITALICS AND QUOTATION MARKS. If a term in italics is possessive, both the apostrophe and the s should be in roman type. Do not add a possessive to a term in quotation marks; rephrase the sentence.

the *Atlantic Monthly*'s editor   admirers of "Ode on a Grecian Urn"

If the term ends in a plural form, add only an apostrophe (in roman type). If it already ends in a possessive form, leave it alone or rephrase.

the *New York Times*' online revenue
Harper's editors (or the editors of *Harper's*)

20.3   Compounds and Words Formed with Prefixes

Compounds come in three forms: hyphenated, open (with a space, not a hyphen, between elements), or closed (spelled as one word). Choosing the right one can be difficult. The best authority is your dictionary. If you cannot find a compound there, follow the principles in the following paragraphs to decide whether or not to hyphenate. If you cannot find the form in either place, leave the compound open.

The patterns outlined below are not hard-and-fast rules. You will have to decide many individual cases on the basis of context, personal taste, or common usage in your discipline. Although much of the suggested hyphenation is logical and aids readability, some is only traditional.

20.3.1   Compounds Used as Adjectives

Some compounds are used only as adjectives. In most cases, hyphenate such a compound when it precedes the noun it modifies; otherwise leave it open.

Before noun	After noun
open-ended question	most of the questions were *open ended*
full-length treatment	treatment is *full length*
well-read students	students who are *well read*
thought-provoking commentary	commentary was *thought provoking*
over-the-counter drug	drug sold *over the counter*
the *third-largest* town	the town was the *third largest*
spelled-out numbers	numbers that are *spelled out*

There are a few exceptions:

- If a compound that would normally be hyphenated is preceded and modified by an adverb (such as *very*), omit the hyphen.

Before noun without adverb	Before noun with adverb
a *well-known* author	a *very well known* author
an *ill-advised* step	a *somewhat ill advised* step

- Hyphenate compounds that begin with *all* or end with *free*.

Before noun	After noun
all-encompassing treatment	treatment was *all-encompassing*
toll-free call	the call was *toll-free*

- Hyphenate compounds that end with the terms *borne*, *like*, and *wide* (both before and after the noun) unless the term is listed as closed in Merriam-Webster.

Hyphenated	Closed (per Merriam-Webster)
food-borne	airborne
bell-like	childlike
Chicago-wide	worldwide

- Comparative constructions beginning with such terms as *more/most*, *less/least*, and *better/best* should be hyphenated only when there may be confusion about whether the comparative term is modifying the adjective that follows within the compound or the noun after the compound.

Modifying adjective	Modifying noun
colleges produce *more-skilled workers*	we hired *more skilled* workers for the holidays

- Constructions that consist of an adverb ending in -ly followed by an adjective are not compounds and should not be hyphenated in any context.

Before noun	After noun
highly developed species	the species was *highly developed*
widely disseminated literature	literature has been *widely disseminated*

20.3.2 Compounds Used as Both Nouns and Adjectives

Some compounds are primarily nouns but can also function as adjectives when they precede and modify another noun. (Unlike some of the examples in 20.3.1, these compounds are rarely used as adjectives after a noun, and then only with a linking verb such as *was* or *are*, as in the third example below.) In most cases, hyphenate such a compound when it precedes a noun that it modifies; otherwise leave it open.

Adjective before noun	Noun, or adjective after noun
a *mountain-climbing* enthusiast	*mountain climbing* became her specialty
a *continuing-education* course	a program of *continuing education*
a *middle-class* neighborhood	her neighborhood was *middle class*

There are a few exceptions:

- Some compounds are common enough to appear as nouns in standard dictionaries either as one word or hyphenated.

birthrate	decision-making
smartphone	head-hunting

- For a compound that begins with *e* (short for *electronic*), *ex*, or *self*, use a hyphen in all contexts. Two exceptions: *email* is spelled without the hyphen, and if *self* is preceded by *un*, the compound should be closed (as in *unselfconscious*).

  ex-husband   self-destructive   e-book

  but

  email

- For a compound that ends with *elect*, use a hyphen in all contexts when the name of the office is only one word, but leave it open when the name is two or more words.

  president-elect   district attorney elect

- For a compound formed by two coordinated nouns that could be joined by *and*, use a hyphen in all contexts.

  actor-singer   *mother-daughter* relationship
  city-state   *parent-teacher* conference

- For a compound composed of directional words, use a closed compound when the term describes a single direction. Use a hyphen if the compound consists of coordinated nouns that could be joined with *and* or *by*.

  northeast   a street running *north-south*
  southwest   *east-southeast* winds

- Compounds that identify family relationships vary in whether they are closed up or hyphenated. When in doubt, consult your dictionary. (For the plural and possessive forms of *in-law* compounds, see 20.1.2 and 20.2.2, respectively.)

  grandfather   stepdaughter   step-grandmother   great-grandmother   son-in-law

- Some familiar phrases are always hyphenated.

  stick-in-the-mud   jack-of-all-trades

20.3.2.1 COMPOUNDS INCLUDING PROPER NOUNS. Leave open most compounds that include proper nouns, including names of ethnic groups.

Adjective before noun	*Noun, or adjective after noun*
African American culture	an *African American* has written
French Canadian explorer	the explorer was *French Canadian*
Middle Eastern geography	the geography of the *Middle East*
State Department employees	employed by the *State Department*
Korean War veterans	veterans of the *Korean War*

If, however, the first term is shortened, use a hyphen.

Indo-European languages   origins that were *Indo-European*

If coordinated terms could be joined by *and*, hyphenate them.

Israel-Egypt peace treaty   *Spanish-English* dictionary

20.3.2.3 COMPOUNDS INCLUDING NUMBERS. If a compound includes a number, hyphenate it if it precedes a noun that it modifies; otherwise leave it open. (For the use of numerals versus spelled-out numbers, see chapter 23.)

Adjective before noun	Noun, or adjective after noun
fifty-year project	the project took *fifty years*
twenty-one-year-old student	the student was *twenty-one years old*
twentieth-century literature	studied the literature of the *twentieth century*
third-floor apartment	she lived on the *third floor*
214-day standoff	standoff that lasted *214 days*

There are a few exceptions:

■ Always hyphenate an age term used as a noun.

   a *twenty-one-year-old*   three *six-year-olds*

■ Always leave open a compound including the word *percent*, and give the number in arabic numerals (see 23.1.3).

   a *15 percent* increase   increased by *15 percent*

■ Always use a hyphen to spell a fraction with words. (See 23.1.3 for use of numerals versus spelled-out numbers in fractions.)

   a *two-thirds* majority   a majority of *two-thirds*

■ For a fraction beginning with *half* or *quarter*, use a hyphen when it precedes a noun that it modifies; otherwise leave it open.

Adjective before noun	Noun, or adjective after noun
a *half-hour* session	after a *half hour* had passed
a *quarter-mile* run	ran a *quarter mile*

■ When the second part of a hyphenated expression is omitted, the suspended hyphen is retained, followed by a space (or, in a series, by a comma). But if the compounds are joined by *to* (as in a span of numbers), hyphenate the whole expression.

fifteen- and *twenty-year* mortgages   *five-, ten-,* and *twenty-dollar* bills

but

a *three-to-five-year* gap (a single range)

20.3.3   Words Formed with Prefixes

Words formed with prefixes are normally closed, whether they are nouns (*postmodernism*), verbs (*misrepresent*), adjectives (*antebellum*), or adverbs (*prematurely*). Use a hyphen, however, in these cases:

- when the prefix is combined with a capitalized word

sub-Saharan	*but*	subdivision
pro-Asian	*but*	pronuclear

- when the prefix is combined with a numeral

pre-1950	*but*	predisposed
mid-80s	*but*	midlife

- to separate two i's, two a's, or other combinations of letters or syllables that might cause misreading

anti-intellectual	*but*	antidepressant
intra-arterial	*but*	intramural

- when the prefix precedes a compound word that is hyphenated or open

non-coffee-drinking	*but*	nonbelief
post-high school	*but*	postgame

- to separate repeated terms in a double prefix

  sub-subentry

- when a prefix stands alone

  pre- and postwar   macro- and microeconomics

These patterns apply to words formed with the following prefixes, among others.

ante	extra	meta	over	semi	un
anti	hyper	micro	post	socio	under
bi	infra	mid	pre	sub	
bio	inter	mini	pro	super	
co	intra	multi	proto	supra	
counter	macro	neo	pseudo	trans	
cyber	mega	non	re	ultra	

Where two prefixes apply to the same word, use a hyphen followed by a space for the first prefix.

over- and underused

20.4 Line Breaks

20.4.1 Breaks within Words

For most papers, the only words that should be hyphenated at the ends of lines are those you have deliberately hyphenated, such as compounds (see 20.3). Set your word processor to align text flush left (with a "ragged" right margin), and do not use its automated hyphenation feature.

If, however, you are required to use full justification (where both the left and right margins are aligned), you may have to hyphenate lines to avoid large gaps between words. If you use your word processor's automatic hyphenation feature, set it to limit to three the number of consecutive lines ending with hyphens. As your paper nears completion, review word breaks in case you need to make any exceptions. You may need to turn off hyphenation for individual paragraphs or words. To manually add an end-of-line hyphen, insert an optional hyphen from your word processor's menu for special formatting characters. When in doubt, consult a your dictionary, which should indicate acceptable breaks with centered dots or similar devices in the main word entry.

20.4.2 Breaks over Spaces and Punctuation

Your word processor may allow certain types of undesirable or even unacceptable line breaks to occur over spaces or punctuation. Especially if you will be submitting a PDF file or a printout, it is a good idea to review the final draft of your paper for such breaks.

- *Initials.* If initials are used in place of both a person's first and middle names, include a space between them but do not allow them to break over a line (you can, however, allow a break before the last name). Because lines will reflow as you write your paper, it is best to replace such spaces with nonbreaking spaces, available in most word processors. See also 24.2.1.

M. F. K. Fisher   M. F. K. / Fisher

but not

M. / F. K. Fisher

- *Numbers and dates.* Never allow a line break within numbers expressed as numerals (25,000) or any terms consisting of numerals plus symbols, abbreviations, or units of measure (10%; £6 4s. 6d.; 6:40 p.m.; AD 1895; 245 ml). Use nonbreaking spaces as needed. See chapter 23 for more on numbers and date systems.
- *Punctuation.* Never allow a line to begin with a closing quotation mark, parenthesis, or bracket (and if this happens, it may be a sign of an extra, unneeded space before the mark). Never allow a line to end with an opening quotation mark, parenthesis, or bracket (also a sign of a possible errant space, after the mark). It is also best to avoid ending a line with (*a*) or (1), as at the beginning of a list. Use nonbreaking spaces as needed. See chapter 21 for more on punctuation and 23.4.2 for lists. Never allow an ellipsis (. . .) to break over the line; use your word processor's ellipsis character to prevent this problem. For more on ellipses, see 25.3.2.
- *URLs and email addresses.* Avoid breaking URLs and email addresses over lines. If you have to break one, insert the break *after* a colon or a double slash; *before or after* an equals sign or ampersand; or *before* a single slash, a period, or any other punctuation or symbol. (Avoid inserting a hard return; instead use the optional break character in your word processor.) Hyphens are frequently included as part of a URL or email address, and it's okay if a URL or email breaks at such a hyphen. To avoid confusion, however, never add a hyphen to indicate the break.

http://
www.press.uchicago.edu

http://www
.press.uchicago.edu

http://www.press.uchicago.edu
/books/subject.html

21 Punctuation

This chapter offers general guidelines for punctuation in the text of your paper. Some rules are clear-cut but others are not, so you often have to depend on sound judgment and a good ear.

Special elements such as abbreviations, quotations, and source citations have their own guidelines for punctuation, which are treated in relevant chapters in this book.

If you are writing a thesis or dissertation, your department or university may have specific requirements for punctuation, which are usually available from the office of theses and dissertations. If you are writing a class paper, your instructor may also ask you to follow certain principles for punctuation. Review these requirements before you prepare your paper. They take precedence over the guidelines suggested here. For style guides in various disciplines, see the bibliography.

21.1   Periods

A period ends a sentence that is a declarative statement, an imperative statement, or an indirect question. A period can also end a sentence fragment, if the context makes its rhetorical function clear, but this usage is rare in academic writing. In all these cases, the period is a *terminal period* and, between sentences, should be followed by a single space.

Consider the advantages of this method.

The question was whether these differences could be reconciled.

Put a period at the end of items in a vertical list only if the items are complete sentences (see 23.4.2). Otherwise, omit terminal periods, even for the last item, and do not capitalize the first words.

The report covers three areas:

1. the securities markets
2. the securities industry
3. the securities industry in the economy

Individual periods can also be used in other contexts, including abbreviations (see especially 24.1.3) and citations (16.1.2 and 18.1.2), and also in URLs (20.4.2), where they are often called *dots*. Strings of periods, or dots, can be used in quotations (see 25.3.2), where they are called *ellipses*, and in tables (26.2.6) and front matter pages (A.2.1), where they are called *leaders*.

Do not use periods after chapter and part titles and most subheadings (see A.2.2) or after table titles (26.2.2). For periods in figure captions, see 26.3.2.

21.2 Commas

Commas separate items within a sentence, including clauses, phrases, and individual words. They are especially important when a reader might mistake where a clause or phrase ends and another begins:

Before leaving the members of the committee met in the assembly room.

Before leaving, the members of the committee met in the assembly room.

For use of commas in numbers, see 23.2.2. For use of commas in citations, see 16.1.2 and 18.1.2.

21.2.1 Independent Clauses

In a sentence containing two or more independent clauses joined by a coordinating conjunction (*and, but, or, nor, for, so, yet*), put a comma before the conjunction. This is not a hard-and-fast rule; no comma is needed between two short independent clauses with no internal punctuation.

Students around the world want to learn English, and many young Americans are eager to teach them.

The senator arrived at noon and the president left at one.

In a sentence containing three or more short and simple independent clauses with no internal punctuation, separate the clauses with commas and add a coordinating conjunction before the last one. (Always include a comma before the coordinating conjunction.) If the clauses are longer and more complex, separate them with semicolons (see 21.3)—or, better, rewrite the sentence.

The committee designed the questionnaire, the field workers collected responses, and the statistician analyzed the results.

The committee designed the questionnaire, which was short; the field workers, who did not participate, collected responses; and the statistician analyzed the results, though not until several days later.

Ordinarily, do not insert a comma before a conjunction joining two subjects or two predicates.

The agencies that design the surveys and the analysts who evaluate the results should work together.

They do not condone such practices but attempt to refute them theoretically.

When a sentence with two independent coordinate clauses opens with a phrase or dependent clause that modifies both, put a comma after the introductory element but not between the two independent clauses.

Within ten years, interest rates surged and the housing market declined.

21.2.2 Series

In a series consisting of three or more words, phrases, or clauses with no internal punctuation of their own, separate the elements with commas. Always use a comma before the conjunction that introduces the last item.

The governor wrote his senators, the president, and the vice president.

Attending the conference were Fernandez, Sullivan, and Kendrick.

The public approved, the committee agreed, but the measure failed.

Do not use commas when all the elements in a series are joined by conjunctions.

The palette consisted of blue and green and orange.

If a series of three or more words, phrases, or clauses ends with an expression indicating continuation (*and so forth*, *and so on*, *and the like*, or *etc.*), punctuate that final expression as though it were the final item in the series. You may, however, add a comma after the continuation expression to prevent confusion after a long series.

They discussed movies, books, plays, and the like until late in the night.

Using such techniques, management can improve not only productivity but also hours, working conditions, training, benefits, and so on, without reducing wages.

Use semicolons to separate the items in a series if one or more includes commas, or if the items are long and complex (see 21.3). If such a series comes before the main verb of a sentence, however, rephrase the sentence.

The three cities that we compare are Hartford, Connecticut; Kalamazoo, Michigan; and Pasadena, California.

but not

Hartford, Connecticut; Kalamazoo, Michigan; and Pasadena, California, are the three cities that we compare.

21.2.3 Nonrestrictive Clauses and Phrases

Use paired commas to set off a nonrestrictive clause. A clause is nonrestrictive if it is not necessary to uniquely identify the noun it modifies.

These five books, which are on reserve in the library, are required reading.

Here the noun phrase *These five books* uniquely identifies the books that the writer has in mind; the nonrestrictive clause is not necessary to identify the books further. On the other hand, in the following sentence, the dependent clause (*that are required reading*) is restrictive, because it identifies a specific subset of books that are on reserve at the library. Commas are therefore not used around the clause.

The books that are required reading are on reserve in the library.

Although *which* is often used with restrictive clauses, American writers generally preserve the distinction between restrictive *that* (no comma) and nonrestrictive *which* (comma).

The principles delineated above apply also to restrictive and nonrestrictive phrases.

The president, wearing a red dress, attended the conference.

The woman wearing a red dress is the president.

21.2.4 Other Uses

Commas are used in a variety of other situations. (For commas in dates, see 23.3.1.)

■ *Introductory words and phrases.* When you begin a sentence with an introductory element of more than a few words, follow it with a comma. A comma is not necessary after a short prepositional phrase unless the sentence could be misread without one.

If the insurrection is to succeed, the army and police must stand side by side.

Having accomplished her mission, she returned to headquarters.

To Anthony, Blake remained an enigma.

After this week the commission will be able to write its report.

■ *Two or more adjectives preceding a noun.* Separate two or more adjectives preceding a noun with commas when they could, without affecting meaning, be joined by *and*. Do not use a comma if one or more of the adjectives is essential to (i.e., forms a unit with) the noun. (Test: if it feels awkward to change the order of the adjectives, do not use commas.)

It was a large, well-placed, beautiful house.

They strolled out into the warm, luminous night.

She refused to be identified with a traditional political label.

- *Clarifying comments.* Words and phrases such as *namely, that is,* and *for example,* which usually introduce a clarifying comment, should be followed by a comma but preceded by something stronger (such as a semicolon or a period). When you use *or* in the sense of "in other words," put a comma before it. (These and similar expressions may be set off by dashes or parentheses instead; see 21.7.2 and 21.8.1.)

  Many people resent accidents of fate; that is, they look on illness or bereavement as undeserved.

  The compass stand, or binnacle, must be visible to the helmsman.

- *Appositives.* A word or phrase is said to be in apposition to a noun when it follows the noun and provides an explanatory equivalent for it. Nonrestrictive appositives are set off by commas; restrictive appositives are not (see 21.2.3).

  Chua, a Harvard College graduate, taught at Duke for several years.

  Kierkegaard, the Danish philosopher, asked, "What is anxiety?"

  but

  The Danish philosopher Kierkegaard asked, "What is anxiety?"

- *Place-names.* Use commas to set off multiple individual elements in names of places. (For commas in addresses, see 23.1.7.)

  Cincinnati, Ohio, is on the Ohio River.

  The next leg of the trip was to Florence, Italy.

- *Interjections and conjunctive adverbs.* Set off interjections, conjunctive adverbs, and the like to suggest a break in the flow of thought or the rhythm of the sentence. But omit commas when such elements do not break the continuity of the sentence.

  Nevertheless, it is a matter of great importance.

  It is, perhaps, the best that could be expected.

  Perhaps it is therefore clear that no deposits were made.

- *Contrasted elements.* Put commas around an interjected phrase beginning with *not, not only,* or similar expressions. But when such a phrase consists of two components (*not . . . but, not only . . . but also,* and the like), commas are usually unnecessary. Use a comma between clauses of *the more . . . the more* type unless they are very short.

The idea, not its expression, is significant.

She was delighted with, but also disturbed by, her new freedom.

He was not only the team's president but also a charter member.

The more it stays the same, the less it changes.

The more the merrier.

- *Parenthetical elements.* Use paired commas to set off a parenthetical element between a subject and a verb or a verb and its object. If you find yourself setting off more than one such interrupting element in a sentence, consider rewriting the sentence.

The Quinn Report was, to say the least, a bombshell.

Wolinski, after receiving instructions, left for Algiers.

- *Repeated words.* Use a comma to separate identical words. An exception is normally made for the word *that.*

They marched in, in twos.

Whatever is, is right.

but

She implied that that did not matter.

21.3 Semicolons

A semicolon is stronger than a comma and marks a greater break in the continuity of a sentence. Use a semicolon in a compound sentence to separate independent clauses that are not connected by a coordinating conjunction (*and, but, or, nor, yet, for, so*).

One hundred communities are in various stages of completion; more are on the drawing board.

You can also use a semicolon with a coordinating conjunction if the clauses are long and have commas or other punctuation within them. But if the result seems unwieldy, consider replacing the semicolon with a period.

Although productivity per capita in the United States is much higher than it is in China, China has an increasingly well educated young labor force; but the crucial point is that knowledge—which is transferable between peoples—has become the most important world economic resource.

Use a semicolon before the words *then, however, thus, hence, indeed, accordingly, besides,* and *therefore* when those words are used transitionally between two independent clauses.

Some think freedom always comes with democracy; however, many voters in many countries have voted for governments that they know will restrict their rights.

When items in a series have internal punctuation, separate them with semicolons (see also 21.2.2).

The original version of the chart included three colors: green, for vegetation that remained stable; red, for vegetation that disappeared; and yellow, for new vegetation.

Semicolons are also sometimes used in titles (see 17.1.2 and 19.1.3) and to separate citations to more than one source (see 16.3.5.1 and 18.3.2.5).

21.4   Colons

A colon introduces a clause, phrase, or series of elements that expands, clarifies, or exemplifies the meaning of what precedes it. Between independent clauses, it functions much like a semicolon, though more strongly emphasizing balance or consequence.

People expect three things of government: peace, prosperity, and respect for civil rights.

Chinese culture is unrivaled in its depth and antiquity: it is unmatched in its rich artistic and philosophical records.

Use a colon to introduce illustrative material or a list. A colon should follow only a complete independent clause; often an introductory element such as *the following* or *as follows* should precede the colon. (See also 23.4.2.)

The qualifications are as follows: a doctorate in economics and an ability to communicate statistical data to a lay audience.

but not

The qualifications are: a doctorate in economics . . .

Note that the first word following a colon within a sentence is generally not capitalized unless it is a proper noun or unless the colon introduces more than one sentence. For capitalization in quotations introduced by a colon, see chapter 25.

Colons are also used in titles (see 17.1.2 and 19.1.3), in notations of time (23.1.5), in URLs (20.4.2), and in various ways in citations.

21.5 Question Marks

Put a question mark at the end of a complete sentence phrased as a question.

Who would lead the nation in its hour of need?

Put a question mark after a clause phrased as a question and included as part of a sentence. Do not use quotation marks unless the question is a quotation and the rest of the sentence is not.

Would the union agree? was the critical question.

If the included question is at the end of the sentence, do not add a period after the question mark. You are not required to capitalize the first word of the included question, but an initial capital helps readers identify the question, especially if it includes internal punctuation. If the sentence becomes awkward, you may instead rephrase the question as a declarative statement.

Several legislators raised the question, Can the fund be used in an emergency, or must it remain dedicated to its original purpose?

Several legislators raised the question of using the fund in an emergency, which was not its original purpose.

A question mark may also indicate doubt or uncertainty, as in a date.

The painter Niccolò dell'Abbate (1512?–71) assisted in the decorations at Fontainebleau.

21.6 Exclamation Points

Exclamation points are rarely appropriate for academic writing, except when they are part of quoted material or part of the title of a work (the musical *Oklahoma!*). See also 21.12.2.1.

21.7 Hyphens and Dashes

21.7.1 Hyphens

Hyphens are used in a variety of contexts, including compound words (see 20.3) and inclusive numbers (23.2.4).

21.7.2 Dashes

A dash is an elongated hyphen used to set off text in a way similar to but more prominent than commas (see 21.2) or parentheses (21.8.1). Also called an *em dash* (because in most fonts it is approximately the width of the capital letter M), this character is available in all word processors.[1] It can be represented with two consecutive hyphens, but most word processors can be set to convert double hyphens to em dashes automatically. Do not leave space on either side of the dash.

When you use dashes to set off a parenthetical element, pair them as you would commas or parentheses. But avoid using more than one pair in any one sentence; instead, use parentheses for the second layer of parenthetical information.

The influence of three impressionists—Monet (1840-1926), Sisley (1839-99), and Degas (1834-1917)—is obvious in her work.

You can also use a single dash to set off an amplifying or explanatory element.

It was a revival of a most potent image—the revolutionary idea.

Use a dash or a pair of dashes enclosing a phrase to indicate a strong break in thought that also disrupts the sentence structure.

Rutherford—how could he have misinterpreted the evidence?

Some characters in *Tom Jones* are "flat"—if you do not object to this borrowing of E. M. Forster's somewhat discredited term—because they are caricatures of their names.

A dash may also introduce a summarizing subject after a list of several elements.

The statue of the discus thrower, the charioteer at Delphi, the poetry of Pindar—all represent the great ideal.

21.7.3   Multiple Dashes

When you quote from a mutilated or illegible text, indicate a missing word or missing letters with a 2-em dash (formed with two consecutive em dashes, or four hyphens). For a missing word, leave a space on either side of the dash; for missing letters, leave no space between the dash and the existing part of the word.

The vessel left the —— of July.

H——h? [Hirsch?]

---

1. There is a second type of dash, called an *en dash* (because it is approximately the width of the capital letter N), that is used in published works to mean "through," usually in connection with numbers or dates (e.g., 1998–2008). It can also be used in other contexts, as discussed in 6.78–84 of *The Chicago Manual of Style*, 17th edition (2017). If your local guidelines require it, this character is available in most word processors; otherwise use a hyphen in these contexts. Note that this book uses en dashes where they are appropriate, as in the preceding reference to *CMOS*.

The same technique can be used when you want to obscure a particular word.

It was a d—— shame.

A 3-em dash (formed with three consecutive em dashes, or six hyphens) is used in bibliographies and reference lists to represent the repeated name of an author or editor (see 16.2.2 and 18.2.1).

21.8 Parentheses and Brackets

21.8.1 Parentheses

Parentheses usually set off explanatory or interrupting elements of a sentence, much like paired commas (see 21.2) and dashes (21.7.2). In general, use commas for material closely related to the main clause, dashes and parentheses for material less closely connected. The abbreviations *e.g.* and *i.e.*, which may introduce a clarifying comment (see 24.7), are used only in parentheses or in notes.

The conference has (with some malice) divided into four groups.

Each painting depicts a public occasion; in each—a banquet, a parade, a coronation (though the person crowned is obscured)—crowds of people are pictured as swarming ants.

There are tax incentives for "clean cars" (e.g., gasoline-electric hybrids and vehicles powered by compressed natural gas and liquefied propane).

Parentheses can also be used with citations (see chapters 16 and 18) and to set off the numbers or letters in a list or an outline (see 23.4.2).

21.8.2 Brackets

Brackets are most often used in quotations, to indicate changes made to a quoted passage (see 25.3 for examples); similarly, brackets are used in source citations to enclose an author's name or a date or other substantive information not present in the source itself (see 17.1.1.5 or 19.1.1.5 for an example). They can also be used to enclose a second layer of parenthetical material within parentheses.

He agrees with the idea that childhood has a history (first advanced by Philippe Ariès [1914–84] in his book *Centuries of Childhood* [1962]).

21.9 Slashes

The forward slash (/) is used in a few contexts, such as fractions (see 23.1.3) and quotations of poetry (see 25.2.1.2). Single and double slashes appear in URLs and other electronic identifiers (see 20.4.2). The backward slash (or backslash, \) has various meanings in different computer languages and operating systems.

21.10 Quotation Marks

For the use of quotation marks in quoted material, see 25.2.1.2. For use in titles and other special situations, see 22.3.2. For use in citations, see 16.1.4 and 18.1.4.

Some fields—linguistics, philosophy, and theology, for example—use single quotation marks to set off words and concepts. The closing quotation mark should precede a comma or period in this case (compare 21.12.2).

kami 'hair, beard'

The variables of quantification, 'something,' 'nothing', . . .

In most other fields, follow the guidelines in 22.2 for using quotation marks and italics with definitions of terms.

21.11 Apostrophes

For the use of apostrophes in plural and possessive forms, see 20.1 and 20.2. Apostrophes are also used in forming contractions (*don't*). If your word processor is enabled to use directional or "smart" quotation marks, make sure not to confuse an apostrophe for a left single quotation mark ('*twas*, not '*twas*).

21.12 Multiple Punctuation Marks

The guidelines given throughout this chapter sometimes call for the use of two punctuation marks together—for example, a period and a closing parenthesis. The guidelines below show when to omit one of the marks and the order of the marks when both are used.

21.12.1 Omission of Punctuation Marks

Except for ellipses, never use two periods together, even when a period in an abbreviation ends a sentence. Keep the abbreviation period when a sentence ends with a question mark or an exclamation point.

The exchange occurred at 5:30 p.m.

Could anyone match the productivity of Rogers Inc.?

If a situation calls for both a comma and a stronger punctuation mark, such as a question mark or a dash, omit the comma.

"What were they thinking?" he wondered to himself.

While the senator couldn't endorse the proposal—and he certainly had doubts about it—he didn't condemn it.

An exception can be made for titles of works that end in a question mark or an exclamation point. Because such punctuation is not strictly related to the rest of the sentence, retain commas where needed.

"Are You a Doctor?," the fifth story in *Will You Please Be Quiet, Please?,* treats modern love.

Films such as *Airplane!*, *This Is Spinal Tap*, and *Austin Powers* offer parodies of well-established genres.

21.12.2 Order of Punctuation Marks

Adjacent marks of punctuation most often occur with quotation marks, parentheses, or brackets. American usage follows a few reliable guidelines for ordering multiple marks.

21.12.2.1 WITH QUOTATION MARKS. A final comma or period nearly always precedes a closing quotation mark, whether it is part of the quoted matter or not.

In support of the effort "to bring justice to our people," she joined the strike.

She made the argument in an article titled "On 'Managing Public Debt.' "

There are two exceptions. When single quotation marks are used to set off special terms in certain fields, such as linguistics, philosophy, and theology (see 21.10), put a period or comma after the closing quotation mark.

Some contemporary theologians, who favored 'religionless Christianity', were proclaiming the 'death of God'.

And if a computer file name or command must be put in quotation marks, a period or comma that is not part of the name or the command should come after the closing mark.

Click on Save As; name your file "appendix A, v. 10".

Question marks and exclamation points precede a closing quotation mark if they are part of the quoted matter. They follow the quotation mark if they apply to the entire sentence in which the quotation appears.

Her poem is titled "What Did the Crow Know?"

Do we accept Jefferson's concept of "a natural aristocracy"?

Semicolons and colons always follow quotation marks. If the quotation ends with a semicolon or a colon, change it to a period or a comma (or delete it) to fit the structure of the main sentence (see 25.3.1).

He claimed that "every choice reflects an attitude toward Everyman"; his speech then enlarged on the point in a telling way.

The Emergency Center is "almost its own city": it has its own services and governance.

21.12.2.2 WITH PARENTHESES AND BRACKETS. When you enclose a complete sentence in parentheses, put the terminal period (or other terminal punctuation mark) for that sentence before the last parenthesis. However, put the period outside when material in parentheses, even a grammatically complete sentence, is included within another sentence. The same principles apply to material in brackets.

We have noted similar motifs in Japan. (They can also be found in Korean folktales.)

Use periods in all these situations (your readers will expect them).

Myths have been accepted as allegorically true (by the Stoics) and as priestly lies (by Enlightenment thinkers).

(The director promised completion "on time and *under budget*" [italics mine].)

For terminal punctuation with citations given parenthetically, see 25.2.

22 Names, Special Terms, and Titles of Works

This chapter offers general guidelines for presenting names, special terms, and titles of works, including advice on when to use capital letters and when to use quotation marks or italic type (as opposed to regular roman type) to set off words, phrases, or titles.

If you are writing a thesis or dissertation, your department or university may have specific requirements for presenting names, special terms, and titles. Those requirements are usually available from the office of theses and dissertations. If you are writing a class paper, your instructor may also ask you to follow certain principles for presenting such items. Review these requirements before you prepare your paper. They take precedence over the guidelines suggested here. For style guides in various disciplines, see the bibliography.

22.1 Names

Proper nouns, or names, are always capitalized, but it is sometimes difficult to distinguish a name from a generic term. This section covers the most common cases. For more detailed information, see chapter 8 of *The Chicago Manual of Style*, 17th edition (2017).

In text, names are normally presented in roman type, but there are a few exceptions noted in 22.1.3.

22.1.1 People, Places, and Organizations

In general, capitalize the first letter in each element of the names of specific people, places, and organizations. However, personal names that contain particles (such as *de* and *van*) or compound last names may vary in capitalization. When in doubt, consult the biographical listings from Merriam-Webster or another reliable authority. Prepositions (*of*) and conjunctions (*and*) that are parts of names are usually lowercase, as is *the* when it precedes a name. For possessive forms of names, see 20.2. For abbreviations with names, see 24.2. For names with numbers, see 23.1.6.

Eleanor Roosevelt	the United States Congress
W. E. B. Du Bois	the State Department
Ludwig van Beethoven	the European Union
Victoria Sackville-West	the University of North Carolina
Chiang Kai-shek	the Honda Motor Company
Sierra Leone	Skidmore, Owings & Merrill
Central America	the University of Chicago Press
New York City	the National Conference for Community and Justice
the Atlantic Ocean	the Roman Catholic Church
the Republic of Lithuania	the Allied Expeditionary Force

A professional title that immediately precedes a personal name is treated as part of the name and should be capitalized. If you use the title alone or after the personal name, it becomes a generic term and should be lowercased. The same principle applies to other generic terms that are part of place or organization names.

President Harry Truman announced	the president announced
Professors Liu and Prakash wrote	the professors wrote
next to the Indian Ocean	next to the ocean
students at Albion College	students at the college

Names of ethnic and national groups are also capitalized. Terms denoting socioeconomic level, however, are not. (For hyphenation of compounds of both types, see 20.3.2.)

Arab Americans	the middle class
Latinos	white-collar workers

Capitalize adjectives derived from names, unless they have lost their literal associations with particular persons or places and have become part of everyday language.

Machiavellian scheme	french fries
Roman and Arabic art	roman and arabic numerals

22.1.2 Historical Events, Cultural Terms, and Designations of Time

The names of many historical periods and events are traditionally capitalized; more generic terms usually are not, unless they include names. Follow the conventions of your discipline.

the Bronze Age	ancient Rome
the Depression	the nineteenth century
the Industrial Revolution	the Shang dynasty
Prohibition	the colonial period
the Seven Years' War	the baby boom

Nouns and adjectives designating cultural styles, movements, and schools are generally capitalized only when derived from names or when they need to be distinguished from generic terms (as in *Stoicism*). Again, follow the conventions of your discipline.

classical	Aristotelian reasoning
impressionism	Dadaism
modernism	Hudson River school
deconstruction	Romanesque architecture

Names of days of the week, months, and holidays are capitalized, but names of seasons are not. For more on date systems, see 23.3.

Tuesday	September	Independence Day	spring

22.1.3 Other Types of Names

Other types of names also follow specific patterns for capitalization, and some require italics.

■ *Academic courses and subjects.* Capitalize the names of specific courses but not of general subjects or fields of study, except for the names of languages.

Archaeology 101	art history
Topics in Victorian Literature	English literature

■ *Acts, treaties, and government programs.* Capitalize the formal or accepted titles of acts, treaties, government programs, and similar documents or entities, but lowercase informal or generic titles.

the United States (or US) Constitution	the due process clause
the Treaty of Versailles	the treaty
Head Start	

▪ *Brand names.* Capitalize the brand names of products, but do not use the symbol ® or ™ after such a name. Unless you are discussing a specific product, however, use a generic term instead of a brand name.

Coca-Cola	cola
Xerox	photocopy
iPhone	smartphone

▪ *Electronic technology.* Capitalize branded names of computer hardware and software, networks, browsers, systems, and languages. Most terms that are not trademarked (such as *internet*), however, can be lowercased, as can generic terms (such as *web*) when used alone or in combination with other generic terms.

Apple iOS 11; iPhone
the Camera app in iOS 11; a camera app
the Kindle app for Android; Kindle
Google Chrome
the internet
the World Wide Web Consortium (W3C); World Wide Web; the web; website; web
    page

▪ *Legal cases.* Capitalize and italicize the names of legal cases; italicize the *v.* (versus). You may shorten the case name after a full reference to it (usually to the name of the plaintiff or the nongovernmental party). For citations of legal cases, see 17.11.7 and 19.11.7.

First reference	*Subsequent references*
Miranda v. Arizona	*Miranda*
United States v. Carlisle	*Carlisle*

▪ *Ships, aircraft, and other vessels and vehicles.* Capitalize and italicize the names of ships, individual aircraft, and the like. If the names are preceded by an abbreviation such as USS (United States ship) or HMS (Her [or His] Majesty's ship), do not italicize these abbreviations or use the word *ship* in addition to the name. Capitalize makes, models, and classes of other vehicles but do not italicize them.

USS *Constitution*	the space shuttle *Atlantis*
HMS *Saranac*	Boeing 787 Dreamliner
Spirit of St. Louis	Subaru Forester

▪ *Plants and animals.* In papers in the humanities and social sciences, do not capitalize the names of plants and animals unless they include other proper nouns, such as geographical names. Binomial Latin species names should be italicized, with the genus name capitalized and the species name (or specific epithet) lowercase. The names of phyla, orders, and such should be in roman type. For papers in the sciences, follow the conventions of your discipline.

rhesus monkey   Rocky Mountain sheep   *Rosa caroliniana*   Chordata

22.2 Special Terms

Some special terms require use of italics, quotation marks, and capitalization.

22.2.1 Terms from Other Languages

Italicize isolated words and phrases in languages likely to be unfamiliar to readers of English, and capitalize them as in the original language. (If you are unfamiliar with the capitalization principles of a language, consult a reliable authority such as chapter 11 of *The Chicago Manual of Style*, 17th edition [2017].) For titles of works in languages other than English, see 22.3.1.

This leads to the idea of *Übermensch* and to the theory of the *acte gratuit* and surrealism.

Do not italicize terms from another language that are familiar enough to appear in a standard dictionary.

de facto   vis-à-vis   pasha   eros

Do not italicize proper names from other languages or personal titles that accompany them.

Padre Pio   the Académie Française   the Puerto del Sol

If you define a non-English term, put the definition in parentheses or quotation marks, either following the term in the text or in a note.

The usual phrase was *ena tuainu-iai*, "I wanted to eat."

According to Sartrean ontology, man is always *de trop* (in excess).

For longer quotations from another language, use roman type. (Italicize the quotation as a whole or any words within it only if they are italicized in the original.) Enclose the quotation in quotation marks within the text or use a block quotation following the principles in 25.2.

The confusion of *le pragmatisme* is traced to the supposed failure to distinguish "les propriétés de la valeur en général" from the incidental.

22.2.2 Words Defined as Terms

To emphasize key terms that you define, italicize them on their first use; thereafter use roman type. You can use quotation marks (called *scare quotes*) to alert readers that you are using a term in a nonstandard or ironic way. When overused, both techniques become less effective.

The two chief tactics of this group, *obstructionism* and *misinformation,* require careful analysis.

Government "efficiency" resulted in a huge deficit.

> Italicize a term when you refer to it as a term.

The term *critical mass* is more often used metaphorically than literally.

How did she define the word *existential*?

but

A critical mass of students took existential philosophy.

> Italicize letters referred to as letters, and present them in lowercase. Letters used to denote grades and to identify exemplars should be roman and capitalized. For plural forms of letters used in these ways, see 20.1.2.

Many of the place-names there begin with the letters *h* and *k.*

In her senior year, she received an A and six Bs.

Imagine a group of interconnected persons: A knows B, B knows C, and C knows D.

22.3   Titles of Works

When you cite a work, present its title exactly as it appears in the original work or, if the original is unavailable, in a reliable authority.

Always preserve the original spelling (including hyphenation) in such titles, even if it does not conform to current American usage as described in chapter 20. See 17.1.2 for some permissible changes to the punctuation of titles, such as the use of a colon between a title and a subtitle, and the addition of a comma before dates.

Academic convention prescribes that titles follow specific patterns of capitalization and the use of italics or quotation marks (or neither), regardless of how they appear in the original.

22.3.1 Capitalization

Titles have two patterns of capitalization: headline style and sentence style. Present most titles in headline style. For titles in languages other than English, use sentence style.

Both citation styles described in this manual prescribe headline-style capitalization for English-language titles. See 16.1.3 and 18.1.3.

Also use headline-style capitalization for the title of your paper and the titles of any parts or chapters within it unless your discipline prefers sentence style (see A.1.5).

22.3.1.1 HEADLINE-STYLE CAPITALIZATION. Headline-style capitalization is intended to distinguish titles clearly from surrounding text. In this style, capitalize the first letter of the first and last words of the title and subtitle and all other words, except as follows:

- Do not capitalize articles (*a, an, the*), coordinating conjunctions (*and, but, or, nor, for*), or the word *to* or *as* except as the first or last word in the title or subtitle.
- Do not capitalize prepositions (*of, in, at, above, under*, and so forth) unless they are used as adverbs (*up* in *Look Up*) or adjectives (*on* in *The On Button*).
- Capitalize the second part (or subsequent parts) of a hyphenated compound unless it is an article, preposition, or coordinating conjunction (*and, but, or, nor, for*), or a modifier such as *sharp* or *flat* following a musical key; or unless the first part is a prefix (*anti, pre*, and so forth). (Remember to follow the original hyphenation of a title even if it differs from the principles discussed in 20.3.)
- Lowercase the second part of a species name, such as *fulvescens* in *Acipenser fulvescens*, even if it is the last word in a title or subtitle (see also 22.1.3).
- Do not capitalize parts of proper nouns that are normally in lowercase, as described in 22.1.1 (*van* in *Ludwig van Beethoven*).

The Economic Effects of the Civil War in the Mid-Atlantic States

To Have and to Hold: A Twenty-First-Century View of Marriage

All That Is True: The Life of Vincent van Gogh, 1853–90

Four Readings of the Gospel according to Matthew

Self-Government and the Re-establishment of a New World Order

Global Warming: What We Are Doing about It Today

Still Life with Oranges

From *Homo erectus* to *Homo sapiens*: A Black-and-White History

E-flat Concerto

Although many short words are lowercase in this style, length does not determine capitalization. You must capitalize short verbs (*is, are*), adjectives (*new*), personal pronouns (*it, we*), and relative pronouns (*that*), because they are not among the exceptions listed above. Use lowercase for long prepositions (*according*), since prepositions are among the exceptions.

Two kinds of titles should not be presented in headline style even if you use it for all other titles:

- For titles in languages other than English, use sentence-style capitalization (see 22.3.1.2).
- For titles of works published in the eighteenth century (1700s) or earlier, retain the original capitalization (and spelling), except that words spelled out in all capital letters should be given with an initial capital only.

A Treatise of morall philosophy Contaynyge the sayings of the wyse

22.3.1.2 SENTENCE-STYLE CAPITALIZATION. Sentence-style capitalization is a simpler, though less distinct, way of presenting titles than headline style. In this style, capitalize only the first letter of the first word of the title and subtitle and any proper nouns and proper adjectives thereafter.

Seeing and selling late-nineteenth-century Japan

Natural crisis: Symbol and imagination in the mid-American farm crisis

Religious feminism: A challenge from the National Organization for Women

Starry night

Unless your discipline says otherwise, reserve sentence style for titles of works in languages other than English.

Note that other languages have different conventions for capitalization. For example, German nouns are generally capitalized, whereas German adjectives, even those derived from proper nouns, are not. If you are uncertain about the conventions of a particular language, consult a reliable authority.

Speculum Romanae magnificentiae

Historia de la Orden de San Gerónimo

Reallexikon zur deutschen Kunstgeschichte

Phénoménologie et religion: Structures de l'institution chrétienne

22.3.2 Italics or Quotation Marks

Most titles of works are set off from the surrounding text by italics or quotation marks, depending on the type of work. The guidelines listed here apply not only to titles used in text but also to most titles in source citations (see chapters 15–19).

The examples below are presented with headline-style capitalization, but the guidelines also apply to titles with sentence-style capitalization (see 22.3.1.2).

22.3.2.1 ITALICS. Italicize the titles of most longer works, including the types listed here. For parts of these works and shorter works of the same type, see 22.3.2.2.

- books (*Culture and Anarchy*, *The Chicago Manual of Style*)
- plays (*A Winter's Tale*) and very long poems, especially those of book length (Dante's *Inferno*)
- journals (*Signs*), magazines (*Time*), newspapers (the *New York Times*), and blogs (*Dot Earth*); an initial *The* in periodical titles is normally treated as part of the surrounding text (and omitted in source citations) but may be capitalized and italicized along with the title if it forms an integral part of a name that otherwise consists of a single word (*The Intercept*)
- long musical compositions (*The Marriage of Figaro*) or titles of albums (Michael Jackson's *Thriller*)
- paintings (the *Mona Lisa*), sculptures (Michelangelo's *David*), and other works of art, including photographs (Ansel Adam's *North Dome*)
- movies (*Citizen Kane*) and television (*Sesame Street*) and radio programs (*All Things Considered*)

22.3.2.2 QUOTATION MARKS. Enclose in quotation marks, but do not italicize, the title of a shorter work, whether or not it is part of a longer work (such as those listed in 22.3.2.1).

- chapters ("The Later Years") or other titled parts of books
- short stories ("The Dead"), short poems ("The Housekeeper"), and essays ("Of Books")
- articles or other features in journals ("The Function of Fashion in Eighteenth-Century America"), magazines ("Who Should Lead the Supreme Court?"), newspapers ("Election Comes Down to the Wire"), and websites or blogs ("An Ice Expert Muses on Greenhouse Heat")
- individual episodes of television programs ("The Opposite")
- short musical compositions ("The Star-Spangled Banner") and recordings ("All You Need Is Love")

Also use quotation marks and roman type for titles of whole works that have not been formally published, including the following:

- theses and dissertations ("A Study of Kant's Early Works")
- lectures and papers presented at meetings ("Voice and Inequality: The Transformation of American Civic Democracy")

- titled documents in manuscript collections ("A Map of the Southern Indian District of North America")

22.3.2.3 NEITHER. Capitalize but do not use italics or quotation marks with these special types of titles:

- book series (Studies in Legal History)
- manuscript collections (Egmont Manuscripts)
- scriptures (the Bible) and other revered works (the Upanishads), as well as versions of the Bible (the King James Version) and its books (Genesis; see 24.6 for a complete list)
- musical works referred to by their genre (Symphony no. 41, Cantata BWV 80), though the popular titles for such works should be italicized (the *Jupiter* Symphony) or placed in quotation marks ("Ein feste Burg ist unser Gott") depending on their length, as noted above
- websites (Google Maps, Facebook, Apple.com, the Internet Movie Database, IMDb, Wikipedia), though exceptions may be made for sites that are closely analogous to a type of work listed in 22.3.2.1 (the *Huffington Post*)

Treat generic terms for parts of books or other works as you would any other word. Do not capitalize them or use italics or quotation marks unless you would do the same for an ordinary word (such as at the beginning of a sentence). If a part includes a number, give it in arabic numerals, regardless of its appearance in the original work (see 23.1.8).

in Lionel Trilling's preface
a comprehensive bibliography

as discussed in chapters 4 and 5
killed off in act 3, scene 2

22.3.3 Punctuation

Preserve any punctuation that is part of a title when using the title in a sentence (see 17.1.2). If the title is used as a restrictive clause or in another position in the sentence that would normally be followed by a comma (see 21.2), add the comma.

Love, Loss, and What I Wore was later adapted for an off-Broadway play.

but

Her favorite book, *Love, Loss, and What I Wore*, is an autobiography recounted largely through drawings.

Punctuation within a title should not affect any punctuation called for by the surrounding sentence. One exception: omit a terminal period after a title ending in a question mark or an exclamation point. See also 21.12.2.

"Are You a Doctor?" is the fifth story in *Will You Please Be Quiet, Please?*

23 Numbers

This chapter offers general guidelines for presenting numbers. These guidelines are appropriate for most humanities and social science disciplines, but disciplines that rely heavily on numerical data may have more specific guidelines. If you are writing a paper in the natural or physical sciences, mathematics, or any other very technical field, follow the conventions of the discipline. For style guides in various disciplines, see the bibliography. For advice on numbering the pages and parts of your paper, see the appendix.

If you are writing a thesis or a dissertation, your department or uni-

Table 23.1. Roman numerals

Arabic	Roman	Arabic	Roman	Arabic	Roman
1	I	11	XI	30	XXX
2	II	12	XII	40	XL
3	III	13	XIII	50	L
4	IV	14	XIV	60	LX
5	V	15	XV	70	LXX
6	VI	16	XVI	80	LXXX
7	VII	17	XVII	90	XC
8	VIII	18	XVIII	100	C
9	IX	19	XIX	500	D
10	X	20	XX	1,000	M

Note: Roman numerals are shown capitalized; for lowercase, use the same forms as in letters (i for I, v for V, etc.). For numbers not listed, follow the patterns shown.

versity may have specific requirements for presenting numbers, which are usually available from the office of theses and dissertations. If you are writing a class paper, your instructor may also ask you to follow certain principles for presenting numbers. Review these requirements before you prepare your paper. They take precedence over the guidelines suggested here.

23.1 Words or Numerals?

The most common question in presenting numbers is whether to spell them out in words (twenty-two) or give them in numerals (22). When the number is followed by a unit of measure, you must also decide whether to give that unit in words (percent) or as a symbol (%) or an abbreviation.

The guidelines presented in 23.1–23.3 pertain to numbers used in the text of your paper. For numbers used in tables, figures, and citations, see 23.4.

Unless otherwise specified, *numerals* here means arabic numerals (1, 2, 3, etc.). For roman numerals (i, ii, iii, etc.), see table 23.1.

23.1.1 General Rule

Before you draft your paper, you should decide on a general rule for presenting numbers and follow it consistently. Which rule you choose depends on how often you use numerical data and the conventions of your discipline. For situations in which you might modify this rule, see 23.1.2–23.1.8.

In the humanities and social sciences, if you use numerical data only occasionally, spell out numbers from one through one hundred. If the number has two words, use a hyphen (fifty-five). Also spell out round numbers followed by *hundred, thousand, hundred thousand, million,* and so on (but see 23.1.2.3). For all other numbers, use arabic numerals. Follow this pattern for numbers that are part of physical quantities (distances, lengths, temperatures, and so on), and do not use abbreviations for the units in such quantities (see 24.5).

After seven years of war came sixty-four years of peace.

The population of the three states was approximately twelve million.

He cataloged more than 527 works of art.

Within fifteen minutes the temperature dropped twenty degrees.

If your topic relies heavily on numerical data, follow a different rule: spell out only single-digit numbers and use numerals for all others.

This study of 14 electoral districts over seven years included 142 participants.

He hit the wall at 65 miles per hour, leaving skid marks for nine feet.

In the sciences, your general rule may be to use numerals for all numbers, except when they begin a sentence (see 23.1.2.1). You may also use abbreviations for quantities (see 24.5).

The mean weight proved to be 7 g, which was far less than predicted.

With any of these rules, use the same principles for ordinal numbers (*first, second,* etc.) that you use for standard ones. Add *st, nd, rd,* or *th* as appropriate.

On the 122nd and 123rd days of his trip, he received his eighteenth and nineteenth letters from home.

23.1.2 Special Cases

In a few common situations, the general rule discussed in 23.1.1 requires modification.

23.1.2.1 NUMBERS BEGINNING A SENTENCE. Never begin a sentence with a numeral. Either spell out the number or recast the sentence, especially when there are other numerals of a similar type in the sentence.

Two hundred fifty soldiers in the unit escaped injury; 175 sustained minor injuries.

or, better,

Of the soldiers in the unit, 250 escaped injury and 175 sustained minor injuries.

When spelling out numbers over one hundred, omit the word *and* within the term (not *two hundred and fifty*).

23.1.2.2 RELATED NUMBERS. Ignore the general rule when you have a series of related numbers in the same sentence that are above *and* below the threshold, especially when those numbers are being compared. In these examples, all are expressed in numerals.

Of the group surveyed, 78 students had studied French and 142 had studied Spanish for three years or more.

We analyzed 62 cases; of these, 59 had occurred in adults and 3 in children.

If you are discussing two sets of items in close proximity, ignore the general rule and, for clarity, spell out all numbers in one set and use numerals for all numbers in the other.

Within the program, 9 children showed some improvement after six months and 37 showed significant improvement after eighteen months.

23.1.2.3 ROUND NUMBERS. Spell out a round number (a whole number followed by *hundred, thousand, hundred thousand, million*, and so on) in isolation (see 23.1.1), but give several round numbers close together in numerals. You may also express large round numbers in a combination of numerals and words. (See also 23.1.4.)

Approximately fifteen hundred scholars attended the conference.

but

They sold 1,500 copies in the first year and 8,000 in the second.

These changes will affect about 7.8 million people in New York alone.

23.1.3 Percentages and Decimal Fractions

Use numerals to express percentages and decimal fractions, except at the beginning of a sentence (see 23.1.2.1). Spell out the word *percent*, except when you use many percentage figures and in the sciences, where the symbol % is usually preferred (with no intervening space after the number). Notice that the noun *percentage* should not be used with a number.

Scores for students who skipped summer school improved only 9 percent. The percentage of students who failed was about 2.4 times the usual rate.

Within this system, the subject scored 3.8, or 95%.

but not

The average rose 9 percentage points.

When you use fractional and whole numbers for the same type of item in the same sentence or paragraph, give both as numerals.

The average number of children born to college graduates dropped from 2.4 to 2.

Put a zero in front of a decimal fraction of less than 1.00 if the quantity expressed is capable of exceeding 1.00. When decimal quantities must be 1.00 or less, as in probabilities, correlation coefficients, and the like, omit the zero before the decimal point.

a mean of 0.73   a loss of 0.08 $p < .05$ a .406 batting average

For fractions standing alone, follow the general rule (see 23.1.1) for spelling out the parts. If you spell the parts, include a hyphen between them. Express in numerals a unit composed of a whole number and a fraction. If you use a symbol for the fraction, there is no intervening space between the number and the fraction.

Trade and commodity services accounted for nine-tenths of all international receipts and payments.

One year during the Dust Bowl era, the town received only 15/16 of an inch of rain.

The main carving implement used in this society measured 2½ feet.

23.1.4 Money

23.1.4.1 US CURRENCY. If you refer only occasionally to US currency, follow the general rule (see 23.1.1), and spell out the words *dollars* and *cents*. Otherwise use numerals along with the symbol $ (or, if needed, ¢). Omit the decimal point and following zeros for whole-dollar amounts, unless you refer to fractional amounts as well.

Rarely do they spend more than five dollars a week on recreation.

The report showed $135 collected in fines.

Prices ranged from $0.95 up to $10.00.

Express large round numbers in a combination of numerals and words.

The deficit that year was $420 billion.

23.1.4.2 OTHER CURRENCIES. For currencies other than that of the United States, follow the pattern for the US dollar. Most currencies put unit symbols before numerals. Even though European nations represent decimal points with commas instead of periods, you may use periods, except in direct quotations from sources. In contexts where the symbol $ may refer to non-US currencies, these currencies should be clearly identified.

When she returned, she had barely fifty euros to her name.

The household records show that it cost only £36.50.

Its current estimated worth is ¥377 million.

If you subtract Can$15.69 from US$25.00, . . .

Most European nations now use the unified currency called the euro (€), but if you are writing about topics from the period before 2002, you may encounter such currencies as the French franc (F), German deutsche mark (DM), and Italian lira (Lit). British currency is still expressed in pounds (£) and pence (p.), though before decimalization in 1971, it was expressed in pounds, shillings, and pence (for example, £12 17s. 6d.). Note that *billion* in traditional British usage as well as in certain languages other than English means a million million, not a thousand million; to avoid confusion, be sure to accurately represent such distinctions.

In more technical contexts, it may be best to use the three-letter codes for current and historical currencies defined by the International Organization for Standardization in standard ISO 4217, which is available on the organization's website. Use a space between the code and the amount.

If you subtract EUR 15.69 from USD 25.00, . . .

23.1.5   Time

For references to times of day in even increments of an hour, half hour, or quarter hour, spell out the times, with a hyphen between parts. If necessary, specify *in the morning* or *in the evening*. You may use *o'clock*, although it is now rare in research writing.

The participants planned to meet every Thursday around ten-thirty in the morning.

When emphasizing exact times, use numerals and, if necessary, *a.m.* or *p.m.* (lowercase and roman; see also 24.4.1). Always include zeros after the colon for even hours.

Although scheduled to end at 11:00 a.m., the council meeting ran until 1:37 p.m.

In either situation, use the words *noon* and *midnight* (rather than numerals) to express these specific times of day.

For use of words or numerals in dates, see 23.3.

23.1.6   Names with Numbers

Some types of personal, governmental, and organizational names include numbers given in either words or numerals. (See also 22.1.)

- *Leaders.* Emperors, sovereigns, or popes with the same first name are differentiated by capitalized roman numerals (see table 23.1).

| Charles V | Napoleon III | Elizabeth II | Benedict XVI |

- *Family members.* Male family members with identical full names are often differentiated with roman or arabic numerals (see also 24.2.1). Note that there are no commas between the name and the numeral, unless the name is inverted, as in a list.

Adlai E. Stevenson III   Michael F. Johnson 2nd

but

Stevenson, Adlai E., III

- *Governments and political divisions.* Certain dynasties, governments, governing bodies, political and judicial divisions, and military units are commonly designated by an ordinal number before the noun. Spell out and capitalize numbers through one hundred (with a hyphen between the parts of the number, if relevant); use numerals for those over one hundred.

Nineteenth Dynasty	Fourteenth Congressional District
Fifth Republic	Forty-Seventh Ward
Eighty-First Congress	Tenth Circuit
109th Congress	101st Airborne Division

- *Churches and religious organizations.* Spell out and capitalize numbers before the names of churches or religious organizations in ordinal form (with a hyphen between the parts of the number, if relevant).

Twenty-First Church of Christ, Scientist

- *Secular organizations.* Express local branches of fraternal lodges and unions in numerals following the name.

American Legion, Department of Illinois, Crispus Attucks Post No. 1268
United Auto Workers Local 890

23.1.7 Addresses and Thoroughfares

Follow the general rule (see 23.1.1) for the names of local numbered streets. State, federal, and interstate highways are always designated with numerals, as are street or building addresses and telephone and fax numbers. Note that in text the elements of a full address are separated by commas, except before a zip code. See 24.3.2 for abbreviations in addresses.

The National Park Service maintains as a museum the house where Lincoln died (516 10th Street NW, Washington, DC 20004; 202-426-6924).

Ludwig Mies van der Rohe designed the apartments at 860–880 North Lake Shore Drive.

Interstate 95 serves as a critical transportation line from Boston to Miami.

23.1.8 Parts of Published Works

With the exception of roman-numeral page numbers (as in the front matter of a book; see 16.1.5, 18.1.5), numbers in parts of published works are given in arabic numerals, regardless of the general rule (see 23.1.1) or their appearance in the work itself. See also 22.3.2.3, 23.2.2.

chapter 14   part 2   act 1, scene 3   page 1024

23.1.9 Equations and Formulas

Numbers in equations and formulas are always given as numerals, regardless of the general rule (see 23.1.1). For detailed guidance on presenting mathematical expressions, see chapter 12 of *The Chicago Manual of Style*, 17th edition (2017).

23.2 Plurals and Punctuation

23.2.1 Plurals

Form the plurals of spelled-out numbers like the plurals of other nouns (see 20.1).

Half the men surveyed were in their thirties or forties.

Form the plurals of numbers expressed in numerals by adding s alone (not 's).

The pattern changed in the late 1990s as more taxpayers submitted 1040s online.

To fly 767s, the pilots required special training.

23.2.2 Commas within Numbers

In most numbers of four or more digits, set off thousands, hundreds of thousands, millions, and so on with commas. (In the sciences, commas are often omitted from four-digit numbers.)

1,500   12,275,500   1,475,525,000

Do not use a comma within a four-digit year; do use one for a year with five or more digits (see also 23.3).

2007   10,000 BC

Do not use a comma in page numbers, street addresses, telephone or fax numbers, zip codes, decimal fractions of less than one, or numbers included in organization names.

page 1012   0.1911 centimeters   15000 Elm Street   Committee of 1000

23.2.3 Other Punctuation within Numbers

Numbers sometimes include internal punctuation other than commas. For periods (decimals), see 23.1.3 and 23.1.4; for colons, see 23.1.5; for hyphens, see 23.1.1 and 23.1.3; for dashes, see 23.2.4.

23.2.4 Inclusive Numbers

To express a range of numbers, such as pages or years, give the first and last (or *inclusive*) numbers of the sequence. If the numbers are spelled out, express the range with the words *from* and *to*; if they are expressed in numerals, use either these words or a connecting hyphen with no space on either side. In some settings, such as citations, always use hyphens (see chapters 16–19). Do not combine words and hyphens in expressing inclusive numbers.

from 45 to 50   ***but not***   from 45–50
45–50   ***but not***   forty-five-fifty

For inclusive numbers of one hundred or greater, you may either use full numbers on either side of a hyphen (245–280 or 1929–1994) or abbreviate the second number. Table 23.2 shows one system of abbreviation.

This system works well for page numbers, which never include commas (see 23.2.2). For numbers that include commas, use the system shown in table 23.2, but repeat all digits if the change extends to the thousands place or beyond. Never abbreviate roman numerals (see table 23.1).

6,000–6,018   12,473–79   128,333–129,114   xxv–xxviii

For years, give all digits for a span that includes more than one century. Also give full dates in a system in which dates are counted backward

Table 23.2. *Abbreviation system for inclusive numbers*

First number	Second number	Examples
1-99	*Use all digits*	*3-10, 71-72, 96-117*
100 or multiples of 100	*Use all digits*	*100-104, 1100-1113*
101 through 109, 201 through 209, etc.	*Use changed part only*	*101-8, 808-33, 1103-4*
110 through 199, 210 through 299, etc.	*Use two digits unless more are needed to include all changed parts*	*321-28, 498-532, 1087-89, 1496-500, 11564-615, 12991-3001*

from a specific point (most notably BC, "before Christ," and BCE, "before the common era"). Otherwise use the system shown in table 23.2. See 23.3 for more on date systems.

the years 1933–36

the winter of 1999–2000

15,000–14,000 BCE

115 BC–AD 10

23.3   Date Systems

23.3.1   Month, Day, and Year

Spell out the names of months when they occur in text, whether alone or in dates. Express days and years in numerals, and avoid using them at the beginning of a sentence, where they would have to be spelled out (see 23.1.2.1). Do not abbreviate references to the year ("the great flood of '05"). For abbreviations acceptable in tables, figures, and citations, see 24.4.2.

Every September, we recall the events of 2001.

but not

Two thousand one was a memorable year.

For full references to dates, give the month, the day (followed by a comma), and the year, in accordance with US practices. If you omit the day, omit the comma. Also omit the comma for dates given with seasons instead of months; do not capitalize the names of seasons (see 22.1.2). If you are quoting material that uses British-style dates (15 March 2007), do not alter them.

President John F. Kennedy was assassinated on November 22, 1963.

By March 1865, the war was nearly over.

The research was conducted over several weeks in spring 2006.

Note that within complete dates, days are generally not given as ordinals—that is, the numerals are not followed by *st*, *nd*, *rd*, or *th*. Use these endings only with spelled-out numbers when you specify the day without the month or year.

The date chosen for the raid was the twenty-ninth.

but not

The events occurred on June 11th, 1968.

23.3.2 Decades, Centuries, and Eras

In general, refer to decades using numerals, including the century (see 23.2.1 for plurals). If the century is clear, you may spell out the name of the decade; do not abbreviate numerals ("the '90s"). The first two decades of any century do not lend themselves to either style and, for clarity, should not be referred to in a shortened form.

The 1920s brought unheralded financial prosperity.

During the fifties, the Cold War dominated the headlines.

Many of these discoveries were announced during the first decade of the twenty-first century.

Refer to centuries using either numerals or lowercase spelled-out names (see 23.2.1 for plurals). If the century is spelled out and used as an adjective preceding a noun that it modifies, as in the second example, include a hyphen; otherwise do not (see 20.3.2).

The Ottoman Empire reached its apex in the 1600s.

She teaches nineteenth-century novels but would rather teach poetry from the twentieth century.

The most common designations for eras use the abbreviations BC ("before Christ") and AD (*anno Domini,* "in the year of the Lord"). Some disciplines use different designations, such as BCE and CE (see 24.4.3). AD precedes the year number; the other designations follow it. For inclusive numbers with eras, see 23.2.4.

Solomon's Temple was destroyed by the Babylonians in 586 BC and again by the Romans in AD 70.

23.4 Numbers Used outside the Text

The preceding sections provide guidelines for presenting numbers in the text of your paper. Numbers used in tables, figures, source citations, and lists are subject to some of their own rules. For additional advice, see the appendix.

23.4.1 Numbers in Tables, Figures, and Citations

In general, use arabic numerals to present numerical data in tables and figures. For a discussion of numbers in tables, including table titles, see 26.2; for numbers in figures, including figure captions, see 26.3.

With few exceptions, arabic numerals are also used to cite volume numbers, edition numbers, and page numbers and other locators. For a discussion of numbers in notes-style citations, see 16.1.5 and chapter 17; for numbers in author-date citations, see 18.1.5 and chapter 19.

23.4.2 Enumerations

You may use numerals (and letters) to enumerate points discussed in the text, in appendixes, or in materials related to drafting your paper.

23.4.2.1 LISTS. Your text may contain lists of items that you choose to enumerate for emphasis. When such a list is relatively short, incorporate it into a single sentence. Be sure that all the items are grammatically parallel (all noun phrases, all adjectives, or the like). Each item should be preceded by an arabic numeral in parentheses. If there are more than two items, each should be followed by a comma (or, if the item is complex in structure, a semicolon; see 21.3). If the list is an appositive, use a colon to introduce it; otherwise do not use punctuation in this position (see 21.4).

Wilson's secretary gave three reasons for his resignation: (1) advancing age, (2) gradually failing eyesight, and (3) opposition to the war.

The committee strongly endorsed the policies of (1) complete executive power, except as constitutionally limited; (2) strong legislative prerogatives; and (3) limited judicial authority, especially when it interfered with the committee's own role.

If you are already using arabic numerals in parentheses for other purposes, substitute lowercase letters for the numbers.

Haskin's latest theory has more than one drawback: (a) it is not based on current evidence, and (b) it has a weak theoretical grounding.

If the items in the list are longer or you wish to give them greater emphasis, arrange them in a vertical list. Introduce the list with a complete sentence followed by a colon. Again, be sure that all the items are grammatically parallel, and begin each one with a bullet or with an arabic numeral followed by a period. If the items are complete sentences, capitalize the first letter in each item and use terminal periods; otherwise use lowercase letters and no periods (see 21.1). Align the numerals on the periods and any lines that run over with the first word in the first line.

My research therefore suggests the following conclusions:

1. The painting could not have been a genuine Picasso, regardless of the claims of earlier scholars.
2. It is impossible to identify the true artist without further technical analysis.

23.4.2.2 OUTLINES. In some situations you may include an outline or a similar enumeration in an appendix to your paper, or in a draft stage of the paper (see 6.2.1). Use the following system of notation, consisting of letters and roman and arabic numerals, and indent each level by one further tab (usually a half inch). You should have at least two items to list at each level; if you do not, reconsider the structure of the outline. If the items are phrases, capitalize them sentence-style (see 22.3.1) and do not use terminal punctuation. If they are complete sentences, capitalize and punctuate them as you would any other sentence (see 6.2.1 for an example).

I. Wars of the nineteenth century
   A. United States
      1. Civil War, 1861–65
         a) Cause
            (1) Slavery
               (a) Compromise
                  i) Missouri Compromise
                  ii) Compromise of 1850 . . .
         b) Result

. . . .

II. Wars of the twentieth century
   A. United States
      1. First World War . . .

24 Abbreviations

This chapter offers general guidelines for using abbreviations. Abbreviations in formal writing were once limited to a few special circumstances, but they are now widely used in writing of all kinds. Even so, their use must reflect the conventions of specific disciplines. The guidelines presented here are appropriate for most humanities and social science disciplines. If you are writing a paper in the natural or physical sciences, mathematics, or any other technical field, follow the conventions of the discipline.

The dictionaries from Merriam-Webster include entries for many abbreviations from many fields. Another resource is chapter 10 of *The Chicago Manual of Style*, 17th edition (2017). For style guides in various disciplines, see the bibliography.

If you are writing a thesis or dissertation, your department or university may have specific requirements for using abbreviations, which are usually available from the office of theses and dissertations. If you are writing a class paper, your instructor may also ask you to follow certain principles for using abbreviations. Review these requirements before you prepare your paper. They take precedence over the guidelines suggested here.

24.1 General Principles

24.1.1 Types of Abbreviations

Terms can be shortened, or abbreviated, in several ways. When a term is shortened to only the first letters of each word and pronounced as a single word (NATO, AIDS), it is called an *acronym*; if the letters are pronounced as a series of letters (EU, PBS), it is called an *initialism*. Other terms are shortened through *contraction*: just the first and last letters of the term are retained (Mr., Dr., atty.), or the last letters are dropped (ed., Tues.). This chapter treats all of these forms under the general term *abbreviations*, with distinctions between types noted as relevant.

24.1.2 When to Use Abbreviations

In most papers, use abbreviations only sparingly in text because they can make your writing seem either too informal or too technical. This chapter covers types of abbreviations that are preferred over spelled-out terms and others that are considered acceptable in academic writing if used consistently.

If your local guidelines allow it, you may use abbreviations for names, titles, and other terms used frequently in your paper. Give the full term on first reference, followed by the abbreviation in parentheses. For subsequent references, use the abbreviation consistently. If you use more than a few such abbreviations, consider adding a list of abbreviations to the front matter of the paper to aid readers who might miss your first reference to an abbreviation (see A.2.1).

Abbreviations are more common, and are often required, outside the text of the paper. This chapter discusses some abbreviations that may be used in tables, figures, and citations. For additional discussion of abbreviations in tables and figures, see chapter 26; for abbreviations in notes-style citations, see 16.1.6 and chapter 17; for abbreviations in author-date citations, see 18.1.6 and chapter 19.

24.1.3 How to Format Abbreviations

Although abbreviations follow the general principles discussed here, there are many exceptions.

- *Capitalization.* Abbreviations are given in all capital letters, all lowercase letters, or a combination.

BC	p.	Gov.
CEO	a.m.	Dist. Atty.
US	kg	PhD

- *Punctuation.* In general, abbreviations given in all capital letters do not include periods, while those given in lowercase or a combination of capital and lowercase letters have a period after each abbreviated element. However, as you can see from the examples above, there are exceptions: metric units of measure (see 24.5) are in lowercase without periods; and no periods are used for academic degrees, whether or not they include lowercase letters (see 24.2.3). Other exceptions are noted throughout this chapter.
- *Spacing.* In general, do not leave a space between letters in acronyms (NATO) and initialisms (PBS), but do leave a space between elements in abbreviations formed through shortening (Dist. Atty.), unless the first element is a single letter (S.Sgt.). If an abbreviation contains an ampersand (&), do not leave spaces around it (Texas A&M). For spaces in personal names, see 24.2.1.
- *Italics.* Abbreviations are not normally italicized unless they stand for an italicized term (OED, for *Oxford English Dictionary*).
- *Indefinite articles.* When an abbreviation follows an indefinite article, choose between *a* and *an* depending on how the abbreviation is read aloud. Acronyms (NATO, AIDS) are pronounced as words; initialisms (EU, FDA) are read as a series of letters.

member nation of NATO	a NATO member
person with AIDS	an AIDS patient
member nation of the EU	an EU member
the FDA	an FDA mandate

24.2   Names and Titles

24.2.1   **Personal Names**

In general, do not abbreviate a person's first (Benj. Franklin) or last name. Once you have used a full name in text, use just the person's last name in subsequent references. However, if you are referring to more than one person with that last name, use first names as necessary to avoid confusion (Alice James, William James). If you refer to these names very frequently in your paper, you may instead use abbreviations that you devise (AJ, WJ), but be sure to use these abbreviations as specified in 24.1.2.

Some individuals are known primarily by initials in place of a first and/or middle name. Such initials should be followed by a period and a space. If you abbreviate an entire name, however, omit periods and spaces.

G. K. Chesterton	*but*	JFK
M. F. K. Fisher	*but*	FDR

Social titles such as *Ms.* and *Mr.* should always be abbreviated and capitalized, followed by a period. In most papers, however, you need not use such titles unless there is a possibility of confusion, such as referring to either a husband or a wife.

Write abbreviations such as *Sr., Jr., III* (or *3rd*), and *IV* (or *4th*) without commas before them. Normally these abbreviations are used only after a full name, although royal and religious figures may be known only by a first name. In frequent references to a father and a son, shortened versions may be used (Holmes Sr.), but only after the full name has been presented. Do not spell out the term when it is part of a name (for example, not *John Smith Junior*).

Oliver Wendell Holmes Jr.	William J. Kaufmann III	Mary II

24.2.2   **Professional Titles**

Some individuals have civil, military, or religious titles such as the following along with their personal names. Many of these titles are conventionally abbreviated rather than spelled out in text when they precede and are capitalized as part of a personal name.

Adm.	Admiral	Dr.	Doctor
Ald.	Alderman, Alderwoman	Fr.	Father
Atty. Gen.	Attorney General	Gen.	General
Capt.	Captain	Gov.	Governor
Col.	Colonel	Hon.	Honorable
Dist. Atty.	District Attorney	Lt.	Lieutenant

Lt. Col.	Lieutenant Colonel	Sen.	Senator
Maj.	Major	Sgt.	Sergeant
Pres.	President	S.Sgt.	Staff Sergeant
Rep.	Representative	Sr.	Sister
Rev.	Reverend	St.	Saint

On first reference to an individual with such a title, use the abbreviation with the person's full name. (If you prefer, you may spell out the titles, but do so consistently.) For subsequent references you may usually give just the person's last name, but if you need to repeat the title (to distinguish two people with similar names, or as a disciplinary sign of respect), give the spelled-out title with the last name. Never use *Honorable* or *Hon.* except with a full name. If you spell out *Honorable* or *Reverend* before a full name, the title should be preceded by *the*.

Sen. Richard J. Durbin	Senator Durbin
Adm. Cecil D. Haney	Admiral Haney
Rev. Jane Schaefer	Reverend Schaefer
Hon. Patricia Birkholz	Birkholz

or

the Honorable Patricia Birkholz

If you use one of these titles alone or after a personal name, it becomes a generic term and should be lowercased and spelled out.

the senator from Illinois   Haney served as an admiral

An exception to the general pattern is *Dr.* Use either the abbreviation *Dr.* before the name or the official abbreviation for the degree (see 24.2.3), set off with commas, after the name. Do not use both together.

Dr. Lauren Shapiro discovered the cause of the outbreak.

Lauren Shapiro, MD, discovered . . .

Dr. Shapiro discovered . . .

The doctor discovered . . .

In addition to academic degrees (24.2.3), here are a few professional titles that may be abbreviated following a personal name. Like MD in the example above, such titles should be set off with commas.

JP	justice of the peace
LPN	licensed practical nurse
MP	member of Parliament
SJ	Society of Jesus

24.2.3 Academic Degrees

You may use abbreviations in text and elsewhere for the common academic degrees. Some of the more common degrees are noted in the following list. Most are initialisms (see 24.1.1), which are written in capital letters without periods or spaces. Others contain both initials and shortened terms and therefore both capital and lowercase letters, also without periods or spaces. Traditionally all these forms appeared with periods (M.A., Ph.D., LL.B.), a style still preferred by some institutions.

AB	artium baccalaureus (bachelor of arts)
AM	artium magister (master of arts)
BA	bachelor of arts
BD	bachelor of divinity
BFA	bachelor of fine arts
BM	bachelor of music
BS	bachelor of science
DB	divinitatis baccalaureus (bachelor of divinity)
DD	divinitatis doctor (doctor of divinity)
DMin	doctor of ministry
DO	osteopathic physician (doctor of osteopathy)
EdD	doctor of education
JD	juris doctor (doctor of law)
LHD	litterarum humaniorum doctor (doctor of humanities)
LittD	litterarum doctor (doctor of letters)
LLB	legum baccalaureus (bachelor of laws)
LLD	legum doctor (doctor of laws)
MA	master of arts
MBA	master of business administration
MD	medicinae doctor (doctor of medicine)
MFA	master of fine arts
MS	master of science
PhB	philosophiae baccalaureus (bachelor of philosophy)
PhD	philosophiae doctor (doctor of philosophy)
SB	scientiae baccalaureus (bachelor of science)
SM	scientiae magister (master of science)
STB	sacrae theologiae baccalaureus (bachelor of sacred theology)

24.2.4 Agencies, Companies, and Other Organizations

You may use abbreviations in text and elsewhere for the names of government agencies, broadcasting companies, associations, fraternal and service organizations, unions, and other groups that are commonly known by acronyms or initialisms (see 24.1.1). Spell out the full name on first reference, followed by the abbreviation in parentheses (see 24.1.2). Such abbreviations are in full capitals with no periods. Here is a representative list of such abbreviations; other names within these categories (for example, ABA, CBS, and NEH) should be treated similarly.

AAAS	CNN	NAFTA	TVA
AFL-CIO	EU	NFL	UN
AMA	FTC	NIMH	UNESCO
AT&T	HMO	NSF	WHO
CDC	NAACP	OPEC	YMCA

If a company is not commonly known by an abbreviation, spell out and capitalize its name in the text. The names of some companies contain abbreviations and ampersands. If in doubt about the correct form, look up the company name at its corporate website or, for historical forms, in an authoritative reference. You may omit such terms as *Inc.* or *Ltd.* from the name, and do not capitalize the word *the* at the beginning of the name. Subsequent references can drop terms such as & *Co.* or *Corporation*.

Merck & Co.   RAND Corporation   the University of Chicago Press

In tables, figures, and citations, you may use any of the following abbreviations in company names.

Assoc.	LP (limited partnership)
Bros.	Mfg.
Co.	PLC (public limited company)
Corp.	RR (railroad)
Inc.	Ry. (railway)

24.3   Geographical Terms

24.3.1   Place-Names

In text, always spell out and capitalize the names of countries, states, counties, provinces, territories, bodies of water, mountains, and the like (see 22.1.1).

Always spell out *United States* when using it as a noun. When using it as an adjective, you may either abbreviate it to *US* or spell it out (for a more formal tone).

She was ineligible for the presidency because she was not born in the United States.

His US citizenship was revoked later that year.

In tables, figures, citations, and mailing addresses, abbreviate the names of US states using the two-letter postal codes created by the US Postal Service.

AK	Alaska	MT	Montana
AL	Alabama	NC	North Carolina
AR	Arkansas	ND	North Dakota
AZ	Arizona	NE	Nebraska
CA	California	NH	New Hampshire
CO	Colorado	NJ	New Jersey
CT	Connecticut	NM	New Mexico
DC	District of Columbia	NV	Nevada
DE	Delaware	NY	New York
FL	Florida	OH	Ohio
GA	Georgia	OK	Oklahoma
HI	Hawaii	OR	Oregon
IA	Iowa	PA	Pennsylvania
ID	Idaho	RI	Rhode Island
IL	Illinois	SC	South Carolina
IN	Indiana	SD	South Dakota
KS	Kansas	TN	Tennessee
KY	Kentucky	TX	Texas
LA	Louisiana	UT	Utah
MA	Massachusetts	VA	Virginia
MD	Maryland	VT	Vermont
ME	Maine	WA	Washington
MI	Michigan	WI	Wisconsin
MN	Minnesota	WV	West Virginia
MO	Missouri	WY	Wyoming
MS	Mississippi		

You may also abbreviate the names of Canadian provinces and territories where state names would be abbreviated.

AB	Alberta	NU	Nunavut
BC	British Columbia	ON	Ontario
MB	Manitoba	PE	Prince Edward Island
NB	New Brunswick	QC	Quebec
NL	Newfoundland and Labrador	SK	Saskatchewan
NS	Nova Scotia	YT	Yukon
NT	Northwest Territories		

24.3.2 Addresses

In text, spell out and capitalize terms that are part of addresses, including those listed below and similar ones (other synonyms for *street*, for example). In tables, figures, citations, and mailing addresses, use the abbreviations. Note that all the abbreviations use periods except for the two-letter initialisms (such as NE). See 23.1.7 for an example of an address in text.

Ave.	Avenue	St.	Street
Blvd.	Boulevard	N.	North
Ct.	Court	S.	South
Dr.	Drive	E.	East
Expy.	Expressway	W.	West
Pkwy.	Parkway	NE	Northeast
Rd.	Road	NW	Northwest
Sq.	Square	SE	Southeast
Pl.	Place	SW	Southwest

24.4 Time and Dates

24.4.1 Time

You may use the abbreviations *a.m.* (*ante meridiem,* or before noon) and *p.m.* (*post meridiem,* or after noon) in text and elsewhere to designate specific times. The abbreviations should be lowercase and in roman type. Do not combine them with *in the morning, in the evening,* or *o'clock;* see also 23.1.5.

24.4.2 Days and Months

In text, spell out and capitalize the names of days of the week and months of the year; see also 23.3.1. In tables, figures, and citations, you may abbreviate them if you do so consistently. (Note that some months in this system are not abbreviated.)

Sun.	Wed.	Sat.	Jan.	Apr.	July	Oct.
Mon.	Thur.		Feb.	May	Aug.	Nov.
Tues.	Fri.		Mar.	June	Sept.	Dec.

24.4.3 Eras

There are various systems for designating eras, all of which use abbreviations with numerical dates. *BC* and *AD* are the most common designations, though *BCE* and *CE* may be used instead. To refer to the very distant past, a designation such as *BP* or *MYA* may become necessary. *AD* precedes the year number; the other designations follow it (see also 23.2.4 and 23.3.2).

BC	before Christ
AD	*anno Domini* (in the year of the Lord)
BCE	before the common era
CE	common era
BP	before the present
MYA (*or* mya)	million years ago

24.5 Units of Measure

In the humanities and social sciences, spell out the names of units of measure such as dimensions, distances, volumes, weights, and degrees. Spell out the numbers or use numerals according to the general rule you are following (see 23.1.1).

five miles   150 kilograms   14.5 meters

In the sciences, use standard abbreviations for units of measure when the amount is given in numerals. (You may use abbreviations in other disciplines, depending on your local guidelines.) Leave a space between the numeral and the unit, except where convention dictates otherwise (36°; 10%; see also 23.1.3). Note that abbreviations are the same in singular and plural. Spell out units of measure when they are not preceded by a number or when the number is spelled out (as at the beginning of a sentence; see 23.1.2.1).

We injected 10 µL of virus near the implants.

Results are given in microliters.

Twelve microliters of virus was considered a safe amount.

For a list of abbreviations including common units of measure, see 10.49 of *The Chicago Manual of Style*, 17th edition (2017).

24.6 The Bible and Other Sacred Works

When you refer in text to whole chapters or books of the Bible or the Apocrypha, spell out the names of the books but do not italicize them.

Jeremiah 42–44 records the flight of the Jews to Egypt.

The Revelation of St. John the Divine, known as Revelation, closes the New Testament.

When you cite biblical passages by verse (see 17.5.2 and 19.5.2), abbreviate the names of the books, using arabic numerals if they are numbered (2 Kings). Also use arabic numerals for chapter and verse numbers, with a colon between them. Since versions of the scriptures do not all use the same names and numbers for books, identify the version you are citing. Depending on the context, you may either spell out the name of the version, at least on first occurrence, or use abbreviations (see 24.6.4), as shown here.

Song of Sol. 2:1–5 NRSV   Ruth 3:14 NAB

The following sections list both traditional and shorter abbreviations for the books of the Bible, arranged in alphabetical order. If you are unsure which form of abbreviation is appropriate, consult your instructor. Where no abbreviation is given, use the full form.

24.6.1 Jewish Bible / Old Testament

Note that the abbreviation for Old Testament is OT.

Traditional	Shorter	Full name
Amos	Am	Amos
1 Chron.	1 Chr	1 Chronicles
2 Chron.	2 Chr	2 Chronicles
Dan.	Dn	Daniel
Deut.	Dt	Deuteronomy
Eccles.	Eccl	Ecclesiastes
Esther	Est	Esther
Exod.	Ex	Exodus
Ezek.	Ez	Ezekiel
Ezra	Ezr	Ezra
Gen.	Gn	Genesis
Hab.	Hb	Habakkuk
Hag.	Hg	Haggai
Hosea	Hos	Hosea
Isa.	Is	Isaiah
Jer.	Jer	Jeremiah
Job	Jb	Job
Joel	Jl	Joel
Jon.	Jon	Jonah
Josh.	Jo	Joshua
Judg.	Jgs	Judges
1 Kings	1 Kgs	1 Kings
2 Kings	2 Kgs	2 Kings
Lam.	Lam	Lamentations
Lev.	Lv	Leviticus
Mal.	Mal	Malachi
Mic.	Mi	Micah
Nah.	Na	Nahum
Neh.	Neh	Nehemiah
Num.	Nm	Numbers
Obad.	Ob	Obadiah
Prov.	Prv	Proverbs
Ps. (plural Pss.)	Ps (plural Pss)	Psalms
Ruth	Ru	Ruth
1 Sam.	1 Sm	1 Samuel

2 Sam.	2 Sm	2 Samuel
Song of Sol.	Sg	Song of Solomon (Song of Songs)
Zech.	Zec	Zechariah
Zeph.	Zep	Zephaniah

24.6.2 Apocrypha

The books of the Apocrypha are included in Roman Catholic but not Jewish or Protestant versions of the Bible. Note that the traditional abbreviation for Apocrypha is Apoc. (no shorter abbreviation).

Traditional	Shorter	Full name
Bar.	Bar	Baruch
Bel and Dragon	—	Bel and the Dragon
Ecclus.	Sir	Ecclesiasticus (Sirach)
1 Esd.	—	1 Esdras
2 Esd.	—	2 Esdras
Jth.	Jdt	Judith
1 Macc.	1 Mc	1 Maccabees
2 Macc.	2 Mc	2 Maccabees
Pr. of Man.	—	Prayer of Manasses (Manasseh)
Song of Three Children	—	Song of the Three Holy Children
Sus.	—	Susanna
Tob.	Tb	Tobit
Wisd. of Sol.	Ws	Wisdom of Solomon
—	—	Additions to Esther (Rest of Esther)

24.6.3 New Testament

Note that the abbreviation for New Testament is NT.

Traditional	Shorter	Full name
Acts	—	Acts of the Apostles
Apoc.	—	Apocalypse (Revelation)
Col.	Col	Colossians
1 Cor.	1 Cor	1 Corinthians
2 Cor.	2 Cor	2 Corinthians
Eph.	Eph	Ephesians
Gal.	Gal	Galatians
Heb.	Heb	Hebrews
James	Jas	James
John	Jn	John (Gospel)
1 John	1 Jn	1 John (Epistle)
2 John	2 Jn	2 John (Epistle)
3 John	3 Jn	3 John (Epistle)
Jude	—	Jude

Luke	Lk	Luke
Mark	Mk	Mark
Matt.	Mt	Matthew
1 Pet.	1 Pt	1 Peter
2 Pet.	2 Pt	2 Peter
Phil.	Phil	Philippians
Philem.	Phlm	Philemon
Rev.	Rv	Revelation (Apocalypse)
Rom.	Rom	Romans
1 Thess.	1 Thes	1 Thessalonians
2 Thess.	2 Thes	2 Thessalonians
1 Tim.	1 Tm	1 Timothy
2 Tim.	2 Tm	2 Timothy
Titus	Ti	Titus

24.6.4 Versions of the Bible

These abbreviations cover many standard versions of the Bible. If the version you are citing is not listed here, consult your instructor.

ARV	American Revised Version
ASV	American Standard Version
AT	American Translation
AV	Authorized (King James) Version
CEV	Contemporary English Version
DV	Douay Version
ERV	English Revised Version
EV	English version(s)
JB	Jerusalem Bible
NAB	New American Bible
NEB	New English Bible
NRSV	New Revised Standard Version
RSV	Revised Standard Version
RV	Revised Version
Vulg.	Vulgate

24.6.5 Other Sacred Works

Many sacred works of other religious traditions are divided into parts similar to those of the Bible. Capitalize and set in roman type the names of the works themselves (Qur'an [or Koran], Vedas), but italicize the names of their parts (*al-Baqarah*, *Rig-Veda*). Although there is no widely accepted method for abbreviating the names of these works or their parts, you may punctuate citations from them similarly to those from the Bible (see also 17.5.2 and 19.5.2). If a work has multiple numbered divisions, you may substitute periods or commas for colons or make other adaptations to clarify the location of the cited passage.

Qur'an 2:257 *or* Qur'an 2 (*al-Baqarah*): 257
Mahabharata 1.2.3

If your paper is in religious studies, consult your instructor for more specific guidance.

24.7 Abbreviations in Citations and Other Scholarly Contexts

Many abbreviations are commonly used and even preferred in citations, especially for identifying the roles of individuals other than authors (ed., trans.), the parts of works (vol., bk., sec.), and locating information (p., n.). For guidelines on using abbreviations in citations, see 16.1.6 and chapter 17 or 18.1.6 and chapter 19.

In text it is usually better to spell things out. Common abbreviations like *e.g.*, i.e., and *etc.*, if used, should be confined to parentheses (see 21.8.1).

Following is a list of some of the most common abbreviations encountered in citations and other scholarly contexts. Unless otherwise shown, most form the plural by adding s or es. None of them are normally italicized.

abbr.	abbreviated, abbreviation
abr.	abridged, abridgment
anon.	anonymous
app.	appendix
assn.	association
b.	born
bib.	Bible, biblical
bibliog.	bibliography, bibliographer
biog.	biography, biographer
bk.	book
ca.	*circa*, about, approximately
cap.	capital, capitalize
CD	compact disc
cf.	*confer*, compare
chap.	chapter
col.	color (best spelled out); column
comp.	compiler, compiled by
cont.	continued
corr.	corrected
d.	died
dept.	department

dict.	dictionary
diss.	dissertation
div.	division
DOI	digital object identifier
DVD	digital versatile (or video) disc
ed.	editor, edition, edited by
e.g.	*exempli gratia*, for example
enl.	enlarged
esp.	especially
et al.	*et alii* or *et alia*, and others
etc.	*et cetera*, and so forth
ex.	example
fig.	figure
ff.	and following
fol.	folio
fps	frames per second
frag.	fragment
ftp	file transfer protocol
http	hypertext transfer protocol
ibid.	*ibidem*, in the same place
id.	*idem*, the same
i.e.	*id est*, that is
ill.	illustrated, illustration, illustrator
inf.	*infra*, below
intl.	international
intro.	introduction
1. (*pl.* 11.)	line (best spelled out to avoid confusion with numerals 1 and 11)
loc. cit.	*loco citato*, in the place cited (best avoided)
misc.	miscellaneous
MS (*pl.* MSS)	manuscript
n. (*pl.* nn.)	note (used without periods in citations)
natl.	national
n.b. or NB	*nota bene*, take careful note
n.d.	no date
no.	number
n.p.	no place; no publisher; no page
NS	New Style (dates)
n.s.	new series
op. cit.	*opera citato*, in the work cited (best avoided)
org.	organization
OS	Old Style (dates)
o.s.	old series
p. (*pl.* pp.)	page
para. *or* par.	paragraph
pers. comm.	personal communication

pl.	plate (best spelled out); plural
PS	*postscriptum*, postscript
pseud.	pseudonym
pt.	part
pub.	publication, publisher, published by
q.v.	*quod vide*, which see
r.	*recto*, right
repr.	reprint
rev.	revised, revised by, revision; review, reviewed by
ROM	read-only memory
sd.	sound
sec.	section
ser.	series
sing.	singular
soc.	society
sup.	*supra*, above
supp.	supplement
s.v. (*pl.* s.vv.)	*sub verbo*, *sub voce*, under the word
syn.	synonym, synonymous
t.p.	title page
trans.	translated by, translator
univ.	university
URL	uniform resource locator
usu.	usually
v. (*pl.* vv.)	verse; *verso*, right
viz.	*videlicet*, namely
vol.	volume
vs. *or* v.	versus (in legal contexts, use v.)

25 Quotations

This chapter offers general guidelines for presenting quotations. Although all of the examples are in English, the guidelines also apply to quotations from other languages (see also 22.2.1).

Quoting directly from a source is just one of several options for representing the work of others in your paper; for a discussion of the alternatives and when to use them, see 7.4. Whichever option you choose, you must cite the source of the words or ideas. Chapter 15 provides an introduction to citation practices, and the following chapters describe two common citation styles (chapters 16 and 17, notes style; chapters 18 and 19, author-date style).

If you are writing a thesis or a dissertation, your department or university may have specific requirements for presenting quotations, which are usually available from the office of theses and dissertations. If you are writing a class paper, your instructor may also ask you to follow certain principles for presenting quotations. Review those requirements before you prepare your paper. They take precedence over the guidelines suggested here. For style guides in various disciplines, see the bibliography.

If your dissertation will be submitted to an external dissertation repository, you may need to obtain formal permission from copyright holders for certain types of quotations. See chapter 4 of *The Chicago Manual of Style*, 17th edition (2017).

25.1   Quoting Accurately and Avoiding Plagiarism

Accurate quotation is crucial to the scholarly enterprise, so you must

- use only reliable, relevant sources (see 3.3)
- transcribe words exactly as they are in the original, or modify them only as described in 25.3
- accurately report the sources in your bibliography or reference list (see chapters 16 and 18) so that readers can consult them for themselves

The ethics of scholarship also require that whenever you quote words or rely on tables, graphics, or data from another source, you clearly indicate what you borrowed and from where, using the appropriate citation style (see chapter 15). If you do not, you risk a charge of plagiarism. But even if you do cite a source accurately, you still risk a charge of plagiarism if you use the exact words of the source but fail to identify them as a quotation in one of the ways given in 25.2. For a fuller discussion of plagiarism, see 7.9.

25.2   Incorporating Quotations into Your Text

You can incorporate a quotation into your text in one of two ways, depending on its length. If the quotation is four lines or less, run it into your text and enclose it in quotation marks. If it is five lines or longer, set it off as a block quotation, without quotation marks. Follow the same principles for quotations within footnotes or endnotes.

You may use a block quotation for a quotation shorter than five lines if you want to emphasize it or compare it to a longer quotation.

25.2.1   Run-in Quotations

When quoting a passage of less than five lines, enclose the exact words quoted in double quotation marks. There are several ways to integrate a quotation into the flow of your text; see 7.5. You may introduce it with the name of the author accompanied by a term such as *notes, claims, argues,* or *according to.* (Note that these terms are usually in the present tense, rather than *noted, claimed,* and so forth, but some disciplines follow different practices.) In this case, put a comma before the quotation.

Ricoeur writes, "The boundary between plot and argument is no easier to trace."

As Ricoeur notes, "The boundary between plot and argument is no easier to trace."

If you weave a quotation more tightly into the syntax of your sentence, such as with the word *that,* do not put a comma before it.

Ricoeur warns us that "the boundary between plot and argument is no easier to trace."

If you put the attributing phrase in the middle or at the end of a quotation, set it off with a pair of commas when it occurs in the middle or with a single comma when it occurs at the end.

"The boundary between plot and argument," says Ricoeur, "is no easier to trace."

"The boundary between plot and argument is no easier to trace," says Ricoeur.

For the use of commas, periods, and other punctuation marks relative to quotations, see 21.12.2 and 25.3.1; for permissible changes to capitalization and other elements, see 25.3.1.

25.2.1.1 PLACEMENT OF CITATIONS. If you cite the source of a quotation in a footnote or endnote, where you place the superscript note number (see 16.3.2) depends on where the quotation falls within a sentence. If the quotation is at the end of the sentence, put the number after the closing quotation mark.

According to Litwack, "Scores of newly freed slaves viewed movement as a vital expression of their emancipation."[4]

If the quotation ends in the middle of a sentence, put the number at the end of the clause that includes the quotation, which often is the end of the sentence.

"Scores of newly freed slaves viewed movement as a vital expression of their emancipation," according to Litwack.[4]

Litwack argues that "scores of newly freed slaves viewed movement as a vital expression of their emancipation,"[4] and he proceeds to prove this assertion.

The same placement options apply to citations given parenthetically with either notes-style (16.4.3) or author-date citations (see 18.3.1), with two notable differences:

- If a period or comma would normally precede the closing quotation mark, place it outside the quotation, following the closing parenthesis.

  The authors seek to understand "how people categorize the objects they encounter in everyday situations" (Bowker and Star 1999, 59).

  To determine "how people categorize the objects they encounter in everyday situations" (Bowker and Star 1999, 59), the authors devised a study.

- When the author's name is mentioned in text along with the quotation, place the date next to the author's name, regardless of where it appears relative to the quotation.

"Scores of newly freed slaves viewed movement as a vital expression of their emancipation," according to Litwack (1999, 482).

Litwack's (1999, 482) observation that "scores of newly freed slaves . . ."

25.2.1.2 SPECIAL PUNCTUATION. For a quotation within a quotation, use single quotation marks for the inner set of quoted words.

Rothko, argues Ball, "wanted to make works that wrought a transcendent effect, that dealt with spiritual concerns: 'Paintings must be like miracles,' he once said."

If you run two or more lines of poetry into your text, separate them with a slash (/), with a space before and after it. In most cases, however, use block quotations for poetry (see 25.2.2.2).

They reduce life to a simple proposition: "All things have rest, and ripen toward the grave; / In silence, ripen, fall, and cease."

25.2.2 Block Quotations

25.2.2.1 PROSE. Present a prose quotation of five or more lines as a block quotation. Introduce the quotation in your own words in the text; see 7.5. If you introduce the quotation with a complete sentence, end the sentence with a colon. If you use only an attribution phrase such as *notes*, *claims*, *argues*, or *according to* along with the author's name, end the phrase with a comma. If you weave the quotation into the syntax of your sentence, do not use any punctuation before the quotation if no punctuation would ordinarily appear there (see the second example below).

Single-space a block quotation, and leave a blank line before and after it. Do not add quotation marks at the beginning or end, but preserve any quotation marks in the original. Indent the entire quotation as far as you indent the first line of a paragraph. (In literary studies and other fields concerned with close analysis of texts, you should indent the first line of a block quotation farther than the rest of the quotation if the text is indented in the original; see also 25.3.) For other punctuation and capitalization within the quotation, see 25.3.1.

Jackson begins by evoking the importance of home:

Housing is an outward expression of the inner human nature; no society can be fully understood apart from the residences of its members. A nineteenth-century melody declares, "There's no place like home," and even though she had Emerald City at her feet, Dorothy could think of no place she would rather be than at home in Kansas. Our homes are our havens from the world.[1]

In the rest of his introduction, he discusses . . .

If you quote more than one paragraph, do not add extra line space between them, but indent the first line of the second and subsequent paragraphs farther than the rest of the quotation.

> He observed that
>
> > governments ordinarily perish by powerlessness or by tyranny. In the first case, power escapes them; in the other, it is torn from them.
> >
> > Many people, on seeing democratic states fall into anarchy, have thought that government in these states was naturally weak and powerless. The truth is that when war among their parties has once been set aflame, government loses its action on society. (Tocqueville, 248)

If you cite the source in a footnote or endnote, place the note number as a superscript at the end of the block quotation, as in the first example above (see also 16.3.2). If you cite the source parenthetically, put the citation *after* the terminal punctuation of a block quotation, as in the second example above. (Note that this differs from its placement with a run-in quotation, as explained in 25.2.1.1.)

25.2.2.2   POETRY AND DRAMA. Present a quotation of two or more lines from poetry as a block quotation. Begin each line of the poem on a new line, with punctuation at the ends of lines as in the original. For most papers, indent a block of poetry as you would a prose quotation; if a line is too long to fit on a single line, indent the runover farther than the rest of the quotation. (In a dissertation or other longer paper that includes many poetry quotations, center each left-aligned quotation on the page relative to the longest line.)

> Whitman's poem includes some memorable passages:
>
> > My tongue, every atom of my blood, form'd from this
> >   soil, this air,
> > Born here of parents born here from parents the same,
> >   and their parents the same,
> > I, now thirty-seven years old in perfect health begin,
> > Hoping to cease not till death.

If you are quoting a poem with an unusual alignment, reproduce the alignment of the original to the best of your ability.

> This is what Herbert captured so beautifully:
>
> > > Sure there was wine
> > Before my sighs did drie it: there was corn
> > > Before my tears did drown it.

> Is the yeare onely lost to me?
>> Have I no bayes to crown it?
> No flowers, no garlands gay? all blasted?
>> All wasted?

If you quote two or more lines of dialogue from a dramatic work, set the quotation apart in a block quotation formatted as you would prose. Present each speaker's name so that it is distinct from the dialogue, such as in all capital letters or in a different font. Begin each speech on a new line, and indent runovers farther than the rest of the quotation.

Then the play takes an unusual turn:

> R. ROISTER DOISTER. Except I have her to my wife, I shall run mad.
> M. MERYGREEKE. Nay, "unwise" perhaps, but I warrant you for
> "mad."

25.2.2.3 EPIGRAPHS. An epigraph is a quotation that establishes a theme of your paper. For epigraphs used in the front matter of a thesis or dissertation, see A.2.1. Treat an epigraph at the beginning of a chapter or section as a block quotation. On the line below it, give the author and the title, flush right and preceded by an em dash (or two hyphens; see 21.7.2). You do not need a more formal citation for an epigraph. Leave two blank lines between the source line and the beginning of text. See also figure A.9.

> The city, however, does not tell its past, but contains it like the lines of a hand.
>> —Italo Calvino, *Invisible Cities*

25.3 Modifying Quotations

When you do your research, you must record the exact wording, spelling, capitalization, and punctuation of any text you plan to quote, even if they do not follow the guidelines in this manual. When you incorporate the quotation into your paper, however, you may make minor adjustments to fit the syntax of the surrounding text or to emphasize certain parts of the quotation.

Note that disciplines have different standards for issues discussed in this section, such as modifying initial capital and lowercase letters and using ellipses for omissions. For papers in most disciplines, follow the general guidelines. For papers in literary studies and other fields concerned with close analysis of texts, follow the stricter guidelines given under some topics. If you are not sure which set to follow, consult your local guidelines or your instructor.

25.3.1 Permissible Changes

25.3.1.1 SPELLING. If the original source contains an obvious typographic error, correct it without comment.

Original: These conclusions are not definate, but they are certainly suggestive.

Clayton admits that his conclusions are "not definite."

If, however, such an error reveals something significant about the source or is relevant to your argument, preserve it in your quotation. Immediately following the error, insert the Latin word *sic* ("so"), italicized and enclosed in brackets, to identify it as the author's error. It is considered bad manners to call out errors just to embarrass a source.

Original: The average American does not know how to spell and cannot use a coma properly.

Russell exemplifies her own argument by claiming that the average American "cannot use a coma [*sic*] properly."

When quoting from an older source or one that represents dialect with nonstandard spelling, preserve idiosyncrasies of spelling, and do not use sic. If you modernize or alter all of the spelling and punctuation for clarity, inform your readers in a note or preface.

25.3.1.2 CAPITALIZATION AND PUNCTUATION. In most disciplines you may change the initial letter of a quoted passage from capital to lowercase or from lowercase to capital without noting the change. If you weave the quotation into the syntax of your sentence, begin it with a lowercase letter. Otherwise begin it with a capital letter if it begins with a complete sentence, with a lowercase letter if it does not. You may also make similar changes when you use ellipses; see 25.3.2.

Original: As a result of these factors, the Mexican people were bound to benefit from the change.

Fernandez claims, "The Mexican people were bound to benefit from the change."

Fernandez claims that "the Mexican people were bound to benefit from the change."

Fernandez points out that "as a result of these factors, the Mexican people were bound to benefit from the change."

"The Mexican people," notes Fernandez, "were bound to benefit from the change."

Depending on how you work the quotation in the text, you may also omit a final period or change it to a comma.

Fernandez notes that the Mexicans were "bound to benefit from the change" as a result of the factors he discusses.

"The Mexican people were bound to benefit from the change," argues Fernandez.

Likewise, if the original passage ends with a colon or semicolon, you may delete it or change it to a period or a comma, depending on the structure of your sentence (see 21.12.2.1).

In literary studies and other fields concerned with close analysis of texts, indicate any change in capitalization by putting the altered letter in brackets. (For the use of ellipsis dots in literary studies, see 25.3.2.3.)

". . . [T]he Mexican people were bound to benefit from the change," argues Fernandez.

Fernandez points out that "[a]s a result of these factors, the Mexican people were bound to benefit from the change."

In any discipline, if you put double quotation marks around a passage that already includes double quotation marks, change the internal marks to single quotation marks for clarity (see 25.2.1.2).

25.3.1.3 ITALICS. You may italicize for emphasis words that are not italicized in the original, but you must indicate the change with the notation *italics mine* or *emphasis added*, placed either in the quotation or in its citation. Within the quotation, add the notation in square brackets immediately after the italicized words. In a citation, add the notation after the page number, preceded by a semicolon (see also 16.3.5). In general, avoid adding italics to passages that include italics in the original; if it becomes necessary, you may distinguish these with the notation *italics in original* or, for example, *Flaubert's italics*.

According to Schultz, "By the end of 2010, *every democracy* [emphasis added] will face the challenge of nuclear terrorism."[1]

Brown notes simply that the destruction of the tribes "had all happened in *less than ten years*" (271; italics mine).

25.3.1.4 INSERTIONS. If you need to insert a word or more of explanation, clarification, or correction into a quotation, enclose the insertion in brackets. If you find yourself making many such insertions, consider paraphrasing or weaving smaller quotations into your text instead.

As she observes, "These masters [Picasso, Braque, Matisse] rebelled against academic training."

She observes that Picasso, Braque, and Matisse "rebelled against academic training."

25.3.1.5 NOTES. If you quote a passage that includes a superscript note number but do not quote the note itself, you may omit the note number. On the other hand, parenthetical text references in the original should usually be retained.

25.3.2 Omissions

If you omit words, phrases, sentences, or even paragraphs from a quotation because they seem irrelevant, be careful not to change or misrepresent the meaning of the original source. Not only must you preserve words whose absence might change the entire meaning of the quotation (such as *not, never*, or *always*), but you must also preserve important qualifications. The quotation shown in the following example would be a misrepresentation of the author's meaning. (See also 4.2.4.)

Original: The change was sure to be beneficial once the immediate troubles subsided.

Yang claims, "The change was sure to be beneficial."

25.3.2.1 INSERTING ELLIPSES. To indicate the omission of a word, phrase, or sentence, use ellipsis dots—three periods with spaces between them. To avoid breaking an ellipsis over the line, use your word processor's ellipsis character or, alternatively, use a nonbreaking space before and after the middle dot. You will also need to use a nonbreaking space between the ellipsis and any punctuation mark that follows. (Any mark that precedes the ellipsis, including a period, may appear at the end of the line above.) Since the dots stand for words omitted, they always go inside the quotation marks or block quotation.

How you use ellipses in certain situations depends on your discipline. For most disciplines, follow the general method; for literary studies and other fields concerned with close analysis of texts, follow the textual studies method (see 25.3.2.3). If you are not sure which method to follow, consult your local guidelines or your instructor. See 25.3.1 for adjustments to capitalization and punctuation with omissions.

25.3.2.2 GENERAL METHOD FOR ELLIPSES. You may shorten a quotation such as the following in several different ways.

Original: When a nation is wrong, it should say so and apologize to the wronged party. It should conduct itself according to the standards of international diplomacy. It should also take steps to change the situation.

If you omit words within a sentence, use three ellipsis dots as described above (25.3.2.1).

"When a nation is wrong, it should . . . apologize to the wronged party."

If you omit material between sentences and the material preceding the omission is a grammatically complete sentence, use a terminal punctuation mark immediately following that sentence. Leave a space between that punctuation mark and the first ellipsis dot. Follow this practice even if the omission includes the end of the preceding sentence as long as what is left is grammatically complete (as in the second example here).

"When a nation is wrong, it should say so and apologize to the wronged party. . . . It should also take steps to change the situation."

"When a nation is wrong, it should say so. . . . It should also take steps to change the situation."

If you omit material between sentences so that the material preceding and following the omission combines to form a grammatically complete sentence, do not include terminal punctuation before the ellipsis. To avoid misrepresenting the author's meaning, however, it is generally better to use one of the shortening options above or to use two separate quotations in this situation.

"When a nation is wrong, it should say so and . . . take steps to change the situation."

The same principles apply with other types of punctuation marks, which precede or follow an ellipsis depending on where the words are omitted. In some situations, such as the second example below, consider using a more selective quotation.

"How hot was it? . . . No one could function in that climate."

"The merchant's stock included dry goods and sundry other items . . . , all for purchase by the women of the town."

or

The merchant stocked "dry goods and sundry other items" for the town's women.

Since in many contexts it is obvious when a quotation has been shortened, you need not use ellipsis points in the following situations:

■ before or after a quoted phrase, incomplete sentence, or other fragment from the original that is clearly not a complete sentence; if you omit anything within the fragment, however, use ellipsis points at the appropriate place:

Smith wrote that the president had been "very much impressed" by the paper that stressed "using the economic resources . . . of all the major powers."

- at the beginning of a quotation, even if the beginning of the sentence from the original has been omitted (but see 25.3.2.3 for the textual studies method for ellipses)
- at the end of a quotation, even if the end of the sentence from the original has been omitted

25.3.2.3 TEXTUAL STUDIES METHOD FOR ELLIPSES. The textual studies method uses ellipses more strictly than the general method to represent omissions of material at the beginning and end of quoted sentences. If you use this method, follow the principles of the general method except as noted below.

Original: When a nation is wrong, it should say so and apologize to the wronged party. It should conduct itself according to the standards of international diplomacy. It should also take steps to change the situation.

- If you omit material between sentences but quote the sentence preceding the omission in full, include the terminal punctuation mark from the original. Leave a space between that punctuation mark and the first ellipsis dot, as in the general method, shown in the first example below. However, if the omission includes the end of the preceding sentence (even if what is left is a grammatically complete sentence), put a space instead of a punctuation mark immediately following that sentence. After the space, use three ellipsis dots to represent the omission, followed by a space and the terminal punctuation mark from the original (as in the second example here).

"When a nation is wrong, it should say so and apologize to the wronged party. . . . It should also take steps to change the situation."

but

"When a nation is wrong, it should say so . . . . It should also take steps to change the situation."

- If you begin a quotation with a sentence that is grammatically complete despite an omission at the beginning of the sentence, indicate the omission with an ellipsis. If the first word is capitalized in the quotation but not in the original, indicate the changed letter in brackets (see 25.3.1).

". . . [I]t should say so and apologize to the wronged party."

- If you end a quotation with a sentence that is grammatically complete despite an omission at the end of the sentence, indicate the omission with a space and a three-dot ellipsis, followed by a space and the terminal punctuation from the original, as you would for an omitted ending between sentences.

> "When a nation is wrong, it should say so . . . ."

25.3.2.4 OMITTING A PARAGRAPH OR MORE. The following practice applies to both the general and textual studies methods of handling omissions.

If you omit a full paragraph or more within a block quotation, indicate that omission with a period and three ellipsis dots at the end of the paragraph before the omission. If the quotation includes another paragraph after the omission, indent the first line of the new paragraph. If it starts in the middle of a paragraph, begin with three ellipsis points after the indentation.

> Merton writes:

> A brand-new conscience was just coming into existence as an actual, operating function of a soul. My choices were just about to become responsible. . . .
>
> . . . Since no man ever can, or could, live by himself and for himself alone, the destinies of thousands of other people were bound to be affected.

25.3.2.5 OMITTING A LINE OR MORE OF POETRY. For both the general and textual studies methods, show the omission of one or more complete lines of a poem quoted in a block quotation by a line of ellipsis points about as long as the line above it.

> The key passage reads as follows:

> Weep no more, woeful shepherds, weep no more,
> For Lycidas your sorrow is not dead,
> . . . .
> To all that wander in that perilous flood.

26 Tables and Figures

Many research papers use tables and figures to present data. *Tables* are grids consisting of columns and rows that present numerical or verbal facts by categories. *Figures* include charts, graphs, diagrams, photographs, maps, musical examples, drawings, and other images. All these types of tabular and nontextual materials are collectively referred to as *illustrations* (a term sometimes used interchangeably with *figures*) or *graphics*.

When you have data that could be conveyed in a table or figure, your first task is to choose the most effective of these formats; some kinds of data are better represented in a table, some in a chart, others in a graph. Your choice will affect how your readers respond to your data. These are rhetorical issues, discussed in chapter 8. This chapter focuses on how to construct the particular form you choose, looking specifically at tables and two types of figures—charts and graphs.

Most tables, charts, and graphs are created with software. You cannot rely on software, however, to select the most effective format or to generate such items in the correct style, nor will software ensure logical or formal consistency. Expect to change some default settings before creating tables, charts, and graphs and to fine-tune these items once they are produced.

Your department or university may have specific requirements for formatting tables and figures, usually available from the office of theses and dissertations. If you are writing a class paper, check with your instructor for any special requirements. Review these requirements before you prepare your paper. They take precedence over the guidelines suggested here. For style guides in various disciplines, see the bibliography.

For more information on creating and formatting tables and figures and inserting them into your paper, see A.3.1.

26.1 General Issues

There are several issues common to the presentation of tables and figures in papers.

26.1.1 Position in the Text

Normally you should place a table or figure immediately after the paragraph in which you first mention it. Sometimes, however, such placement will cause a short table to break unnecessarily across the page or a figure to jump to the top of the next page, leaving more than a few lines of white space at the bottom of the previous page. To prevent either of these from happening, you may (a) place the table or figure farther along in the text, as long as it remains within a page of its first mention, or (b) place the table or figure just before the first mention, as long as it appears on the same page as the mention. (Such adjustments are best made after the text of your paper is final.)

You may group smaller tables or figures on a page, as long as they are clearly distinct from one another. Grouped tables generally retain their own titles (see 26.2.2). If grouped figures are closely related, give them a single number and a general caption; otherwise use separate numbers and captions (see 26.3.2). (Depending on your local guidelines, you may instead group tables and figures together in a section labeled *Illustrations* in the back matter of your paper; see A.2.3.1.)

If a table or figure is only marginally relevant to your topic, or if it is too large to put in the text, put it in an appendix in the back matter of your paper (see A.2.3).

For more information on inserting tables and figures into your paper, see A.3.1.

26.1.2   Size

Whenever you can, format tables and figures to fit on one page in normal, or *portrait*, orientation. If they do not fit, try shortening long column heads or abbreviating repeated terms.

If you cannot make a table or figure fit on a page, you have several options.

- *Landscape.* If a table or figure is too wide for a page, turn it ninety degrees so that the left side is at the bottom of the page; this orientation is called *landscape* or *broadside*. Do not put any of your main text on a page containing a landscape table or figure. Set the table title or figure caption in either landscape or portrait orientation. See figure A.13 for an example. (You may need to convert a table into an image file in order to rotate it.)
- *Side by side.* If a table is longer than a page but less than half a page wide, break it in half and position the two halves side by side in one table on the same page. Separate the two halves with a vertical rule, and include the column heads on both sides.
- *Multiple pages.* If a table or figure is too long to fit on a single page in portrait orientation or too wide to fit in landscape, divide it between two (or more) pages. For tables, repeat the stub column and all column heads (see 26.2) on every page. Omit the bottom rule on all pages except the last.
- *Reduction.* If the figure is a photograph or other image, consider reducing it. Consult your local guidelines for any requirements related to resolution, scaling, cropping, and other parameters.
- *Separate items.* If none of the above solutions is appropriate, consider presenting the data in two or more separate tables or figures.
- *Appendix.* If the table or figure consists of supplementary material that cannot be presented in print form, such as a large data set or a multimedia file, treat it as an appendix, as described in A.2.3.

26.1.3   Source Lines

You must acknowledge the sources of any data you use in tables and figures that you did not collect yourself. You must do this even if you present the data in a new form—for example, you create a graph based on data originally published in a table, add fresh data to a table from another source, or combine data from multiple sources by meta-analysis.

Treat a source line as a footnote to a table (see 26.2.7) or as part of a caption for a figure (see 26.3.2). For tables, introduce the source line with the word *Source(s)* (capitalized, in italics, followed by a colon). If the source line runs onto more than one line, the runovers should be flush left, single-spaced. End a source line with a period.

If you are following notes style for your citations, cite the source as in a full note (see chapter 16), including the original table or figure number or the page number from which you took the data. Unless you cite this source elsewhere in your paper, you need not include it in your bibliography.

Source: Data from David Halle, *Inside Culture: Art and Class in the American Home* (Chicago: University of Chicago Press, 1993), table 2.

Sources: Data from Richard H. Adams Jr., "Remittances, Investment, and Rural Asset Accumulation in Pakistan," *Economic Development and Cultural Change* 47, no. 1 (1998): 155–73; David Bevan, Paul Collier, and Jan Gunning, *Peasants and Government: An Economic Analysis* (Oxford: Clarendon Press, 1989), 125–28.

If you are following author-date style for your citations, cite the source as in a parenthetical citation (minus the parentheses) and include full bibliographical information about it in your reference list (see chapter 18).

Source: Data from Halle 1993, table 2.

Sources: Data from Adams 1998, 155–73; Bevan, Collier, and Gunning 1989, 125–28.

If you have adapted the data in any way from what is presented in the original source, include the phrase *adapted from* in the source line, as shown in tables 26.1 and 26.3.

For photographs, maps, and other figures that you did not create yourself, include an acknowledgment of the creator in place of a source line.

Map by Gerald F. Pyle.   Photograph by James L. Ballard.

If your dissertation will be submitted to an external dissertation repository, you may also need to obtain formal permission to reproduce tables or figures protected by copyright. See chapter 4 of *The Chicago Manual of Style*, 17th edition (2017). If you need to include credit lines in connection with such permissions, see *CMOS* 3.29–37 (figures) and 3.77 (tables).

26.2 Tables

In many situations, you may choose to present data in a table. Chapter 8 describes criteria for using tables as well as general design principles for them. This section covers most of the issues you are likely to encounter in their preparation. Tables 26.1–26.3 provide examples of the principles discussed here.

Tables vary widely in the complexity of their content and therefore in their structure, but consistency both within and across tables is essential to ensure that readers will understand your data.

Use arabic numerals for all numerical data in tables unless otherwise

Table 26.1. Selected churches in Four Corners, Boston

Church	Religious tradition	Attendance	Ethnicity/origin	Class
Church of God	Pentecostal	100	Caribbean, mixed	Middle
Church of the Holy Ghost	Pentecostal	10	Southern Black	Working
Faith Baptist	Baptist	70	Southern Black	Middle
Maison d'Esprit	Pentecostal	50	Haitian	Working
Mt. Nebo Apostolic	Apostolic	30	Southern Black	Working/middle

Source: Data adapted from Omar M. McRoberts, *Streets of Glory: Church and Community in a Black Urban Neighborhood* (Chicago: University of Chicago Press, 2003), 53.

noted. To save space, you can use abbreviations and symbols more freely than you can in text, but use them sparingly and consistently. If standard abbreviations do not exist, create your own and explain them either in a footnote to the table (see 26.2.7) or, if there are many, in a list of abbreviations in your paper's front matter (see A.2.1).

26.2.1   Table Structure

A table has elements analogous to horizontal and vertical axes on a graph. On the horizontal axis along the top are *column heads*. On the vertical axis along the left are headings that constitute what is called the *stub column*.

This grid of columns (vertical) and rows (horizontal) in a table usually correlates two sets of variables called *independent* and *dependent*. The independent variables are traditionally defined on the left, in the stub column. The dependent variables are traditionally defined in the column heads. If you include the same set of variables in two or more tables in your paper, be consistent: put them in the same place in each table, as column heads or in the stub.

The data, which may be words, numbers, or both (see table 26.1), are entered in the cells below the column heads and to the right of the stub column.

26.2.2   Table Numbers and Titles

In general, every table should have a number and a title. Place these items flush left on the line above the table, with the word *Table* (capitalized, in roman type), followed by the table number (in arabic numerals), followed by a period. After a space, give the title without a terminal period. Capitalize the title sentence-style (see 22.3.1). If a title runs onto more than one line, the runovers should be flush left, single-spaced.

Table 13. Yen-dollar ratios in Japanese exports, 1995–2005

A simple tabulation that can be introduced clearly in the text, such as a simple two-column list, need not be numbered or titled.

Chicago's population grew exponentially in its first century:

1840	4,470
1870	298,977
1900	1,698,575
1930	3,376,438

26.2.2.1 TABLE NUMBERS. Number tables separately from figures, in the order in which you mention them in the text. If you have only a few tables, number them consecutively throughout the paper, even across chapters. If you have many tables and many chapters, use double numeration: that is, the chapter number followed by a period followed by the table number, as in "Table 12.4."

When you refer to a table in the text, specify the table number ("in table 3") rather than its location ("below") because you may end up moving the table while editing or formatting the paper. Do not capitalize the word *table* in text references to tables.

26.2.2.2 TABLE TITLES. Keep table titles short but descriptive enough to indicate the specific nature of the data and to differentiate tables from one another. For discussion of good titling practices, see 8.3.1. Table titles may be presented in a smaller font than the rest of your text.

26.2.3 Rules

Rules (lines) separate different types of data and text. Too many rules create a confusing image, so use them sparingly and consistently (see also 8.3.2).

- Insert full-width horizontal rules to separate the table's title from the column heads (see 26.2.4), the column heads from the body of the table, and the body of the table from footnotes. A rule above a row of totals is traditional but not essential (see table 26.2). Unnumbered tables run into the text can usually be set with no rules, as long as any column heads are set off typographically.
- Use partial-width horizontal rules to indicate which column heads and columns are governed by special types of heads, if you use them (see 26.2.4, table 26.2).
- Leave enough space between data cells to avoid the need for additional rules. Do not use vertical rules to enclose the table in a box. But if you need to double up a long and narrow table (see 26.1.2), use a vertical rule to separate the two halves.
- Use caution in employing shading or color to convey meaning (see 8.3.2). Even if you print the paper on a color printer or submit it as a PDF, it may

Table 26.2. Election results in Gotefrith Province, 1950–60

Party	1950		1956		1960	
	% of vote	Seats won	% of vote	Seats won	% of vote	Seats won
			Provincial Assembly			
Conservative	35.5	47	26.0	37	30.9	52
Socialist	12.4	18	27.1	44	24.8	39
Christian Democrat	49.2	85	41.2	68	39.2	59
Other	2.9	0	5.7	1[a]	5.1	0
Total	100.0	150	100.0	150	100.0	150
			National Assembly			
Conservative	32.6	4	23.8	3	28.3	3
Socialist	13.5	1	27.3	3	24.1	2
Christian Democrat	52.1	7	42.8	6	46.4	8
Other	1.8	0	6.1	0	1.2	0
Total	100.0	12	100.0	12	100.0	13[b]

Source: Data from Erehwon 1950, 1956, 1960.
[a]This seat was won by a Radical Socialist, who became a member of the Conservative coalition.
[b]Reapportionment in 1960 gave Gotefrith an additional seat in the National Assembly.

be printed or copied later in black and white. If you use shading, make sure it does not obscure the text of the table, and do not use multiple shades, which might not reproduce distinctly.

26.2.4 Column Heads

A table must have at least two columns, each with a *head* or *heading* at the top that names the data in the column below.

- When possible, use noun phrases for column heads. Keep them short to avoid an excessively wide table or heads that take up too many lines.
- Capitalize column heads sentence-style (see 22.3.1).
- Align the stub head flush left (see 26.2.5); column heads can be set flush left or centered over the widest entry in the column below. Align the bottom of all heads horizontally.

You may need to include special types of heads in addition to the column heads. Such a head may apply to two or more columns of data. Center the head over the relevant columns with a partial-width horizontal rule beneath (and, if necessary, above) it. Table 26.2 shows heads both above the main column heads ("1950," "1956," and "1960") and below them ("Provincial Assembly" and "National Assembly").

Heads may have explanatory tags to clarify or to indicate the unit of measure for data in the column below. Enclose such tags in parentheses.

You may use abbreviations and symbols (mpg, km, lb., %, $M, and so on), but be consistent within and among your tables.

Responses (%)   Pesos (millions)

26.2.5 The Stub

The leftmost column of a table, called the *stub*, lists the categories of data in each row.

- Include a column head for the stub whenever possible, even if it is generic ("Typical Characteristic" or "Variable"). Omit the head only if it would merely repeat the table title or if the categories in the stub are too diverse for a single head.
- Make *stub entries* nouns or noun phrases whenever possible, and keep them consistent in form: "Books," "Journal articles," "Manuscripts," rather than "Books," "Articles published in journals," "Manuscripts." Use the same word for the same item in all of your tables (for example, if you use "Former USSR" in one table, do not use "Former Soviet Union" in another).
- Capitalize all stub entries sentence-style (see 22.3.1), with no terminal periods.
- Set the stub head and entries flush left; indent any runover lines, unless you've left enough space between rows to distinguish entries from each other.
- To show the sum of the numbers in a column, include an indented stub entry titled *Total* (see table 26.2).

If the stub column includes subentries as well as main entries (see table 26.3), distinguish them through indentation, italics, or both. Follow the same principles listed above for main entries for capitalization and so forth.

26.2.6 The Body of a Table

The body of a table consists of *cells* containing your data, which may be words, numbers, or both (see table 26.1).

If the data are numerical and all values in a column or in the entire table are in thousands or millions, omit the rightmost zeros and note the unit in an explanatory tag in the relevant column head (see 26.2.4), in the table title (26.2.2), or in a footnote (26.2.7). Indicate an empty cell with three spaced periods (ellipsis dots), centered as in table 26.3.

26.2.6.1 HORIZONTAL ALIGNMENT. Align the data in each row with the stub entry for that row.

Table 26.3. Unemployment rates for working-age New Yorkers, 2000

Unemployment rate	As % of labor force		
	Female	Male	Both sexes
All workers	6.1	5.4	. . .
By education (ages 25–64)			
Less than high school	11.9	5.8	. . .
High school degree	5.4	5.0	. . .
Some college	4.2	4.5	. . .
BA or more	2.6	2.3	. . .
By age			
16–19	. . .	. . .	19.3
20–34	. . .	. . .	6.5
35–54	. . .	. . .	4.7
55–64	. . .	. . .	2.9

Source: Data adapted from Mark Levitan, "It Did Happen Here: The Rise in Working Poverty in New York City," in *New York and Los Angeles: Politics, Society, and Culture—A Comparative View,* ed. David Halle (Chicago: University of Chicago Press, 2003), table 8.2.
Note: "Working age" is defined as ages 16 to 64. Educational level is not tracked below the age of 25 in census data.

- If the stub entry runs over onto two or more lines but the related data does not, align the row with the bottom line of the stub entry.
- If both the stub entry and the data in the same row run over onto two or more lines, align the row with the top line of the stub entry.
- If necessary, insert *leaders* (lines of periods, or dots) to lead the reader's eye from the stub to the data in the first column. (For an example of leaders in a similar context, see fig. A.5.)

26.2.6.2 VERTICAL ALIGNMENT. Align a column of numbers vertically on their real or implied decimal points, so that readers can compare the values in the column. If all numerical values in a column have a zero before a decimal point, you may omit the zeros (see fig. A.13).

Align dollar signs, percent signs, degrees, and so on. But if they occur in every cell in the column, delete them from the cells and give the unit as a tag in the column head (see 26.2.4, table 26.2, and fig. A.13).

If the data consist of words, either center each column under the column head or, especially if the data consist of longer items or items that include runovers, align each column flush left.

26.2.7 Footnotes

If a table has footnotes, position them flush left, single-spaced. Leave a blank line between the bottom rule of the table and the first note, and also between notes. Footnotes may be presented in a smaller font than the rest of the text; consult your local guidelines.

Footnotes for tables can be of four kinds: (1) source lines (discussed in 26.1.3), (2) general footnotes that apply to the whole table, (3) footnotes that apply to specific parts of the table, and (4) notes on levels of statistical significance. If you have more than one kind of note, put them in that order.

26.2.7.1   GENERAL NOTES.   General notes apply to the entire table. They define abbreviations, expand on the table title, specify how data were collected or derived, indicate rounding of values, and so on. Gather all such remarks into a single note. Do not put a note number (or other symbol) anywhere in the table or the table title, or with the note itself. Simply begin the note with the word *Note* (capitalized, in italics, followed by a colon). See also table 26.3.

Note: Since not all data were available, there is disparity in the totals.

SPECIFIC NOTES.   Notes to explain specific items in a table can be attached to any part of the table except the table number or title. Designate such notes with lowercase superscript letters rather than numbers, both within the table and in the note itself. Do not begin the note with the word *note* but with the same superscript letter, with no period or colon following.

[a]Total excludes trade and labor employees.

If you include more than one such note in a table (as in table 26.2), use letters in sequential order, beginning at the upper left of the table, running left to right and then downward, row by row. If a note applies to two or more items in the table, use the same letter for each item; if it applies to all items in a column or row, put the letter in the relevant column head or stub entry.

26.2.7.3   NOTES ON STATISTICAL SIGNIFICANCE.   If you include notes on the statistical significance of your data (also called *probability notes*), and if the significance levels are standard, designate notes with asterisks, both within the table and in the note itself. Use a single asterisk for the lowest level of probability, two for the next higher, and three for the level after that. If, however, you are noting significance levels other than standard ones, use superscript letters instead. Because these footnotes are short and they share a single purpose, you may combine them on the same line, spaced, without intervening punctuation. The letter p (for *probability*, no period after it) should be lowercase and italic. Omit zeros before decimal points (see 23.1.3).

*$p < .05$ **$p < .01$ ***$p < .001$

26.3   Figures

The term *figure* refers to a variety of images, including charts, graphs, diagrams, photographs, maps, musical examples, and drawings. Most such materials can be prepared and inserted into a paper electronically. The technical details are software-specific and too complex to be covered in this book, but some general guidelines are presented in A.3.1.

This section describes some principles for presenting two types of figures created from data: charts and graphs. It also discusses captions for figures of all kinds.

Treat a video, an animation, or any other multimedia file that cannot be presented in print form as an appendix (see A.2.3).

26.3.1   Charts and Graphs

In many situations you may choose to present data in a chart or graph. Chapter 8 lays out criteria for using these graphic forms as well as general design principles for them. It also provides examples of several different types of graphics. For detailed guidance on constructing charts and graphs, consult a reliable authority.

Each chart and graph in your paper should take the form that best communicates its data and supports its claim, but consistency both within and across these items is essential to ensure that readers will understand your data. Keep in mind the following principles when presenting charts and graphs of any type:

- Represent elements of the same kind—axes, lines, data points, bars, wedges—in the same way. Use distinct visual effects only to make distinctions, never just for variety.
- Use arabic numerals for all numerical data.
- Label all axes using sentence-style capitalization. Keep the labels short, following the principles outlined in 8.3.1. Use the figure caption (see 26.3.2) to explain any aspects of the data that cannot be captured in the labels. To save space, you can use abbreviations and symbols more freely than you can in text, but use them sparingly and consistently. If standard abbreviations do not exist, create your own and explain them either in the caption or, if there are many, in a list of abbreviations in your paper's front matter (see A.2.1).
- Label lines, data points, and other items within the chart or graph that require explanation using either all lowercase letters (for single words) or sentence-style capitalization (for phrases). If phrases and single words both appear, they should all be styled the same (as in fig. 8.3). The other principles described above for axis labels also apply to labels of this type.

■ Use caution in employing shading or color to convey meaning (see 8.3.2). Even if you print the paper on a color printer or submit it as a PDF, it may be printed or copied later in black and white. If you use shading, make sure it does not obscure any text in the figure, and do not use multiple shades, which might not reproduce distinctly.

26.3.2 Figure Numbers and Captions

In general, every figure in your paper should have a number and a caption. But if you include only a few figures in your paper and do not specifically refer to them in the text, omit the numbers. Figure captions may be presented in a smaller font than the rest of your text; consult your local guidelines.

On the line below the figure, write the word *Figure* (flush left, capitalized, in roman type), followed by the figure number (in arabic numerals), followed by a period. After a space, give the caption, usually followed by a terminal period (but see 26.3.3.2). If a caption runs onto more than one line, the runovers should be flush left, single-spaced.

Figure 6. The Great Mosque of Córdoba, eighth to tenth century.

An exception: in examples from musical scores, place the figure number and caption above the figure rather than below.

26.3.3.1 FIGURE NUMBERS. Number figures separately from tables, in the order in which you mention them in the text. If you have only a few figures, number them consecutively throughout the paper, even across chapters. If you have many figures and many chapters, use double numeration: that is, the chapter number followed by a period followed by the figure number, as in "Figure 12.4."

When you refer to a figure in the text, specify the figure number ("in figure 3") rather than its location ("below"), because you may end up moving the figure while editing or formatting the paper. Do not capitalize the word *figure* in text references to figures, and do not abbreviate it as *fig.* except in parenthetical references—for example, "(see fig. 10)."

26.3.3.2 FIGURE CAPTIONS. Figure captions are more varied than table titles. In some cases, captions can consist solely of a noun phrase, capitalized sentence-style (see 22.3.1), without a terminal period.

Figure 9. Mary McLeod Bethune, leader of the Black Cabinet

More complex captions begin with a noun phrase followed by one or more complete sentences. Such captions are also capitalized sentence-style but have terminal periods, even after the initial incomplete sentence. If your captions include a mix of both types, you may include a terminal period in those of the first type for consistency.

Figure 16. Benito Juárez. Mexico's great president, a contemporary and friend of Abraham Lincoln, represents the hard-fought triumph of Mexican liberalism at midcentury. Courtesy of Bancroft Library, University of California at Berkeley.

When a figure has a source line, put it at the end of the caption, following the guidelines in 26.1.3.

Figure 2.7. The Iao Valley, site of the final battle. Photograph by Anastasia Nowag.

Figure 11.3. US population growth, 1900–1999. Data from US Census Bureau, "Historical National Population Estimates," revised June 28, 2000, http://www.census.gov /popest/.

Sometimes a caption is attached to a figure consisting of several parts. Identify the parts in the caption with terms such as *top*, *bottom*, *above*, *left to right*, and *clockwise from left* (italicized to distinguish them from the caption itself) or with lowercase italic letters.

Figure 6. *Above left*, William Livingston; *right*, Henry Brockholst Livingston; *below left*, John Jay; *right*, Sarah Livingston Jay.

Figure 15. Four types of Hawaiian fishhooks: *a*, barbed hook of tortoise shell; *b*, trolling hook with pearl shell lure and point of human bone; *c*, octopus lure with cowrie shell, stone sinker, and large bone hook; *d*, barbed hook of human thigh bone.

If the caption for a figure will not fit on the same page as the figure itself, put it on the nearest preceding text page (see A.3.1.4), with placement identification in italics before the figure number and caption.

Next page: Figure 19. A toddler using a fourth-generation iPhone. Refinements in touchscreen technology helped Apple and other corporations broaden the target market for their products.

Appendix: *Paper Format and Submission*

When you are writing a thesis, a dissertation, or a class paper, you must observe certain format and style requirements.[1] For a thesis or dissertation, these requirements are set by your department or your university's office of theses and dissertations; for a class paper, they are set by your instructor. You may also have to follow specific procedures for submitting the paper, whether in hard copy or electronically. If your paper will be submitted to an electronic repository maintained by a service like Pro-Quest or by your university, additional guidelines may apply.

Be particularly aware of these requirements if you are writing a thesis or dissertation. You will be judged on how well you follow the academic conventions of your field. Also, many of the rules for format and submission are intended to make the preserved copy, bound or electronic, as accessible as possible for future readers.

---

[1]. A *thesis* is a paper submitted as part of the requirements for a master's-level or undergraduate degree. A *dissertation*, which is typically longer than a thesis, is a paper submitted toward fulfillment of a doctoral degree.

The guidelines presented here are widely accepted for the format and submission of theses and dissertations, but most universities have their own requirements, which are usually available from the office of theses and dissertations. *Review the current guidelines of your department or university before you submit your thesis or dissertation. Those local guidelines take precedence over the recommendations provided here.*

In general, the requirements for a class paper are less extensive and strict than those for a thesis or dissertation. Such papers usually have fewer elements, and since they are not likely to be bound or preserved electronically, there are fewer submission requirements. Even so, you may be expected to follow certain guidelines set by your instructor or department, and those guidelines take precedence over the guidelines suggested here.

This appendix assumes that you will prepare your paper on a computer and submit it as an electronic file, hard copy, or both. A full-featured word processor like Microsoft Word can be used to set margin size, number pages, place and number footnotes, and insert tables and figures according to the guidelines in this appendix. If you are using a different application, make sure it includes all the formatting options that you will need. And if you are following specific guidelines set by your instructor or institution, make sure to check your paper's format carefully against those guidelines before submitting it; if you are submitting an electronic file and a printout, review the formatting of both.

A.1 General Format Requirements

This section addresses general format issues that apply to your paper as a whole. For discussion of specific elements and their individual format requirements, see A.2. Your instructor, department, or university may have guidelines (or templates) that differ from the advice offered here. If so, those guidelines take precedence.

A.1.1 Margins

Nearly all papers in the United States are produced on standard pages of 8½ × 11 inches, regardless of whether they are submitted electronically or as hard copy. Leave a margin of at least one inch on all four edges of the page. For a thesis or dissertation intended to be bound, you may need to leave a bigger margin on the left side—usually 1½ inches.

Be sure that any material placed in headers or footers, including page numbers and other identifiers (see A.1.4), falls within the margins specified in your local guidelines.

A.1.2 Font

Choose a single, readable, and widely available font (also called typeface), such as Times New Roman or Arial. To ensure your text displays correctly, you may need to embed the font in the electronic file (see also A.3.2). Avoid ornamental fonts, which can distract readers and make your work seem less serious. (For the characteristics of specific fonts, see Robert Bringhurst, *The Elements of Typographic Style*, 4th ed. [Seattle: Hartley and Marks, 2013].) In general, use the equivalent of at least ten-point Arial or twelve-point Times New Roman for the body of the text. (Some fonts, like Arial, take up more space on a line and appear larger than other fonts at the same point size.) Footnotes or endnotes, headings, tables, and other elements might require other type sizes or fonts; check your local guidelines.

A.1.3 Spacing and Indentation

Double-space all text in papers except the following items, which should be single-spaced:

- block quotations (see 25.2.2)
- table titles and figure captions
- lists in appendixes

The following items should be single-spaced internally but with a blank line between items:

- certain elements in the front matter (see A.2.1), including the table of contents and any list of figures, tables, or abbreviations
- footnotes or endnotes
- bibliographies or reference lists

For single spacing, a setting of up to 1.15 lines may be allowed. And some departments or universities allow or require single spacing or one and a half spaces between lines in the body of the text. Check your local guidelines.

Put only one space, not two, between sentences. Use tabs or indents rather than spaces for paragraph indentation and to adjust other content requiring consistent alignment. Block quotations have their own rules for indentation, depending on whether they are prose or poetry (see 25.2.2).

A.1.4 Pagination

A.1.4.1 NUMBERING. If your only front matter is a title page, do not number that page. Number pages in the body of the paper and the back matter with arabic numerals, starting on the first page of text (page 2 if you count the title page).

If you are writing a thesis or dissertation, number front matter separately from the rest of the text. (You may need to insert a section break in your document in order to accomplish this task.)

■ Front matter includes the title page and various other elements (see A.2.1). Number these pages consecutively with lowercase roman numerals (i, ii, iii, etc.; see table 23.1). Every page of front matter except the submission page is usually counted in numbering, but not all of these pages have numbers displayed on them. Departments and universities often provide specific directions for numbering front matter pages; if yours does not, follow the guidelines in this appendix.

■ The rest of the text, including back matter (see A.2.3), is numbered consecutively with arabic numerals (usually starting with page 1).

A.1.4.2   PLACEMENT. Page numbers are usually placed in one of four locations: centered or flush right in the *footer* (at the bottom of the page) or centered or flush right in the *header* (at the top of the page). For class papers, choose one of these locations and follow it consistently.

Traditionally, page numbers for theses and dissertations have been placed in different locations depending on the part of the paper (as shown in the samples in this appendix).

■ *In the footer*: all front matter pages; pages in the text and back matter that bear titles, such as the first page of a chapter or an appendix
■ *In the header*: all other pages in the text and back matter

Many departments and universities have eliminated these distinctions and now require consistent placement of page numbers throughout a thesis or dissertation. Some specify a location, while others allow you to choose. In any position, the number should be at least half an inch from the edge of the page. Check your local guidelines.

A.1.4.3   OTHER IDENTIFIERS. In some settings you may be allowed or even encouraged to include identifying information besides the page number in the header or footer. For a class paper, your instructor may ask you to include your last name, the date of the paper, or a designation such as "First Draft." For longer papers, chapter or section titles help readers keep track of their location in the text. The requirements for headers and footers in theses and dissertations vary, so consult your local guidelines.

A.1.5   Titles

Depending on its complexity, your paper may consist of many elements, as listed in A.2, and most of them should have a title.

Use the same font, type size, and formatting style (bold, italic, etc.) for the titles of like elements. In general, and unless your local guidelines say otherwise, titles should appear in bold. A more traditional method calls for full capitalization (LIKE THIS), but this has the undesirable effect of obscuring the capitalization of individual words in a title.

On the title page, center each element and use headline-style capitalization for all, including the title of your paper. (Your local guidelines may require sentence-style capitalization for the title of your paper; see 22.3.1 for the two styles.)

Titles for the front and back matter are also typically centered, as are chapter number designations and chapter titles. For chapter titles, use headline-style capitalization unless your local guidelines specify sentence style.

All such elements may be in a larger type size than the text of your paper. Check your local guidelines. For subheadings within chapters, see A.2.2.4.

If your local guidelines are flexible, you may use different typography and format from those described here for various types of titles, as long as you are consistent. Titles of larger divisions (parts, chapters) should be more visually prominent than subheadings. In general, titles are more prominent when larger or centered (or both), in bold or italic type, or capitalized headline-style than when flush left, in regular type, or capitalized sentence-style.

The most efficient way to ensure consistency in titles is to use your word processor to define and apply a unique style (specifying font, size, bold or italic, position, line spacing, and so forth) for each type of title. See also A.3.1.2.

A.2 Format Requirements for Specific Elements

In addition to the general requirements outlined in A.1, specific elements of a paper have specific format requirements. This section describes elements most commonly found in class papers, theses, and dissertations, and it provides samples of many of them. All of the samples except figures A.1 and A.8 are pages drawn from dissertations written at the University of Chicago. As needed, the pages have been edited to match the style and format recommendations in this manual. If your instructor, department, or university has specific guidelines that differ from these samples, they take precedence.

Most long papers and all theses and dissertations have three main divisions: (1) front matter, (2) the text of the paper itself, and (3) back matter. The front and back matter are also divided into elements that will vary depending on your paper.

In a class paper, the front matter will probably be a single title page and the back matter just a bibliography or reference list.

A.2.1   Front Matter

The front matter of your thesis or dissertation may include some or all of the following elements. Departments and universities usually provide specific directions for the order of elements; if yours does not, follow the order given here.

A.2.1.1   SUBMISSION PAGE. Most theses and dissertations include a submission page, usually as the first page of the document. If it appears in this position, it does not bear a page number and is not counted in paginating the front matter.

The submission page states that the paper has been submitted in partial fulfillment of the requirements for an MA (or MS) or PhD degree (the wording varies), and it includes space for the signatures of the examining committee members. Most departments and universities provide model submission pages that should be followed exactly for wording and form. In electronic submissions the signatures may need to be omitted and submitted separately on paper. Consult your local guidelines.

A.2.1.2   TITLE PAGE. Class papers should begin with a title page (but some put the title on the first page of the text; consult your instructor). Place the title of the paper a third of the way down the page, usually centered (see A.1.5). If the paper has both a main title and a subtitle, put the main title on a single line, followed by a colon, and begin the subtitle on a new line with an intervening line space. Several lines below it, place your name along with any information requested by your instructor, such as the course title (including its department and number) and the date. Figure A.1 shows a sample title page for a class paper. For most such papers, this is the only front matter needed.

For a thesis or dissertation, most departments and universities provide model title pages that should be followed exactly for wording and form. Otherwise use figure A.2 as a model. Count the title page as page i, but do not put that number on it.

A.2.1.3   COPYRIGHT PAGE. In a thesis or dissertation, insert a copyright page after the title page. Count this page as page ii, but do not put that number on it unless directed by your local guidelines. Include the copyright notice near the top of this page, usually flush left, in this form:

You need not apply for a formal copyright. However, in cases of infringement formal registration provides additional protections. For more information, see chapter 4 in *The Chicago Manual of Style* (17th ed., 2017).

A.2.1.4 ABSTRACT. Most departments and universities require that a thesis or dissertation include an abstract summarizing its contents (including any supplementary materials; see A.2.3.2). Abstracts of papers submitted to ProQuest will be featured as part of its Dissertations and Theses database. Count the first page of the abstract as page iii, and number all pages. Label the first page *Abstract* at the top of the page. Leave two blank lines between the title and the first line of text. Double-space the text of the abstract, and format it to match the main text. Most departments or universities have specific models for abstracts that you should follow exactly for content, word count, format, placement, and pagination. The abstract may also need to be submitted as a separate document, usually as part of an online submission form (see also A.3.2). At the same time, a list of keywords may be required. Consult your local guidelines.

A.2.1.5 DEDICATION. If your department or university allows dedications, you may include a brief one to acknowledge someone who has been especially important to you. Number the dedication page with a roman numeral. Place the dedication a third of the way down the page, centered, and set it in regular type with no terminal punctuation. You need not include the word *dedication* or *dedicated*; simply say *to*:

To Jamillah

You may identify the person to whom you dedicate the work ("To my father, Sebastian Wells") and give other information such as birth and death dates.

A.2.1.6 EPIGRAPH. If your department or university allows epigraphs, you may include a brief one in addition to or instead of a dedication. An epigraph is a quotation that establishes a theme of the paper. It is most appropriate when its words are especially striking and uniquely capture the spirit of your work. Number the epigraph page with a roman numeral. You should not include the word *epigraph* on the page.

Place the epigraph a third of the way down the page, either centered or treated as a block quotation (see 25.2.2). Do not enclose it in quotation marks. Give the source on a new line, set flush right and preceded by an em dash (see 21.7.2). Often the author's name alone is sufficient, but you may also include the title of the work (see 22.3.2) and, if it seems relevant, the date of the quotation.

> Thus out of small beginnings greater things have been produced by His hand . . . and, as one small candle may light a thousand, so the light here kindled hath shone unto many, yea in some sort to our whole nation.
>
> —William Bradford

> Some people think the women are the cause of modernism, whatever that is.
>
> —*New York Sun*, February 13, 1917

Epigraphs may also appear at the beginning of a chapter or section; see 25.2.2.3 and figure A.9.

A.2.1.7   TABLE OF CONTENTS. All papers divided into chapters require a table of contents. Number all pages of this element with roman numerals. Label the first page *Contents* at the top of the page. Leave two blank lines between the title and the first item listed. Single-space individual items listed, but add a blank line after each item. Between the lists for the front and back matter and the chapters, or between parts, leave two blank lines. Two blank lines can also intervene between an introduction and the first chapter or between the last chapter and a conclusion.

A table of contents does not list pages that precede it (submission page, title page, copyright page, abstract, dedication, epigraph) or the table of contents itself but should begin with the front matter pages that follow it. Following these items, list in order the parts, chapters, or other units of the text, and then the elements of the back matter. If you have subheads in the text (see A.2.2.4), you need not include them in your table of contents. If you do include them, list only the first level unless further levels are specific enough to give readers an accurate overview of your paper. Be sure that the wording, capitalization, number style (arabic, roman, or spelled out), and punctuation of all titles (see A.1.5) and subheads match exactly those in the paper.

Give page numbers only for the first page of each listed item (not the full span of pages), and use lowercase roman or arabic numerals as on the pages themselves. List page numbers flush right, and, if you choose, use a line of periods or dots (called *leaders*, a feature available from the tab setting of most word processors) to lead a reader's eye from each title to the page number.

To ensure consistency between the table of contents and the items that it lists, you can use your word processor to generate the table of contents automatically. This will also ensure that the page-number listings

One Hundred Acres and a Mule:

The Sutpen Family as Allegory for the Old South in *Absalom, Absalom!*

Melinda Lopez

English 390: William Faulkner and the Southern Renaissance

March 16, 2018

Figure A.1. Title page for a class paper

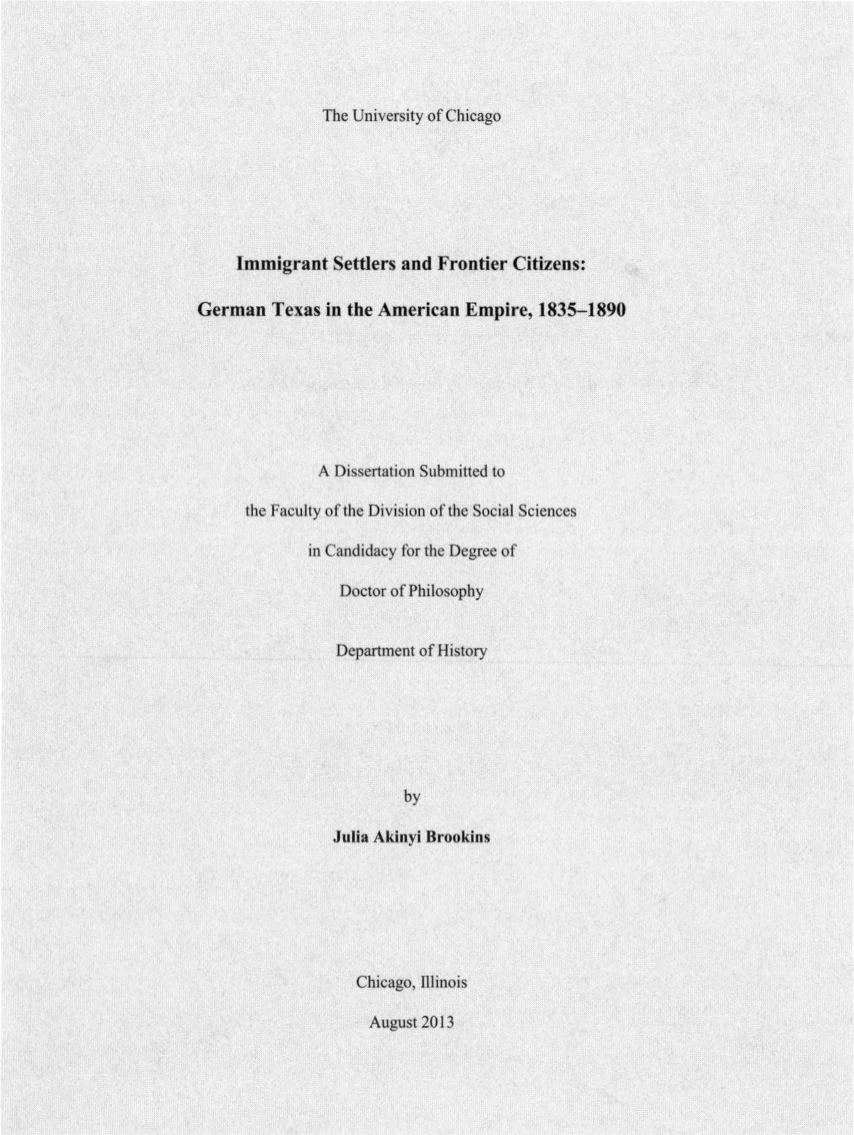

The University of Chicago

Immigrant Settlers and Frontier Citizens:

German Texas in the American Empire, 1835–1890

A Dissertation Submitted to

the Faculty of the Division of the Social Sciences

in Candidacy for the Degree of

Doctor of Philosophy

Department of History

by

Julia Akinyi Brookins

Chicago, Illinois

August 2013

Figure A.2. Title page for a dissertation. Reprinted with permission from Julia Akinyi Brookins, "Immigrant Settlers and Frontier Citizens: German Texas in the American Empire, 1835–1890" (PhD diss., University of Chicago, 2013).

remain accurate. Just be sure to double-check for proper formatting and to make sure that no items have been inadvertently omitted.

Figure A.3 shows a sample table of contents for a paper with a simple structure. Chapter titles appear flush left, with page numbers flush right.

For a more complex paper, follow the logic of your paper's organization unless your local guidelines require a specific format. Figure A.4 shows the first page of a long table of contents. To distinguish chapter titles from subheadings, you may indent the subheadings, with each level consistently indented half an inch to the right of the preceding level.

A.2.1.8   LIST OF FIGURES, TABLES, OR ILLUSTRATIONS.   If your thesis or dissertation (or long class paper) includes figures, tables, or both, you may choose to list them in the front matter. Number all pages of such a list with roman numerals. If your paper includes only figures (see chapter 26 for definitions), label the first page *Figures* at the top of the page; if it includes only tables, label it *Tables* instead. Leave two blank lines between the title and the first item listed. Single-space individual items listed, but leave a blank line between items. Figure A.5 shows a sample list of tables.

If your paper includes both figures and tables, you may provide a separate list for each, or your local guidelines may allow you to combine them into a single list. In the latter case label the list *Illustrations* (following the pattern described above), but divide it into two sections labeled *Figures* and *Tables*, as in figure A.6.

Give each table or figure number in arabic numerals, and vertically align the list on the last digit. If you are using double numeration (as in fig. A.5), align the numbers on the decimals instead. (Your word processor should allow you to set a right- or decimal-aligned tab stop as needed.)

Figure captions and table titles should match the wording and capitalization of those in the paper itself, but if they are very long, shorten them in a logical way for the entries in the list. (See 26.2.2 and 26.3.2 for more on table titles and figure captions.) List page numbers flush right and, if you choose, use leader dots (see A.2.1.7) to connect the captions and titles to page numbers.

A.2.1.9   PREFACE.   In a thesis or dissertation you may include a preface to explain what motivated your study, the background of the project, the scope of the research, and the purpose of the paper. The preface may also include acknowledgments, unless they are so numerous and detailed that they merit their own section (see A.2.1.10). Number all pages of this element with roman numerals. Label the first page *Preface* at the top of the page. Leave two blank lines between the title and the first line of text. Double-space the text of the preface, and format it to match the main text.

Contents

iv

Figure A.3. Table of contents. Reprinted with permission from Daniel W. Pratt, "Aesthetic Selves: Non-narrative Constructions of Identity in Central Europe" (PhD diss., University of Chicago, 2014).

Contents

iv

Figure A.4. First page of a table of contents with part number and subheadings. Reprinted with permission from Julia Akinyi Brookins, "Immigrant Settlers and Frontier Citizens: German Texas in the American Empire, 1835–1890" (PhD diss., University of Chicago, 2013).

Tables

Figure A.5. List of tables. Reprinted with permission from Mary Channen Caldwell, "Singing, Dancing, and Rejoicing in the Round: Latin Sacred Songs with Refrains, circa 1000–1582" (PhD diss., University of Chicago, 2013).

Illustrations

Figure A.6. List of illustrations. Reprinted with permission from Julia Akinyi Brookins, "Immigrant Settlers and Frontier Citizens: German Texas in the American Empire, 1835–1890" (PhD diss., University of Chicago, 2013).

A.2.1.10 ACKNOWLEDGMENTS. In a thesis or dissertation you may have a separate section of acknowledgments in which you thank mentors and colleagues or name the individuals or institutions that supported your research or provided special assistance (such as consultation on technical matters or aid in securing special equipment and source materials). You may also be required to acknowledge the owners of copyrighted material who have given you permission to reproduce their work. If your only acknowledgments are for routine help by an advisor or a committee, include them in the preface (see A.2.1.9) or omit them entirely. Number all pages of the acknowledgments with roman numerals. Label the first page *Acknowledgments* at the top of the page. Leave two blank lines between the title and the first line of text. Double-space the text of the acknowledgments, and format it to match the main text.

A.2.1.11 LIST OF ABBREVIATIONS. If your thesis or dissertation (or long class paper) includes an unusual number of abbreviations other than the common types discussed in chapter 24, list them in the front matter. Examples of items to include would be abbreviations for sources cited frequently (see 16.4.3) or for organizations that are not widely known (24.1.2).

Number all pages of such a list with roman numerals. Label the first page *Abbreviations* at the top of the page. Leave two blank lines between the title and the first item listed. Single-space individual items listed, but leave a blank line between items. Figure A.7 shows a sample list of abbreviations. (The abbreviations in this sample are italic only because they correspond to titles of published works.)

Note that the items are arranged alphabetically by the abbreviation, not by the spelled-out term. The abbreviations themselves are flush left; spelled-out terms (including runovers) are set on a consistent indent that allows about half an inch of space between the longest abbreviation in the first column and the first word in the second column.

A.2.1.12 GLOSSARY. You may need a glossary if your thesis or dissertation (or long class paper) includes many words from other languages or technical terms and phrases that may be unfamiliar to your readers. Some departments and universities allow or require the glossary to be placed in the back matter, after any appendixes and before the endnotes and bibliography or reference list. If you are free to choose, put it in the front matter only if readers must know the definitions before they begin reading. Otherwise put it in the back matter (see A.2.3.3).

If it appears in the front matter, number all pages of a glossary with roman numerals. Label the first page *Glossary* at the top of the page. Leave

Abbreviations

AH   *Analecta hymnica medii aevi.* Edited by Guido Maria Dreves and Clemens Blume. 55 vols. Leipzig, 1886–1922. All references, unless otherwise noted, are from *Analecta hymnica Medii Aevi Digitalia,* Erwin Rauner Verlag, http://webserver.erwin-rauner.de/.

CAG   *Saint Augustine: Opera Omnia—Corpus Augustinianum Gissense.* Electronic edition, http://www.nlx.com/collections/11.

CANTUS   *CANTUS: A Database for Latin Ecclesiastical Chant.* Faculty of Music, University of Western Ontario. http://cantusdatabase.org/.

CAO   *Corpus antiphonalium officii.* Edited by René-Jean Hesbert. 6 vols. Rerum Ecclesiasticarum Documenta. Series maior, Fontes 7–12. Rome, 1963–79.

CCCM   *Corpus Christianorum: Continuatio Mediaevalis.* Brepols Publishers, Turnhout, 1966. http://www.brepolis.net.

CCSL   *Corpus Christianorum: Series Latina.* Brepols Publishers, Turnhout, 1953–. http://www.brepolis.net.

CGM   *Catalogue général des manuscrits des bibliothèques publiques de France.* Paris: Bibliothèque Nationale, 1849–.

COGD   *Conciliorum Oecumenicorum Generaliumque Decreta.* Brepols Publishers, Turnhout, 1973–. From Brepol's CETEDOC Library of Christian Latin Texts, http://www.brepolis.net.

CPI   *CPI Conductus.* Catalogue of conductus by *Cantum pulcriorem invenire*: Thirteenth-Century Music and Poetry research group at the University of Southampton. http://catalogue.conductus.ac.uk.

CSEL   *Corpus scriptorum ecclesiasticorum Latinorum.* Vienna: Apud C. Geroldi filium and Hoelder-Pichler-Tempsky, 1866–. From CETEDOC Library of Christian Latin Texts, http://www.brepolis.net.

DIAMM   Andrew Wathey and Margaret Bent, directors. *Digital Image Archive of Medieval Music.* http://www.diamm.ac.uk.

Gloss.   *Glossarium mediae et infimae latinitatis.* Edited by Charles du Fresne, sieur du Cange. Niort: L. Favre et al., 1883–87. From Éditions en ligne de l'École des chartes, http://ducange.enc.sorbonne.fr.

Figure A.7. List of abbreviations. (The abbreviations are italicized because they correspond to titles of published works.) Reprinted with permission from Mary Channen Caldwell, "Singing, Dancing, and Rejoicing in the Round: Latin Sacred Songs with Refrains, circa 1000–1582" (PhD diss., University of Chicago, 2013).

two blank lines between the title and the first item listed. Single-space individual items listed, but leave a blank line between items. Figure A.8 shows a sample glossary.

Note that the terms are arranged alphabetically, flush left and followed by a period (a colon or dash is sometimes used). You may put the terms in bold type to make them stand out. The translation or definition follows, with its first word capitalized and a terminal period. If, however, the definitions consist of only single words or brief phrases, do not use terminal periods. If a definition is more than one line, indent the runovers by half an inch.

A.2.1.13 **EDITORIAL OR RESEARCH METHOD.** If your thesis or dissertation requires an extensive preliminary discussion of your editorial method (such as your choices among variant texts) or research method, include it as a separate element. You can also briefly discuss method in the preface. If all you need to clarify is that you have modernized capitalization and punctuation in quoted sources, put that in the preface or in a note attached to the first such quotation.

Number all pages of a discussion on method with roman numerals. Label the first page *Editorial Method* or *Research Method* at the top of the page. Leave two blank lines between the title and the first line of text. Double-space the text of this section, and format it to match the main text.

A.2.2 **Text**

The text of a paper includes everything between the front matter and the back matter. It begins with your introduction and ends with your conclusion, both of which may be as short as a single paragraph or as long as several pages. In a thesis or dissertation, the text is usually separated into chapters and sometimes into parts, sections, and subsections. Many longer class papers are also divided in this way.

Since most of the text consists of paragraphs laying out your findings, there are few format requirements for the body of the text. The only additional issues are how to begin divisions of the text, how to format notes or parenthetical citations, and how to position tables and figures within the text.

Begin the arabic numbering of your paper with the first page of the text (normally page 1 or 2; see A.1.4.1).

A.2.2.1 **INTRODUCTION.** Many theses and dissertations (and some long class papers) begin with a section that previews the contents and argument

Glossary

arabic numeral. One of the familiar digits used in arithmetical computation (1, 2, 3, etc.).

block quotation. Quoted material set off typographically from the text by indentation.

boldface type. Type that has a darker and heavier appearance than regular type (**like this**).

italic type. Slanted type suggestive of cursive writing (*like this*), as opposed to roman type.

lowercase letter. An uncapitalized letter of a font (a, b, c, etc.).

roman numeral. A numeral formed from a traditional combination of roman letters, either capitals (I, II, III, etc.) or lowercase (i, ii, iii, etc.).

roman type. The primary type style (like this), as opposed to italic type.

run-in quotation. Quoted material set continuously with text, as opposed to a block quotation.

vii

Figure A.8. Glossary

of the entire paper and is so distinct that the writer separates it from the rest of the paper. (The background of the project and any issues that informed the research should be covered in the preface; see A.2.1.9.) If you begin with such an introduction, label the first page *Introduction* at the top of the page. Leave two blank lines between the title and the first line of text. If the substance of your introductory material is not clearly distinct from the chapters that follow it, consider incorporating it into your first chapter.

A.2.2.2 **PARTS.** If you divide the text of your thesis or dissertation into two or more parts, each including two or more chapters, begin each part with a part-title page. The first part-title page follows the introduction (even if the introduction is labeled chapter 1). Count a part-title page in paginating, but do not put a page number on it except in the case described below or unless directed by your local guidelines. Label this page *Part* followed by the part number at the top of the page. Depending on your local guidelines, give the part number either in capitalized roman numerals (II) or spelled out (Two); be sure to number the chapters in a different style (see A.2.2.3). If the part has a descriptive title in addition to its number, place this title two lines down, following a blank line.

If you include text introducing the contents of the part on the part-title page, number the page with an arabic numeral. Leave two blank lines between the title and the first line of text.

Follow a consistent format for all of your part-title pages: if one part has a descriptive title in addition to a number, then give all parts descriptive titles; if one part has introductory text, then include introductory text in all parts.

A.2.2.3 **CHAPTERS.** Most theses and dissertations, and many long class papers, consist of two or more chapters. Each chapter begins on a new page. Label this page *Chapter* followed by the chapter number at the top of the page. You may give the chapter number either in arabic numerals (4) or spelled out (Four). If your paper has parts, choose a different style of numbering for the chapter numbers (for example, Part II *but* Chapter Four). If the chapter has a descriptive title in addition to its number, place this title two lines down, following a blank line. Leave two blank lines between the title and the first line of text. Figure A.9 shows a sample first page of a chapter with an epigraph (see 25.2.2.3 and A.2.1.6).

An alternative format is to omit the word *Chapter* and use only the chapter number and title, which can then appear on the same line, separated by a colon. Do not use this format, however, if your paper has parts

Chapter 5

Libertas Decembrica: **Singing Songs in the Christmas Season**

Everyone has some liking for those curiously-fashioned little songs which come into brief prominence for a season at the end of the year. . . . In the multitudinous choice of carols it is disconcerting to note how the same stock-pieces crop up year after year, to the exclusion of other and better things. We are too easily put off with the expedient in art; our children do not properly prepare their little programme; our choirmasters all too naturally reach down the old, time-worn sheets that have done duty so long.

—Edmondstoune Duncan, "Christmas Carols"

Christmas carols have long held an ambivalent position within contemporary culture, as the above epigraph suggests with its "old, time-worn sheets" of Christmas songs that "crop up year after year."[1] Shopping malls, dentist offices, and radio stations resound untiringly from Thanksgiving to Christmas with the strains of "Away in a Manger" and "Silent Night,"[2] while in our increasingly multicultural and international communities, nonreligious holiday songs, such as "Rudolph the Red-Nosed Reindeer," are gradually replacing sacred carols. For those, however, for whom the year concludes with Christmas, the familiar refrains of "We Wish You a Merry Christmas" and "The First Nowell" are still recalled and sung from year to year without fail, whether caroling in the streets, worshipping in churches, or sitting around the piano at home. Many of the still-performed carols and hymns can be traced back to the nineteenth century—if not earlier—and can be found in numerous translations and adaptations, resulting in a relatively limited repertory, albeit one with international appeal. While it is a rare occurrence to be able to connect any current carols with those of the Middle Ages or Renaissance, there is no question

---

1. Edmondstoune Duncan, "Christmas Carols," *Musical Times* 55, no. 862 (1914): 687.

2. Hugh Keyte and Andrew Parrott, eds., *The New Oxford Book of Carols* (Oxford: Oxford University Press, 1992), 300–305 and 59–61.

527

Figure A.9. First page of a chapter. Reprinted with permission from Mary Channen Caldwell, "Singing, Dancing, and Rejoicing in the Round: Latin Sacred Songs with Refrains, circa 1000–1582" (PhD diss., University of Chicago, 2013).

as well as chapters, if it does not have chapter titles, or if there is any possibility of confusing a new chapter with any other division of the paper.

A.2.2.4   **SECTIONS AND SUBSECTIONS.**   Long chapters in theses, dissertations, and long class papers may be further divided into sections, which in turn may be divided into subsections, and so on. If your paper, or a chapter within it, has only a few sections, you may signal the division between sections informally by centering three spaced asterisks (* * *) on their own line.

If you create formal sections in a paper or in its chapters, you may give each one its own title, also called a *subheading* or *subhead*. You may have multiple levels of subheads, which are designated *first-level*, *second-level*, and so on. Unless you are writing a very long and complex paper, think carefully before using more than two or three levels of subheads. Rather than being helpful, they can become distracting. You should have at least two subheads at any level within a chapter; if you do not, your divisions may not be logically structured. Two consecutive subhead levels may appear together without intervening text.

Unless your local guidelines have rules for subheads, you may devise your own typography and format for them. Each level of subhead should be consistent and different from all other levels, and higher-level subheads should be more visually prominent than lower-level ones. In general, subheads are more prominent when centered, in bold or italic type, or capitalized headline-style than when flush left, in regular type, or capitalized sentence-style. Except for run-in subheads (see *fifth level*, below), put more space before a subhead than after (up to two blank lines before and one line, or double line spacing, after) and do not end a subhead with a period. To maintain consistency, use your word processor to define a style for each level.

Here is one plan for five levels of subheads.

- *First level*: centered, boldface or italic type, headline-style capitalization

Contemporary Art

- *Second level*: centered, regular type, headline-style capitalization

What Are the Major Styles?

- *Third level*: flush left, boldface or italic type, headline-style capitalization

Abstract Expressionism

- *Fourth level*: flush left, regular type, sentence-style capitalization

Major painters and practitioners

■ *Fifth level*: run in at beginning of paragraph (no blank line after), boldface or italic type, sentence-style capitalization, terminal period

Pollock as the leader. The role of leading Abstract Expressionist painter was filled by Jackson Pollock . . .

Never end a page with a subhead. Set your word processor to keep all headings attached to the ensuing paragraph. (The built-in heading styles may already be set to stay with the next paragraph by default.)

A.2.2.5 **NOTES OR PARENTHETICAL CITATIONS.** If you are using notes-style citations with footnotes, see 16.3 for a discussion of how to format footnotes. Figure A.10 shows a sample page of text with footnotes.

If you are using author-date citations, see 18.3 for a discussion of how to format parenthetical citations. Figure A.11 shows a sample page of text with parenthetical citations.

A.2.2.6 **TABLES AND FIGURES.** If your paper includes tables or figures, see chapter 26 for a discussion of how to format tables, some types of figures, and figure captions, and see A.3.1 for information about inserting these elements into your paper. Figure A.12 shows a sample page of text with a figure positioned on it, and figure A.13 shows a sample of a table in landscape orientation on its own page.

A.2.2.7 **CONCLUSION.** In a thesis or dissertation (or, in some cases, a long class paper), you will probably end with a conclusion that is long enough to treat as a separate element. If you include such a conclusion, label the first page *Conclusion* at the top of the page. Leave two blank lines between the title and the first line of text.

You may also make the conclusion the last numbered chapter of your paper if you want to emphasize its connection to the rest of your text. If so, treat the word *Conclusion* as a chapter title (see A.2.2.3).

A.2.3   Back Matter

The back matter of your paper may consist of all or some or none of the following elements. Departments and universities usually provide specific directions for the order of elements; if yours does not, follow the order given here. Number the back matter continuously with the text using arabic numerals.

A.2.3.1 **ILLUSTRATIONS.** If you group all of your illustrations together at the end of your thesis or dissertation (or long class paper) instead of including them in the text (see 26.1.1), make them the first element in the back

51

earlier voyage. Then Rosa, her new husband, parents, five more of her siblings, one sister-in-law,

a fiancée to another brother (these two women were sisters), and Kleberg's own brother Louis

followed in the fall of 1834.[22]

Many years later, Robert Kleberg reflected without regret on his decision to migrate:

> I wished to live under a republican form of Government, with unbounded personal,
> religious and political liberty, free from the petty tyrannies and the many disadvantages
> and evils of the old countries. Prussia smarted at that time under an offensive military
> despotism. I was (and have ever remained) an enthusiastic lover of republican
> institutions, and I expected to find in Texas, above all other countries, the blessed land
> of my most fervent hopes.[23]

In December of 1834, Rosa and Robert Kleberg's ship wrecked at Galveston, then a

largely uninhabited island, instead of landing at the port of Brazoria as planned. Louis von

Roeder and Robert Kleberg, who was the only one of the party who already spoke English, left

Rosa and the others to watch their considerable baggage and set off on foot to find their relatives

who had emigrated earlier. An Indian man helped the party to find them near the location of Cat

Spring. Rosa recalled, "He belonged to a troop of Indians who were camping in the

neighborhood and from whom our relations had been in the habit of obtaining venison in

exchange for ammunition. They found our people in a wretched condition. My sister and one

brother had died, while the two remaining brothers were very ill with the fever." Kleberg and the

von Roeders rented accommodations in the city of Harrisburg through the winter and until they

were all together again, and eventually settled fifty miles west of there, near where the advance

party had been living at Cat Spring.[24]

---

22. Rosa Kleberg, "Some of My Early Experiences in Texas," *Quarterly of the Texas State Historical Association* 1, no. 4 (April 1898): 297–302; *Handbook of Texas Online*, s.vv. "Kleberg, Rosalie von Roeder," and "Kleberg, Robert Justus [I]," accessed Sept. 28, 2010, http://www.tshaonline.org/; Tiling, 24–25.

23. Kleberg notes, 1876, as excerpted in Tiling, 24. Originals in the Rudolph Kleberg Family Papers, 1829–1966, Dolph Briscoe Center for American History (hereafter CAH).

24. Rosa Kleberg, 297–98.

Figure A.10. Page of text with footnotes. Reprinted with permission from Julia Akinyi Brookins, "Immigrant Settlers and Frontier Citizens: German Texas in the American Empire, 1835–1890" (PhD diss., University of Chicago, 2013).

320

The DPP was successful in attracting an important number of votes in the 1990s, during

the first rounds of multiparty elections in Taiwan. Those DPP candidates who campaigned in

favor of the country's independence and sovereignty were the most successful ones: "In 1989,

eight members of the New Tide Faction joined together to form the pro-independence New

National Alliance to contest seats in the December legislative election. All eight were elected, a

stunning accomplishment" (Rigger 2001, 124). The party was successful in "stealing" votes from

the dominant KMT: in 1991 the DPP obtained 23.9 percent of the vote for the National

Assembly elections, and by 1996 this percentage had increased to 29.8 (data in Taiwan-

Communiqué 1996). Following the logic of the theory of programmatic capacity, I end this

section noting that in the 1990s the KMT adopted many of the policies advocated by the DPP:

> By the mid-1990s, all of the concrete items on the DPP's reform agenda had been
> achieved, and the party was forced to find new issues to attract members and voters.
> . . . *The KMT has tended to co-opt DPP issue positions that prove popular with voters*,
> including domestic policy proposals such as national health care and foreign policy
> initiatives such as the U[nited] N[ations] bid. (Rigger 2001, 151; emphasis added)

Turkey's Democrat Party

Mustafa Kemal founded the Republican People's Party (RPP) in 1923, an organization

that would dominate Turkish politics for a quarter of a century. The RPP was, like the PRI in

Mexico, a conglomerate of different political groups, including the urban middle class, the state

bureaucracy, landowners, and army officers (Ahmad 1977, 1–2). However, unlike the Mexican

dominant party, the RPP was never able to develop a structure capable of effectively fostering

elite collective action or incorporating the population—via corporatist arrangements—into the

party organization. The reason for this was that, contrary to what Calles did in Mexico in 1929,

Kemal "felt little need to develop the party organization. The [RPP] leaders did not devote

considerable energy to opening up branches across the country. . . . Throughout the 1920s, the

Figure A.11. Page of text with parenthetical citations. Reprinted with permission from José Antonio Hernández Company, "The Legacies of Authoritarianism: Party Origins and the Development of Programmatic Capacity in Mexico" (PhD diss., University of Chicago, 2015).

136

Figure 3.1. *Helpers in a Georgia Cotton Mill*. Photograph by Lewis W. Hine, January 19, 1909. The National Child Labor Committee Collection, Library of Congress Prints and Photographs Division, Washington, DC. LC-DIG-nclc-01581.

percent of the total.[21] In both regions, mill children as young as six or seven were engaged in "doffing," spinning, and other forms of casual labor.[22] To compensate for their shorter height, child doffers would stand on top of electric looms to reach the top shelf, where spindles were located (fig. 3.1). The first contact children usually had with mill labor was while accompanying older siblings or parents as they worked. Typically, very young children would begin an informal training whereby they would "help" their relatives, but this regular assistance would soon

21. Hugh D. Hindman, *Child Labor: An American History* (New York: M. E. Sharpe, 2002), 153.

22. Jacquelyn Dowd Hall et al, *Like a Family: The Making of a Southern Cotton Mill World* (New York: W. W. Norton, 1987), 61.

Figure A.12. Page with text and a figure. Reprinted with permission from Marjorie Elizabeth Wood, "Emancipating the Child Laborer: Children, Freedom, and the Moral Boundaries of the Market in the United States, 1853–1938" (PhD diss., University of Chicago, 2011).

Table 2.2. The largest regions by employment

	Rank	Number of subcenters	Fraction of regional employment			Mean annual earnings ($)			
			CBD	Center city	Subcenters	CBD	Center city	Subcenters	Region
New York	1	38	.19	.83	.47	47,217	34,781	37,360	33,984
Los Angeles	2	62	.04	.49	.21	38,238	30,228	31,770	29,719
Chicago	3	67	.09	.44	.16	39,968	30,133	28,137	29,355
Washington	4	46	.08	.33	.22	40,156	35,657	32,329	32,556
Dallas	5	72	.06	.40	.34	35,391	29,107	28,959	27,902
Philadelphia	6	58	.10	.55	.34	32,614	28,393	28,805	27,696
Houston	7	47	.06	.77	.19	37,379	27,863	30,784	27,493
Detroit	8	38	.05	.23	.22	32,219	28,606	32,270	29,305
San Francisco	9	35	.12	.40	.35	37,651	33,559	33,256	31,098
Atlanta	10	38	.07	.55	.19	30,548	28,567	29,210	27,800
Minneapolis	11	52	.08	.22	.30	31,671	27,534	27,918	25,962
Boston	12	37	.14	.39	.24	38,285	33,620	27,653	30,684
San Diego	13	26	.05	.58	.19	29,482	26,973	27,113	25,307
Baltimore	14	32	.10	.46	.25	29,926	26,887	27,223	26,191
Saint Louis	15	36	.08	.29	.24	29,923	26,383	28,503	25,147
Phoenix	16	32	.02	.58	.18	29,529	25,147	24,734	24,600
Denver	17	43	.07	.47	.29	32,725	28,072	26,990	26,305
Miami	18	32	.07	.44	.26	28,345	24,539	24,800	24,462
Seattle	19	18	.12	.50	.25	30,177	27,565	29,579	27,574
Cleveland	20	16	.11	.40	.19	32,461	27,972	29,607	26,108
Pittsburgh	21	26	.14	.42	.28	30,801	26,596	26,561	24,968
Tampa	22	36	.05	.36	.29	27,650	23,974	22,825	22,812
Kansas City	23	34	.07	.43	.18	29,578	25,897	24,835	24,925
Milwaukee	24	20	.11	.47	.19	28,434	24,400	26,176	24,086
Portland, OR	25	32	.12	.48	.18	28,319	25,287	23,317	25,458
Sacramento	26	31	.10	.46	.28	29,996	27,995	26,240	27,118
Orlando	27	37	.05	.30	.31	28,089	22,963	22,476	22,629
Indianapolis	28	17	.11	.80	.22	27,004	25,264	26,930	24,693
Columbus	29	30	.13	.74	.30	29,546	26,046	25,294	26,307
Cincinnati	30	21	.14	.54	.13	30,358	27,615	23,093	25,900

Source: Data from US Bureau of the Census 1990.

Note: The portion of CTPP-defined regions that are closest to the CBD of the largest city defines the geography. This definition does not result in exact matches with metropolitan areas in some cases.

39

Figure A.13. Page with a landscape table. Reprinted with permission from Nathaniel Baum-Snow, "Essays on the Spatial Distribution of Population and Employment" (PhD diss., University of Chicago, 2005).

matter. Label the first page of such a section *Illustrations* at the top of the page. For information about inserting figures into your paper, see A.3.1.

If some illustrations are placed in the text, however, any that are grouped in the back matter must be placed in an appendix; see A.2.3.2.

A.2.3.2 **APPENDIXES.** If your thesis or dissertation (or long class paper) includes essential supporting material that cannot be easily worked into the body of your paper, put the material in one or more appendixes in the back matter. (Do not put appendixes at the ends of chapters.) Examples of such material would be tables and figures that are marginally relevant to your topic or too large to put in the text; schedules and forms used in collecting materials; copies of documents not available to the reader; and case studies too long to put into the text.

Label the first page *Appendix* at the top of the page. Leave two blank lines between the title and the first line of text or other material.

If the appendix material is of different types—for example, a table and a case study—divide it among two or more appendixes. In this case, give each appendix a number or letter and a descriptive title. The numbers can be either arabic numerals (1, 2) or spelled out (One, Two), or you may use single letters of the alphabet in sequential order (A, B). Put the number or letter following the word *Appendix*, and place the descriptive title on the next line. (If your paper has only one appendix, you may also give it a descriptive title, but do not give it a number or letter.)

If the appendix consists of your own explanatory text, double-space it and format it to match the main text. If it is in list form or consists of a primary document or a case study, you may choose to single-space the text, especially if it is long.

Treat supporting material that cannot be presented in print form, such as a large data set or a multimedia file, as an appendix. Include a brief description of the material and its location, including a hyperlink (if relevant). Such supplementary materials may also need to be described in your abstract (see A.2.1.4). Consult your local guidelines for specific requirements for file format, presentation, and submission; see also A.3.1.

A.2.3.3 **GLOSSARY.** If your thesis or dissertation (or long class paper) needs a glossary (see A.2.1.12), you may include it in either the front or back matter, where it follows any appendixes and precedes endnotes and the bibliography or reference list. All of the special format requirements described in A.2.1.12 apply, except that the back-matter glossary pages should be numbered with arabic instead of roman numerals. Figure A.8 shows a sample glossary (paginated for the front matter).

A.2.3.4 ENDNOTES. If you are using notes-style citations, and unless your local guidelines require footnotes or end-of-chapter notes, you may include notes in the back matter as endnotes. Label the first page of this element *Notes* at the top of the page. Leave two blank lines between the title and the first note, and one blank line between notes. The notes themselves should be single-spaced, with a standard paragraph indent at the start of each one. If you restart numbering for each chapter, add a subheading before the first note to each chapter. Figure A.14 shows a sample page of endnotes for a paper divided into chapters. See also 16.3.3 and A.2.2.4.

If you are using author-date citations, you will not have endnotes.

A.2.3.5 BIBLIOGRAPHY OR REFERENCE LIST. If you are using notes-style citations, you will probably include a bibliography in the back matter. Label the first page of this element *Bibliography* at the top of the page. Leave two blank lines between the title and the first entry, and one blank line between entries. The entries themselves should be single-spaced, with runovers indented half an inch. Figure A.15 shows a sample page of a bibliography.

For some types of bibliographies you should use a different title, such as *Sources Consulted*. If you do not arrange the bibliography alphabetically by author, include a headnote, subheadings (formatted consistently), or both to clarify the arrangement. See 16.2 for these variations.

If you are using author-date citations, you must include a reference list in the back matter. Label the first page of the list *References* at the top of the page. Leave two blank lines between the title and the first entry, and one blank line between single-spaced entries. Indent runovers half an inch (use a hanging indent). Figure A.16 shows a sample page of a reference list.

In the rare case that you do not arrange the reference list alphabetically by author (see 18.2.1), include a headnote, subheadings (formatted consistently), or both to clarify the arrangement.

A.3 File Preparation and Submission Requirements

A.3.1 Preparing Your Files

By following some basic practices for good electronic file management and preparation, you can avoid problems and produce a legible, properly formatted paper. These practices apply whether you will be submitting your paper electronically, as hard copy, or both.

A.3.1.1 FILE MANAGEMENT. Try to minimize the risk that your data will be lost or corrupted at some point.

804

213. László Dobszay, *Liber ordinarius Agriensis: 1509* (Budapest: MTA Zenetudományi intézet, 2001), 147n39. "The procedure according to which the exultant nature of the hymn is enhanced by the 'Fulget dies' acclamation inserted between the various lines is exceptional. The same is prescribed by the Ordinal of Esztergom for Holy Innocent's Day. Christmas hymns with written out 'Fulget' can be found in the intonation book of Zagreb cathedral (Zagreb, University Library, MR 10)."

214. Doutrepont, *Les noëls wallons*, 197–201.

215. The following information is drawn from Wulf Arlt, "Einstimmige Lieder des 12. Jahrhunderts und Mehrstimmiges in französischen Handschriften des 16. Jahrhunderts aus Le Puy," *Schweizer Beiträge zur Musikwissenschaft* 3:23–24.

216. *Le Puy A*, folios 87v–88r.

217. The refrains are transcribed for comparison in appendix F. For a comparison of all the songs, see Arlt, "Einstimmige Lieder," 23–24.

218. Haines, *Medieval Song*, 70.

219. For an overview of solar symbolism and Christmas, see Thomas J. Talley, *The Origins of the Liturgical Year*, 2nd ed. (Collegeville, MN: Liturgical Press, 1991), 99–103. On solstitial rituals associated not with winter but with summer, see Anderson, "Fire, Foliage, and Fury."

Chapter 6

1. "1. Sole brevem Iani lucem / Incoante, renovante, / Revoluto circulo / 2. Christo novas atolamus / Laudes grates referamus / Canticis et modulo." Edited (with one correction made here) and transcribed in Gordon A. Anderson, ed., *Notre-Dame and Related Conductus: Opera Omnia*, vol. 4, *Two-Part Conductus in the Central Sources* (Henryville, PA: Institute of Mediaeval Music, 1986), xxxi.

2. A. R. Wright and T. E. Lones, *British Calendar Customs: England*, 3 vols. (London: W. Glaisher, 1936–40), 2:1.

3. In particular, Offices composed for the Feast of the Circumcision, which was also at times the date for the Feast of Fools, often seem to skirt the boundaries between sacred and secular; see, however, the most recent study of the Feast of Fools by Max Harris, who argues for a more Christian perspective on the feast. Max Harris, *Sacred Folly: A New History of the Feast of Fools* (Ithaca, NY: Cornell University Press, 2011).

4. For the earliest questions of when the New Year began in Christianity, see Talley, *Liturgical Year*, 80–82, 129–34.

Figure A.14. Endnotes. Reprinted with permission from Mary Channen Caldwell, "Singing, Dancing, and Rejoicing in the Round: Latin Sacred Songs with Refrains, circa 1000–1582" (PhD diss., University of Chicago, 2013).

392

Breuilly, John, ed. *Nineteenth-Century Germany: Politics, Culture, and Society, 1780–1918.* London: Arnold, 2001.

Briscoe, Eugenia Reynolds. *City by the Sea: A History of Corpus Christi, Texas, 1519–1875.* New York: Vantage Press, 1985.

Brister, Louis E. "William von Rosenberg's 'Kritik': A History of the Society for the Protection of German Immigrants to Texas." *Southwestern Historical Quarterly* 85, no. 2 (October, 1981): 161–86.

Brooks, James F. *Captives and Cousins: Slavery, Kinship, and Community in the Southwest Borderlands.* Chapel Hill: University of North Carolina Press, 2002.

Brown, Richard Maxwell. *No Duty to Retreat: Violence and Values in American History and Society.* New York: Oxford University Press, 1991.

Brubaker, Rogers. *Citizenship and Nationhood in France and Germany.* Cambridge, MA: Harvard University Press, 1992.

Buchenau, Jürgen. *Tools of Progress: A German Merchant Family in Mexico City, 1865– Present.* Albuquerque: University of New Mexico Press, 2004.

Buenger, Walter L. *The Path to a Modern South: Northeast Texas between Reconstruction and the Great Depression.* Austin: University of Texas Press, 2001.

———. "Secession and the Texas German Community: Editor Lindheimer vs. Editor Flake." *Southwestern Historical Quarterly* 82, no. 4 (April 1979): 379–402.

———. *Secession and the Union in Texas.* Austin: University of Texas Press, 1984.

Bungert, Heike. "Demonstrating the Values of 'Gemütlichkeit' and 'Cultur': The Festivals of German Americans in Milwaukee, 1870–1910." In *Celebrating Ethnicity and Nation: American Festive Culture from the Revolution to the Early 20th Century*, edited by Jürgen Heideking, Geneviève Fabre, and Kai Dreisbach, 175–92. New York: Berghahn Books, 2001.

———. "Feste und das ethnische Gedächtnis: Die Festkultur der Deutsch-Amerikaner im Spannungsfeld zwischen deutscher und amerikanischer Identität, 1848–1914." Habilitation, Universität zu Köln, 2004.

Burchell, R. A. "Irish Property-Holding in the West in 1870." *Journal of the West* 31, no. 2 (April 1992): 9–16.

Bushick, Frank H. *Glamorous Days.* San Antonio, TX: Naylor, 1934.

Figure A.15. Bibliography. Reprinted with permission from Julia Akinyi Brookins, "Immigrant Settlers and Frontier Citizens: German Texas in the American Empire, 1835–1890" (PhD diss., University of Chicago, 2013).

343

Lerner, Victoria. 1979a. "Historia de la reforma educativa, 1933–1945." *Historia Mexicana* 29, no. 1 (July–September): 91–132.

———. 1979b. *Historia de la Revolución Mexicana, 1934–1940.* Vol. 17, *La educación socialista.* Mexico City: El Colegio de México.

Levendusky, Matthew. 2009. *The Partisan Sort: How Liberals Became Democrats and Conservatives Became Republicans.* Chicago: University of Chicago Press.

Levitsky, Steven. 1998. "Institutionalization and Peronism. The Concept, the Case, and the Case for Unpacking the Concept." *Party Politics* 4, no. 1 (January): 77–92.

Levitsky, Steven, and Lucan A. Way. 2010. *Competitive Authoritarianism: Hybrid Regimes after the Cold War.* Cambridge: Cambridge University Press.

Lieberman, Evan S. 2005. "Nested Analysis as a Mixed-Method Strategy for Comparative Research." *American Political Science Review* 99, no. 3 (August): 435–52.

Lijphart, Arend. 1975. "The Comparable-Cases Strategy in Comparative Research." *Comparative Political Studies* 8, no. 2 (July): 158–77.

Loaeza, Soledad. 1988. *Clases medias y política en México: La querella escolar, 1959–1963.* Mexico City: El Colegio de México.

———. 1999. *El Partido Acción Nacional: La larga marcha, 1939–1994; Oposición leal y partido de protesta.* Mexico City: Fondo de Cultura Económica.

———. 2005. "Gustavo Díaz Ordaz: El colapso del Milagro Mexicano." In *Una historia contemporánea de México: Actores,* edited by Ilán Bizberg and Lorenzo Meyer, 117–55. Mexico City: Océano.

Lujambio, Alonso. 2001. "Democratization through Federalism? The National Action Party Strategy, 1939–2000." In *Party Politics and the Struggle for Democracy in Mexico: National and State-Level Analyses of the Partido Acción Nacional,* edited by Kevin Middlebrook, 47–94. La Jolla: Center for US-Mexican Studies at the University of California, San Diego.

Lujambio, Alonso, and Fernando Rodríguez Doval. 2009. "La idea, el liderazgo y la coyuntura: Manuel Gómez Morin y la fundación del Partido Acción Nacional en 1939." In *La democracia indispensable: Ensayos sobre la historia del Partido Acción Nacional,* edited by Alonso Lujambio, 19–97. Mexico City: DGE Equilibrista.

Luna, Juan Pablo. 2010. "Segmented Party-Voter Linkages in Latin America: The Case of the UDI." *Journal of Latin American Studies* 42, no. 2 (May): 325–56.

Figure A.16. Reference list. Reprinted with permission from José Antonio Hernández Company, "The Legacies of Authoritarianism: Party Origins and the Development of Programmatic Capacity in Mexico" (PhD diss., University of Chicago, 2015).

- Prepare your paper as a single electronic file, regardless of its length. Working with a single file makes it easier to use your word processor to number pages, footnotes, and the like and to define and apply styles consistently (see A.3.1.2). Working in a single file will also make it easier to search and make global changes. Papers submitted electronically must almost always consist of a single file (though certain supplementary materials may need to be prepared and submitted as separate files; see A.2.3.2). You may need to use your word processor to divide your document into sections to meet certain formatting requirements, such as presenting notes at the end of a chapter (as chapter endnotes) or changing the way page numbers display in headers or footers in different parts of the document.
- Name the file simply and logically. If you save different versions of the file over time, name them consistently (always ending in the date, for example) to avoid any confusion. Before final submission, check your local guidelines for naming conventions that apply to the file for the paper and to any supplemental materials.
- If possible, stick with the same application to draft and edit your paper. Conversions always involve some risk of formatting errors and lost data, even when moving between word processors that are supposed to be compatible.
- Save your work often during each writing session.
- Back up your work in more than one location after each writing session. In addition to a local drive, save it to a network or cloud storage service.
- Print out the file for your paper or convert it to the required electronic format before your submission date. Look it over carefully for any formatting glitches, such as special characters that are not displaying properly, while there is time to correct them. Label the printout or name the new file "Draft" and keep it at least until you submit the final version. In an emergency (such as a computer problem or a serious illness), you can use it to show that you did indeed produce a draft.

For considerations related to citation management tools, see 15.6.

A.3.1.2 **TEXT COMPONENTS.** Present all components of your text clearly and consistently.

- Format each text component consistently, including regular text, block quotations, footnotes, and each type of title and subhead. The most efficient way to ensure consistency is to use your word processor to define and apply a unique style (specifying font, size, position, line spacing, and so forth) for each component.

- Set your word processor to align text flush left with a ragged right margin unless your local guidelines recommend otherwise, and do not use its automated hyphenation feature (see 20.4.1).
- To avoid stranding headings at the bottom of the page, use your word processor to define them to keep with the next element. And to avoid stranding single lines of text at the top or bottom of the page, use your word processor's option for widow and orphan control.
- Use your word processor's menu for special characters (also called symbols) to insert letters with accents and other diacritics, characters from Greek and other non-Latin alphabets, mathematical operators (but see below), paragraph or section symbols, and the like. If a particular character is not available, you may need to select a different font for that character.
- Insert any linked cross-references (for the table of contents, figure references, or other elements) and external hyperlinks (for cited sources and the like) that your local guidelines recommend.
- Avoid font colors other than black. Even if you submit your paper as a PDF or print it on a color printer, it may be printed or copied later in black and white, and the color might not reproduce well.
- Create equations and formulas with the equation editor in your word processor, if possible. If not, create these items in another application and insert them into your file as images (see A.3.1.3). Leave at least one blank line between the equation and the text both above and below.

A.3.1.3 **TABLES.** Use your software to present tables that are clear, well formatted, and easily readable. For more information, see 8.3.

- Create tables with the table editor in your word processor, if possible. If not, create them in a spreadsheet program and insert them into your file as unlinked (embedded) tables. Format them to match the surrounding text. See chapter 26 for discussion of table structure, format, and placement in text.
- Place a table number and title on the line above each numbered table (see 26.2.2). Run the title the full width of the table.
- Put any source notes, general notes, or footnotes under the bottom rule of a table, with a blank line between the rule and the first note, and also between notes. Notes to tables may be presented in a smaller font than the text of your paper; consult your local guidelines.
- Leave at least one blank line (and preferably two) between the table title and any text above it on the page, and also between the bottom rule (or last note) and any text below it.

- Use caution in employing shading or color to convey meaning. Even if you print the paper on a color printer or submit it as a PDF, it may be printed or copied later in black and white. If you use shading, make sure it does not obscure the text of the table, and do not use multiple shades, which might not reproduce distinctly.

- Repeat the stub column and all column heads (see 26.2.4 and 26.2.5) on every page of a multipage table. Omit the bottom rule on all pages except the last.

- Remain within your paper's standard margins for a table that takes up an entire page or is in landscape orientation (see 26.1.2). Do not put any regular text on a page containing a landscape table. Set the table title in either landscape or portrait orientation, and include a page number (preferably in portrait orientation, so that it lines up with the rest of the page numbers in your paper).

- Keep a table that cannot be presented in print form, such as one containing a large data set, as a separate file, and treat it as an appendix to your paper (see A.2.3.2).

A.3.1.4 FIGURES. Take care that your graphics are easy to read, accurate, and to the point. For more information, see 8.3.

- Some charts, graphs, and diagrams can be created with the tools built in to your word processor. If you create them in a different application, insert them into your file as images. Format them to match the surrounding text. See chapter 26 for discussion of figure types, format, and placement in text.

- Insert photographs, maps, and other types of figures into your file as images. If an item is available to you only in hard copy, scan and insert it if possible.

- Put a figure number and caption on the line below the figure (see 26.3.2). (An exception: with examples from musical scores, put the number and caption on the line above the figure rather than below.) Run the caption the full width of the figure. If there is not enough room for both figure and caption within the margins of a page, put the caption at the bottom (or, if necessary, the top) of the nearest preceding text page.

- Leave at least one blank line (and preferably two) between the figure and any text above it on the page, and also between the caption and any text below it.

- Use caution in employing shading or color to convey meaning. Even if you print the paper on a color printer or submit it as a PDF, it may be printed or copied later in black and white. If you use shading, make sure it does not obscure any text in the figure, and do not use multiple shades, which might not reproduce distinctly.

- Consult your local guidelines for any requirements related to resolution, scaling, cropping, and other parameters.
- Remain within your paper's standard margins for a figure that takes up an entire page or is in landscape orientation (see 26.1.2). Do not put any regular text on a page containing a landscape figure. Set the figure caption in either landscape or portrait orientation, and include a page number (preferably in portrait orientation, so that it lines up with the rest of the page numbers in your paper).
- Keep a figure that cannot be presented in print form, such as a multimedia file, as a separate file, and treat it as an appendix to your paper (see A.2.3.2).

A.3.2 Submitting Electronic Files

Most departments and universities now require electronic submission of a thesis or dissertation instead of or in addition to hard copy (see A.3.3). Instructors may also request electronic copies of class papers. For class papers, consult your instructor regarding acceptable file types.

The requirements for theses and dissertations are more stringent. Well in advance of the deadline, review the specific guidelines of your department or university regarding any forms or procedures that must be completed before you can submit your paper. If possible, get an official to review your paper for proper format and other requirements before you submit the final copy.

Most dissertations and some theses will be submitted to an electronic repository. Many universities work with ProQuest Dissertations and Theses, a commercial repository; others maintain their own. In either case, follow your university's guidelines for formatting your paper and creating the electronic file. Most papers will need to be submitted as a single PDF document. To ensure that all text displays correctly for other readers, make sure that all fonts used in your paper have been embedded according to the guidelines provided by ProQuest or your university. If a copy of your abstract will be submitted separately, double-check formatting and special characters to make sure they have been maintained in the copy. If your paper includes supplemental files that cannot be included in the PDF (see A.2.3.2), follow all applicable guidelines for preparing and submitting them.

Once the full text of your paper is published in an electronic repository, others will have access to your work. You may be given the option to publish "traditionally" or to provide free, open access to your work online, sometimes in conjunction with a Creative Commons license that specifies how others may use or distribute your work. If you choose a traditional publishing option, your paper may still be visible to search engines, and readers may have free access to your abstract and in some cases a portion of your text; full access is typically provided through a subscription database or a library. If you are concerned about limiting access to your paper for a specific period, you may be able to apply for an embargo; check your local guidelines.

Whichever publishing option you select, copyright restrictions apply. If you include copyrighted material beyond the conventions of fair use, you must obtain written permission from the copyright holder, and you may be required to submit that documentation with your paper. Failure to provide such material may delay acceptance or publication of your dissertation. Consult your local guidelines and those offered by the repository. For more information, see chapter 4 in *The Chicago Manual of Style*, 17th ed. (2017), or *Copyright and Your Dissertation or Thesis: Ownership, Fair Use, and Your Rights and Responsibilities*, by Kenneth D. Crews, available online from ProQuest.

A.3.3 Submitting Hard Copy

Even if you submit your paper electronically (A.3.2), you may also be asked to submit one or more hard copies of the full paper or of specific pages. In some cases you may be asked to submit only the hard copy. If you are writing a class paper, submitting it may be as simple as printing out a single copy and handing it in to your instructor. Or you may instead be asked to submit multiple copies to multiple individuals (your classmates, or other faculty members). Follow instructions exactly, and always keep both a hard copy and the electronic file for your records. All copies should exactly match the original.

The requirements for theses and dissertations are more stringent, in part because such papers may be preserved in bound form by the university or by a commercial repository. Well in advance of the deadline, review the specific guidelines of your department or university regarding such matters as the number of copies required and any paperwork or procedures that must be completed before you can submit your paper. (If your thesis or dissertation is very long, your department or university may bind it in multiple volumes. Check your local guidelines.) If possible, get an official to review your paper for proper format before you produce the final copies.

Follow your university's recommendations for paper stock. Most will specify a paper that is 8½ × 11 inches (in US universities) and suitable for long-term preservation of the work. If the guidelines do not specify the paper stock, follow the American Library Association's recommendation for twenty-pound weight, neutral-pH (acid-free) paper that is labeled either "buffered" or as having a minimum 2 percent alkaline reserve. Some but not all stock referred to as "dissertation bond" meets these requirements, so be sure to examine the paper specifications before making any copies. Unless your guidelines specify otherwise, print your paper on only one side of each page.

Bibliography

There is a large literature on finding and presenting information, only some of which can be listed here. For a larger and more current selection, consult the Library of Congress catalog or an online bookseller. URLs are provided here for sources that are available online (in addition to or in place of traditional print formats). Other sources may also be available online or in an e-book format; consult your library. This list is divided as follows:

For most of those areas, six kinds of resources are listed:

1. specialized dictionaries that offer short essays defining concepts in a field
2. general and specialized encyclopedias that offer more extensive overviews of a topic
3. guides to finding resources in different fields and using their methodologies
4. bibliographies, abstracts, and indexes that list past and current publications in different fields
5. writing manuals for different fields
6. style manuals that describe required features of citations in different fields

Internet Databases (Bibliographies and Indexes)

General

Academic OneFile. Farmington Hills, MI: Gale Cengage Learning, 2006–. http://www.gale.com/.

Academic Search Premier. Ipswich, MA: Ebsco Information Services, 1975–. https://www.ebscohost.com/academic/academic-search-premier.

ArticleFirst. Dublin, OH: OCLC, 1990–. http://www.oclc.org/.

Booklist Online. Chicago: American Library Association, 2006–. http://www.booklistonline.com/.

Clase and Periódica. Mexico City: UNAM, 2003–. http://www.oclc.org/.

CQ Researcher. Washington, DC: CQ Press, 1991–. http://library.cqpress.com/cqresearcher/.

ERIC (Educational Resources Information Center). Washington, DC: US Department of Education, Institute of Education Sciences, 2004–. http://www.eric.ed.gov/.

Essay and General Literature Index (H. W. Wilson). Ipswich, MA: EBSCO Publishing, 2000s–. http://www.ebscohost.com/wilson/.

General OneFile. Farmington Hills, MI: Gale Cengage Learning, 2006–. http://www.gale.cengage.com/.

ISI Web of Science (formerly Web of Knowledge). New York: Thomson Reuters, 1990s–. http://wokinfo.com/.

LexisNexis Academic. Dayton, OH: LexisNexis, 1984–. http://www.lexisnexis.com/.

Library Literature and Information Science Full Text (H. W. Wilson). Ipswich, MA: EBSCO Publishing, 1999–. http://www.ebscohost.com/wilson/.

Library of Congress Online Catalog. Washington, DC: Library of Congress. https://catalog.loc.gov/.

Omnifile Full Text Select (H. W. Wilson). Ipswich, MA: EBSCO Publishing, 1990–. http://www.ebscohost.com/wilson/.

Periodicals Index Online. ProQuest Information and Learning, 1990–. http://www.proquest
.com.

ProQuest Dissertations and Theses. Ann Arbor, MI: ProQuest Information and Learning,
2004–. http://www.proquest.com/.

ProQuest Research Library. Ann Arbor, MI: ProQuest Information and Learning, 1998–.
http://www.proquest.com/.

Reference Reviews. Bradford, UK: MCB University Press, 1997–. http://www.emeraldinsight
.com/journals.htm?issn=0950-4125.

WorldCat. Dublin, OH: Online Computer Library Center. http://www.oclc.org/worldcat/.

Humanities

Arts and Humanities Citation Index. Philadelphia: Institute for Scientific Information,
1990s–. http://ip-science.thomsonreuters.com/mjl/.

Humanities Full Text (H. W. Wilson). Ipswich, MA: EBSCO Publishing, 2011–. http://www
.ebscohost.com/wilson/.

Humanities International Index (formerly *American Humanities Index*). Ipswich, MA: EBSCO
Publishing, 2005–. http://www.ebscohost.com/academic/.

U.S. History in Context. Farmington Hills, MI: Gale Group, 2007–. http://www.gale.com/.

Social Sciences

Anthropological Literature. Cambridge, MA: Tozzer Library, Harvard University, 1984–. http://
hcl.harvard.edu/libraries/tozzer/anthrolit/anthrolit.cfm.

AnthroSource. Arlington, VA: American Anthropological Association. http://www.aaanet
.org/publications/anthrosource/.

Anthropology Plus. Rutgers, NJ: Rutgers University Library. http://www.libraries.rutgers
.edu/indexes/anthropology_plus.

APA PsycNET. Washington, DC: American Psychological Association, 1990s–. http://www
.apa.org/pubs/databases/psycnet/.

ASSIA: Applied Social Sciences Index and Abstracts. Rutgers, NJ: Rutgers University Library.
http://www.libraries.rutgers.edu/indexes/assia.

PAIS International with Archive. Public Affairs Information Service; CSA Illumina. Bethesda,
MD: CSA, 1915–. http://www.proquest.com/.

Political Science. Research Guide. Ann Arbor: University of Michigan. http://guides.lib
.umich.edu/polisci/.

Social Sciences Abstracts (H. W. Wilson). Ipswich, MA: EBSCO Publishing, 1990s–. http://www
.ebscohost.com/wilson/.

Social Sciences Citation Index. Philadelphia: Institute for Scientific Information, 1990s–.
http://wokinfo.com/.

Sociological Abstracts. Sociological Abstracts; Cambridge Scientific Abstracts. Bethesda,
MD: ProQuest CSA, 1990s–. http://www.proquest.com/.

Natural Sciences

Applied Science and Technology Index (H. W. Wilson). Ipswich, MA: EBSCO Publishing, 1997–.
http://www.ebscohost.com/wilson/.

NAL Catalog (AGRICOLA). Washington, DC: National Agricultural Library, 1970–. http://
agricola.nal.usda.gov/.

PubMed.gov. US National Library of Medicine, National Institutes of Health. http://www
.ncbi.nlm.nih.gov/pubmed.

Web of Science. Philadelphia: Institute for Scientific Information, 1990s–. http://wokinfo
.com/.

Print and Electronic Resources

General

1. *American National Biography*. New York: Oxford University Press, 2000–. http://www.anb
.org/.
1. Bowman, John S., ed. *The Cambridge Dictionary of American Biography*. Cambridge: Cambridge University Press, 1995.
1. *World Biographical Information System*. [Munich:] Thomson Gale, n.d. http://db.saur.de
/WBIS/.
1. Matthew, H. C. G., and Brian Howard Harrison, eds. *Oxford Dictionary of National Biography,
in Association with the British Academy: From the Earliest Times to the Year 2000*. New York:
Oxford University Press, 2004. Also at http://www.oxforddnb.com/.
2. Jackson, Kenneth T., Karen Markoe, and Arnie Markoe, eds. *The Scribner Encyclopedia of
American Lives*. 8 vols. covering 1981–2008. New York: Charles Scribner's Sons, 1998–
2010.
2. Lagassé, Paul, ed. *The Columbia Encyclopedia*. 6th ed. New York: Columbia University Press,
2008.
2. *New Encyclopaedia Britannica*. 16th ed. 32 vols. Chicago: Encyclopaedia Britannica, 2010.
Also at http://www.britannica.com/.
3. Abbott, Andrew Delano. *Digital Paper: A Manual for Research and Writing with Library and
Internet Materials*. Chicago: University of Chicago Press, 2014.
3. Balay, Robert, ed. *Guide to Reference Books*. 11th ed. Chicago: American Library Association,
1996.
3. Hacker, Diana, and Barbara Fister. *Research and Documentation in the Digital Age, with 2016
MLA Update*. 6th ed. Boston: Bedford / St. Martin's, 2016.
3. Kane, Eileen, and Mary O'Reilly-de Brún. *Doing Your Own Research*. London: Marion Boyars,
2001.
3. Kieft, Robert, ed. *Guide to Reference*. Chicago: American Library Association, 2008–16.
3. Lipson, Charles. *Doing Honest Work in College: How to Prepare Citations, Avoid Plagiarism, and
Achieve Real Academic Success*. 2nd ed. Chicago: University of Chicago Press, 2008.
3. Mann, Thomas. *Oxford Guide to Library Research*. 4th ed. New York: Oxford University Press,
2015.
3. *Reference Universe*. Sterling, VA: Paratext, 2002–. http://refuniv.odyssi.com/.
3. Rowely, Jennifer, and John Farrow. *Organizing Knowledge: An Introduction to Managing Access
to Information*. 4th ed. Aldershot, Hampshire, UK: Ashgate Publishing, 2008.
3. Sears, Jean L., and Marilyn K. Moody. *Using Government Information Sources: Electronic and
Print*. 3rd ed. Phoenix: Oryx Press, 2001.
4. *Alternative Press Index*. Chicago: Alternative Press Centre; Ipswich, MA: EBSCO Publishing,
1969–. https://www.ebscohost.com/academic/alternative-press-index.
4. *Bibliographic Index Plus*. Ipswich, MA: EBSCO Publishing; Bronx: H. W. Wilson, 2003.
4. *Book Review Digest Plus*. New York: H. W. Wilson; Ipswich, MA: EBSCO Publishing, 2002–.
http://www.ebscohost.com/wilson/.

4. *Book Review Digest Retrospective: 1903–1982 (H. W. Wilson)*. Bronx: H. W. Wilson Co.; Ipswich, MA: EBSCO Publishing, 2011–. http://www.ebscohost.com/wilson/.

4. *Book Review Index*. Detroit: Gale Research, 1965–. Also at http://www.gale.com.

4. *Books in Print*. New Providence, NJ: R. R. Bowker, 2011. Also at http://www.booksinprint.com/.

4. Brigham, Clarence S. *History and Bibliography of American Newspapers, 1690–1820*. 2 vols. Westport, CT: Greenwood Press, 1976.

4. *Conference Papers Index*. Bethesda, MD: Cambridge Scientific Abstracts, 1978–.

4. Farber, Evan Ira, ed. *Combined Retrospective Index to Book Reviews in Scholarly Journals, 1886–1974*. 15 vols. Arlington, VA: Carrollton Press, 1979–82.

4. Gregory, Winifred, ed. *American Newspapers, 1821–1936: A Union List of Files Available in the United States and Canada*. New York: H. W. Wilson, 1937.

4. *Kirkus Reviews*. New York: Kirkus Media, 1933–. Also at http://www.kirkusreviews.com/.

4. *National Newspaper Index*. Menlo Park, CA: Information Access, 1982–2011.

4. *Newspapers in Microform*. Washington, DC: Library of Congress, 1948–83. Also at https://www.loc.gov/.

4. *New York Times Index*. New York: New York Times, 1913–.

4. *Periodicals Index Online*. Ann Arbor, MI: ProQuest Information and Learning, 1990–. http://proquest.com/pio.

4. Poole, William Frederick, and William Isaac Fletcher. *Poole's Index to Periodical Literature*. Rev. ed. Gloucester, MA: Peter Smith, 1971.

4. *Popular Periodical Index*. Camden, NJ: Rutgers University, 1973–93.

4. *Readers' Guide to Periodical Literature (H. W. Wilson)*. Ipswich, MA: EBSCO Publishing, 2003–. http://www.ebscohost.com/wilson/.

4. *Reference Books Bulletin*. Chicago: American Library Association, 1989. Also at http://www.ala.org/offices/reference-books-bulletin.

4. *Serials Review*. New York: Taylor and Francis, 1975–2013. Also at http://www.sciencedirect.com/science/journal/00987913.

4. *Subject Guide to Books in Print*. New York: R. R. Bowker, 1957–. Also at http://www.booksinprint.com/.

5. Bolker, Joan. *Writing Your Dissertation in Fifteen Minutes a Day: A Guide to Starting, Revising, and Finishing Your Doctoral Thesis*. New York: H. Holt, 1998.

5. Crews, Kenneth D. *Copyright Law and Graduate Research: New Media, New Rights, and Your Dissertation*. Ann Arbor, MI: UMI, 2002.

5. Eco, Umberto. *How to Write a Thesis*. Translated by Caterina Mongiat Farina and Geoff Farina. Cambridge, MA: Massachusetts Institute of Technology, 2015.

5. Few, Stephen. *Show Me the Numbers: Designing Tables and Graphs to Enlighten*. Burlingame, CA: Analytics Press, 2012.

5. Miller, Jane E. *The Chicago Guide to Writing about Numbers*. 2nd ed. Chicago: University of Chicago Press, 2015.

5. Sternberg, David. *How to Complete and Survive a Doctoral Dissertation*. New York: St. Martin's Griffin, 1981.

5. Strunk, William, and E. B. White. *The Elements of Style*. 50th anniversary ed. New York: Pearson Longman, 2009.

5. Williams, Joseph M., and Joseph Bizup. *Style: Lessons in Clarity and Grace*. 11th ed. Boston: Pearson Longman, 2014.

6. *The Chicago Manual of Style*. 17th ed. Chicago: University of Chicago Press, 2017. Also at http://www.chicagomanualofstyle.org/.

Visual Representation of Data (Tables, Figures, Posters, Etc.)

2. Harris, Robert L. *Information Graphics: A Comprehensive Illustrated Reference*. New York: Oxford University Press, 2000.

3. Cleveland, William S. *The Elements of Graphing Data*. Rev. ed. Summit, NJ: Hobart Press, 1994.

3. Cleveland, William S. *Visualizing Data*. Summit, NJ: Hobart Press, 1993.

3. Monmonier, Mark. *Mapping It Out: Expository Cartography for the Humanities and Social Sciences*. Chicago: University of Chicago Press, 1993.

3. Tufte, Edward R. *Envisioning Information*. Cheshire, CT: Graphics, 1990.

3. Tufte, Edward R. *The Visual Display of Quantitative Information*. 2nd ed. Cheshire, CT: Graphics Press, 2001.

3. Tufte, Edward R. *Visual and Statistical Thinking: Displays of Evidence for Making Decisions*. Cheshire, CT: Graphics Press, 1997.

3. Wainer, Howard. *Visual Revelations: Graphical Tales of Fate and Deception from Napoleon Bonaparte to Ross Perot*. New York: Psychology Press, 2014.

5. Alley, Michael. *The Craft of Scientific Presentations: Critical Steps to Succeed and Critical Errors to Avoid*. 2nd ed. New York: Springer, 2013.

5. Briscoe, Mary Helen. *Preparing Scientific Illustrations: A Guide to Better Posters, Presentations, and Publications*. 2nd ed. New York: Springer, 1996.

5. Esposito, Mona, Kaye Marshall, and Fredricka L. Stoller. "Poster Sessions by Experts." In *New Ways in Content-Based Instruction*, edited by Donna M. Brinton and Peter Master, 115–18. Alexandria, VA: Teachers of English to Speakers of Other Languages, 1997.

5. Kosslyn, Stephen M. *Elements of Graph Design*. New York: W. H. Freeman, 1994.

5. Larkin, Greg. "Storyboarding: A Concrete Way to Generate Effective Visuals." *Journal of Technical Writing and Communication* 26, no. 3 (1996): 273–89.

5. Nicol, Adelheid A. M., and Penny M. Pexman. *Displaying Your Findings: A Practical Guide for Creating Figures, Posters, and Presentations*. 6th ed. Washington, DC: American Psychological Association, 2010.

5. Nicol, Adelheid A. M., and Penny M. Pexman. *Presenting Your Findings: A Practical Guide for Creating Tables*. 6th ed. Washington, DC: American Psychological Association, 2010.

5. Rice University, Cain Project in Engineering and Professional Communication. "Designing Scientific and Engineering Posters" [2003]. http://www.owlnet.rice.edu/~cainproj/ih_posters.html.

5. Robbins, Naomi B. *Creating More Effective Graphs*. New York: John Wiley and Sons, 2005. Paperback reprint, Houston, TX: Chart House, 2013.

5. Ross, Ted. *The Art of Music Engraving and Processing: A Complete Manual, Reference, and Text Book on Preparing Music for Reproduction and Print*. Miami: Hansen Books, 1970.

5. Zweifel, Frances W. *A Handbook of Biological Illustration*. 2nd ed. Chicago: University of Chicago Press, 1988.

6. CBE Scientific Illustration Committee. *Illustrating Science: Standards for Publication*. Bethesda, MD: Council of Biology Editors, 1988.

Humanities

General

1. Hornblower, Simon, and Antony Spawforth, eds. *The Oxford Classical Dictionary*. 4th ed. Oxford: Oxford University Press, 2012. Also at http://www.oxfordreference.com/.

1. Murphy, Bruce, ed. *Benét's Reader's Encyclopedia.* 5th ed. New York: HarperCollins, 2008.

3. Kirkham, Sandi. *How to Find Information in the Humanities.* London: Library Association, 1989.

4. *Arts and Humanities Citation Index.* Philadelphia: Institute for Scientific Information, 1976–. Compact disc ed. 1994. Also at http://ip-science.thomsonreuters.com/mjl/.

4. Blazek, Ron, and Elizabeth Aversa. *The Humanities: A Selective Guide to Information Sources.* 5th ed. Englewood, CO: Libraries Unlimited, 2000.

4. *British Humanities Index.* London: Library Association; Bethesda, MD: Cambridge Scientific Abstracts, 1963–. Also at http://www.proquest.com/.

4. Harzfeld, Lois A. *Periodical Indexes in the Social Sciences and Humanities: A Subject Guide.* Metuchen, NJ: Scarecrow Press, 1978.

4. *An Index to Book Reviews in the Humanities.* Williamston, MI: P. Thomson, 1960–90.

4. *Index to Social Sciences and Humanities Proceedings.* Philadelphia: Institute for Scientific Information, 1979–. Also at http://wokinfo.com/.

4. *L'année philologique.* Paris: Belles Lettres, 1928–. Also at http://www.annee-philologique .com/.

4. *Walford's Guide to Reference Material.* Vol. 3, *Generalia, Language and Literature, the Arts,* edited by Anthony Chalcraft, Ray Prytherch, and Stephen Willis. 8th ed. London: Library Association, 2000.

5. Northey, Margot, and Maurice Legris. *Making Sense in the Humanities: A Student's Guide to Writing and Style.* Toronto: Oxford University Press, 1990.

Art

1. Chilvers, Ian, ed. *The Oxford Dictionary of Art and Artists.* 5th ed. Oxford: Oxford University Press, 2015. https://doi.org/10.1093/acref/9780191782763.001.0001.

1. Myers, Bernard L., and Trewin Copplestone, eds. *The Macmillan Encyclopedia of Art.* Rev. ed. London: Basingstroke Macmillan, 1981.

1. Myers, Bernard S., and Shirley D. Myers, eds. *McGraw-Hill Dictionary of Art.* 5 vols. New York: McGraw-Hill, 1969.

1. *Oxford Art Online.* Oxford: Oxford University Press, 2007–. http://www.oxfordartonline .com/.

1. *Oxford Reference Online: Art and Architecture.* Oxford: Oxford University Press, 2002–. http:// www.oxfordreference.com/.

1. Sorensen, Lee. *Dictionary of Art Historians.* Durham, NC: Duke University Press. http://www .dictionaryofarthistorians.org/.

2. Myers, Bernard S., ed. *Encyclopedia of World Art.* 17 vols. New York: McGraw-Hill, 1959–87.

3. Arntzen, Etta, and Robert Rainwater. *Guide to the Literature of Art History.* Chicago: American Library Association, 1980.

3. Jones, Lois Swan. *Art Information and the Internet: How to Find It, How to Use It.* Phoenix: Oryx Press, 1999.

3. Jones, Lois Swan. *Art Information: Research Methods and Resources.* 3rd ed. Dubuque, IA: Kendall/Hunt, 1994.

3. Marmor, Max, and Alex Ross. *Guide to the Literature of Art History 2.* Chicago: American Library Association, 2005.

3. Minor, Vernon Hyde. *Art History's History.* 2nd ed. Upper Saddle River, NJ: Prentice Hall; London: Pearson Education [distributor], 2000.

4. *Art Abstracts (H. W. Wilson).* Ipswich, MA: EBSCO Publishing, 1990s–. http://www.ebscohost .com/wilson/.

4. *Art Index (H. W. Wilson).* Ipswich, MA: EBSCO Publishing, 1990s–. http://www.ebscohost.com/wilson/.

4. *Art Index Retrospective: 1929–1984 (H. W. Wilson).* Ipswich, MA: EBSCO Publishing, 1990s. http://www.ebscohost.com/wilson/.

4. *International Bibliography of Art.* Lost Angeles: J. Paul Getty Trust; Ann Arbor, MI: ProQuest CSA, 2008–. http://www.proquest.com.

5. Barnet, Sylvan. *A Short Guide to Writing about Art.* 11th ed. Upper Saddle River, NJ: Prentice Hall, 2015.

History

1. Cook, Chris. *A Dictionary of Historical Terms.* 3rd ed. Houndmills, UK: Macmillan, 1998.

1. Ritter, Harry. *Dictionary of Concepts in History.* Westport, CT: Greenwood Press, 1986.

2. Bjork, Robert E., ed. *The Oxford Dictionary of the Middle Ages.* 4 vols. Oxford: Oxford University Press, 2010.

2. Breisach, Ernst. *Historiography: Ancient, Medieval, and Modern.* 3rd ed. Chicago: University of Chicago Press, 2007.

2. *The Cambridge Ancient History.* 14 vols. Cambridge: Cambridge University Press, 1970–2005. Also at http://histories.cambridge.org/.

2. Grendler, Paul F., ed. *Encyclopedia of the Renaissance.* 6 vols. New York: Scribner's, 1999.

2. Hillerbrand, Hans J., ed. *The Oxford Encyclopedia of the Reformation.* 4 vols. New York: Oxford University Press, 1996.

2. *The New Cambridge Medieval History.* 7 vols. Cambridge: Cambridge University Press, 1995–2005.

2. *The New Cambridge Modern History.* 14 vols. Cambridge: Cambridge University Press, 1957–90.

3. Benjamin, Jules R. *A Student's Guide to History.* 13th ed. Boston: Bedford / St. Martin's, 2016.

3. Bentley, Michael, ed. *Companion to Historiography.* London: Routledge, 1997.

3. Brundage, Anthony. *Going to the Sources: A Guide to Historical Research and Writing.* 5th ed. Chichester, UK: Wiley-Blackwell, 2013.

3. Frick, Elizabeth. *History: Illustrated Search Strategy and Sources.* 2nd ed. Ann Arbor, MI: Pierian Press, 1995.

3. Fritze, Ronald H., Brian E. Coutts, and Louis Andrew Vyhnanek. *Reference Sources in History: An Introductory Guide.* 2nd ed. Santa Barbara, CA: ABC-Clio, 2004.

3. Higginbotham, Evelyn Brooks, Leon F. Litwack, and Darlene Clark Hine, eds. *The Harvard Guide to African-American History.* Cambridge, MA: Harvard University Press, 2001.

3. Kyvig, David E., and Myron A. Marty. *Nearby History: Exploring the Past around You.* 3rd ed. Walnut Creek, CA: AltaMira Press, 2010.

3. Norton, Mary Beth, and Pamela Gerardi, eds. *The American Historical Association's Guide to Historical Literature.* 3rd ed. 2 vols. New York: Oxford University Press, 1995.

3. Prucha, Francis Paul. *Handbook for Research in American History: A Guide to Bibliographies and Other Reference Works.* 2nd ed. rev. Lincoln: University of Nebraska Press, 1996.

4. *America: History and Life.* Ipswich, MA: EBSCO Publishing, 1990s–. http://www.ebscohost.com/academic/.

4. Blazek, Ron, and Anna H. Perrault. *United States History: A Multicultural, Interdisciplinary Guide to Information Sources.* 2nd ed. Westport, CT: Libraries Unlimited, 2003.

4. Danky, James Philip, and Maureen E. Hady. *African-American Newspapers and Periodicals: A National Bibliography.* Cambridge, MA: Harvard University Press, 1998.

4. *Historical Abstracts.* Ipswich, MA: EBSCO Publishing, 1990s–. http://www.ebscohost.com/academic/.

4. Kinnell, Susan K., ed. *Historiography: An Annotated Bibliography of Journal Articles, Books, and Dissertations.* 2 vols. Santa Barbara, CA: ABC-Clio, 1987.

4. Mott, Frank Luther. *A History of American Magazines.* 5 vols. Cambridge, MA: Harvard University Press, 1930–68.

5. Barzun, Jacques, and Henry F. Graff. *The Modern Researcher.* 6th ed. Belmont, CA: Thomson/Wadsworth, 2004.

5. Marius, Richard, and Melvin E. Page. *A Short Guide to Writing about History.* 9th ed. New York: Pearson Longman, 2015.

Literary Studies

1. Abrams, M. H., and Geoffrey Galt Harpham. *A Glossary of Literary Terms.* 11th ed. Boston: Wadsworth Cengage Learning, 2015.

1. Baldick, Chris, ed. *The Concise Oxford Dictionary of Literary Terms.* 4th ed. Oxford: Oxford University Press, 2015.

1. Brogan, Terry V. F., ed. *The New Princeton Handbook of Poetic Terms.* Princeton, NJ: Princeton University Press, 1994.

1. Greene. Roland, and Stephen Cushman, ed. *Princeton Handbook of Poetic Terms.* Princeton, NJ: Princeton 2016.

1. Groden, Michael, Martin Kreiswirth, and Imre Szeman, eds. *The Johns Hopkins Guide to Literary Theory and Criticism.* 2nd ed. Baltimore: Johns Hopkins University Press, 2005. Also at http://litguide.press.jhu.edu/.

2. Birch, Dinah, ed. *The Oxford Companion to English Literature.* 7th ed. New York: Oxford University Press, 2009. Also at http://www.oxfordreference.com/.

2. Hart, James D., and Phillip W. Leininger, eds. *The Oxford Companion to American Literature.* 7th ed. New York: Oxford University Press, 2009. Also at http://www.oxfordreference.com/.

2. Lentricchia, Frank, and Thomas McLaughlin, eds. *Critical Terms for Literary Study.* 2nd ed. Chicago: University of Chicago Press, 1995.

2. Parini, Jay, ed. *The Oxford Encyclopedia of American Literature.* 4 vols. New York: Oxford University Press, 2004. Also at http://www.oxfordreference.com/.

2. Ward, Sir Adolphus William, A. R. Waller, William Peterfield Trent, John Erskine, Stuart Pratt Sherman, and Carl Van Doren. *The Cambridge History of English and American Literature: An Encyclopedia in Eighteen Volumes.* New York: G. P. Putnam's Sons, 1907–21. Bartleby .com, 2000. At http://www.bartleby.com/cambridge/.

3. Altick, Richard Daniel, and John J. Fenstermaker. *The Art of Literary Research.* 4th ed. New York: W. W. Norton, 1993.

3. Harner, James L. *Literary Research Guide: An Annotated Listing of Reference Sources in English Literary Studies.* 6th ed. New York: Modern Language Association of America, 2014.

3. Klarer, Mario. *An Introduction to Literary Studies.* 2nd ed. London: Routledge, 2004.

3. Vitale, Philip H. *Basic Tools of Research: An Annotated Guide for Students of English.* 3rd ed., rev. and enl. New York: Barron's Educational Series, 1975.

4. *Abstracts of English Studies.* Boulder, CO: National Council of Teachers of English, 1958–91. Reprint, New Castle, DE: Oak Knoll Press, 2003. Also at http://catalog.hathitrust.org /Record/000521812.

4. Blanck, Jacob, Virginia L. Smyers, and Michael Winship. *Bibliography of American Literature.* 9 vols. New Haven, CT: Yale University Press, 1955–91. Also at http://collections .chadwyck.co.uk/.

4. *Index of American Periodical Verse.* Metuchen, NJ: Scarecrow Press, 1971–2006.

4. *MLA International Bibliography.* New York: Modern Language Association of America. https://www.mla.org/Publications/MLA-International-Bibliography.

5. Barnet, Sylvan, and William E. Cain. *A Short Guide to Writing about Literature.* 12th ed. New York: Longman/Pearson, 2011.

6. Griffith, Kelley. *Writing Essays about Literature: A Guide and Style Sheet.* 9th ed. Boston: Wadsworth Cengage Learning, 2014.

6. *MLA Handbook for Writers of Research Papers.* 8th ed. New York: Modern Language Association of America, 2016.

Music

1. *Oxford Music Online.* New York: Oxford University Press, 2001–. Includes *Grove Music Online.* http://www.oxfordmusiconline.com/.

1. Randel, Don Michael, ed. *The Harvard Dictionary of Music.* 4th ed. Cambridge, MA: Belknap Press of Harvard University Press, 2003.

1. Sadie, Stanley, and John Tyrrell, eds. *The New Grove Dictionary of Music and Musicians.* 2nd ed. 29 vols. New York: Grove, 2001. Also at http://www.oxfordmusiconline.com/ (as part of *Grove Music Online*).

2. Netti, Bruno, Ruth M. Stone, James Porter, and Timothy Rice, eds. *The Garland Encyclopedia of World Music.* 10 vols. New York: Garland, 1998–2013. Also at http://alexanderstreet .com/.

3. Brockman, William S. *Music: A Guide to the Reference Literature.* Littleton, CO: Libraries Unlimited, 1987.

3. Duckles, Vincent H., Ida Reed, and Michael A. Keller, eds. *Music Reference and Research Materials: An Annotated Bibliography.* 5th ed. New York: Schirmer Books, 1997.

4. *The Music Index.* Ipswich, MA: EBSCO Publishing, 2000s–. http://www.ebscohost.com /academic/.

4. *RILM Abstracts of Music Literature.* New York: RILM, 1967–. Also at http://www.ebscohost .com/academic/.

5. Druesedow, John E., Jr. *Library Research Guide to Music: Illustrated Search Strategy and Sources.* Ann Arbor, MI: Pierian Press, 1982.

5. Herbert, Trevor. *Music in Words: A Guide to Researching and Writing about Music.* 2nd ed. London: ABRSM, 2012.

5. Wingell, Richard. *Writing about Music: An Introductory Guide.* 4th ed. Upper Saddle River, NJ: Pearson Prentice Hall, 2009.

6. Bellman, Jonathan. *A Short Guide to Writing about Music.* 2nd ed. New York: Pearson Longman, 2006.

6. Holoman, D. Kern. *Writing about Music: A Style Sheet.* 3rd ed. Berkeley: University of California Press, 2014.

Philosophy

1. Blackburn, Simon. *The Oxford Dictionary of Philosophy.* 3rd ed. Oxford: Oxford University Press, 2016. Also at http://www.oxfordreference.com/.

1. Wellington, Jean Susorney. *Dictionary of Bibliographic Abbreviations Found in the Scholarship of Classical Studies and Related Disciplines.* Rev. ed. Westport, CT: Praeger, 2004.

2. Borchert, Donald, ed. *The Encyclopedia of Philosophy.* 8 vols. 2nd ed. Detroit: Macmillan Reference USA, 2006.

2. Craig, Edward, ed. *Routledge Encyclopedia of Philosophy.* 10 vols. New York: Routledge, 1998. Also at http://www.rep.routledge.com/.

2. Parkinson, George H. R. *The Handbook of Western Philosophy.* New York: Macmillan, 1988.

2. Schrift, Alan D., ed. *The History of Continental Philosophy.* 8 vols. Chicago: University of Chicago Press, 2010.

2. Urmson, J. O., and Jonathan Rée, eds. *The Concise Encyclopedia of Western Philosophy and Philosophers.* 3rd ed. London: Routledge, 2005.

2. Zalta, Edward N. *Stanford Encyclopedia of Philosophy.* Stanford, CA: Stanford University, 1997–. http://plato.stanford.edu/.

3. List, Charles J., and Stephen H. Plum. *Library Research Guide to Philosophy.* Ann Arbor, MI: Pierian Press, 1990.

4. Bourget, David, and David Chalmers, eds. *PhilPapers.* London: Institute of Philosophy at the University of London, 2008–. Also at http://philpapers.org/.

4. *L'année philologique.* Paris: Belles Lettres, 1928–. Also at http://www.annee-philologique.com/.

4. *The Philosopher's Index.* Bowling Green, OH: Philosopher's Information Center, 1968–. Also at http://philindex.org/.

5. Watson, Richard A. *Writing Philosophy: A Guide to Professional Writing and Publishing.* Carbondale: Southern Illinois University Press, 1992.

6. Martinich, A. P. *Philosophical Writing: An Introduction.* 4th ed. Malden, MA: Wiley-Blackwell, 2015.

Social Sciences

General

1. Calhoun, Craig, ed. *Dictionary of the Social Sciences.* New York: Oxford University Press, 2002. Also at http://www.oxfordreference.com/.

1. *Statistical Abstract of the United States.* Washington, DC: US Census Bureau, 1878–2011. Also at https://www.census.gov/library/publications/time-series/statistical_abstracts.html.

2. Darity, William, ed. *International Encyclopedia of the Social Sciences.* 2nd ed. 9 vols. Detroit: Macmillan, 2008.

3. Herron, Nancy L., ed. *The Social Sciences: A Cross-Disciplinary Guide to Selected Sources.* 3rd ed. Englewood, CO: Libraries Unlimited, 2002.

3. Light, Richard J., and David B. Pillemer. *Summing Up: The Science of Reviewing Research.* Cambridge, MA: Harvard University Press, 1984.

3. Øyen, Else, ed. *Comparative Methodology: Theory and Practice in International Social Research.* London: Sage, 1990.

4. *Bibliography of Social Science Research and Writings on American Indians.* Compiled by Russell Thornton and Mary K. Grasmick. Minneapolis: Center for Urban and Regional Affairs, University of Minnesota, 1979.

4. *Book Review Index to Social Science Periodicals.* 4 vols. Ann Arbor, MI: Pierian Press, 1978–81.

4. *Communication and Mass Media Complete.* Ipswich, MA: EBSCO Publishing, 2004–. https://www.ebscohost.com/wilson/.

4. *C.R.I.S.: The Combined Retrospective Index Set to Journals in Sociology, 1895–1974.* With an introduction and user's guide by Evan I. Farber; executive editor, Annadel N. Wile; assistant editor, Deborah Purcell. Washington, DC: Carrollton Press, 1978.

4. *Current Contents: Social and Behavioral Sciences.* Philadelphia: Institute for Scientific Information, 1974–. Also at http://ip-science.thomsonreuters.com/mjl/scope/scope_ccsbs/.

4. *Document Retrieval Index.* US Dept. of Justice, Law Enforcement Assistance Administration, National Institute of Law Enforcement and Criminal Justice, 1978–. Microfiche.

4. Grossman, Jorge. *Índice general de publicaciones periódicas latinoamericanas: Humanidades y ciencias sociales / Index to Latin American Periodicals: Humanities and Social Sciences.* Metuchen, NJ: Scarecrow Press, 1961–70.

4. Harzfeld, Lois A. *Periodical Indexes in the Social Sciences and Humanities: A Subject Guide.* Metuchen, NJ: Scarecrow Press, 1978.

4. *Index of African Social Science Periodical Articles.* Dakar, Senegal: Council for the Development of Economic and Social Research in Africa, 1989–.

4. *Index to Social Sciences and Humanities Proceedings.* Philadelphia: Institute for Scientific Information, 1979–. Also at http://ip-science.thomsonreuters.com/mjl/scope/scope_cpci-ssh/.

4. Lester, Ray, ed. *The New Walford.* Vol. 2, *The Social Sciences.* London: Facet, 2008.

4. *PAIS International in Print.* New York: OCLC Public Affairs Information Service, 1991–. Also at http://www.proquest.com/.

4. *Social Sciences Citation Index.* Philadelphia: Institute for Scientific Information, 1969–. Also at http://wokinfo.com/.

4. *Social Sciences Index.* New York: H. W. Wilson, 1974–. Also at http://www.ebscohost.com /wilson/ (as *Social Science Abstracts*).

5. Becker, Howard S. *Writing for Social Scientists: How to Start and Finish Your Thesis, Book, or Article.* 2nd ed. Chicago: University of Chicago Press, 2007.

5. Bell, Judith, and Stephen Waters. *Doing Your Research Project: A Guide for First-Time Researchers in Education, Health, and Social Science.* 6th ed. rev. Maidenhead, UK: McGraw-Hill Open University Press, 2014.

5. Krathwohl, David R., and Nick L. Smith. *How to Prepare a Dissertation Proposal: Suggestions for Students in Education and the Social and Behavioral Sciences.* Syracuse, NY: Syracuse University Press, 2005.

5. Northey, Margot, Lorne Tepperman, and Patrizia Albanese. *Making Sense: A Student's Guide to Research and Writing; Social Sciences.* 6th ed. Don Mills, ON: Oxford University Press, 2015.

Anthropology

1. Barfield, Thomas, ed. *The Dictionary of Anthropology.* 13th pr. Malden, MA: Blackwell, 2009.

1. Winthrop, Robert H. *Dictionary of Concepts in Cultural Anthropology.* New York: Greenwood Press, 1991.

2. Barnard, Alan, and Jonathan Spencer, eds. *Routledge Encyclopedia of Social and Cultural Anthropology.* 2nd ed. London: Routledge, 2012.

2. Ember, Melvin, Carol R. Ember, and Ian A. Skoggard, eds. *Encyclopedia of World Cultures: Supplement.* New York: Gale Group / Thomson Learning, 2002.

2. Ingold, Tim, ed. *Companion Encyclopedia of Anthropology: Humanity, Culture, and Social Life.* London: Routledge, 2007.

2. Levinson, David, ed. *Encyclopedia of World Cultures.* 10 vols. Boston: G. K. Hall, 1991–96.

2. Levinson, David, and Melvin Ember, eds. *Encyclopedia of Cultural Anthropology.* 4 vols. New York: Henry Holt, 1997.

3. Bernard, H. Russell. *Research Methods in Anthropology: Qualitative and Quantitative Approaches.* 5th ed. Lanham, MD: AltaMira Press, 2011.

3. Bernard, H. Russell, ed. *Handbook of Methods in Cultural Anthropology.* Walnut Creek, CA: AltaMira Press, 2000.

3. *Current Topics in Anthropology: Theory, Methods, and Content.* 8 vols. Reading, MA: Addison-Wesley, 1971–75.

3. Glenn, James R. *Guide to the National Anthropological Archives, Smithsonian Institution.* Rev.

and enl. ed. Washington, DC: National Anthropological Archives, 1996. Revised and amended, as *Guide to the Collections of the National Anthropological Archives*, at http://anthropology.si.edu/naa/guide/_toc.htm.

3. Poggie, John J., Jr., Billie R. DeWalt, and William W. Dressler, eds. *Anthropological Research: Process and Application*. Albany: State University of New York Press, 1992.

4. *Abstracts in Anthropology*. Amityville, NY: Baywood Publishing, 1970–. Also at http://anthropology.metapress.com/.

4. *Annual Review of Anthropology*. Palo Alto, CA: Annual Reviews Inc., 1972–. Also at http://www.annualreviews.org/journal/anthro.

4. *The Urban Portal*. Chicago: University of Chicago Urban Network. http://urban.uchicago.edu/.

Business

1. Friedman, Jack P. *Dictionary of Business Terms*. 4th ed. Hauppauge, NY: Barron's Educational Series, 2012.

1. Link, Albert N. *Link's International Dictionary of Business Economics*. Chicago: Probus, 1993.

1. Nisberg, Jay N. *The Random House Dictionary of Business Terms*. New York: Random House, 1992.

1. Wiechmann, Jack G., and Laurence Urdang, eds. *NTC's Dictionary of Advertising*. 2nd ed. Lincolnwood, IL: National Textbook, 1993.

2. Folsom, W. Davis, and Stacia N. VanDyne, eds. *Encyclopedia of American Business*. Rev. ed. 2 vols. New York: Facts on File, 2011. Also at http://www.infobasepublishing.com/.

2. *The Lifestyle Market Analyst: A Reference Guide for Consumer Market Analysis*. Wilmette, IL: Standard Rate and Data Service, 1989–2008.

2. McDonough, John, and Karen Egolf, eds. *The Advertising Age Encyclopedia of Advertising*. 3 vols. New York: Fitzroy Dearborn, 2003.

2. Vernon, Mark. *Business: The Key Concepts*. New York: Routledge, 2002.

2. Warner, Malcolm, and John P. Kotter, eds. *International Encyclopedia of Business and Management*. 2nd ed. 8 vols. London: Thomson Learning, 2002.

3. Bryman, Alan, and Emma Bell. *Business Research Methods*. 4th ed. New York: Oxford University Press, 2015.

3. Daniells, Lorna M. *Business Information Sources*. 3rd ed. Berkeley: University of California Press, 1993.

3. Moss, Rita W., and David G. Ernsthausen. *Strauss's Handbook of Business Information: A Guide for Librarians, Students, and Researchers*. 3rd ed. Westport, CT: Libraries Unlimited, 2012.

3. Sekaran, Uma, and Roger Bougie. *Research Methods for Business: A Skill Building Approach*. 7th ed. New York: John Wiley and Sons, 2016.

3. Woy, James B., ed. *Encyclopedia of Business Information Sources*. 33rd ed. 2 vols. Detroit: Gale Cengage Learning, 2016.

4. *Business Periodicals Index*. New York: H. W. Wilson, 1958–. Also at http://www.ebscohost.com/academic/ (as *Business Periodicals Index Retrospective*).

5. Farrell, Thomas J., and Charlotte Donabedian. *Writing the Business Research Paper: A Complete Guide*. Durham, NC: Carolina Academic Press, 1991.

6. Vetter, William. *Business Law, Legal Research, and Writing: Handbook*. Needham Heights, MA: Ginn Press, 1991.

6. Yelin, Andrea, and Hope Viner Samborn. *The Legal Research and Writing Handbook: A Basic Approach for Paralegals*. New York: Aspen Publishers, 2009.

Communication, Journalism, and Media Studies

1. Horak, Ray. *Webster's New World Telecom Dictionary*. Indianapolis: Wiley Technology, 2008.
1. Miller, Toby, ed. *Television: Critical Concepts in Media and Cultural Studies*. London: Routledge, 2003.
1. Newton, Harry. *Newton's Telecom Dictionary*. 30th ed. New York: Telecom Publishing, 2016.
1. Watson, James, and Anne Hill. *A Dictionary of Communication and Media Studies*. 9th ed. New York: Bloomsbury Academic, 2015.
1. Weik, Martin H. *Communications Standard Dictionary*. 3rd ed. New York: Chapman and Hall, 1996.
2. Barnouw, Erik, ed. *International Encyclopedia of Communications*. 4 vols. New York: Oxford University Press, 1989.
2. Johnston, Donald H., ed. *Encyclopedia of International Media and Communications*. 4 vols. San Diego, CA: Academic Press, 2003.
2. Jones, Steve, ed. *Encyclopedia of New Media: An Essential Reference to Communication and Technology*. Thousand Oaks, CA: Sage, 2003.
2. Stern, Jane, and Michael Stern. *Jane and Michael Stern's Encyclopedia of Pop Culture: An A to Z Guide of Who's Who and What's What, from Aerobics and Bubble Gum to Valley of the Dolls and Moon Unit Zappa*. New York: HarperPerennial, 1992.
2. Vaughn, Stephen L. *Encyclopedia of American Journalism*. New York: Routledge, 2008.
3. Clark, Vivienne, James Baker, and Eileen Lewis. *Key Concepts and Skills for Media Studies*. London: Hodder and Stoughton, 2003.
3. Stokes, Jane. *How to Do Media and Cultural Studies*. 2nd ed. London: Sage, 2012.
3. Storey, John. *Cultural Studies and the Study of Popular Culture*. 3rd ed. Edinburgh: Edinburgh University Press, 2010.
4. Block, Eleanor S., and James K. Bracken. *Communication and the Mass Media: A Guide to the Reference Literature*. Englewood, CO: Libraries Unlimited, 1991.
4. Blum, Eleanor, and Frances Goins Wilhoit. *Mass Media Bibliography: An Annotated Guide to Books and Journals for Research and Reference*. 3rd ed. Urbana: University of Illinois Press, 1990.
4. Cates, Jo A. *Journalism: A Guide to the Reference Literature*. 3rd ed. Westport, CT: Libraries Unlimited, 2004.
4. *CD Review*. Hancock, NH: WGE Publishing, 1989–96.
4. *Communications Abstracts*. Los Angeles: Dept. of Journalism, University of California, Los Angeles, 1960–. Also at http://www.ebscohost.com/academic/.
4. *Film Review Annual*. Englewood, NJ: J. S. Ozer, 1981–2002.
4. Matlon, Ronald J., and Sylvia P. Ortiz, eds. *Index to Journals in Communication Studies through 1995*. Annandale, VA: National Communication Association, 1997.
4. *Media Review Digest*. Ann Arbor, MI: Pierian Press, 1974–2006.
4. *New York Theatre Critics' Reviews*. New York: Critics' Theatre Reviews, 1943–95.
4. *New York Times Directory of the Film*. New York: Arno Press, 1971–.
4. *Records in Review*. Great Barrington, MA: Wyeth Press, 1957–.
4. Sterling, Christopher H., James K. Bracken, and Susan M. Hill, eds. *Mass Communications Research Resources: An Annotated Guide*. Mahwah, NJ: Erlbaum, 1998.
6. Christian, Darrell, Sally Jacobsen, and David Minthorn, eds. *Associated Press Stylebook and Briefing on Media Law*. Updated annually. New York: Associated Press. Also at http://www.apstylebook.com/.

Economics

1. Pearce, David W., ed. *MIT Dictionary of Modern Economics*. 4th ed. Cambridge, MA: MIT Press, 1992.

2. Durlauf, Steven N., and Lawrence E. Blume, eds. *The New Palgrave Dictionary of Economics*. 8 vols. 2nd ed. New York: Palgrave Macmillan, 2008. Also at http://www.dictionaryof economics.com/dictionary.

2. Greenwald, Douglas, ed. *The McGraw-Hill Encyclopedia of Economics*. 2nd ed. New York: McGraw-Hill, 1994.

2. Mokyr, Joel, ed. *The Oxford Encyclopedia of Economic History*. 5 vols. Oxford: Oxford University Press, 2003. Also at http://www.oxfordreference.com/.

3. Fletcher, John, ed. *Information Sources in Economics*. 2nd ed. London: Butterworths, 1984.

3. Johnson, Glenn L. *Research Methodology for Economists: Philosophy and Practice*. New York: Macmillan, 1986.

4. *Journal of Economic Literature*. Nashville: American Economic Association, 1969–. Also at https://www.aeaweb.org/journals/jel.

5. McCloskey, Deirdre N. *Economical Writing*. 2nd ed. Prospect Heights, IL: Waveland Press, 2000.

5. Thomson, William. *A Guide for the Young Economist*. 2nd ed. Cambridge, MA: MIT Press, 2011.

Education

1. Barrow, Robin, and Geoffrey Milburn. *A Critical Dictionary of Educational Concepts: An Appraisal of Selected Ideas and Issues in Educational Theory and Practice*. 2nd ed. New York: Harvester Wheatsheaf, 1990.

1. Collins, John Williams, and Nancy P. O'Brien, eds. *The Greenwood Dictionary of Education*. 2nd ed. Santa Barbara, CA: Greenwood, 2011.

1. Gordon, Peter, and Denis Lawton. *Dictionary of British Education*. 3rd rev. ed. London: Woburn Press, 2003.

2. Alkin, Marvin C., ed. *Encyclopedia of Educational Research*. 6th ed. 4 vols. New York: Macmillan, 1992.

2. Guthrie, James W., ed. *Encyclopedia of Education*. 2nd ed. 8 vols. New York: Macmillan Reference USA, 2002.

2. Levinson, David L., Peter W. Cookson Jr., and Alan R. Sadovnik, eds. *Education and Sociology: An Encyclopedia*. New York: RoutledgeFalmer, 2002.

2. Peterson, Penelope, Eva Baker, and Barry McGaw, eds. *The International Encyclopedia of Education*. 3rd ed. 8 vols. Oxford: Elsevier, 2010.

2. Unger, Harlow G. *Encyclopedia of American Education*. 3rd ed. 3 vols. New York: Facts on File, 2007. Also at http://www.infobasepublishing.com/.

3. Bausell, R. Barker. *Advanced Research Methodology: An Annotated Guide to Sources*. Metuchen, NJ: Scarecrow Press, 1991.

3. Keeves, John P., ed. *Educational Research, Methodology, and Measurement: An International Handbook*. 2nd ed. New York: Pergamon, 1997.

3. Tuckman, Bruce W., and Brian E. Harper. *Conducting Educational Research*. 6th ed. Lanham, MD: Rowman and Littlefield, 2012.

4. *Education Index*. New York: H. W. Wilson, 1929–. Also at http://www.ebscohost.com/wilson/ (as *Education Index Retrospective* and *Education Abstracts*).

4. *ERIC Database*. Lanham, MD: Educational Resources Information Center, 2004–. http://www.eric.ed.gov/.

4. O'Brien, Nancy P., and Lois Buttlar. *Education: A Guide to Reference and Information Sources.* 2nd ed. Englewood, CO: Libraries Unlimited, 2000.
5. Carver, Ronald P. *Writing a Publishable Research Report: In Education, Psychology, and Related Disciplines.* Springfield, IL: C. C. Thomas, 1984.

Geography

1. Witherick, M. E., Simon Ross, and John Small. *A Modern Dictionary of Geography.* 4th ed. London: Arnold, 2001.
1. *The World Factbook.* Washington, DC: Central Intelligence Agency, 1990s–. https://www.cia .gov/library/publications/the-world-factbook/.
2. Dunbar, Gary S. *Modern Geography: An Encyclopedic Survey.* New York: Garland, 1991.
2. McCoy, John, ed. *Geo-Data: The World Geographical Encyclopedia.* 3rd ed. Detroit: Thomson/ Gale, 2003. Also at http://www.gale.com/.
2. Parker, Sybil P., ed. *World Geographical Encyclopedia.* 5 vols. New York: McGraw-Hill, 1995.
3. *Historical GIS Clearinghouse and Forum.* Washington, DC: Association of American Geographers. http://www.aag.org/.
3. Walford, Nigel. *Geographical Data: Characteristics and Sources.* New York: John Wiley and Sons, 2002.
4. Conzen, Michael P., Thomas A. Rumney, and Graeme Wynn. *A Scholar's Guide to Geographical Writing on the American and Canadian Past.* Chicago: University of Chicago Press, 1993.
4. *Current Geographical Publications.* New York: American Geographical Society, 1938–2006.
4. *Geographical Abstracts.* Norwich, UK: Geo Abstracts, 1966–.
4. Okuno, Takashi. *A World Bibliography of Geographical Bibliographies.* Tsukuba, Japan: Institute of Geoscience, University of Tsukuba, 1992.
5. Durrenberger, Robert W., John K. Wright, and Elizabeth T. Platt. *Geographical Research and Writing.* New York: Crowell, 1985.
5. Northey, Margot, David B. Knight, and Dianne Draper. *Making Sense: A Student's Guide to Research and Writing; Geography and Environmental Sciences.* 6th ed. Don Mills, ON: Oxford University Press, 2015.

Law

1. Garner, Bryan A., ed. *Black's Law Dictionary.* 10th ed. St. Paul, MN: Thomson/West, 2014.
1. Law, Jonathan, and Elizabeth A. Martin, eds. *A Dictionary of Law.* 8th ed. Oxford: Oxford University Press, 2015.
1. Richards, P. H., and L. B. Curzon. *The Longman Dictionary of Law.* 8th ed. New York: Pearson Longman, 2011.
2. Baker, Brian L., and Patrick J. Petit, eds. *Encyclopedia of Legal Information Sources.* 2nd ed. Detroit: Gale Research, 1993.
2. *Corpus Juris Secundum.* Brooklyn: American Law Book; St. Paul, MN: West, 1936–.
2. *Gale Encyclopedia of American Law.* 3rd ed. 14 vols. Detroit: Gale Cengage Learning, 2011. Also at http://www.gale.cengage.com/.
2. Hall, Kermit, and David Scott Clark, eds. *The Oxford Companion to American Law.* New York: Oxford University Press, 2002. Also at http://www.oxfordreference.com/.
2. Patterson, Dennis M., ed. *A Companion to Philosophy of Law and Legal Theory.* Oxford: Blackwell, 1999.
3. Campbell, Enid Mona, Lee Poh-York, and Joycey G. Tooher. *Legal Research: Materials and Methods.* 4th ed. North Ryde, Australia: LBC Information Services, 1996.

3. *Online Legal Research: Beyond LexisNexis and Westlaw.* Los Angeles: University of California. http://libguides.law.ucla.edu/onlinelegalresearch.

4. *Current Index to Legal Periodicals.* Seattle: University of Washington Law Library, 1948–. Also at http://lib.law.washington.edu/cilp/cilp.html.

4. *Current Law Index.* Los Altos, CA: Information Access; Farmington Hills, MI: Gale Cengage Learning, 1980–.

4. *Index to Legal Periodicals and Books.* New York: H. W. Wilson, 1924–. Also at http://www .ebscohost.com/wilson/.

5. Bast, Carol M., and Margie Hawkins. *Foundations of Legal Research and Writing.* 5th ed. Clifton Park, NY: Delmar Cengage Learning, 2012.

5. Garner, Bryan A. *The Elements of Legal Style.* 2nd ed. New York: Oxford University Press, 2002.

6. *The Bluebook: A Uniform System of Citation.* 20th ed. Cambridge, MA: Harvard Law Review Association, 2015. Also at https://www.legalbluebook.com/.

6. *The Maroonbook: The University of Chicago Manual of Legal Citation.* Chicago: University of Chicago, 2013.

Political Science

1. Robertson, David. *A Dictionary of Modern Politics.* 4th ed. London: Routledge, 2007.

2. *The Almanac of American Politics.* Washington, DC: National Journal, 1972–. Also at http:// nationaljournal.com/almanac.

2. Hawkesworth, Mary E., and Maurice Kogan, eds. *Encyclopedia of Government and Politics.* 2nd ed. 2 vols. London: Routledge, 2004.

2. Lal, Shiv, ed. *International Encyclopedia of Politics and Laws.* 17 vols. 5th ed. New Delhi: Election Archives, 1992.

2. Miller, David, ed. *The Blackwell Encyclopaedia of Political Thought.* Oxford: Blackwell, 2004.

3. Green, Stephen W., and Douglas J. Ernest, eds. *Information Sources of Political Science.* 5th ed. Santa Barbara, CA: ABC-Clio, 2005.

3. Johnson, Janet Buttolph, and H. T. Reynolds. *Political Science Research Methods.* 8th ed. Los Angeles: Congressional Quarterly Press, 2015.

4. *ABC Pol Sci.* Santa Barbara, CA: ABC-Clio, 1969–2000.

4. Hardy, Gayle J., and Judith Schiek Robinson. *Subject Guide to U.S. Government Reference Sources.* 2nd ed. Englewood, CO: Libraries Unlimited, 1996.

4. *PAIS International Journals Indexed.* New York: Public Affairs Information Service, 1972–. Also at http://www.proquest.com/.

4. *United States Political Science Documents.* Pittsburgh: University of Pittsburgh, University Center for International Studies, 1975–91.

4. *Worldwide Political Science Abstracts.* Bethesda, MD: Cambridge Scientific Abstracts, 1976–. Also at http://www.proquest.com/.

5. Biddle, Arthur W., Kenneth M. Holland, and Toby Fulwiler. *Writer's Guide: Political Science.* Lexington, MA: D. C. Heath, 1987.

5. LaVaque-Manty, Mika, and Danielle LaVaque-Manty. *Writing in Political Science: A Brief Guide.* New York: Oxford University Press, 2016.

5. Lovell, David W., and Rhonda Moore. *Essay Writing and Style Guide for Politics and the Social Sciences.* Rev. ed. Canberra: Australasian Political Studies Association, 1993.

5. Schmidt, Diane E. *Writing in Political Science: A Practical Guide.* 4th ed. Boston: Longman, 2010.

5. Scott, Gregory M., and Stephen M. Garrison. *The Political Science Student Writer's Manual*. 7th ed. Boston: Pearson, 2012.

6. American Political Science Association. APSA *Style Manual for Political Science*. Rev. ed. Washington, DC: American Political Science Association, 2006. http://www.apsanet.org /files/APSAStyleManual2006.pdf.

Psychology

1. Colman, Andrew M. A *Dictionary of Psychology*. 4th ed. Oxford: Oxford University Press, 2015. Also at http://www.oxfordreference.com/.

1. Eysenck, Michael W., ed. *The Blackwell Dictionary of Cognitive Psychology*. Oxford: Blackwell, 1997.

1. Hayes, Nicky, and Peter Stratton. A *Student's Dictionary of Psychology*. 4th ed. London: Arnold, 2003.

1. Wolman, Benjamin B., ed. *Dictionary of Behavioral Science*. 2nd ed. San Diego, CA: Academic Press, 1989.

2. Colman, Andrew M., ed. *Companion Encyclopedia of Psychology*. 2 vols. London: Routledge, 1997.

2. Craighead, W. Edward, Charles B. Nemeroff, and Raymond J. Corsini, eds. *The Corsini Encyclopedia of Psychology and Behavioral Science*. 4th ed. 4 vols. New York: John Wiley and Sons, 2010.

2. Kazdin, Alan E., ed. *Encyclopedia of Psychology*. 8 vols. Washington, DC: American Psychological Association; Oxford: Oxford University Press, 2000.

2. Weiner, Irving B., and W. Edward Craighead, eds. *The Corsini Encyclopedia of Psychology*. 4th ed. 4 vols. Hoboken, NJ: Wiley, 2010.

3. Breakwell, Glynis M., Sean Hammond, Chris Fife-Schaw, and Jonathan A. Smith. *Research Methods in Psychology*. 4th ed. London: Sage, 2012.

3. Elmes, David G., Barry H. Kantowitz, and Henry L. Roediger III. *Research Methods in Psychology*. 9th ed. Belmont, CA: Wadsworth Cengage Learning, 2012.

3. Reed, Jeffrey G., and Pam M. Baxter. *Library Use: A Handbook for Psychology*. 3rd ed. Washington, DC: American Psychological Association, 2003.

3. Shaughnessy, John J., Eugene B. Zechmeister, and Jeanne S. Zechmeister. *Research Methods in Psychology*. 10th ed. Boston: McGraw-Hill, 2014.

3. Wilson, Christopher. *Research Methods in Psychology: An Introductory Laboratory Manual*. Dubuque, IA: Kendall-Hunt, 1990.

4. *Annual Review of Psychology*. Palo Alto, CA: Annual Reviews, 1950–. Also at http://arjournals .annualreviews.org/journal/psych.

4. *APA PsycNET*. Washington, DC: American Psychological Association, 1990s–. http://www .apa.org/pubs/databases/psycnet/.

4. *NASPSPA Abstracts*. Champaign, IL: Human Kinetics Publishers, 1990s–. Also at http:// journals.humankinetics.com/.

4. *PubMed*. Bethesda, MD: US National Library of Medicine. http://www.ncbi.nlm.nih.gov /pubmed/.

4. *Science Citation Index*. Philadelphia: Institute for Scientific Information, 1961–. Also at http://wokinfo.com/.

5. Solomon, Paul R. A *Student's Guide to Research Report Writing in Psychology*. Glenview, IL: Scott Foresman, 1985.

5. Sternberg, Robert J., and Karin Sternberg. *The Psychologist's Companion: A Guide to Writing*

Scientific Papers for Students and Researchers. 6th ed. Cambridge: Cambridge University Press, 2016.

6. *Publication Manual of the American Psychological Association*. 6th ed. Washington, DC: American Psychological Association, 2009.

Religion

1. Bowker, John, ed. *The Concise Oxford Dictionary of World Religions*. New ed. Oxford: Oxford University Press, 2007. Also at http://www.oxfordreference.com/.
1. Pye, Michael, ed. *Continuum Dictionary of Religion*. New York: Continuum, 1994.
2. Cesari, Jocelyne. *Encyclopedia of Islam in the United States*. London: Greenwood Press, 2007.
2. Freedman, David Noel, ed. *The Anchor Yale Bible Dictionary*. 6 vols. New Haven, CT: Yale University Press, 2008.
2. Jones, Lindsay, ed. *Encyclopedia of Religion*. 2nd ed. 15 vols. Detroit: Macmillan Reference USA, 2005.
2. Martin, Richard C., ed. *Encyclopedia of Islam and the Muslim World*. 2 vols. New York: Macmillan Reference USA, 2003.
2. Routledge Encyclopedias of Religion and Society (series). New York: Routledge.
2. Skolnik, Fred, and Michael Berenbaum, eds. *Encyclopaedia Judaica*. 2nd ed. 22 vols. Detroit: Macmillan Reference USA, 2007.
3. Kennedy, James R., Jr. *Library Research Guide to Religion and Theology: Illustrated Search Strategy and Sources*. 2nd ed., rev. Ann Arbor, MI: Pierian, 1984.
4. Brown, David, and Richard Swinburne. *A Selective Bibliography of the Philosophy of Religion*. Rev. ed. Oxford: Sub-faculty of Philosophy, 1995.
4. Chinyamu, Salms F. *An Annotated Bibliography on Religion*. [Lilongwe,] Malawi: Malawi Library Association, 1993.
4. *Guide to Social Science and Religion in Periodical Literature*. Flint, MI: National Library of Religious Periodicals, 1970–88.
4. *Index of Articles on Jewish Studies (RAMBI)*. Jerusalem: Jewish National and University Library, 2002–. http://jnul.huji.ac.il/rambi/.
4. *Index to Book Reviews in Religion*. Chicago: American Theological Library Association, 1990–. Also at http://ebscohost.com/academic (as *ATLA Religion Database*).
4. *Islamic Book Review Index*. Berlin: Adiyok, 1982–.
4. O'Brien, Betty A., and Elmer J. O'Brien, eds. *Religion Index Two: Festschriften, 1960–1969*. Chicago: American Theological Library Association, 1980.
4. *Religion Index One: Periodicals*. Chicago: American Theological Library Association, 1977–. Also at https://ebscohost.com/academic (as *ATLA Religion Database*).
4. *Religion Index Two: Multi-author Works*. Chicago: American Theological Library Association, 1976–. Also at https://ebscohost.com/academic (as *ATLA Religion Database*).
6. *CNS Stylebook on Religion: Reference Guide and Usage Manual*. 4th ed. Washington, DC: Catholic News Service, 2012.

Sociology

1. Abercrombie, Nicholas, Stephen Hill, and Bryan S. Turner. *The Penguin Dictionary of Sociology*. 5th ed. London: Penguin, 2006.
1. Johnson, Allan G. *The Blackwell Dictionary of Sociology: A User's Guide to Sociological Language*. 2nd ed. Oxford: Blackwell, 2002.
1. Scott, John, and Marshall Gordon, eds. *A Dictionary of Sociology*. 4th ed. rev. Oxford: Oxford University Press, 2009. Also at http://www.oxfordreference.com/.

2. Beckert, Jens, and Milan Zafirovksi, eds. *International Encyclopedia of Economic Sociology*. London: Routledge, 2006.

2. Borgatta, Edgar F., and Rhonda J. V. Montgomery, eds. *Encyclopedia of Sociology*. 2nd ed. 5 vols. New York: Macmillan Reference USA, 2000.

2. Levinson, David L., Peter W. Cookson, and Alan R. Sadovnik, eds. *Education and Sociology: An Encyclopedia*. New York: RoutledgeFalmer, 2014.

2. Ritzer, George, ed. *Encyclopedia of Social Theory*. 2 vols. Thousand Oaks, CA: Sage, 2005.

2. Smelser, Neil J., and Richard Swedberg, eds. *The Handbook of Economic Sociology*. 2nd ed. Princeton, NJ: Princeton University Press, 2005.

3. Aby, Stephen H., James Nalen, and Lori Fielding, eds. *Sociology: A Guide to Reference and Information Sources*. 3rd ed. Westport, CT: Libraries Unlimited, 2005.

3. Lieberson, Stanley. *Making It Count: The Improvement of Social Research and Theory*. Berkeley: University of California Press, 1987.

4. *Annual Review of Sociology*. Palo Alto, CA: Annual Reviews, 1975–. Also at http://www .annualreviews.org/journal/soc.

4. *Applied Social Sciences Index and Abstracts (ASSIA)*. Bethesda, MD: Cambridge Scientific Abstracts, 1987–. Also at http://www.proquest.com/.

4. *Social Science Research*. San Diego, CA: Academic Press, 1972–. Also at http://www.science direct.com/science/journal/0049089X/.

4. *Sociological Abstracts*. Bethesda, MD: Sociological Abstracts, 1952–. Also at http://www .proquest.com/.

5. Smith-Lovin, Lynn, and Cary Moskovitz. *Writing in Sociology: A Brief Guide*. New York: Oxford University Press, 2016.

5. Sociology Writing Group. *A Guide to Writing Sociology Papers*. 7th ed. New York: Worth, 2013.

5. Tomovic, Vladislav A., ed. *Definitions in Sociology: Convergence, Conflict, and Alternative Vocabularies; A Manual for Writers of Term Papers, Research Reports, and Theses*. St. Catharines, ON: Diliton Publications, 1979.

Women's Studies

1. Bataille, Gretchen M., and Laurie Lisa, eds. *Native American Women: A Biographical Dictionary*. 2nd ed. New York: Routledge, 2001.

1. Hendry, Maggy, and Jennifer S. Uglow, eds. *The Palgrave Macmillan Dictionary of Women's Biography*. 4th ed. New York: Palgrave Macmillan, 2005.

1. Mills, Jane. *Womanwords: A Dictionary of Words about Women*. New York: H. Holt, 1993.

1. Salem, Dorothy C., ed. *African American Women: A Biographical Dictionary*. New York: Garland, 1993.

2. Hine, Darlene Clark, ed. *Black Women in America*. 2nd ed. 3 vols. New York: Oxford University Press, 2005.

2. Kramarae, Cheris, and Dale Spender, eds. *Routledge International Encyclopedia of Women: Global Women's Issues and Knowledge*. 4 vols. New York: Routledge, 2000.

2. Tierney, Helen, ed. *Women's Studies Encyclopedia*. Rev. ed. 3 vols. Westport, CT: Greenwood Press, 2007.

2. Willard, Frances E., and Mary A. Livermore, eds. *Great American Women of the 19th Century: A Biographical Encyclopedia*. Amherst, NY: Humanity Books, 2005.

3. Carter, Sarah, and Maureen Ritchie. *Women's Studies: A Guide to Information Sources*. Jefferson, NC: McFarland, 1991.

3. Searing, Susan E. *Introduction to Library Research in Women's Studies*. 2nd ed. Boulder, CO: Westview Press, 1998.

4. *Studies on Women and Gender Abstracts.* Abingdon, Oxfordshire, UK: Carfax, 1983–.

4. *ViVa: A Bibliography of Women's History in Historical and Women's Studies Journals.* Amsterdam: International Institute of Social History, 1995–. http://www.iisg.nl/womhist/viva home.php/.

4. *Women's Review of Books.* Wellesley, MA: Wellesley College Center for Research on Women, 1983–. Also at http://www.oldcitypublishing.com/journals/wrb-home/.

4. *Women Studies Abstracts.* Rush, NY: Rush Publishing, 1972–. Also at http://www.ebscohost.com/academic/ (as *Women's Studies International*).

Natural Sciences

General

1. *McGraw-Hill Dictionary of Scientific and Technical Terms.* 7th ed. New York: McGraw-Hill, 2017. Also at http://www.accessscience.com/.

1. Morris, Christopher, ed. *Academic Press Dictionary of Science and Technology.* San Diego, CA: Academic, 1992.

1. Porter, Roy, and Marilyn Bailey Ogilvie, eds. *The Biographical Dictionary of Scientists.* 3rd ed. 2 vols. New York: Oxford University Press, 2000.

1. Walker, Peter M. B., ed. *Chambers Dictionary of Science and Technology.* London: Chambers, 2000.

2. Considine, Glenn D., and Peter H. Kulik, eds. *Van Nostrand's Scientific Encyclopedia.* 10th ed. 3 vols. Hoboken, NJ: Wiley, 2008. https://doi.org/10.1002/9780471743989.

2. Heilbron, J. L., ed. *The Oxford Companion to the History of Modern Science.* Oxford: Oxford University Press, 2003. Also at http://www.oxfordreference.com/.

2. *McGraw-Hill Encyclopedia of Science and Technology.* 11th ed. 20 vols. New York: McGraw-Hill, 2012. Also at http://www.accessscience.com/.

2. *Nature Encyclopedia: An A–Z Guide to Life on Earth.* New York: Oxford University Press, 2001.

3. *Directory of Technical and Scientific Directories: A World Bibliographic Guide to Medical, Agricultural, Industrial, and Natural Science Directories.* 6th ed. Phoenix: Oryx Press, 1989.

3. Hurt, Charlie Deuel. *Information Sources in Science and Technology.* 3rd ed. Englewood, CO: Libraries Unlimited, 1998.

3. Nielsen, Harry A. *Methods of Natural Science: An Introduction.* Englewood Cliffs, NJ: Prentice-Hall, 1967.

4. *Applied Science and Technology Index.* New York: H. W. Wilson, 1913–. Also at http://www.ebscohost.com/wilson/.

4. *Book Review Digest.* New York: H. W. Wilson, 1905–. Also at http://www.ebscohost.com/wilson/.

4. *British Technology Index.* London: Library Association, 1962–80.

4. *Compumath Citation Index.* Philadelphia: Institute for Scientific Information, 1981–2006.

4. *General Science Index.* New York: H. W. Wilson, 1978–. Also at http://www.ebscohost.com/wilson/ (as *General Science Full Text*).

4. *Genetics Citation Index: Experimental Citation Indexes to Genetics with Special Emphasis on Human Genetics.* Compiled by Eugene Garfield and Irving H. Sher. Philadelphia: Institute for Scientific Information, 1963.

4. *Index to Scientific Reviews: An International Interdisciplinary Index to the Review Literature of Science, Medicine, Agriculture, Technology, and the Behavioral Sciences.* Philadelphia: Institute for Scientific Information, 1974.

4. *Science and Technology Annual Reference Review.* Phoenix: Oryx Press, ca. 1989–.

4. *Science Citation Index*. Philadelphia: Institute for Scientific Information, 1961–. Also at http://wokinfo.com/.

4. *Technical Book Review Index*. New York: Special Libraries Association, 1935–88.

5. Booth, Vernon. *Communicating in Science: Writing a Scientific Paper and Speaking at Scientific Meetings*. 2nd ed. Cambridge: Cambridge University Press, 1993.

5. Montgomery, Scott L. *The Chicago Guide to Communicating Science*. Chicago: University of Chicago Press, 2003.

5. Valiela, Ivan. *Doing Science: Design, Analysis, and Communication of Scientific Research*. 2nd ed. Oxford: Oxford University Press, 2009.

5. Wilson, Anthony, et al. *Handbook of Science Communication*. Bristol, UK: Institute of Physics, 1998. https://doi.org/10.1201/9780849386855.

6. Rubens, Phillip, ed. *Science and Technical Writing: A Manual of Style*. 2nd ed. New York: Routledge, 2001.

Biology

1. Allaby, Michael, ed. *The Oxford Dictionary of Natural History*. Oxford: Oxford University Press, 1985.

1. Cammack, Richard et al., eds. *Oxford Dictionary of Biochemistry and Molecular Biology*. 2nd ed. Oxford: Oxford University Press, 2008. Also at http://www.oxfordreference.com/.

1. Lackie, John M., ed. *The Dictionary of Cell and Molecular Biology*. 5th ed. Amsterdam: Elsevier/AP, 2013.

1. Lawrence, Eleanor, ed. *Henderson's Dictionary of Biology*. 16th ed. New York: Benjamin Cummings, 2016.

1. Martin, Elizabeth, and Robert S. Hine, eds. *A Dictionary of Biology*. 7th ed. Oxford: Oxford University Press, 2015. Also at http://www.oxfordreference.com/.

1. Singleton, Paul, and Diana Sainsbury. *Dictionary of Microbiology and Molecular Biology*. 3rd ed. rev. New York: Wiley, 2006. https://doi.org/10.1002/9780470056981.

2. Creighton, Thomas E., ed. *Encyclopedia of Molecular Biology*. 4 vols. New York: John Wiley and Sons, 1999. https://doi.org/10.1002/047120918X.

2. Dulbecco, Renato, ed. *Encyclopedia of Human Biology*. 3rd ed. 10 vols. San Diego, CA: Academic Press, 2008.

2. Eldredge, Niles, ed. *Life on Earth: An Encyclopedia of Biodiversity, Ecology, and Evolution*. 2 vols. Santa Barbara, CA: ABC-Clio, 2002.

2. Hall, Brian Keith, and Wendy M. Olson, eds. *Keywords and Concepts in Evolutionary Developmental Biology*. Rev. ed. Cambridge, MA: Harvard University Press, 2006.

2. Huber, Jeffrey T., and Susan Swogger, eds. *Introduction to Reference Sources in the Health Sciences*. 6th ed. Chicago: ALA Neal-Schuman Publishers, 2014.

2. Pagel, Mark D., ed. *Encyclopedia of Evolution*. 2 vols. Oxford: Oxford University Press, 2002. Also at http://www.oxfordreference.com/.

3. Wyatt, H. V., ed. *Information Sources in the Life Sciences*. 4th ed. London: Bowker-Saur, 1997.

4. *Biological Abstracts*. Philadelphia: BioSciences Information Service of Biological Abstracts, 1926–. Also at http://www.ebscohost.com/academic/biological-abstracts/.

4. *Biological and Agricultural Index*. New York: H. W. Wilson, 1964–. Also at http://www.ebscohost.com/wilson/.

4. *Environmental Sciences and Pollution Management*. Bethesda, MD: Cambridge Scientific Abstracts. Also at http://www.proquest.com/.

4. *Genetics Citation Index: Experimental Citation Indexes to Genetics with Special Emphasis on Hu-*

man Genetics. Compiled by Eugene Garfield and Irving H. Sher. Philadelphia: Institute for Scientific Information, 1963.

5. McMillan, Victoria E. *Writing Papers in the Biological Sciences.* 6th ed. Boston: Bedford / St. Martin's, 2016.

5. Roldan, Leslie Ann, and Mary-Lou Pardue. *Writing in Biology: A Brief Guide.* New York: Oxford University Press, 2016.

6. Council of Science Editors. *Scientific Style and Format: The CSE Manual for Authors, Editors, and Publishers.* 8th ed. Chicago: University of Chicago Press, 2014.

Chemistry

1. Hawley, Gessner Goodrich, and Richard J. Lewis Sr. *Hawley's Condensed Chemical Dictionary.* 16th ed. New York: Wiley, 2016.

2. Haynes, William M., ed. *CRC Handbook of Chemistry and Physics.* 97th ed. Boca Raton, FL: CRC Press, 2016.

2. *Kirk-Othmer Encyclopedia of Chemical Technology.* 5th ed. 2 vols. Hoboken, NJ: Wiley-Interscience, 2007. https://doi.org/10.1002/0471238961.

2. Meyers, Robert A., ed. *Encyclopedia of Physical Science and Technology.* 3rd ed. 18 vols. San Diego, CA: Academic, 2002. Also at http://www.sciencedirect.com/science/referenceworks /9780122274107/.

3. Leslie, Davies. *Efficiency in Research, Development, and Production: The Statistical Design and Analysis of Chemical Experiments.* Cambridge: Royal Society of Chemistry, 1993.

3. Wiggins, Gary. *Chemical Information Sources.* New York: McGraw-Hill, 1991. Also at http:// en.wikibooks.org/wiki/Chemical_Information_Sources.

4. *ACS Publications.* Columbus, OH: American Chemical Society. http://pubs.acs.org/.

4. *Chemical Abstracts.* Columbus, OH: American Chemical Society, 1907–. Also at http://www .cas.org/.

4. *Composite Index for CRC Handbooks.* 3rd ed. 3 vols. Boca Raton, FL: CRC Press, 1991.

4. *CrossFire Beilstein.* San Leandro, CA: MDL Information Systems, 1996–. Also at https://www .reaxys.com/.

4. *Reaxys.* New York: Elsevier Science. Also at http://www.elsevier.com/solutions/reaxys.

4. *ScienceDirect.* New York: Elsevier Science, 1999–. http://www.sciencedirect.com/.

5. Davis, Holly B., Julian F. Tyson, and Jan A. Pechenik. *A Short Guide to Writing about Chemistry.* Boston: Longman, 2010.

5. Ebel, Hans Friedrich, Claus Bliefert, and William E. Russey. *The Art of Scientific Writing: From Student Reports to Professional Publications in Chemistry and Related Fields.* 2nd ed. Weinheim, Germany: Wiley-VCH, 2004.

5. Schoenfeld, Robert. *The Chemist's English, with "Say It in English, Please!"* 3rd rev. ed. New York: Wiley-VCH, 2001.

6. Dodd, Janet S., ed. *The ACS Style Guide: Effective Communication of Scientific Information.* 3rd ed. Washington, DC: American Chemical Society, 2006.

Computer Sciences

1. Gattiker, Urs E. *The Information Security Dictionary: Defining the Terms That Define Security for E-Business, Internet, Information, and Wireless Technology.* Boston: Kluwer Academic, 2004.

1. LaPlante, Phillip A. *Dictionary of Computer Science, Engineering, and Technology.* Boca Raton, FL: CRC Press, 2001.

1. Pfaffenberger, Bryan. *Webster's New World Computer Dictionary.* 10th ed. Indianapolis: Wiley, 2003.

1. *Random House Concise Dictionary of Science and Computers.* New York: Random House Reference, 2004.
1. South, David W. *The Computer and Information Science and Technology Abbreviations and Acronyms Dictionary.* Boca Raton, FL: CRC Press, 1994.
2. Henderson, Harry. *Encyclopedia of Computer Science and Technology.* Rev. ed. New York: Facts on File, 2009. Also at http://www.infobasepublishing.com/.
2. Narins, Brigham, ed. *World of Computer Science.* 2 vols. Detroit: Gale Group / Thomson Learning, 2002.
2. Wah, Benjamin W., ed. *Wiley Encyclopedia of Computer Science and Engineering.* 5 vols. Hoboken, NJ: Wiley, 2009.
3. Ardis, Susan B., and Jean A. Poland. *A Guide to the Literature of Electrical and Electronics Engineering.* Littleton, CO: Libraries Unlimited, 1987.
4. *Directory of Library Automation Software, Systems, and Services.* Medford, NJ: Learned Information, 1993–2007.
5. Eckstein, C. J. *Style Manual for Use in Computer-Based Instruction.* Brooks Air Force Base, TX: Air Force Human Resources Laboratory, Air Force Systems Command, 1990. Also at http://www.dtic.mil/dtic/tr/fulltext/u2/a226959.pdf.

Geology and Earth Sciences

1. *McGraw-Hill Dictionary of Geology and Mineralogy.* 2nd ed. New York: McGraw-Hill, 2003.
1. Neuendorf, Klaus K. E., et al., eds. *Glossary of Geology.* 5th ed. rev. Alexandria, VA: American Geological Institute, 2011.
1. Smith, Jacqueline, ed. *The Facts on File Dictionary of Earth Science.* Rev. ed. New York: Facts on File, 2006. Also at http://www.infobasepublishing.com/.
2. Bishop, Arthur C., Alan R. Woolley, and William R. Hamilton. *Cambridge Guide to Minerals, Rocks, and Fossils.* Rev. ed. Cambridge: Cambridge University Press, 2001.
2. Bowes, Donald R., ed. *The Encyclopedia of Igneous and Metamorphic Petrology.* New York: Van Nostrand Reinhold, 1989.
2. Dasch, E. Julius, ed. *Macmillan Encyclopedia of Earth Sciences.* 2 vols. New York: Macmillan Reference USA, 1996.
2. Good, Gregory A., ed. *Sciences of the Earth: An Encyclopedia of Events, People, and Phenomena.* 2 vols. New York: Garland, 1998.
2. Hancock, Paul L., and Brian J. Skinner, eds. *The Oxford Companion to the Earth.* Oxford: Oxford University Press, 2000. Also at http://www.oxfordreference.com/.
2. Nierenberg, William A., ed. *Encyclopedia of Earth System Science.* 4 vols. San Diego, CA: Academic Press, 1992.
2. Selley, Richard C., et al., eds. *Encyclopedia of Geology.* 5 vols. Amsterdam: Elsevier Academic, 2005.
2. Seyfert, Carl K., ed. *The Encyclopedia of Structural Geology and Plate Tectonics.* New York: Van Nostrand Reinhold, 1987.
2. Singer, Ronald, ed. *Encyclopedia of Paleontology.* 2 vols. Chicago: Fitzroy Dearborn, 1999.
2. Steele, John H., S. A. Thorpe, and Karl K. Turekian, eds. *Encyclopedia of Ocean Sciences.* 2nd ed. 6 vols. Boston: Elsevier, 2009. Also at http://www.sciencedirect.com/science/reference works/9780122274305/.
4. *Bibliography and Index of Geology.* Alexandria, VA: American Geological Institute, 1966–2005. Also at http://www.proquest.com/ (as *GeoRef*).
4. *Geobase.* New York: Elsevier Science. Also at http://www.elsevier.com/online-tools /engineering-village/geobase/.

4. Wood, David N., Joan E. Hardy, and Anthony P. Harvey. *Information Sources in the Earth Sciences.* 2nd ed. London: Bowker-Saur, 1989.
5. Bates, Robert L., Marla D. Adkins-Heljeson, and Rex C. Buchanan, eds. *Geowriting: A Guide to Writing, Editing, and Printing in Earth Science.* Rev. 5th ed. Alexandria, VA: American Geological Institute, 2004.
5. Dunn, J., et al. *Organization and Content of a Typical Geologic Report.* Rev. ed. Arvada, CO: American Institute of Professional Geologists, 1993.

Mathematics

1. Borowski, E. J., and J. M. Borwein, eds. *Collins Dictionary: Mathematics.* 2nd ed. Glasgow: HarperCollins, 2002.
1. Nelson, David, ed. *The Penguin Dictionary of Mathematics.* 4th ed. London: Penguin, 2008.
1. Nicholson, James. *The Concise Oxford Dictionary of Mathematics.* 5th ed. Oxford: Oxford University Press, 2014.
1. Schwartzman, Steven. *The Words of Mathematics: An Etymological Dictionary of Mathematical Terms Used in English.* Washington, DC: Mathematical Association of America, 1994.
2. Darling, David J. *The Universal Book of Mathematics: From Abracadabra to Zeno's Paradoxes.* Hoboken, NJ: Wiley, 2004.
2. Ito, Kiyosi, ed. *Encyclopedic Dictionary of Mathematics.* 2nd ed. 2 vols. Cambridge, MA: MIT Press, 1993.
2. Weisstein, Eric W. *CRC Concise Encyclopedia of Mathematics.* 3rd ed. Boca Raton, FL: Chapman and Hall / CRC, 2009.
3. Pemberton, John E. *How to Find Out in Mathematics: A Guide to Sources of Information.* 2nd rev. ed. Oxford: Pergamon, 1969.
4. *DoD Public Access Search.* Fort Belvoir, VA: Defense Technical Information Center. https://publicaccess.dtic.mil/padf_public/.
4. *Mathematical Reviews: 50th Anniversary Celebration.* Providence, RI: American Mathematical Society, 1990.
4. *MathSci.* Providence, RI: American Mathematical Society. Also at http://www.ams.org/mathscinet/.
5. *A Manual for Authors of Mathematical Papers.* Rev. ed. Providence, RI: American Mathematical Society, 1990.
5. Miller, Jane E. *The Chicago Guide to Writing about Multivariate Analysis.* 2nd ed. Chicago: University of Chicago Press, 2013.

Physics

1. Basu, Dipak, ed. *Dictionary of Pure and Applied Physics.* Boca Raton, FL: CRC Press, 2001.
1. Daintith, John, ed. *A Dictionary of Physics.* 7th ed. Oxford: Oxford University Press, 2015. Also at http://www.oxfordreference.com/.
1. Sube, Ralf. *Dictionary: Physics Basic Terms; English-German.* Berlin: A. Hatier, 1994.
1. Thewlis, James. *Concise Dictionary of Physics and Related Subjects.* 2nd ed. rev. and enl. Oxford: Pergamon, 1979.
2. Lerner, Rita G., and George L. Trigg, eds. *Encyclopedia of Physics.* 3rd ed. Weinheim, Germany: Wiley-VCH, 2005.
2. *McGraw-Hill Concise Encyclopedia of Physics.* New York: McGraw-Hill, 2005.
2. Meyers, Robert A., ed. *Encyclopedia of Modern Physics.* San Diego, CA: Academic Press, 1990.
2. Trigg, George L., ed. *Encyclopedia of Applied Physics.* 23 vols. Weinheim, Germany: Wiley-VCH, 2004. https://doi.org/10.1002/3527600434.

2. Woan, Graham. *The Cambridge Handbook of Physics Formulas*. 2003 ed. Cambridge: Cambridge University Press, 2003.

3. Shaw, Dennis F. *Information Sources in Physics*. 3rd ed. London: Bowker-Saur, 1994.

4. American Institute of Physics. Journals. College Park, MD: AIP. http://aip.scitation.org/.

4. *Astronomy and Astrophysics Abstracts*. Berlin: Springer-Verlag, 1969–.

4. *Current Physics Index*. New York: American Institute of Physics, 1975–2005. Also at http://aip.scitation.org.

4. *IEEE Xplore*. New York: Institute of Electrical and Electronics Engineers. http://ieeexplore.ieee.org/Xplore/.

4. *Inspec*. Stevenage, UK: Institution of Electrical Engineers. Also at http://www.ebscohost.com/academic/.

4. Institute of Physics. Journals. London: IOP. http://iopscience.iop.org/journals/.

4. *Physics Abstracts*. London: Institution of Electrical Engineers, 1967–.

5. Katz, Michael J. *Elements of the Scientific Paper*. New Haven, CT: Yale University Press, 1985.

6. American Institute of Physics. *AIP Style Manual*. 4th ed. New York: American Institute of Physics, 1990.

Authors

Kate L. Turabian (1893–1987) was the graduate school dissertation secretary at the University of Chicago for nearly three decades. She is the original author of this work and the *Student's Guide to Writing College Papers*, also published by the University of Chicago Press and currently in its fourth edition (2010).

Wayne C. Booth (1921–2005) was the George M. Pullman Distinguished Service Professor Emeritus at the University of Chicago, where he taught in the English Department, the Committee on Ideas and Methods, and the College. His many books include *The Rhetoric of Fiction*, *A Rhetoric of Irony*, *Critical Understanding*, *The Vocation of a Teacher*, and *For the Love of It: Amateuring and Its Rivals*, all published by the University of Chicago Press.

Gregory G. Colomb (1951–2011) was professor of English at the University of Virginia and the author of *Designs on Truth: The Poetics of the Augustan Mock-Epic*.

Joseph M. Williams (1933–2008) was professor emeritus of English and linguistics at the University of Chicago. He is the author of *Style: Lessons in Clarity and Grace*. Colomb and Williams jointly wrote *The Craft of Argument*.

Joseph Bizup is associate professor of English and associate dean for undergraduate academic programs and policies in the College of Arts & Sciences at Boston University. He is the author of *Manufacturing Culture*, coeditor of recent editions of the *Norton Reader*, and editor of recent editions of Williams's *Style*.

William T. FitzGerald is associate professor of English and director of the Writing Program and the Teaching Matters and Assessment Center at Rutgers University–Camden. He is the author of *Spiritual Modalities*.

Together Booth, Colomb, and Williams authored *The Craft of Research*, which Bizup and FitzGerald revised for its fourth edition (University of Chicago Press, 2016). And first Colomb and Williams, and now Bizup and FitzGerald, have revised Turabian's *Student's Guide*.

The University of Chicago Press Editorial Staff produces *The Chicago Manual of Style*, currently in its seventeenth edition (2017).

Index

References are to section numbers except where specified as page (p.), figure (fig.), table, or note (n) number.